Each volume of this series of companions to major philosophers contains specially commissioned essays by an international team of scholars, together with a substantial bibliography, and will serve as a reference work for students and non-specialists. One aim of the series is to dispel the intimidation such readers often feel when faced with the work of a difficult and challenging thinker.

Michel Foucault, one of the most important of contemporary French thinkers, exerted a profound influence on philosophy, history, and social theory. Foucault attempted to reveal the historical contingency of ideas that present themselves as necessary truths. He carried out this project in a series of original and strikingly controversial studies on the origins of modern medical and social scientific disciplines. These studies have raised fundamental philosophical questions about the nature of knowledge and its relation to power structures that have become major topics of discussion throughout the humanities and social sciences.

This volume presents a systematic and comprehensive overview of Foucault's major themes and texts, from his early work on madness through his history of sexuality, and relates his work to significant contemporary movements such as critical theory and feminism. The volume includes the first English translation of George Canguilhem's much cited essay on *The Order of Things*, and a pseudonymous dictionary entry on Foucault that was probably written by Foucault himself shortly before his death.

New readers and nonspecialists will find this the most convenient, accessible guide to Foucault currently available. Advanced students and specialists will find a conspectus of recent developments on the interpretation of Foucault.

D0162470

THE CAMBRIDGE COMPANION TO

FOUCAULT

The Cambridge Companion to
FOUCAULT

Edited by Gary Gutting
University of Notre Dame

PUBLISHED BY THE PRESS SYNDICATE OF THE UNIVERSITY OF CAMBRIDGE
The Pitt Building, Trumpington Street, Cambridge, United Kingdom

CAMBRIDGE UNIVERSITY PRESS
The Edinburgh Building, Cambridge CB2 2RU, UK   http: //www.cup.cam.ac.uk
40 West 20th Street, New York, NY 10011-4211, USA   http: //www.cup.org
10 Stamford Road, Oakleigh, Melbourne 3166, Australia

First published 1994
Reprinted 1994, 1995, 1996, 1998, 1999

Printed in the United States of America

Chapter 3 is a translation of "Mort de l'homme ou épuisement du
cognito?" Critique 24 (1967), pp. 599-618.

Typeset in Trump Mediaeval

A catalogue record for this book is available from the British Library

Library of Congress Cataloguing-in-Publication Data is available

ISBN 0-521-40332-4 hardback
ISBN 0-521-40887-3 paperback

CONTENTS

v

PREFACE

It is unlikely that any collection of academic essays could fulfill all the expectations stirred by the engaging term "companion." We think of a combined friend and cicerone, knowledgeable and charming, who leads us with easy clarity to an appreciation of the important features of a major site – in short, an informed and personable *guide vert* to a three-star French philosophical monument. Without pretending to the intimacy and charm our title might suggest, this set of essays does hope to provide an informed and reasonably accessible guide to most of Foucault's major works and themes. My introduction issues a warning (perhaps not endorsed by all of my fellow contributors) against general interpretations of Foucault's work, and sketches a few of his specific achievements as a maker of histories, theories, and myths.

Since almost all Foucault's books are in one way or another histories, it seemed sensible to begin the collection with Thomas Flynn's overview of the successive forms Foucault's historical project has taken, from archaeology to genealogy to problematization. The next five essays cover in turn Foucault's major writings from 1961 to his death in 1984. My piece approaches *The History of Madness* (1961) through an account of and reflection on its reception by professional historians. Next comes the first English translation (by Catherine Porter) of Georges Canguilhem's perceptive and influential review of *Les mots et les choses* (1966). Joseph Rouse provides an interpretation of the account of power, knowledge, and their essential relations that is at the heart of Foucault's book on the prison, *Discipline and Punish* (1975) and the first volume (1976) of his *History of Sexuality*. Arnold Davidson treats the work on Greek and Roman sexuality in the next two volumes of this history, *The Use of Pleasure*

vii

(1984) and *The Care of the Self* (1984). James Bernauer and Michael Mahon discuss the ethical viewpoint Foucault developed throughout the *History of Sexuality*.

The next five essays place Foucault in relation to a variety of thinkers and movements that are particularly important for understanding his work and its impact. Christopher Norris discusses Foucault's attitude toward the Enlightenment (particularly Kant) and toward postmodern critiques of the Enlightenment project. Paul Rabinow reflects on the connections – and essential differences – between Foucault's thought and that of Heidegger. David Ingram develops a fruitful confrontation between Foucault and Jürgen Habermas that reveals both important convergences and major disagreements. Stephen Watson's essay situates Foucault amid the complexities of twentieth-century French philosophical thought. Jana Sawicki analyses and evaluates the reception of Foucault's work by contemporary feminist theorists.

The final piece in this volume is Catherine Porter's translation of an entry on Michel Foucault in the *Dictionnaire des philosophes*, edited by Denis Huisman (Presses Universitaires de France, 1984). ' The article is signed with the name "Maurice Florence," a personage of whom I can find no other trace on the French philosophical scene. There is, in fact, good reason to think that "Maurice Florence" is a pseudonym and that Michel Foucault was himself the author (or involved in the authorship) of the piece; certainly, the perspective of the article is very close to that of his last published works. I am happy to think that our volume gives the last word to Foucault himself.

CONTRIBUTORS

JAMES BERNAUER is professor of Philosophy at Boston College. A former student of Foucault, he is the author of *Michel Foucault's Force of Flight: Toward an Ethics for Thought* (Humanities Press, 1990). He is also the editor of *The Final Foucault* (MIT Press, 1988) and *Amor Mundi: Explorations in the Faith and Thought of Hannah Arendt* (Nijhoff, 1987).

GEORGE CANGUILHEM was, until his retirement, director of the Institut d'Histoire des Sciences at the Sorbonne. His works available in English include *On the Normal and the Pathological* (Zone Books, 1989) and *Ideology and Rationality in the History of the Life Sciences* (MIT Press, 1988).

ARNOLD DAVIDSON is Professor of Philosophy at the University of Chicago and the editor of *Critical Inquiry*.

THOMAS FLYNN is Samuel Candler Dobbs Professor of Philosophy at Emory University. His publications include *Sartre and Marxist Existentialism: The Test Case of Collective Responsibility* (University of Chicago Press, 1984) and essays on Sartre and Foucault. He also contributed to the Sartre volume in the "Companions to the Philsophers" series.

GARY GUTTING is Professor of Philosophy at the University of Notre Dame. He is the author of *Michel Foucault's Archaeology of Scientific Knowledge* (Cambridge University Press, 1989) and editor of *The American Philosophical Quarterly*.

DAVID INGRAM is Professor of Philosophy at Loyola University of Chicago. His publications include *Habermas and the Dialectic of Reason* (Yale University Press, 1987); *Critical Theory and Philoso-*

phy (Paragon House, 1990); and *Reason, History, and Politics: The Communitarian Grounds of Legitimation in the Modern Age* (SUNY Press, 1994). He and his wife, Julia Simon-Ingram, edited *Critical Theory: The Essential Readings* (Paragon House, 1991).

MICHAEL MAHON is Assistant Professor of Humanities at the College of General Studies, Boston University. He is the author of *Foucault's Nietzschean Genealogy: Truth, Power, and the Subject* (SUNY Press, 1992).

CHRISTOPHER NORRIS is Professor of English at the University of Wales at Cardiff. He has published many books on philosophy and the history of ideas, most recently *Spinoza and the Origins of Modern Critical Theory* (1990) and *The Truth About Postmodernism* (1993).

CATHERINE PORTER is Professor of French at the State University of New York, College at Cortland. She is the English translator of Foucault's "What Is Enlightenment?"

PAUL RABINOW is Professor of Anthropology at the University of California at Berkeley. He is the author of *French Modern: Norms and Forms of the Social Environment* (MIT Press, 1989) and is currently working on a history of the polymerase chain reaction and a book of essays on the cultural implications of biotechnology.

JOSEPH ROUSE is Professor of Philosophy and Science in Society at Wesleyan University. He is the author of *Knowledge and Power: Toward a Political Philosophy of Science* (Cornell University Press, 1987) and is currently completing a book entitled *The Dynamics of Scientific Knowledge: Beyond Realism, Rationality, and Social Constructivism.*

JANA SAWICKI is Associate Professor of Philosophy and Women's Studies at Williams College, where she serves as Chair of Women's Studies. She is the author of *Disciplining Foucault: Feminism, Power, and the Body* (Routledge, 1991). She is currently at work on a series of articles on feminist models of self-reflection and liberation that explore the empowering dimension of confessional narratives.

STEPHEN WATSON is Professor of Philosophy at the University of Notre Dame. He is the author of *Extensions: Essays on Interpretation, Rationality, and the Closure of Modernism* (SUNY, 1992) and numerous articles in recent Continental philosophy.

1962	Becomes Professor of Philosophy at Clermont-Ferrand.
1966	Visiting Professor in Tunisia at University of Tunis.
1967	Chosen Professor at the University of Paris at Nanterre, but returns to Tunisia when the Ministry of Education delays ratification of the choice.
1968	Chairman of Philosophy Department at new experimental university at Vincennes.
1969	Elected to the Collège de France, choosing to designate his chair as in the "History of Systems of Thought." Gives inaugural lecture, "L'ordre de discours," on December 2, 1970.
1970	First lectures in the United States and in Japan.
1971	Helps found the Groupe d'information sur les prisions (GIP), an organization for scrutinizing and criticizing prison conditions in France.
1972	Another trip to the United States, including a visit to the New York State prison at Attica.
1973	Lectures in New York, Montreal, and Rio de Janeiro.
1975	Takes part in protests against Franco's executions of militants.
1976	Visits Brazil and California.
1978	Reports on the Iranian revolution for an Italian newspaper. Visits Japan.
1981	Active in protests against the Communist government of Poland and in support of Solidarity.
1983	Teaches at the University of California at Berkeley as part of an agreement to visit there every year.
1984	Dies in Paris, June 25, 1984.

The above chronology is based on Daniel Defert, "Quelques repères chronologique" in J.-C. Hug, *Michel Foucault: Une Histoire de la Vérité* (Paris: Syros, 1985), 109–114; and James Bernauer, "Michel Foucault: A Biographical Chronology" in James Bernauer and David Rasmussan, eds., *The Final Foucault* (Cambridge: MIT Press, 1988), 159–66. For further information on Foucault's life, see the biographies by Didier Eribon and James Miller and the "témoinages" collected in *Le débat* 41 (Sept.–Nov., 1986).

BIOGRAPHICAL CHRONOLOGY

1926   Born October 15 in Poitiers; named (after his father) Paul-Michel Foucault
1936   Enrolls at the Lycée Henri-IV in Poitiers.
1940   Enrolls at the Jesuit secondary school, Collège St. Stanislas.
1945   Studies in Paris at Lycée Henri-IV to prepare for entrance examination to École normale supérieure; taught philosophy by Jean Hyppolite.
1946   Admitted to École normale supérieure, where he receives the *licence de philosophie* (1948), the *licence de psychologie* (1949), and the *agrégation de philosophie* (1952).
1952   Employed in the Faculty of Letters at the University of Lille; receives *Diplôme de psycho-pathologie* from the Institut de psychologie at Paris.
1955–1958   Teaches in Sweden at University of Uppsala.
1958   Director of French Center at University of Warsaw.
1959   Director of the French Institute in Hamburg, Germany.
1960   Teaches psychology at the University of Clermont-Ferrand.
1961   Receives Doctorat ès lettres (primary thesis: *Histoire de la folie à l'âge classique*, published by Plon, 1961; thèse complémentaire: introduction to and translation (with notes) of Kant's *Anthropologie in pragmatischer Hinsicht*; translation and notes published by Vrin, 1964.

Introduction
Michel Foucault: A user's manual

AGAINST INTERPRETATION

For all Foucault's reservations about modernity and authorship, his writings are typical of a modernist author in their demand for interpretation. Any writing, of course, requires some interpretation as part of our efforts to evaluate, refine, extend, or appreciate its achievement; or to provide special background that readers outside the author's culture or historical period may require. But certain authors – in literature, the twentieth-century modernists are among the best examples – present themselves as so immediately and intrinsically "difficult" as to require special interpretative efforts even for those well equipped to understand them. *The Wasteland, Cantos,* and *Finnegans Wake,* for example, require explanation, even for culturally and historically attuned readers, in a way that *Paradise Lost,* the *Essay on Man,* and *Emma* do not. Philosophy, at least since Kant and Hegel, has also provided its share of "intrinsically obscure" writing. Although it may not be easy to formulate the precise difference, it is clear that Wittgenstein, the later Heidegger, and Derrida require a sort of interpretation that Russell, Dewey, and Quine do not.

Foucault's penchant, particularly prior to *Discipline and Punish,* for the modernist obscure explains much of the demand for interpretations of his work. But the need to interpret Foucault sits ill with his own desire to escape general interpretative categories. More important, as the enterprise of interpretation is usually understood, interpreting Foucault is guaranteed to distort his thought. Interpretation typically means finding a unifying schema through which we can make overall sense of an author's works. Interpretations of Foucault, accordingly, single out some comprehensive unity or defini-

I

tive achievement that is thought to provide the key to his work. They claim to have attained a privileged standpoint that provides the real meaning or significance of his achievement.[1]

Interpretation distorts because Foucault's work is at root ad hoc, fragmentary, and incomplete. Each of his books is determined by concerns and approaches specific to it and should not be understood as developing or deploying a theory or a method that is a general instrument of intellectual progress. In Isaiah Berlin's adaptation of Archilochus's metaphor, Foucault is not a hedgehog but a fox.[2]

Foucault's writings tempt us to general interpretation along two primary axes. In the first dimension he appears as a philosophical historian, progressively developing a series of complementary historical methods: an archaeology of discourse in *The History of Madness, The Birth of the Clinic, The Order of Things,* and *The Archaeology of Knowledge;* a genealogy of power relations in *Discipline and Punish* and *The History of Sexuality I;* and a problematization of ethics in *The Use of Pleasure* and *The Care of the Self.* In the second dimension he appears as a historicist philosopher, offering, parallel to his methodological innovations, successively deeper and mutually supporting theories of knowledge, power, and the self. It is natural to combine these two dimensions in an overall interpretation of Foucault's work as a new comprehensive understanding of human reality supported by new methods of historical analysis.

One of the most intelligent and interesting general interpretations of Foucault is that of Hubert Dreyfus and Paul Rabinow.[3] They present Foucault as developing a "new method" (both historical and philosophical) whereby he "goes beyond" structuralism and hermeneutics. This method they term "interpretative analytics": *analytics* because it shares Kant's critical concern of determining "the sources and legitimate uses" of our concepts; *interpretative* because it seeks "a pragmatically guided reading of the coherence of the practices" in which the concepts are expressed.[4] Dreyfus and Rabinow agree that interpretative analytics "is not a general method," since it recognizes that it itself is practiced within a historically contingent context and that its practitioner "realizes that he himself is produced by what he is studying; consequently he can never stand outside it."[5] Nonetheless, Dreyfus and Rabinow do see Foucault's method as occupying a privileged position on the contemporary scene:

since we still take the problems of our culture seriously, . . . we are drawn
ineluctably to a position like Foucault's. In a sense, it is the only position
left that does not regress to a tradition that is untenable. . . . This does not
mean that one is forced to agree with Foucault's specific diagnosis of our
current situation. . . . But . . . some form of interpretative analytics is currently the most powerful, plausible and honest option available.[6]

Dreyfus and Rabinow offer a general interpretation in that they read
the whole of Foucault's work as directed toward the development of
a single historico-philosophical method that has a privileged role in
contemporary analyses. Even if this method is not ahistorically universal, they clearly present it as Foucault's definitive achievement
for our time: the preferred instrument for current social and cultural
analysis.

I am uneasy with this and other general interpretations of Foucault because they deny the two things that, to my mind, are most
distinctive and most valuable in his voice: its specificity and its
marginality. It is striking that Foucault's books hardly ever refer
back to his previous works. *The Birth of the Clinic* never mentions
The History of Madness, even though the two books share the common ground of the history of medicine in the nineteenth century;
The Order of Things describes the episteme of the Classical Age
with scarcely a hint of the author's previous extensive dealings with
that period in *The History of Madness* and *The Birth of the Clinic*;
The History of Sexuality I, for all its conceptual, methodological,
and topical similarities to *Discipline and Punish*, refuses to acknowledge any connection; and *The Use of Pleasure* and *The Care of the
Self*, although formally the second and third volumes of a history of
sexuality, acknowledge the first volume only to note their divergence from it. This lack of self-citation is not mere coyness. Each of
Foucault's books strikes a specific tone that is muffled and distorted
if we insist on harmonizing it with his other books. In examining
psychiatry, medicine, the social sciences, and other contemporary
disciplines, his goal was always to suggest liberating alternatives to
what seem to be inevitable conceptions and practices. But his analyses are effective precisely because they are specific to the particular
terrain of the discipline he is challenging, not determined by some
general theory or methodology. As we shall see, Foucault does not

hesitate to construct theories and methods, but the constructions are always subordinated to the tactical needs of the particular analysis at hand. They are not general engines of war that can be deployed against any target. This is why each of Foucault's books has the air of a new beginning.

General interpretations of Foucault suppress his marginality by presenting his work as the solution to the problems of an established discipline or as the initiation of some new discipline. This ignores the crucial fact that disciplines are precisely the dangers from which Foucault is trying to help us save ourselves. His attacks are on the apparently necessary presuppositions (such as that madness is mental illness, that imprisonment is the only humane punishment for criminals, that ending sexual repression is the key to human liberation) that define disciplines. Therefore, they can be launched only from the peripheral areas where the defining assumptions begin to lose hold. To present Foucault as working within an established discipline or, even worse, as attempting to found one himself is to contradict the basic thrust of his efforts.[7]

Resisting our inclination to general interpretation accords not only with the direction of Foucault's work but also with some of his own explicit pronouncements. For example, in "What Is an Author?" and elsewhere,[8] he challenges the unifying categories (author, works, etc.) presupposed by general interpretation. And in an anonymous interview, "The Masked Philosopher," he describes his dream that books would not be subjected to totalizing judgments but would rather find "a criticism of scintillating leaps of the imagination [that] would not be sovereign or dressed in red [but would] catch the sea-foam in the breeze and scatter it."[9]

On the other hand, it is only fair to note that Foucault himself was prone to providing overall interpretations of his work. Thus, in 1969 he characterizes all his previous books (*The History of Madness*, *The Birth of the Clinic*, and *The Order of Things*) as "imperfect sketches" of the archaeological method for analyzing discursive formations that is explained in *The Archaeology of Knowledge*.[10] But then in 1977 he says, "When I think back now, I ask myself what else was I talking about in [*The History of Madness*] or *The Birth of the Clinic*, but power?"[11] By 1982 he is saying: "it is not power, but the subject, which is the general theme of my research."[12]

The ambivalence of Foucault's view of his own work is particularly apparent in a discussion at the end of *The Archaeology of Knowledge*. Foucault imagines a critic who suggests that archaeology is

> yet another of those discourses that would like to be taken as a discipline still in its early stages . . . yet another of those projects that justify themselves on the basis of what they are not, . . . disciplines for which one opens up possibilities, outlines a programme, and leaves the future development to others. But no sooner have they been outlined than they disappear together with their authors. And the field they were supposed to tend remains sterile forever.[13]

Foucault first responds with forthright denials of "scientific" pretensions: "I have never presented archaeology as a science, or even as the beginning of a future science. . . . The word archaeology is not supposed to carry any suggestion of anticipation; it simply indicates a possible line of attack for the analysis of verbal performances."[14] But he then goes on to emphasize the close connection of archaeology to current sciences. They are, he says, a primary object of archaeological analysis; its methods are closely related to those of some sciences – especially generative grammar; and its topics are closely correlated to those of disciplines such as psychoanalysis, epistemology, and sociology. Foucault even suggests that a "general theory of productions" would, if developed, be an "enveloping theory" for archaeology. He goes on to say that he is perfectly aware that "my discourse may disappear with the figure that has borne it so far." But he also says, "It may turn out that archaeology is the name given to a part of our contemporary theoretical conjuncture" and suggests as one possibility that "this conjuncture is giving rise to an individualizable discipline, whose initial characteristics and overall limits are being outlined here."[15] It is clear that, at least when he wrote *The Archaeology of Knowledge*, Foucault was tempted by the hope of becoming the founder of a new discipline.

General interpretations of Foucault are tempting because, for all their distortion, they can put us on to some important truths. My suggestion is not that we renounce them but that we regard them as nonunique and developed for specific purposes. (Had Foucault lived, he would have surely continued to produce them as an accompaniment to his ever-changing specific concerns.) Without becoming obsessed with finding the general interpretation that will give us the "final truth" about Foucault's work, we should be prepared to use a variety of such interpretations to elucidate, for particular purposes, specific aspects of his writings. For example, the methodological axis of interpretation, which sees Foucault moving from archaeology through genealogy to ethics, is useful for appreciating his contribution to historical method and hence relating his work to the *Annales* school, French history and philosophy of science, the "new historians," disputes about the role of events in history, etc.[16] The topical axis of interpretation, which views him as starting with the study of knowledge, coming to see the inextricable connection of knowledge to power, and finally subordinating both to a primary concern with the self, shows how to read Foucault as contributing to recent discussions in the epistemology and philosophy of science (particularly social epistemology and "postmodern" philosophy of science) and in social theory.[17]

It is, however, less risky and even more profitable to regard Foucault as an intellectual artisan, someone who over the years constructed a variety of artifacts, the intellectual equivalents of the material objects created by a skilled goldsmith or cabinetmaker. We need to take account of the specific circumstance occasioning the production of each artifact in order to understand and appreciate it. But each artifact may also have further uses not explicitly envisaged by its creator, so that we also need to examine it with a view to employment for our own purposes. Foucault was particularly adept at crafting three sorts of intellectual artifacts: histories, theories, and myths. As an alternative to a general interpretation of his work, I propose to discuss some examples of these productions.

FOUCAULT'S HISTORIES

Foucault wrote book-length histories of madness, clinical medicine, the social sciences, the prison, and ancient and modern sexuality. Although much has been made of his archaeological and genealogical methods, his approach to each topic is driven much more by the specific historical subject matter than by prior methodological commitments. "Archaeology" and "genealogy" are primarily retrospective (and usually idealized) descriptions of Foucault's complex efforts to come to terms with his historical material. His "discourse on method," *The Archaeology of Knowledge*, is a reconstruction, with a not insignificant amount of trimming and shaping, of what went on in the three histories that preceded it.[18]

An appreciation of Foucault's histories requires locating them on a finer grid than that defined by the two dimensions of archaeology and genealogy. I propose tracking Foucaultian histories along four dimensions: histories of ideas, histories of concepts, histories of the present, and histories of experience.

Although Foucault's explicit mentions of standard history of ideas are at best disdainful, we need to keep in mind that he himself frequently offers the sorts of textual interpretations and comparisons that are the mainstay of orthodox history of ideas. Central to *The History of Madness*, for example, is his reading of the passage in the *Meditations* in which Descartes dismisses the possibility that he is mad as a grounds for doubt.[19] Similarly, crucial claims of *The Order of Things* are based on interpretations of scientific and philosophical texts from Paracelsus and Aldrovandi to Smith and Kant. Moreover, despite Foucault's particular disdain for historians of ideas' concern with attributions of originality, key points of his argument in *The Order of Things* depend on showing that, for example, Cuvier rather than Lamarck developed the basic framework for evolutionary theory and that Marx's work in economics is really just a variant on Ricardo's. Much of Foucault's last two volumes, on ancient sexuality, also need to be read and evaluated by the norms of standard interpretative history of ideas. On at least one important level, they are simply explications of texts by Galen, Xenophon, and Plato, among others.

Much of Foucault's historiography falls in the genre of "the history of concepts," as that has been understood by his friend and mentor Georges Canguilhem. This approach flows from an insistence on the distinction between the concepts that interpret scientific data and the theories that explain them. By contrast, the standard Anglo-American view (shared by both positivists such as Hempel and their critics such as Kuhn) is that theories are interpretations of data and therefore define the concepts in terms of which data are understood. On Canguilhem's view, concepts give us a preliminary understanding of data that allows us to formulate scientifically fruitful questions about how to explain the data as conceptualized. Theories then provide different – and often conflicting – answers to these questions. For example, Galileo introduced a new concept of the motion of fall-

ing bodies (in opposition to Aristotle's); then he, Descartes, and Newton provided competing theories to explain the motion so conceived.
As long as concepts are regarded as functions of theories, their history
will be identical with that of the development of theoretical formulations. But for Canguilhem concepts are "theoretically polyvalent";
the same concept can function in quite different theoretical contexts.
This opens up the possibility of histories of concepts that are distinct
from the standard histories that merely trace a succession of theoretical formulations.

Canguilhem himself demonstrated the power of this approach in
his history of the concept of reflex action.[20] The standard view is
that this concept was first introduced by Descartes in his _Traité de
l'homme._ Such a view is natural if we do not make Canguilhem's
distinction between concepts and theories. The concept of reflex
action is at the heart of modern mechanistic theories in physiology,
and Descartes was the first to describe reflex phenomena and try to
account for them mechanistically. But Canguilhem is able to show
that, even though Descartes anticipates modern physiology in offering a mechanistic explanation of the reflex, he does not in fact have,
either explicitly or implicitly, the modern concept of the reflex. His
explanation is of the phenomenon conceived quite differently than
modern physiology conceives it. By contrast, Canguilhem shows,
the modern concept of the reflex is fully present in the (distinctly
nonmodern) vitalistic physiology of Thomas Willis.[21]

Foucault makes a similar use of the history of concepts in _The
Order of Things_ when he argues that the Darwinian idea of an evolution of species is implicit in Cuvier but not in Lamarck. He admits
that Lamarck's developmental theory recognizes biological change in
a way that Cuvier's fixist theory does not. But, Foucault argues, it is
Cuvier and not Lamarck who introduces the fundamental idea that
biological species are productions of historical forces rather than in-
stantiations of timeless, a priori possibilities. Lamarckian "evolution" is merely a matter of living things successively occupying pre-
established niches that are quite independent of historical forces,
such as natural selection. But for Cuvier the fact that species do not
change over time is itself a result of the historical forces that have led
to their production. Lamarckian change is just a superficial play of
organisms above the eternally fixed structure of species; Cuvier's
fixism is a historical stability produced by radically temporal biologi-

cal processes. Accordingly, Foucault maintains that Cuvier rather than Lamarck provides the conceptual framework that makes Darwin's theory of evolution possible.

Of all Foucault's books, *The Birth of the Clinic* (written for a series edited by Canguilhem) comes the closest to a pure history of concepts, the concept in question being that of physical illness as it developed from the end of the eighteenth century through the first third of the nineteenth. *The Order of Things* also makes extensive use of Canguilhem's approach. Foucault's accounts of the empirical sciences of the eighteenth and nineteenth centuries are simply histories of the relevant concepts. But *The Order of Things* also extends and transforms Canguilhem's method. For Canguilhem concepts correspond to disciplines, and the history of a concept is written within the confines of the relevant discipline. But Foucault links apparently very different disciplines by showing similarities in their basic concepts. He argues, for example, that the Classical empirical sciences of general grammar, natural history, and analysis of wealth share a common conceptual structure that makes them much more similar to one another than any one of them is to its modern successor (respectively: philology, biology, and economics). Even more important, Foucault maintains that such philosophical concepts as *resemblance, representation*, and *man* pervade all the disciplines of a given period, a view that leads him to the notion of an episteme as the system of concepts that defines knowledge for a given intellectual era.

These extensions of Canguilhem's history of concepts transform it by moving to a level where the historian is no longer required to define a discipline in its own terms. As a historian of biology, Canguilhem deals with concepts (such as reflex action) explicitly deployed by contemporary biology. Foucault focuses not only on such first-order biological concepts but also on concepts (such as representation and historicity) that are conditions of possibility for the first-order concepts.

This analysis of the "intellectual subconscious" of scientific disciplines is precisely Foucault's famous archaeological approach to the history of thought. Archaeology is an important alternative to standard history of ideas, with its emphasis on the theorizing of individual thinkers and concern with their influence on one another. Foucault suggests (and shows how the suggestion is fruitful) that the play of individuals' thought, in a given period and disciplinary context, takes place in a space with a structure defined by a system of rules more fundamental than the assertions of the individuals thinking in the space. Delineating the structures of this space (the goal of the archaeology of thought) often gives a more fundamental understanding of the history of thought than do standard histories centered on the individual subject (which Foucault disdainfully labels "doxology").

Many of Foucault's histories fall under the category he designated "history of the present." Of course history is, by definition, about the past, but Foucault's histories typically begin from his perception that something is terribly wrong in the present. His motive for embarking on a history is his judgment that certain current social circumstances – an institution, a discipline, a social practice – are "intolerable."[22] His primary goal is not to understand the past but to understand the present; or, to put the point with more nuance, to use an understanding of the past to understand something that is intolerable in the present. In this sense his characterization of *Discipline and Punish* as "history of the present" (30–31) applies to all his histories.

Apart from the paradoxical language, there is really nothing extraordinary in Foucault's project of trying to understand the present in terms of the past; in one way or another, this is what most historians are up to. But Foucault reverses a standard polarity of this enterprise. Whereas much traditional history tries to show that where we are is inevitable, given the historical causes revealed by its account, Foucault's histories aim to show the contingency – and hence surpassability – of what history has given us. Intolerable practices and institutions present themselves as having no alternative: How could we do anything except set up asylums to treat the mentally ill? How deal humanely with criminals except by imprisoning them? How attain sexual freedom except by discovering and accepting our sexual orientation? Foucault's histories aim to remove this air of necessity by showing that the past ordered things quite differently and that the processes leading to our present practices and institutions were by no mean inevitable.

Foucault's history of madness, for example, is an assault on our conception of madness as mental illness and the practice of psychiatry based on this conception. We tend to think that people who shout unprovoked obscenities in public places or refuse to eat anything other than cat food are by definition mentally ill and require the care of qualified medical professionals. Mental illness is the inevitable diagnosis of such behavior, and psychiatric treatment the only way of dealing with it. Foucault's history of madness is designed to show first that there have been alternative conceptions of mad behavior with at least as much cognitive respectability as ours. In particular, during the Classical Age (about 1650 to 1800), Europeans viewed madness not as an illness requiring medical treatment but as a moral fault that reduced human beings to a level of animality that could only be isolated and contained, not cured. Foucault maintains that this is not a false conception, refuted by the truth of modern psychiatry. Rather, both the Classical and the modern conceptions of madness are social constructions, intelligible and apparently compelling in their own periods, but with no privileged access to the truth of madness.

Foucault further maintains that the modern conception of madness as mental illness was unwittingly constructed from two key elements of the Classical conception. The notion that the mad are animals was transformed into the modern view of madness as a natural phenomenon, governed by biological and psychological laws, while the Classical moral condemnation of madness was retained through the asylum system of confinement, which surreptitiously imposed bourgeois values on its inmates. He reads the emergence of modern psychiatry not as an ineluctable triumph of compassion based on scientific objectivity, but as the product of scientifically and morally suspect forces peculiar to the social and intellectual structures of the nineteenth and twentieth centuries.

In *The Order of Things* Foucault offers a similar analysis of the modern social sciences. He maintains that all social scientific knowledge is based on a particular conception of human reality, the conception of *man*. Man is defined as that entity for which representations of objects exist. To assert the reality of man in this special sense is to posit a being with a puzzling dual status; something that is both an object in the world and an experiencing subject through which the world is constituted. Modern thought takes this conception of man as definitive of human reality as such, but Foucault maintains that it is just one contingent construal of that reality – and one that will soon pass.

The Order of Things can be read broadly as a historical critique of the modern concept of man. First, Foucault begins by trying to show that the concept had no role during the immediately preceding Classical period. That age simply identified thought with representation; to think of something was just to represent it as an item in a table of genera and species. But that meant that there could be no Classical thought of representation itself. To think of representation would require representing it, which would in turn require placing it as one species in the table of kinds of thought. But this was impossible, since representation was regarded as identical with thought. It was, accordingly, impossible for the Classical Age to think of representation and therefore impossible for it to form the concept of man, which is defined in terms of representation. In this sense man did not exist for the Classical Age. The concept, Foucault argues, emerges only at the end of the eighteenth century, when Kant for the first time treats representation as just one form of thought and seeks the conditions that make it possible.

Foucault also details ways in which the viability of the concept of man has come into question during the modern period. His discussion of "the analytic of finitude" highlights the failure of modern philosophical efforts (from Kant through Heidegger) to forge a coherent understanding of an entity that is somehow both the source of the world and an object in the world. And he argues that the more successful efforts of the human sciences to attain knowledge of human beings have led to "counter-sciences," such as Lacan's psychoanalysis and Lévi-Strauss's anthropology, that undermine the concept of man.

We have seen how Foucault's archaeological method is an outgrowth of his use of Canguilhem's history of concepts. Similarly, his genealogical method can be understood in terms of his desire to write histories of the present. In fact, in one use of the term, Foucault simply identifies genealogy with history of the present, regarding it as any effort to question the necessity of dominant categories and procedures. More narrowly, genealogy is a history of the present specifically concerned with the complex casual antecedents of a socio-intellectual reality (in contrast to archaeology, which is concerned only with the conceptual structures subtending the reality). *Discipline and Punish* is the fullest expression of genealogy in this narrow sense, since it, more than any other of Foucault's books, is concerned with practices and institutions rather than experiences and ideas.[23]

Foucault frequently referred to his historical analyses as "histories of experience." Such reference is especially prominent in *The History of Madness*, which continually speaks of the Renaissance, Classical, and modern experiences of madness, and in the two volumes on the ancient history of sexuality, which Foucault explicitly presents as "a history of the experience of sexuality" (*The Use of Pleasure*, 4). But the idea is present throughout Foucault's histories. The Preface to *The Order of Things*, for example, presents that work as an analysis of "the pure experience of order and of its modes of being" (xxi).

"History of experience" does not, however, have a univocal sense throughout Foucault's historical writings. In *The History of Madness*, which is still significantly marked by Foucault's early attraction to existential phenomenology, the talk of experience evokes, as Foucault himself later noted,[24] the notion of an anonymous subject of an age's thought and perception. The account of *The History of Madness* accordingly often suggests a quasi-Hegelian *Phänomenologie des kranken Geistes*. Subsequent references (for example, to the experience of order in *The Order of Things* or to the "gaze" in *The Birth of the Clinic*) are more appropriately read in terms of the nonsubjective linguistic structures (discursive formations) Foucault theorizes about in *The Archaeology of Knowledge*. The "experience" of the last two volumes of the history of sexuality signals a return of the subject, although not the quasi-Hegelian specter of *The History of Madness*. Now the experience is located in individual persons, who are themselves, however, situated in the fields of knowledge and the systems of normativity that are the respective objects of archaeology and genealogy.

These four dimensions define the field on which Foucault's histories take their diverse forms. Rather than taking any single book as the monotone development of a particular method or strategy, we should read each of Foucault's historical studies as the marshaling of a variety of historical approaches to come to terms with a particular historical reality. The precise combination of approaches depends on the object of inquiry. The history of concepts is most appropriate for disciplines well past the "threshold of scientificity"[25] and so is particularly prominent in *The Birth of the Clinic*'s treatment of medicine and *The Order of Things*'s treatment of the social sciences and their predecessors. All of Foucault's studies are histories of the present in that their subject matter corresponds to some contemporary ideas and practices that he finds especially dangerous. But the approach is paramount in *The History of Madness, Discipline and Punish*, and *The History of Sexuality I*, where there is a specific and well-entrenched institutional locus (the asylum, the prison, governmental bio-power) of the danger. The history of experience is most prominent in *The History of Madness* and *The Use of Pleasure* and *The Care of the Self*, where, although in very different ways, Foucault recognizes a central role for the subject.

Foucault's distinctiveness as an historian of thought lies less in his invention of new methods than in his willingness to employ whatever methods seem required by his specific subject matter. Archaeology and genealogy are innovations of some importance. The former, developed out of Canguilhem's history of concepts, writes a history of thought centered not in the individual subject but in the linguistic structures defining the fields in which individual subjects operate. The latter, as a particular version of history of the present, undermines grand narratives of inevitable progress by tracing the origins of practices and institutions from a congeries of contingent "petty causes." But neither method is the exclusive vehicle of any given Foucaultian analysis, and neither has precisely the same sense in its various applications.

Further, despite the imperial tone of some Foucaultian rhetoric, neither of these methods eliminates the need for historical work of a more standard sort. Archaeology is a useful supplement and, in some cases, a necessary corrective to standard (subject-centered) approaches to intellectual history, but it can hardly stand as a substitute for such work. Its weakness is the obverse of its strength: the bracketing or decentering of the subject. The power of archaeology is apparent from what it finds in the conceptual structures that lie beneath and outside the consciousness of individual subjects. Its limitation is its abstraction from the intellectual lives of subjects, which are not purely foam spewed up by the archaeological ocean but the most concrete and original locus of intellectual achievement. Similarly, the microanalyses of Foucault's genealogy usefully undermine the apparent inevitability of many large-scale accounts. But there are relevant factors operative at the macro-level that the close focus of genealogy is too narrow to detect.

There are those who suggest that Foucault is not really a historian and that his work should not be evaluated by the standard norms and canons of historiography.[26] They are correct in the sense that a Foucaultian history often has its distinctive agenda, with goals quite different from that of standard historiography. His histories of the present, for example, do not aim at a full and balanced reconstruction of past phenomena in their own terms. They focus selectively on just those aspects of the past that are important for understanding our present intolerable circumstances. Such histories may suggest comprehensive schemata that either intrigue or outrage orthodox historians, who have every right to develop or refute Foucault's general claims about, for example, the status of the mad in eighteenth-century Europe or the fundamental mentality of the Classical Age. But even if, read as standard history, his accounts are found inaccurate, they may still be adequate to their task of grounding a historical critique of current malpractices. For example, reservations regarding the overall adequacy of Foucault's account of Tuke's "moral therapy" may not affect the validity of his conclusions about modern psychiatry's lack of moral neutrality.

Foucault's histories of experience provide an example of another sort. Here he is concerned to describe the basic categories that structure the way a given age perceived and thought about objects such as madness or disease. Such a description is derived from historical facts about discourse and behavior during the given age, but Foucault's claims about the "mentality" of an age do not require that he be right about every fact he puts forward to illustrate them. For example, historians such as Roy Porter have rightly challenged Foucault's assertions about the extent of confinement of the mad in eighteenth-century Europe without thereby subverting his view that the attitudes behind confinement were central to the Classical experience of madness.

Although Foucault's particular focus may sometimes allow him to escape from criticisms that would refute a more orthodox historical account, this is not because his enterprise falls outside the standard disciplinary norms of historiography. Histories of experience, of concepts, or of the present do need to be justified by historical evidence, as Foucault is entirely aware. But just what sort of evidence is appropriate depends on the precise sort of historical claim being made. If a history of the present is confused with a global account of the past for its own sake or if a history of an experience is mistaken for a set of empirical generalizations about what people in the past said or did, then Foucault is being evaluated by the wrong sort of norms. But every one of his historical claims needs to be justified on the basis of some set of facts accessible to standard historiography. Otherwise Foucault's claims will be either gratuitous or not really historical.

FOUCAULT'S THEORIES

Foucault is an impressive theoretician who builds complex analytic structures with rare facility and acuity. His theorizing is typically not for its own sake but in response to the demands of a specific historical or critical project. Moreover, the theories devised are not intended as permanent structures, enduring in virtue of their universal truth. They are temporary scaffoldings, erected for a specific purpose, that Foucault is happy to abandon to whomever might find them useful, once he has finished his job.

Consider, for example, Foucault's uses of theories of language. His two most extensive treatments of language are in *The Order of Things* and *The Archaeology of Knowledge;* and although these books were separated by only three years, it would be hard to imagine more thoroughly different approaches. *The Order of Things* deals with language in a broadly Heideggerian framework of historical ontology. The question is how the being of language has varied over time, and the answer is given by describing the diverse ways that language has both existed in and referred to the world.

During the Renaissance, according to Foucault, language had "been set down in the world and form[ed] a part of it, both because things themselves hide and manifest their enigma like a language and because words offer themselves to men as things to be deciphered" (*The Order of Things*, 35). As a result, the Renaisssance studied language as it would any other natural object. Ramus, for example, did not regard etymology as having to do with the meanings of words but with the intrinsic properties of letters, syllables, and words. And his syntax was concerned with the consequences of these intrinsic properties for combinations of words, not with criteria for the meaningfulness of such combinations. For the Renaissance, "language is not what it is because it has a meaning; its representative content . . . has no role to play here" (*The Order of Things*, 35).

With the Classical Age, there is a radical change in the ontological status of language: "language, instead of existing as the material writing of things, was to find its area of being restricted to the general organization of representative signs" (*The Order of Things*, 42). Language is no longer intertwined with the world, a subsystem of resemblances ontologically on a par with the nonlinguistic resemblances that constitute the overall system of reality. Language is now a separate ontological realm, related to but sharply distinct from the world it describes. "The profound kinship of language with the world was . . . dissolved. . . . Discourse was still to have the task of speaking that which is, but it was no longer to be anything more than what it said" (*The Order of Things*, 43). The entire reality of language was exhausted in its function of representing objects.

With the modern period (roughly, following Kant), the transparent, purely representative character of language is lost and language becomes once again just one part of the world. Now, however, its reality is not that of an eternal, divinely contrived system of resemblances but that of complexly dispersed historical phenomena. No longer the golden key to understanding the world, language has become our unavoidable but profoundly recalcitrant means of expression – recalcitrant precisely because of the historical sedimentations that constrain and distort everything we try to say. Foucault sees formalization and hermeneutical interpretation, the two apparently opposed instruments of modern philosophical analysis, as in fact complementary efforts to overcome the obstacles language poses to knowledge.

With the modern age, as Foucault suspects, ending, the being of language is once again undergoing a fundamental shift. The final result is still undetermined and unpredictable, although Foucault suggests that it may involve a rebirth of language as a unified plentitude. In any case, he has no doubt that the question of language is "where the whole curiosity of our thought now resides" (*The Order of Things*, 306).

In *the Archaeology of Knowledge* there are only a few hints of Heideggerian historical ontology. Languages are historical in the sense that the thought of different periods arises from different sets of linguistic systems ("discursive formations"). But language itself is characterized by an atemporal basic structure characteristic of all discursive formations. This structure is given by Foucault's elaborate typology of the rules governing the statements (*énoncés*) that are the basic elements of a discursive formation. Classical natural history and modern biology are very different modes of thought because the discursive rules governing their statements are very different. But in the schema of *The Archaeology of Knowledge* there is no suggestion that language as such has undergone any fundamental transformation from the Classical to the modern age. In both periods it is a system of statements governed by rules that instantiate Foucault's atemporal type of a discursive formation.

It might seem then that in *The Archaeology of Knowledge* Foucault renounces the Heideggerianism of *The Order of Things* in favor of a structuralist theory of language, despite his intemperate disavowals of the structuralist label. And, indeed, when (in the conclusion of *The Archaeology of Knowledge*) Foucault imagines a critic objecting "You have refused to see that discourse, unlike a particular language [*langue*] perhaps, is essentially historical" he replies, "You are quite right" (*The Archaeology of Knowledge*, 200, translation modified). My suggestion, however, is that what happens from *The Order of Things* to *The Archaeology of Knowledge* is not Foucault's conversion to a new position but his selection of a new intellectual tool. In *The Order of Things* Foucault's concern is eschatological: he sets himself up as the prophet of the end of one epistemic age and the beginning of another. In casting his gaze over all that has preceded the coming transformation, he sees new conceptions of language as central in each stage of development. A Heideggerian picture of language as a historico-ontological presence is a natural and effective vehicle for presenting such a viewpoint. In *The Archaeology of Knowledge* Foucault's concern is methodological: he is trying to construct a general approach to the history of thought that does not presuppose the centrality of the phenomenological subject. For this purpose it is natural and effective to present language as an atemporal structure of rules. To ask Foucault which theory of language is really right is like asking the quantum physicist whether light is really a wave or a system of particles. The only sensible answer is that there are particular contexts in which each view has distinctive advantages.

My suggestion is not that Foucault need be an antirealist in principle about theories, any more than the quantum physicist who refuses to choose between a wave and a particle picture need be an antirealist in principle. The physicist may well think that there is some ultimate truth about the nature of light, even while maintaining that the choice between the wave and the particle picture is not relevant to the question of what this truth is. Such a physicist might even think that the question of a theory's ultimate truth was of no concern to him or her as a physicist, on the grounds that physics aims only at accounts that are empirically adequate. Similarly, my suggestion is not that Foucault thinks he has philosophical grounds for rejecting the very idea of a true theory, but that he is concerned about values theories may have quite apart from questions about their ultimate truth.

This nonrealist approach is also helpful in thinking about Foucault's famous and controversial account of power. This account is laid out, generally and abstractly it seems, in a series of propositions in *The History of Sexuality I*. For example: "power is exercised from innumerable points, in the interplay of nonegalitarian and mobile relations. . . . Power comes from below; that is, there is no binary and all-encompassing opposition between rulers and ruled at the root of power relations. . . . Power relations are both intentional and nonsubjective" (*The History of Sexuality I*, 94).

Charles Taylor, most effectively among many others, has criticized Foucault's theory of power as a gross over-simplification:

His espousal of the reversal of Clauswitz's aphorism, which makes us see politics as war carried on by other means, can open insights in certain situations. But to make this one's basic axiom for the examination of modern power as such leaves out too much. Foucault's opposition between the old model of power, based on sovereignty/obedience, and the new one based on domination/subjugation leaves out everything in Western history which has been animated by civic humanism or analogous movements. . . . Without this in one's conceptual armoury Western history and societies become incomprehensible.[27]

But it is not at all clear that the theory Foucault propounds is, as Taylor suggests, intended to elucidate anything as grand as "Western history and societies." The chapter of *The History of Sexuality I* in which Foucault lays down his propositions about power is not titled "The Nature of Power," but simply "Method," the question being, as Foucault explicitly puts it, one "of forming a different grid of historical decipherment by starting from a different theory of power" (*The*

History of Sexuality I, 90–91). Further, this theory will not be put forward as an independent construct; it will be a matter of "advancing little by little toward a different conception of power through a closer examination of an entire historical material" (91), namely, the very specific material that makes up the body of Foucault's projected history of modern sexuality. Foucault's goal, then, is not to provide a universally applicable theory of modern power but to find a theory that will help us understand "a certain form of knowledge regarding sex" (92). He is after nothing more than what Taylor agrees he has: a theory that "can open insights in certain situations."

Certainly, Foucault is also interested in deploying his theory of power in other relevant domains. He first developed it in his study of the modern prison in *Discipline and Punish*, where he also showed how the theory elucidated a range of modern institutions, from armies to schools, that had a "carceral" structure. But Foucault sees such extensions as demonstrating the fruitfulness of a method rather than the universality of a picture. Moreover, he makes no claims about the exclusive validity of his approach, even to the domains in which he thinks it particularly enlightening. According to his theory, power is a matter of the subtle and meticulous control of bodies rather than the influence of ethical and judicial ideas and institutions. Nonetheless, he says that "it is certainly legitimate to write a history of punishment against the background of moral ideas or legal structures." His point is just that there remains the question (which his work purports to answer positively), "Can one write such a history against the background of a history of bodies?" (*Discipline and Punish*, 25). It is, then, not surprising that, when formulating "four rules" expressing the consequences of his theory of power for writing a history of sexuality, Foucault emphasizes that they "are not intended as methodological imperatives; at most they are cautionary prescriptions" (*The History of Sexuality I*, 98).

FOUCAULT'S MYTHS

The power of Foucault's writing is due not only to his carefully wrought histories and theories; it also derives from the much less consciously developed, deeply emotional myths that inform many of his books. These myths take the traditional form of a struggle between monsters and heroes. *The History of Madness*, for example, is built on the struggle between the terrors inflicted on the mad by moralizing psychiatrists and the dazzling transgressions of mad artists such as Nietzsche, van Gogh, and Artaud. As so often, the horrors of the monsters are the most effectively portrayed. Rage against them periodically cracks the mannered surface of Foucault's subtle and learned prose with outbursts of derision, sarcasm, and moral indignation. He denounces the moral psychiatry of the nineteenth-century reformers, which "substituted for the free terror of madness the stifling anguish of responsibility; fear no longer reigned on the other side of the prison gates, it now raged under the seals of conscience" (582, 247); "the insane individual . . . far from being protected, [was] kept in a perpetual anxiety, ceaselessly threatened by Law and Transgression" (580, 245). Foucault presents such psychiatry as a "gigantic moral imprisonment" that can be called liberation "only by way of antiphrasis."[28] *The History of Sexuality I* expresses a similar disdain at the liberation from repression allegedly effected by modern sciences of sexuality: "The irony of this deployment is in having us believe that our 'liberation' is in the balance" (159). Even the generally detached analysis of *The Birth of the Clinic* is laced with venom toward the alleged compassion of "medical humanism": "the mindless phenomenologies of understanding mingle the sand of their conceptual desert with this half-baked notion" (xiv).

Although Foucault's monsters take different forms from book to book, all are manifestations of the grand bogeyman of French intellectuals since Flaubert: bourgeois society. Hatred of the institutions of this society – particularly the family and conventional morality – gives power and intensity to Foucault's prose. But it also renders him uncharacteristically insensitive to the complexities and nuances of the despised phenomena. They remain little more than scarecrows on his historical landscapes, and their logical function is, appropriately, that of straw men.

Until the 1970s, Foucault opposed his bourgeois scarecrows to the heroic monuments of the great deviant artists. In his historical studies, these most often appear simply as names in honorific litanies. But beneath these brief liturgical evocations, there is a rather well developed view of avant garde (modernist and postmodernist) literature and art, sketched toward the end of *The History of Madness* and at various points of *The Order of Things* and more fully articulated in his book on Raymond Roussel and in a series of essays published during the 1960s, mostly in *Tel Quel*. Foucault's artists exemplify the two primary components of his positive morality: transgression and intensity. Human fulfillment requires first an opening up of possibilities that lie beyond the limits of prevailing norms. This he understands in terms of Bataille's concept of transgression, a notion developed with great subtlety in his essay on Bataille.[29] For the Foucault of the 1960s, art – particularly writing – is the primary locus of transgression. Writing "implies an action that is always testing the limits of its regularity, transgressing and reversing an order that it accepts and manipulates. Writing unfolds like a game that inevitably moves beyond its own rules and finally leaves them behind. . . . It is primarily concerned with creating an opening where the writing subject endlessly disappears."[30]

For Foucault, transgression is neither a denial of existing values and the limits corresponding to them (it contains, he says, "nothing negative") nor an affirmation of some new realm of values and limits. It is (and here Foucault employs Blanchot's term) a "contestation" of values that "carries them all to their limits." In Nietzschean terms, transgression is an affirmation of human reality, but one made with the stark realization that there is no transcendent meaning or ground of this reality. "To contest [transgress] is to proceed until one reaches the empty core where being achieves its limit and where the limit defines being. There, at the transgressed limit, the 'yes' of contestation reverberates, leaving without echo the heehaw of Nietzsche's braying ass."[31]

Foucault sees transgression as essentially tied to intensity; it "is like a flash of lightning in the night which, from the beginning of time, gives a dense and black intensity to the night it denies."[32] Such intensity is the direct consequence of a transgression that by its very nature places us beyond the deadening and consoling certainties of conventional life. But it also is something that was – and remained – of major importance to Foucault in much more personal terms. In an uncharacteristically revelatory comment to an interviewer in 1983, he noted: "I'm not able to give myself and others those middle-range pleasures that make up everyday life. Such pleasures are nothing for me and I'm not able to organize my life in order to make place for them. . . . A pleasure must be something incredibly intense. . . . Some drugs are really important for me because they are the mediation to those incredibly intense joys that I am looking for."[33]

James Miller's recent biography takes Foucault's fascination with intensity – particularly with what Miller calls "limit-experiences" and relates to Foucault's use of drugs and participation sado-masochistic sexual rituals – as the biographical key to his work.[34] Although intensity is, as we have just seen, an important category in Foucault's thought, Miller overemphasizes it to the point of distortion. This occurs on two levels. On what we might call the microlevel, Miller systematically misreads specific texts by attributing to Foucault himself (on the basis of meagre biographical information) views that the text explicitly attributes to someone else. (David Halperin offers some clear examples in his critique of Miller.)[35] In support of his interpretative method, Miller cites Jean Starobinski's much admired work on Rousseau.[36] But whereas Starobinski had available voluminous autobiographical and other confessional materials, in the case of Foucault there is really nothing beyond some anecdotes from friends and acquaintances and occasional brief remarks Foucault made in interviews or other conversations. When there are vast tracts of someone's personal life about which we know virtually nothing and when the knowledge we have of most other areas is at best sketchy, the effort to read the texts in terms of the life can only be an exercise in speculation. Miller is simply projecting his own ideas about what certain thoughts, feelings, situations, or actions might mean, with no reason for thinking that this is what they did mean for Foucault.[37]

On the macrolevel, Miller simply ignores or dismisses large chunks of Foucault's work that do not admit of analysis in terms of his biographical reading. He ignores almost all the central historical discussion of *The History of Madness* in favor of a focus on the preface to the first edition (which Foucault dropped from later editions) and the discussion of the mad artist toward the end of the book. He passes over the subtle epistemological and linguistic analyses of *The Birth of the Clinic* and pays attention only to the brief discussions of death. And he dismisses out of hand almost all of *The Order of Things* and of *The Archaeology of Knowledge*. Even *Discipline and Punish* and the three volumes of *The History of Sexuality*, which might seem to be especially relevant to Foucault's personal life, receive little attention because they have so little to do with "limit-experiences." We would hardly expect an interpretative master key to fit so few locks.

As John Rajchman has very effectively argued in *Discipline and Punish* and related writings, Foucault moved away from his assertion of the ethical centrality of modernist art.[38] As a result, his heroes take a new form. Hope is no longer primarily in the lightning flashes of artistic genius but in the struggles and suffering of marginalized individuals and groups: the parricide (Pierre Rivière), the hermaphrodite (Herculine Barbin), protesting prisoners, Maoist students. Transgression and intensity remain fundamental ethical categories, but they are now increasingly rooted more in lived social and political experiences than in refined aesthetic sensitivity. Foucault begins to move from heroic myth to mundane reality, although there is still considerable idealization and romanticizing of the marginalized. Similarly, the bourgeois monsters of the 1960s take on the more realistic cast (no less evil for that) of the structures and functionaries of complex power networks.

In the last books on ancient sexuality, however, Foucault's style and tone abruptly change. The volcanic subtexts of mythological struggles almost entirely disappear in favor of the cool exploration of alternative aesthetic forms of human existence. It is impossible for us to know the significance of this shift. Perhaps it was the beginning of what would have become a fundamentally new attitude and approach in Foucault's work; perhaps it merely reflects his view of the particular historical materials he was dealing with; or perhaps it exhibits his way of facing death. In any case, Foucault's last writings attain a calm humanity not found in his previous work.

NOTES

1 Here I am taking "interpretation" to mean "general interpretation" in order to emphasize that interpretative efforts typically put forward some single unifying method or vision as the key to understanding an author's oeuvre. There is, of course, a weaker sense of interpretation as any sort of comment on or explication of a text, with which I have no quarrel in principle.

2 A fragment of the archaic Greek poet Archilochus runs, "The fox knows many things, but the hedgehog knows one big thing." Berlin uses this

image to divide thinkers into two classes: those (the hedgehogs) "who relate everything to a central vision ... in terms of which they understand, think, and feel – a single, universal, organizing principle in terms of which alone all that they are and say has significance," and those (the foxes) "who pursue many ends, often unrelated and even contradictory, connected, if at all, only in some *de facto* way, for some psychological or physiological cause, related by no moral or aesthetic principle" (*Russian Thinkers*, London: Penguin, 1979, 22).

3 *Michel Foucault: Beyond Structuralism and Hermeneutics*, 2nd ed.

4 Ibid., 122, 124.

5 124–25.

6 Ibid.

7 To this extent, I agree with Allan Megill's claim that Foucault's work is antidisciplinary ("The Reception of Foucault by Historians"). I do not, however, agree with the suggestion that this means Foucault's work cannot be evaluated by the standards of existing disciplines, particularly history. The fact that disciplines are dangerous (that is, possible sources of domination) does not mean that they are not valid sources of knowledge. They are in fact all the more dangerous because of the knowledge they embody. Consequently, an effective challenge to a discipline will have to make a case that can be made plausible in the discipline's own terms, even though the case works against the disciplinary grain. I return to this topic at the end of the following section, "Foucault's Theories."

8 "What Is an Author?" in Donald Bouchard, ed., *Language, Counter-Memory, Practice: Selected Essays and Interviews*, 113–38. See also Foucault's *The Archaeology of Knowledge*, 21–26.

9 In Lawrence Kritzman, *Politics, Philosophy, Culture: Interviews and Other Writings, 1977–1984*, 323–30.

10 *The Archaeology of Knowledge*, 14–15.

11 "Truth and Power" in Colin Gordon, ed., *Power/Knowledge: Selected Interviews and Other Writings, 1972–1977*, 115.

12 "The Subject and Power," appendix to Dreyfus and Rabinow, 209.

13 *Archaeology of Knowledge*, 206.

14 Ibid.

15 Ibid., 207–8.

16 On these topics, particularly Foucault's connection with the French tradition in history and philosophy of science, see Gary Gutting, *Michel Foucault's Archaeology of Scientific Reason*.

17 For this approach to Foucault, see Joseph Rouse's excellent treatment in *Knowledge and Power: Toward a Political Philosophy of Science*; and in "Foucault and the Natural Sciences," in J. Caputo and M. Yount, eds.,

Institutions, Normalization, and Power (State College: Pennsylvania State University Press, 1993).

18 Foucault remarked that he saw the possibility of regarding these three books – *The History of Madness, The Birth of the Clinic,* and *The Order of Things* – as part of a unified project only after he had finished the last of them. See "La naissance d'un monde" (interview with J.-M. Palmier), *Le Monde,* May 3, 1969.

19 See *The History of Madness,* 55–58. Much more than his other works, *The History of Madness* makes claims regarding social and political history, such as the dates and extent of confinement of the mad in various European countries. For a discussion of *The History of Madness*'s historical adequacy, see my "Foucault and the History of Madness," this volume.

20 *La formation du concept de reflex aux XVIIe et XVIIIe siècles,* 2nd ed. (Paris: Vrin, 1970).

21 For a more thorough discussion of these issues, see Gutting, *Michel Foucault's Archaeology of Scientific Reason,* 32–37.

22 See André Glucksmann's discussion of Foucault and the intolerable in "Michel Foucault's Nihilism" in *Michel Foucault: Philosopher,* trans. Timothy Armstrong (London: Routledge, 1992), 336–39.

23 For a discussion of the development of Foucault's genealogical method and its role in his work, see Gary Gutting, "Foucault's Genealogical Method," in French, Uehling, and Wettstein, eds., *Midwest Studies in Philosophy* 15: 327–44.

24 *The Archaeology of Knowledge,* 16.

25 For this notion, see *The Archaeology of Knowledge,* 186–89.

26 Allan Megill, "The Reception of Foucault by Historians," 133–34; Jan Goldstein, review of *Discipline and Punish, Journal of Modern History* 51 (1979): 117.

27 Charles Taylor, "Foucault on Freedom and Truth" in David Hoy, ed., *Foucault: A Critical Reader,* 82–83.

28 Foucault's antipathy to psychiatry is very apparent in his essay "La recherche scientifique and la psychologie" in Morère, ed., *Des chercheurs franćais s'interrogent,* 171–201.

29 Foucault, "A Preface to Transgression" in Bouchard, ed., *Language, Counter-memory, and Practice,* 29–52.

30 Foucault, "What Is an Author?" in Bouchard, ed., *Language, Counter-Memory, Practice,* 116.

31 "A Preface to Transgression" in Bouchard, ed., *Language, Counter-Memory, Practice,* 35, 36.

32 Ibid., 35.

33 "The Minimalist Self," interview with Stephen Riggins, in L. Kritzman, ed., *Politics, Philosophy, Culture* 13, 12.

34 James Miller, *The Passion of Michel Foucault*.

35 David Halperin, "Bringing out Michel Foucault," *Salmagundi* (Winter 1993): 79–82. Another striking example, not discussed by Halperin, is Miller's interpretation of Foucault's 1969 article "Death of the Author": "Foucault sought out 'limit-experiences' for himself, trying to glimpse Dionysus beneath Apollo, hazarding the risk of 'a sacrifice, an actual sacrifice of life,' as he put in 1969, 'a voluntary obliteration that does not have to be represented in books because it takes place in the very existence of the writer' " (*The Passion of Michel Foucault*, 32). Miller's clear implication is that Foucault is saying that he himself has risked his life (persumably in S/M practices), seeking "voluntary obliteration." But the text of Foucault's essay makes it absolutely clear that he is not saying anything about his own views or practices; he is explaining what he takes to be the new relation between death and writing in modern literature. "This conception of a spoken or written narrative as a protection against death [for example, in Greek epic or the Arabian Nights] has been transformed by our culture. Writing is now linked to sacrifice and to the sacrifice of life itself . . . Where a work had the duty of creating immortality, it now attains the right to kill, to become the murderer of its author. Flaubert, Proust, and Kafka are obvious examples of this reversal." (*Language, Counter-memory, and Practice*, 117). Even if we suppose that Foucault agrees with this modern conception of writing (not implausible) and that he regards his own work as an instance of the sort of writing he has in mind (less plausible), there is no reason to think that his talk of "sacrifice of life" and of "right to kill" has the literal meaning required by a connection of it to S/M. Such an interpretation requires us to believe an evident absurdity: that Foucault thought Flaubert, Kafka, and Proust were literally risking their lives through their writing.

36 James Miller, "Policing Discourse: A Response to David Halperin," *Salmagundi* (Winter 1993): 97.

37 For example, Miller cites anecdotal evidence (*The Passion of Michel Foucault*) that Foucault's father, a surgeon, was a strong disciplinarian with whom his son had frequent conflicts. He immediately reads this in terms of contemporary clichés about the medical personality, authoritarian fathers, and rebellious youth. But if we know anything about Foucault, it is that he was a very unusual and complicated person – someone of whom our clichés are very unlikely to be true.

38 John Rajchman, *Michel Foucault: The Freedom of Philosophy*, Chapter I.

I am grateful to Anastasia Gutting for helpful comments on the penultimate draft of this introduction.

1   Foucault's mapping of history

All of Foucault's major works are histories of a sort, which is enough to make him a historian of a sort. The challenge is to determine what sort of history he does and thus what kind of historian he is. It is fortunate that Foucault has adopted distinctive terms for his specific approaches at different phases of his career. His early works, the ones that earned him his reputation, were called "archaeologies," the subsequent ones "genealogies"; and the volumes on the history of sexuality that appeared at the time of his death he called "problematizations."

These approaches do not exclude each other. Rather, like successive waves breaking on the sand, each is discovered after the fact to have been an implicit interest of the earlier one, for which it served as the moving force. Thus Foucault insists that the question of power relations, which characterizes his genealogies, was what his archaeologies were really about and, subsequently, that the issue of truth and subjectivity, the explicit focus of his final works, had been his basic concern all along. Although these avowals reveal a greater desire for consistency and coherence than Foucault is supposed to have possessed, much less to have been able to warrant, they hypothesize a unity among the three approaches that enables us to present each in more than sequential order. Accordingly, after a survey of these three modes of "history" in their turn, I shall address four issues that give Foucault's approach to history its distinctive character, namely, the topics of nominalism, the historical event, the spatialization of Reason, and the nature of problematization. I shall argue that these themes serve to criticize, respectively, Platonists, historians of culture, dialecticians, and traditional historians of the battles-and-treaties variety. My

28

concluding remarks will assess Foucault as a "postmodern" philosopher of history.[1]

Discounting a brief neomarxian study of psychology published in
1954[2] and a lengthy Introduction to the French translation of Ludwig Binswanger's *Dream and Existence* (1954), which shows his
youthful fascination with existential phenomenology,[3] Foucault's
first major works were "archaeologies" of madness, clinical medicine, and the social sciences, respectively. Rather than study the
"arche," or origin, these archaeologies examine the "archive," by
which he means "systems that establish statements (*énoncés*) as
events (with their own conditions and domain of appearance) and as
things (with their own possibility and field of use)" (*AK*, 128). More
simply put, the archive is "the set (*l'ensemble*) of discourses actually
pronounced" (*FL*, 45); not just any discourses, but the set that conditions what counts as knowledge in a particular period. The archive is
discourse not only as events having occurred but as "things," with
their own economies, scarcities, and (later in his thought) strategies
that continue to function, transformed through history and providing the possibility of appearing for other discourses.

This linguistic understanding of the archive is modified by reference to discursive *practices*, specifically, any set of basic practices
that constitute the "conditions for existence" for other discursive
practices. Even in what is arguably Foucault's most "structuralist"
text, *The Archaeology of Knowledge*, he insists that the "discursive
relations" he is studying obtain "at the limit of discourse" considered as language. They pertain not to the language (*langue*) of discourse, but to "discourse itself *as practice*" (*AK*, 46, emphasis mine).
As he explains, "my object is not language but the archive, that is to
say the accumulated existence of discourse. Archaeology, as I intend
it, is kin neither to geology (as analysis of the sub-soil), nor to genealogy (as descriptions of beginning and sequences); it's the analysis of
discourse in its modality of *archive*" (*FL*, 25). That modality is the
"historical a priori" of a discourse. The contradictory form of this
expression evinces the tension that Foucault's position generates
between relativism ("historical") and objectivity ("a priori") in archaeology. Analysis of discourse in its archival mode (archaeology) is

the search for those enabling and unifying "forms" – a term he continues to use in this context in his very last works (see *UP*, 14).

Like any original method, archaeology has its proper object, namely, discursive and nondiscursive *practices*, although the nondiscursive receive little attention until the genealogies. Similar to Wittgenstein's "game," a practice is a preconceptual, anonymous, socially sanctioned body of rules that govern one's manner of perceiving, judging, imagining, and acting. From the vantage point of his subsequent genealogies, Foucault describes practice as "the point of linkage (*enchaînement*) of what one says and what one does, of the rules one prescribes to oneself and the reasons one ascribes, of projects and of evidences" (*IP*, 42). Neither a disposition nor an individual occurrence, a practice forms the intelligible background for actions by its twofold character as *judicative* and *"veridicative."* That is, on the one hand, practices establish and apply norms, controls, and exclusions; on the other, they render true/false discourse possible. Thus the practice of legal punishment, for example, entails the interplay between a "code" that regulates ways of acting – such as how to discipline an inmate – and the production of true discourse that legitimates these ways of acting (*IP*, 47). The famous power/knowledge dyad in Foucault's larger schema merely elaborates these judicative and veridicative dimensions of "practice." An archive is the locus of the rules and prior practices forming the conditions of inclusion or exclusion that enable certain practices and prevent others from being accepted as "scientific," or "moral," or whatever other social rubric may be in use at a particular epoch. In other words, archaeologies need not be confined to the sciences. Foucault suggests possible archaeological studies of discursive practices in the ethical, the aesthetic, and the political fields (see *AK*, 192–95). His subsequent studies pursue those suggestions.

Reference to "epoch" is crucial, for these archives are time-bound and factual; they are discovered, not deduced; they are the locus of practices as "positivities" to be encountered, not as "documents" to be interpreted. Foucault can thus characterize the archive paradoxically as a "historical a priori." The claim that these practices are to be registered as facts, not read as the result of intentions of some sort, gives his archaeology its "positivist" tilt, an inclination he continued to favor.

Inspired by the work of his teacher George Canguilhem, Foucault's early studies are archaeologies of those discursive practices that tread the borderline of the scientific. These "histories" of science are chartings of the epistemic breaks that account for the sudden appearance of new disciplines and the equally rapid demise of certain old ones. But if there is a post factum "necessity" about these breaks ("fittingness" is perhaps the better word, except that it rings too aesthetic for this stage in Foucault's career), it is only in the sense that some areas of scientific investigation arise in precisely those spaces where earlier practices had proved weak or absent, although this could not have been predicted from the *status quo ante*. As Foucault explains in his programmatic Inaugural Lecture at the Collège de France, his intent is to restore "chance as a category in the production of events" (*AK*, 231). This respect for the aleatory becomes even more pronounced in his genealogies.

This early emphasis on *epistemes* (roughly, those conditions that constitute the "veridicative" function of a practice, its claim to the status of scientific knowledge) led many to link Foucault with the structuralists – an association he vigorously rejected. There is little doubt that the immense success of *The Order of Things* was due in part to its being perceived by the public as a structuralist tour de force. Although Foucault shared many concepts with the structuralists as well as a common enemy (subjectivist, humanist thought), his nominalism and "positivism," not to mention the Nietzschean tenor of his writing overall, are clearly post-structuralist.

When one views together the four works that constitute Foucault's archaeological period, namely, *The History of Madness, The Birth of the Clinic, The Order of Things*, and *The Archaeology of Knowledge*, one senses a curious unity-within-diversity. All four address the practices of exclusion that constitute the discourse that will bear the honorific "science." All manifest a profound respect for the period surrounding the French Revolution and its immediate aftermath as the watershed for apparently unrelated discursive and nondiscursive practices. And they all reveal a sense of the unspoken and unspeakable relationships that the archaeologist has been the first to discover between such apparently disjointed areas as clinical medicine, medicalization of madness, and the scientific status of various social inquiries – which are pronounced to have more in common with each other than with their presumed precursors in traditional historical accounts.

In this sense, archaeology is both *counter*-history and social critique. It is counter-history because it assumes a contrapuntal relationship to traditional history, whose conclusions it more rearranges than denies and whose resources it mines for its own purposes. In *The Birth of the Clinic*, subtitled "An Archaeology of Medical Perception," for example, Foucault offers us an alternative account of many of the same facts that anchored the received view of how anatomo-clinical medicine came to replace the "medicine of species" that had dominated thought and practice in the Classical Age. What others had taken as crucial in the history of this displacement, such as the use of corpses in pathological anatomy, Foucault argues, was symptomatic of a more basic and far-reaching change at the level of epistemology. The well-known opposition to the use of corpses in pathology, he notes, was not due to religious or moral scruples, as was commonly believed, but resulted from the epistemic conviction of classificatory medicine that cadavers would be of little use. After the epistemic break (a concept Foucault adopts from the philosopher of science Gaston Bachelard), attention focused on the surface of a lesion, the site of a disease; clinicians were now interested in "geography" rather than in "history"; their question was no longer the essentialist "What is wrong with you?," but the nominalistic "Where does it hurt?"

But archaeology is social critique as well. It radicalizes our sense of the contingency of our dearest biases and most accepted necessities, thereby opening up a space for change. In its appeal to discursive practices, it underlines the close link between perceiving, conceiving, saying, and doing. It is not that Classical physicians had refused to admit the evidence that lay before them; they simply perceived the object differently from their modern successors. Indeed, this epistemic shift would result in the emergence of a new object for their investigation. Foucault will make a similar claim for the rise of the delinquent in the face of a science of criminology. In both instances traditional accounts, by trying to get "beneath" the surface of the positivities in question, confused the conditioned with its conditions.

In viewing the archaeologies, one notes a pattern in Foucault's approach to historical topics that will continue throughout the next phases of his career. He begins with a powerful image, an iconic statement of the thesis he intends to unveil: the *Narrenschiff* with its cargo of madmen; Pomme treating a hysteric with baths, ten or twelve hours a day for ten months; Velasquez attempting to depict representation. One could call this the "phenomenological" or descriptive moment in his method. This is followed by a bold claim that counters the received opinion. Then begins the rearrangement of the evidence into a new configuration. The result is an alternative reading that yields new insights: Enlightenment reason, far from liberating madness, confines it; Classical medicine is blind to the individual cases it studies; nineteenth-century political economy is shown to have more in common epistemically with biology and philology of the same period than with eighteenth-century analyses of wealth.

Whether these alternatives are intended to replace or simply to complement the standard accounts is unclear. In an interview with a group of historians, Foucault asserts the latter (*IP*, 41), but his vigorous advocacy of epistemic shifts in *The Order of Things*, for example, suggests the former. In fact, his claims regarding the extent of epistemic or archival boundaries become more modest as time goes on. Thus, in *The Order of Things* he insists there is only one episteme for a given epoch (*OT*, 168), whereas in the Foreword to the English edition of that same work four years later, he cautions that the work is "a strictly 'regional' study" and that such terms as "thought" or "Classical science" refer "practically always to the particular discipline under consideration" (*OT*, x). He exemplifies the latter view by locating the epistemological break for the life sciences, economics, and languages at the beginning of the nineteenth century and that for history and politics at the middle (*FL*, 15). He is explicit in distinguishing his *episteme* from a Kantian category and insists that the term simply denotes "all those relationships which existed between the various sectors of science during a given epoch" (*FL*, 76).

GENEALOGIES OF THE PRESENT

No more than archaeology is genealogy a return to origins, a project that Foucault associates with Platonic essentialism. Rather, its concern is the descent (*Herkunft*) of practices as a series of events. Unlike the continuities of a theory of origins, genealogy underscores the jolts and surprises of history, the chance occurrences, in order to "maintain passing events in their proper dispersion" (*LCP*, 146). To this extent it resembles archaeology.

It moves beyond the earlier method in its explicit focus on power and bodies. Genealogy "poses the problem of power and of the body (of bodies), indeed, its problems begin from the imposition of power upon bodies."[4] As Foucault notes, "The body – and everything that touches it: diet, climate, and soil – is the domain of the *Herkunft* [genealogy]" (*LCP*, 148). This emphasis on the body as the object of discipline and control gives Foucault's genealogical studies of the practice of punishment (*Discipline and Punish*) and of sexuality (*History of Sexuality, I*) their distinctive character. His genealogy of the carceral system centers on the way "the body as the major target of penal repression disappeared" at a certain point in history (*DP*, 8), only to be subjected to more subtle control by the "normalizing" techniques of the social sciences in the nineteenth century. And the first volume of his genealogy of sexuality reveals "the encroachment of a type of power on bodies and their pleasures" that the Victorian proliferation of "perversions" produced (*HS*, 48). As we should now expect, this focus on the body continues in his subsequent work. A chapter in the second volume of his history of sexuality, which appeared just before he died, is entitled "Dietetics" to underscore the greater concern of the classical Greeks for sex in the context of diet and physical regimen than with sex as primarily a moral matter.

Power relations underwrite all Foucault's genealogies. This translates "history" from a project of meaning and communication toward a "micro-physics of power," in Foucault's telling phrase (*DP*, 139). It likewise shifts the model for historical understanding from Marxist science and ideology, or from hermeneutical text and interpretation, to strategy and tactics. "The history which bears and determines us," he writes, "has the form of a war rather then that of a language: relations of power, not relations of meaning" (*P/K*, 114).

Given the major role that the concept plays in Foucault's genealogies, it is unfortunate that he offers no definition of "power" as such. Of course, as befits a historical nominalist, he insists that "power" does not exist, that there are only individual relations of domination and control. Moreover, he cautions us, "power" should not be taken in a pejorative sense. It is in fact a positive concept, functioning in our divisions of the true and the false, the good and the evil, as well as in the distinction and control of ourselves and one another. He is

particularly intent on unmasking the prevalent legalistic understanding of "power."

This inevitability of power relations led critics such as Jürgen
Habermas to list Foucault among the "neoconservatives." While it
is true that this usage figures in his anti-utopian thinking and that
its stark realism, if that's the word, separates him from Marxist and
other optimists, his claim that every exercise of power is accompanied by or gives rise to resistance opens a space for possibility and
freedom in any context. This stance leaves him remarkably close to
Jean-Paul Sartre, whose maxim was that we can always make something out of what we have been made into. The historical (not to
mention the ethical) problem is what role genealogy, much less archaeology, leaves for individual initiative in these matters. In fact, it
seems to leave very little. The genealogies operate on strategies without a strategist.[5] The "dialectic of emancipation" that Foucault sees
at work in Enlightenment theories of history, including those of
Marx and the Marxists, has no place in a postmodern account – a
point to which we shall return in conclusion.

There is an archaeological dimension to his genealogy of the modern penal system. It consists in uncovering those discursive and
nondiscursive practices that make it possible, indeed natural, to
speak of surveillance, re-education, and training – words from the
military and scholastic vocabulary – in the context of judicial punishment. The descriptive aspect of his enterprise reveals a rapid and
widespread change in the penal practices of the European and North
American communities between 1791 and 1810. Prior to that, governments inflicted on criminals any of a vast array of punishments,
most of them corporal. These ranged from flogging and the pillory to
the gruesome torture and execution of a would-be regicide, an account of which opens Foucault's book. Yet within two decades this
multiplicity of punishments had been reduced to one: detention.
Foucault asks why.

In addressing this question, he adopts Lord Acton's distinction
between the history of a period and that of a problem. The former
would address the ideological movements, economic changes, social
conditions, and, of course, the individual agents that fashioned this
dramatic shift in practice. It is a work of erudition. Foucault's focus,
however, is on the problem: What made this transformation possible? Description has revealed a radical break, the kind that interests

the archaeologist, who will analyze it to discover a transformation and displacement of discursive and nondiscursive practices. What genealogy adds to this inquiry is a specific interest in the new economy of power relations at work in this practice of high-minded penal reform. As genealogist, Foucault thus joins Marx, Nietzsche, and Freud as a "master of suspicion," uncovering the unsavory provenance (*pudenda origo*) of ostensibly noble enterprises.

Two terms that recur at crucial junctures throughout Foucault's histories are "transformation" and "displacement." In *The Archaeology of Knowledge*, he pointed out that he "held in suspense the general, empty category of [historical] change in order to reveal transformations at different levels" (*AK*, 200). His opposition to traditional history is in part the rejection of a uniform model of temporalization. *Discipline and Punish*, for example, superimposes on the standard history of nineteenth-century penal practices the transformation in the way the body is related to power, a real but unconscious shift in what he terms the "political technology of the body" (*DP*, 24). This "radical event," in the language of *Archaeology*, is not attributable to any individual, such as a founder or a reformer, and yet its temporal parameters can be charted with relative precision.

Foucault follows his former teacher Louis Althusser in adopting the Freudian term "displacement" to characterize this new "economy of power." It is significant that this is a spatial, not a temporal, term. The vocabulary and the very objects of practical and theoretical concern in the realm of punishment, even if retained in the new dispensation, are altered in meaning and use by the "punitive reason" that becomes operative in the early nineteenth century and the "carceral system" it serves to legitimate. What he calls the "technology of power" mediates the humanization of punishment and the rise of the social sciences – a new perspective on the archaeological thesis of *The Order of Things*. As before the displacement, the object is ostensibly the body of the criminal, but now that body is confined for the sake of *discipline*. It is the individual's body as a social instrument that must be rendered a docile and pliable tool of economic productivity. This, rather than the vengeance of the sovereign, is the goal of the "reformed" techniques of punishment.

The architectural emblem for this displacement of punishment is

Bentham's Panopticon. Symbol and instrument of constant surveillance, it assured the automatic application of power by rendering the
prisoner perpetually visible; since the overseers could not be seen,
the inmates became their own guards – the ideal of a carceral society. Panopticism, Foucault concludes, "is the general principle of
this new 'political anatomy' whose object and end are not the relations of sovereignty [as before the break] but the relations of discipline" (*DP*, 208).

PROBLEMATIZATIONS

In an interview with his research assistant François Ewald, published shortly before his death, Foucault characterizes his current
work as "problematization." The term denotes "the ensemble of
discursive and nondiscursive practices that makes something enter
into the play of the true and the false and constitutes it an object of
thought (whether in the form of moral reflection, scientific knowledge, political analysis or the like)."[6] The mention of practices and
of epistemic value (the true and the false) harkens back to archaeology, and talk of control of self and others (elsewhere in the interview)
indicates that genealogy is still at work here. But reference to play
and, specifically, to "truth games" (*les jeux de vérité*) introduces a
new phase of his approach to history and affords yet another perspective on his previous work. What truth game is the person playing, for
example, who regards himself as insane or sick? As a living, speaking, working being? As a criminal or the subject of sexual desire?
Each of Foucault's successive books is now seen as addressing these
questions.[7]

The change occurred during the eight-year gap between the first
and the next two volumes of his *History of Sexuality*. As Foucault
explains in a lengthy Introduction to Volume Two, his previous
investigations were the fruit of "theoretical shifts" by which he
analyzed the cognitive and the normative relations of "experience"
in modern Western society. These are the "veridicative" and judicative dimensions mentioned earlier as the domains of archaeology
and genealogy, respectively. It is worth noting, however, that they
are now described as dimensions of "experience," not simply of
"discourse" nor of discursive practice. "It appeared that I now had to
undertake a third shift," he acknowledges, "in order to analyze what

is termed 'the subject.' It seemed appropriate to look for the forms and modalities of the relation to self by which the individual constitutes and recognizes himself *qua* subject" (*UP*, 6). How one constitutes oneself and is constituted the subject of sexuality (or a political subject) – what he calls "subjectivation" – now becomes his concern. In this work he asks why sexual conduct became an object of moral solicitude. Why this "problematization"?

Typically, he rereads his previous work in light of this question. His archaeologies are said to have examined the forms of problematization; the genealogies enabled him to examine the practices involved in their formation. Now he wishes to focus on the problematizing of sexual activity and pleasure via "practices of the self" by appeal to the criteria of an "aesthetic of existence." He acknowledges both an archaeological and a genealogical dimension to the experience he analyzes. But the distinctive question is the problematizing of sexual activity in the constitution of the moral self. He studies the relation between "technologies of the self" and the regulation of sexual practices and (later) desires in the context of the "truth games" being played by the relevant participants.

Problematization, in effect, is an important complement to the other two approaches to an historical issue, the charting of the experience in question along a third axis. Foucault insists that none of the axes along which he plots the events in question is the complete story. Indeed, there is no such thing as the "whole" picture. There is simply a multiplication of events (and presumably of axes, as well), which elsewhere he terms a "polyhedron of intelligibility," to mix spatial metaphors, the number of whose sides is indefinite.

FOUCAULT'S HISTORICAL CARTOGRAPHY

To chart Foucault's distinctive approach to history, it will help to select four coordinates that lend a certain coherence to what might better be termed a philosophical "style" à la Nietzsche than a theory. Rather than circumscribe the work of so polymorphous a thinker, these topics designate four overlapping fields on which he simultaneously pursued his investigations. Their superimposition should clarify the kind of history that Foucault was engaged in.

Historical nominalism

Foucault's method is radically anti-Platonic and individualistic. His sympathy with the Sophists, Cynics, and other philosophical "outsiders" is based on a profound distrust of essences, natures, and other kinds of unifying, totalizing, and exclusionary thought that threaten individual freedom and creativity. That is to say, his misgivings are moral (in the broad sense) as well as epistemological, as becomes clear from his numerous remarks about an "aesthetic of existence" toward the end of his life.

What Foucault calls his "nominalism" is a form of methodological individualism. It treats such abstractions as "man" and "power" as reducible for purposes of explanation to the individuals that comprise them. This is the context of his claim, for example, that "power does not exist," that there are only individual instances of domination, manipulation, edification, control, and the like. His infamous assertion that "man" did not exist before the nineteenth century, even when tempered by appeal to the social sciences that generated the category (which, in turn, served to legitimize them), must be interpreted in the additional sense that "man" is a mere *flatus vocis* even for the social sciences. Failure to respect Foucault's underlying nominalism has frustrated the critics who have complained about the elusive character of his concept of power.

It is the historian's task to uncover discursive and nondiscursive practices in their plurality and contingency, in order to reveal the *fields* that render intelligible an otherwise heterogeneous collection of events. There is no foundational principle, no originating or final cause. Such words as "influence" and "author" dissolve under nominalistic scrutiny. "History," as Foucault writes it, is the articulation of the series of practices (archive, historical a priori) that accounts for our current practices, where "account" means assigning the relevant transformations (differentials) and displacements or charting the practice along an axis of power, knowledge, or "subjectivation." Thus Foucault's program offers the "new historians" too much and too little: too many diverse relations, too many lines of analysis; but not enough unitary necessity. We are left with a plethora of intelligibilities and a lack of necessity. But he resolutely refuses, as he puts it, to place himself "under the sign of unique necessity" (*IP*, 46).[8]

The event

In selecting this topic, we can assess Foucault in terms of the controversy that arose among historians during the 1960s and 1970s regarding the comparative merits of "history of events" (*histoire événementielle*) and "non-event–oriented history" (*histoire nonévénementielle*). Defenders of the former traditional approach considered themselves humanists, employing hermeneutical methods in ascertaining the meaning of documents; whereas those in the latter camp were closer to the social sciences, favoring comparativist or structuralist insights, statistical arguments, and computer techniques. Foucault, who criticized the "confused, understructured, and ill-structured domain of the history of ideas" (*BC*, 195), was commonly linked with the latter, and his "histories" were judged to be "structuralist" attacks on humanist values.

It is not by accident, therefore, that he chose to make the concept of event the center of his historical analyses. But his peculiar use of "event" serves to distinguish him from old and new historians alike. Practices are events in the Foucaultian sense; so too are statements. The famous epistemological breaks of his archaeologies are events, as are the "micro" exercises of power in the "capillaries" of the body politic. Appeal to "event" enables Foucault to avoid such "magical" concepts as historical "influence" and vague notions like "continuity" by proliferating events without number. An event, he explains, "is not a decision, a treaty, a reign, or a battle, but the reversal of a relationship of forces, the usurpation of power, the appropriation of a vocabulary turned against those who had one used it, a feeble domination that poisons itself as it grows lax, the entry of a masked 'other' " (*LCP*, 154). It is precisely "the singular randomness of events" that enables him to reintroduce the central role of chance into historical discourse. His ironic defense against "structuralist" charges is that no one favors the history of events more than he! In fact, a close reading of his work reveals that the concept of event broadens to bridge the gap between these two schools of historiography.[9]

Spatialization of reason

Foucault's spatialized thinking extends far beyond his well-known use of spatial metaphors to include the use of lists, tables, geometrical configurations, and illustrations. These are not merely ancillary to his approach but pertain to the core of his historical method, which is "diagnostic" and, as such, comparatist and differential. He seems to have adopted as a general rule what he characterized in *The Birth of the Clinic* as "the diacritical principle of medical observation," namely, that "the only pathological fact is a comparative fact" (*BC*, 134). What we described earlier as "counter" history is Foucault's use of a comparatist and differential method. This not only frees him from historical "realism" that seeks to ascertain the truth "as it actually happened" but also liberates him from the confines of dialectical thinking. His shift from time to space as the paradigm guiding his approach to historical topics counters the totalizing, teleological method favored by standard histories of ideas, with their appeal to individual and collective consciousness and to a "tangled network of influences" (*OT*, 63).

The best known examples of Foucault's spatialized thinking are his analysis of Velasquez's "Las Meninas" in *The Order of Things* and of Bentham's "Panopticon" in *Discipline and Punish*. In the former, like an art critic, he leads us along the path of argument by repeatedly calling our attention to the singular image before us. We are drawn to the graphic conclusion that representation cannot represent itself, that "the very being of that which is represented is now going to fall outside representation itself" (*OT*, 240). By a powerful iconic argument, Foucault has shown that "representation has lost the power [it enjoyed in the Classical period] to provide a foundation ... for the links that can join its various elements together" (*OT*, 238–239). That connection will next be sought in "man" and, failing that, in the very differential that Foucault, as postmodern historian, both practices and preaches.

Foucault's famous description of Jeremy Bentham's Panopticon relates power and knowledge, norm and surveillance, in an interplay of architecture and social science to reveal the self-custodial nature of modern society, where "prisons resemble factories, schools, barracks, hospitals, which all resemble prisons" (*DP*, 228). Again the demonstrative force of his analyses depends on the spatial organization of the institutions he discusses. As with the Velasquez painting, one is constantly referred back to the visual evidence, to the plans, the prospects, the models. But now the line of sight is *strategic*, not just descriptive; the contours inscribe the relations of control, not just forms of intelligibility. The space has become genealogical.[10]

Problematization

Foucault's interest in contrast and difference does not imply commitment to an underlying unity. This was evident in his focus on the event. The redescription of his histories as problematizations and their linkage with differential or spatialized thought emphasizes this fact.

The freeing of difference requires thought without contradiction, without dialectics, without negation; thought that accepts divergence; affirmative thought whose instrument is disjunction; thought of the multiple – of the nomadic and dispersed multiplicity that is not limited or confined by the constraints of similarity. . . . What is the answer to the question? The problem. How is the problem resolved? By displacing the question. . . . We must think problematically rather than question and answer dialectically. (*LCP,* 185–186).

We have seen how writing the history of a "problem" rather than of a "period" frees Foucault from the obligation to exhaustive research of the historical sources. Not that he can ignore the "facts"; rather, he is warranted to consider only those events that are relevant to the problem at issue, its transformation and displacement, the strategies it exhibits, and the truth games it involves. This also relieves him of the need to "totalize" or "synthesize" in the Sartrean and Hegelian senses, respectively. Such an approach, he insists, would be considered anti-historical only by "those who confuse history with the old schemas of evolution, living continuity, organic development, the progress of consciousness or the project of existence" (*P/K,* 70).

POSTMODERN HISTORY

Although we could speak of "post-structuralist" history just as easily,[11] "postmodern" seems the more appropriate term to designate the histories of someone who drew sharp epistemic lines between modernity, its predecessor, and its successor, and then proceeded to fill in all three spaces with description and analysis. Like the term "existentialist," the use and abuse of which it is coming to resemble, "postmodern" is notoriously difficult to define. Prudence counsels that we fashion a cluster of themes and concepts whose crisscrossing and overlapping will reveal a family resemblance among the uses of the term. In Foucault's case, this postmodern cluster includes the four topics just discussed.

His nominalism is not of itself distinctive. The historian Paul Veyne reads Henri Irène Marrou as supporting Foucault's claim that "nothing is more reasonable than a nominalist conception of history."[12] In this respect, both share what was probably Aristotle's view of the profession. But the radicalization of this position to the point of evacuating the historical subject, coupled with a Nietzschean appeal to relations of power and resistance, gives Foucaultian history an "agonistic" character that Jean-François Lyotard considers characteristic of "postmodern" logic.[13]

The dispersion of events and multiplicity of lines of "explanation" is another feature of the postmodern. In this regard, Lyotard speaks of the end of "master narratives" like the Marxist and the evolutionary. Foucault's "polyhedron of intelligibility" and his exclusion of any "dialectic of emancipation," such as Enlightenment thinking is supposed to have bequeathed us, are rightly seen as postmodern in spirit. This is obviously the case if one takes the Habermasian defense of modernity as paradigmatic of the genre.[14]

What is most distinctive of Foucault as a postmodern thinker is what I have called his "spatialization of reason" as studied in his histories and exhibited in his writings. His implicit appeal to space, with its transformations and displacements as well as its comparativist and diacritical method, rather than time as the model for historical explanation undermines the telic nature of traditional historical accounts, even as it restores the dispersive, "Dionysian" character to time, which had been tamed by existentialists and other narrativists.

Foucault's focus on problematization supports numerous regional studies and discourages larger undertakings. His more limited understanding of "episteme," as well as his nominalist use of "power," has a similar, particularizing effect. In fact, his writings consistently counter the Aristotelian prohibition against a "science of the singular" by appeal to the case study method of modern (!) medicine, which he employs throughout his histories.

Finally, his move away from explanation toward diagnosis is typically postmodern in its eschewal of foundations, origins, ultimates, and grand theories in favor of practical, moral (in the broad sense) concerns. Assuming the demise of representational thinking, which he subjected to a profound critique in *The Order of Things*, Foucault has no intention of grasping the event-fact "as it actually occurred." Rather, he writes a "history of the present" that, in effect, seeks to diagnose and suggest alternative avenues of behavior, or at least their possibility. Such is his postmodern understanding of history, which "has more in common with [modern] medicine than [modern] philosophy" (*LCP*, 156).

Given the breadth and boldness of Foucault's approach, it is liable to criticism from a variety of quarters. There is something of the poet in his easy way with striking examples at the price of tedious factual corroboration. Indeed, in a famous phrase he once avowed, "I am well aware that I have not written anything but fictions," but then hastened to add, "which is not to say they have nothing to do with the truth" (*P/K*, 193). Professional historians, for example, who specialize in the fields he covers, have been quick to take issue with his list of historical facts.[15] The price of being an historian *suo modo* seems to be that he is not entirely at home either with professional historians or with philosophers. His greatest influence to date appears to have been on scholars working in literature and in the social sciences.

Many philosophers will question the tenability of Foucault's radically nominalistic claims. This is an ancient quarrel, which need not be rehearsed here. But its central role in his philosophy demands a defense or at least an explicit discussion, which is never forthcoming. If nominalism fails, so too do many of Foucault's assertions about power, truth, and subjectivation.

Perhaps the most controversial aspect of the spatialization of history is its freeing of the discipline from its moorings in philosophical anthropology, the famous "death of man" thesis that caused so much ink to spill after the appearance of *The Order of Things*. Speaking of archaeology as "diagnosis," Foucault claims that it "does not establish the fact of our identity by the play of distinctions. [Rather], it establishes that we are difference, that our reason is the difference of discourses, our history the difference of times, our selves the difference of masks." That difference, he concludes, "far from being the forgotten and recovered origin, is this dispersion that we are and make" (*AK*, 131). A condition of the existence of this dispersion is spatialized language that dissolves the unity of the self, dissipates projects by chance events, and multiplies rationalities.[16] But this, of course, also generates a "counter-anthropology" to undergrid Foucault's counter-history. And the ethical implications of that position were just beginning to be worked out at the time of Foucault's death. Whether it can advance beyond a certain aestheticism is not yet clear.

But the chief difficulty with the Foucaultian project as history arises from the fact that, to speak like a nominalist, the lived, experienced time of the responsible agent is too firmly entrenched; it is, to use more comfortable terms, an essential ingredient in our human condition. As exhibited in our ability to recount and follow narratives, this experience lies at the heart of what we call "history," whether of the agents and forces that condition it or of the historians who fashion its form. No doubt Foucault has indicated the inadequacy of any simple narrative account, although he has done so with great rhetorical (narrative) skill. Doubtless, too, he has chastened those who would look for a single meaning-direction to history or who wish to single out its atomic agents or root causes. But his suspicions have not rooted out the experiential basis of historical narrative. Indeed, his own narratives have served to underscore its inevitability.[17]

It has been said that the kind of music aestheticians analyze is the kind no one can hear. *Mutatis mutandis*, might not something similar be said of Foucault's "postmodern" history?

NOTES

1 The following abbreviations are used in citing Foucault's writings. (Full references are given in the Bibliography of this volume.)

   AK: *The Archaeology of Knowledge*
   BC: *The Birth of the Clinic*
   DP: *Discipline and Punish*
   FL: *Foucault Live*
   HS: *History of Sexuality, Vol. I: An Introduction*
   IP: *L'Impossible Prison*
   LCP: *Language, Counter-Memory, Practice*
   OT: *The Order of Things*
   P/K: *Power/Knowledge*
   UP: *The Use of Pleasure*

2 *Maladie mentale et personnalité* (Paris: PUF, 1954). A revised version

(PUF, 1962) was translated by Alan Sheridan as *Mental Illness and Psychology*.

3 English translation by Forrest Williams, "Dream, Imagination, and Existence," *Review of Existential Psychology and Psychiatry* 19, 1 (1984–1985): 29–78.

4 François Ewald, "Anatomie et corps politique," 1229.

5 In this too he is remarkably close to the later Sartre, who saw the possibility of "totalization without a totalizer" as *the* question about the meaning of history.

6 Interview with François Ewald, "Le Souci de la vérité," 18.

7 See my "Truth and Subjectivation in the Later Foucault," 531–40.

8 For a development of this argument, see my "Foucault and Historical Nominalism," in H.A. Durfee and D.F.T. Rodier, eds., *Phenomenology and Beyond: The Self and Its Language*, 134–47. Portions of this essay have been included here with permission.

9 An extended discussion of this topic occurs in my "Foucault and the Career of the Historical Event," Dauenhauer, ed., *At the Nexus of Philosophy and History*, 178–200. Portions of this piece have been used here with permission.

10 See my "Foucault and the Spaces of History," 165–86.

11 See Derek Attridge et al., eds., *Post-Structuralism and the Question of History* (Cambridge: Cambridge University Press, 1987). Foucault, in fact, observes: "While I see clearly that behind what was known as structuralism, there was a certain problem – broadly speaking, that of the subject and the recasting of the subject – I do not understand what kind of problem is common to the people we call post-modern or post-structuralist" (*PPC*, 34).

12 Paul Veyne, *Writing History*, trans. Mina Moore-Rinvolucri (Middletown, Conn.: Wesleyan University Press, 1984), 43.

13 See Jean-François Lyotard, *The Postmodern Conditions: A Report on Knowledge*, trans. Geoff Bennington and Brian Massumi (Minneapolis: University of Minnesota Press, 1984), 10.

14 See, for example, Richard J. Bernstein, ed., *Habermas and Modernity* (Cambridge: MIT Press, 1985).

15 See, for example, Jacques Proust et al., "Entretiens sur Foucault," *La Pensée* 137 (February 1968): 4–37; as well as Gary Gutting, *Michel Foucault's Archaeology of Scientific Reason* 175–79.

16 Flynn, "Foucault and the Spaces of History," 181.

17 These and similar objections are developed at length in Paul Ricoeur, *Time and Narrative*, 3 vols. (Chicago: University of Chicago Press, 1984–88); and in David Carr, *Time, Narrative, and History* (Bloomington: Indiana University Press, 1986).

2 Foucault and the history of madness

"I am not a professional historian; nobody is perfect."
Michel Foucault[1]

FOUCAULT AMONG THE HISTORIANS – PART I

Foucault's work always had an ambivalent relation to established academic disciplines, but almost all his books are at least superficially classifiable as histories. His first major work, in particular, seems to proclaim its status in the title: *Histoire de la folie à l'âge classique*.[2] One plausible way of trying to understand and evaluate this seminal book is by assessing its status as a work of history.

The reactions of professional historians to *Histoire de la foile* seem, at first reading, sharply polarized.[3] There are many acknowledgments of its seminal role, beginning with Robert Mandrou's early review in *Annales*, characterizing it as a "beautiful book" that will be "of central importance for our understanding of the Classical period."[4] Twenty years later, Michael MacDonald confirmed Mandrou's prophecy: "Anyone who writes about the history of insanity in early modern Europe must travel in the spreading wake of Michel Foucault's famous book, *Madness and Civilization*."[5] Later endorsements have been even stronger. Jan Goldstein: "For both their empirical content and their powerful theoretical perspectives, the works of Michel Foucault occupy a special and central place in the historiography of psychiatry."[6] Roy Porter: "Time has proved *Mad-*

47

ness and Civilization far the most penetrating work ever written on the history of madness."[7] More specifically, Foucault has recently been heralded as a prophet of "the new cultural history."[8]

But criticism has also been widespread and often bitter. Consider H.C. Eric Midelfort's conclusion from his very influential assessment of Foucault's historical claims: "What we have discovered in looking at *Madness and Civilization* is that many of its arguments fly in the face of empirical evidence, and that many of its broadest generalizations are oversimplifications. Indeed, in his quest for the essence of an age, its *episteme,* Foucault seems simply to indulge in a whim for arbitrary and witty assertion so often that one wonders why so much attention and praise continue to fall his way."[9] Many of Midelfort's criticisms, if not always his overall assessment, have been widely endorsed by, for example, Peter Sedgwick, Lawrence Stone, Ian Hacking, and Dominick LaCapra.[10]

From the above juxtaposition of texts, it would seem that historians are sharply split in their view of the value of Foucault's work. But the division pretty much disappears on closer scrutiny. Those who applaud Foucault have primarily in mind what we may call his meta-level claims about how madness should be approached as a historiographical topic. They are impressed by his view of madness as a variable social construct, not an ahistorical scientific given, and of the history of madness as an essential part of the history of reason. These views are now generally accepted by historians of psychiatry,[11] and Foucault was one of the first to put them forward. In this sense he is a widely and properly revered father of the new history of psychiatry. But on the "object-level" of specific historical facts and interpretations, the consensus of even favorably disposed historians is that Foucault's work is seriously wanting. Andrew Scull, whose own work shares much of the general spirit of Foucault's, nonetheless endorses what he rightly says is "the verdict of most Anglo-American specialists: that *Madness and Civilization* is a provocative and dazzlingly written prose poem, but one resting on the shakiest of scholarly foundations and riddled with errors of fact and interpretation."[12] Similarly, Patricia O'Brien, in an article expressing great enthusiasm for Foucault's work, agrees tht "historians who are willing to admit that Foucault was writing history find it bad history, too general, too unsubstantiated, too mechanistic."[13]

Even historians who have a more favorable view of Foucault's specific historical claims are reluctant to accept him as a member of their tribe. Jan Goldstein, after maintaining that "Foucault used historical material to great advantage" and that "his historical sense was extraordinarily acute," goes on to note that "Foucault always considered himself at least as much a philosopher as a historian, whose epistemological and political project required that he challenge the ordinary canons of history writing."[14] Consequently, as she remarks in a review of *Discipline and Punish*, "the usual criteria of historical scholarship cannot be used to assess" Foucault's work.[15] MacDonald is similarly ambivalent: "Much of what Foucault has to say seems to me to be correct, in spite of his rejection of the prevailing standards of historical discourse" (xi). Allan Megill goes even further. For him, not only does Foucault's work fall outside the discipline of history, "he is *anti*disciplinary, standing outside all disciplines and drawing from them only in the hope of undermining them."[16]

At least one Foucaultian, Colin Gordon, has opposed this consensus, arguing that historians have rejected Foucault's conclusions because they have not properly understood him. The difficulties of *Histoire de la folie* and, especially, the greatly abridged nature of its English translation have led to misinformed criticism. "*Histoire de la folie* has been a largely unread or misread book."[17] If, he suggests, we read Foucault's full text with care, we will find most of the standard criticisms to be misplaced and recognize his work as a rich source of detailed historical insight.

We have, then, three suggestions regarding Foucault's history of madness. The consensus of working historians is that it is bad history. To this Colin Gordon responds that it is good history (or, at least, that there are not yet sufficient grounds for thinking it is bad). And, questioning the presupposition of both these views, is the claim of Goldstein and Megill that it is not history at all.

Gordon is clearly right that many of the standard historical criticisms of *Histoire de la folie* are misdirected. Midelfort, because of his wide influence, is the best example. He says that

considered as history, Foucault's argument rests on four basic contentions. The first . . . is the forceful parallel between the medieval isolation of leprosy and the modern isolation of madness. . . . Second is Foucault's contention that in the late Middle Ages and early Renaissance the mad led an 'easy wandering life,' madness having been recognized as part of truth. . . . The third major contention . . . is that this openness [of the Middle Ages and Renaissance to madness] disappeared in the Age of the Great Confinement, beginning in the mid-seventeenth century. . . . The fourth and final contention posits a transition to madness as mental illness, in which Foucault examines the work of the reformers, Tuke and Pinel, and concludes that they "invented" mental illness.[18]

The reader of Foucault's book is immediately struck by the oddity of claiming that these are its "basic contentions." Although Foucault explicitly offered a history of madness in the Classical Age, it seems that three of his four central claims are about other periods. In fact, neither of the first two contentions is central to Foucault's argument. He begins his book by suggesting that leprosy in the Middle Ages bore some striking functional parallels to madness in the Classical Age: both lepers and the mad were objects of fear and repulsion; both were isolated in houses designed more for separation from society than for cures; both were used as joint signs of divine justice and mercy; and in some cases funds and institutions originally meant for lepers came to be used for the mad. There is, Foucault thinks, a nice parallel between the two phenomena, a parallel he uses as a rhetorically effective opening of his book. But as far as historical substance goes, the leprosy discussion is entirely nonessential. Leave it out and the core of Foucault's argument about the nature of Classical madness and its relation to modern psychiatry is unaffected.

To some extent, the same is true of the contrast Foucault sets up between the integration of madness into medieval and Renaissance existence and its exclusion by the Classical Age. The main point is that exclusion and confinement were distinctive features of the Classical Age's attitude toward madness. Foucault sketches an ingenious and provocative story about the medieval and Renaissance viewpoints, but no central argument depends on this account. The needful point is merely that exclusion and confinement distinguish the Classical Age in a fundamental way from the preceding centuries. Beyond this, Foucault's hypotheses as to what went on in the Middle Ages and the Renaissance are just intriguing marginalia.

In any case, the specific objections Midelfort raises to Foucault's claims about the pre-Classical period are of little weight. He points out, for example, that the mad were isolated from society during this period, particularly when they posed a threat to others or themselves, and that there were special hospitals for the mad in Spain during the fifteenth century. Here Midelfort mistakes a claim about the fundamental attitude of a period with a claim about the first introduction of a practice. Finding examples of confinement that precede the Classical Age does not count against the claim that confinement had a unique role in that period. One could just as well argue against the secular character of modern society by citing examples of medieval and Renaissance free-thinking. Midelfort also misunderstands Foucault's position when he urges against it that "instances of harsh treatment of the mad [during pre-Classical periods] could be multiplied *ad nauseam*."[19] This evidence counts against Foucault's view only on the assumption that the pre-Classical inclusion of madness as part of the "truth of human existence" entailed humane treatment of the mad. But such an assumption makes a travesty of Foucault's account, on which Renaissance madness, for example, is either the critically ironic inverse of reason or a tragic and horrifying encounter with monstrous truths.[20] In either case, madness is an integral but disconcerting aspect of human life, essential but by no means welcomed.[21]

What Midelfort presents as Foucault's fourth basic contention – the "invention" of mental illness by the nineteenth-century reformers – is indeed central. His history of madness in the Classical Age is intended as a basis for showing that madness as mental illness was a social construction foreign to that period and original with the nineteenth century. Midelfort's criticism of this contention, however, is based on fundamental misunderstandings of Foucault's position. He says, for example, that "Foucault frequently implies that prior to the nineteenth century madness was not a medical problem." As he notes, such an "assertion seems deliberately preposterous" (256), but no more so than Midelfort's attribution of it to Foucault, who has frequent and detailed discussions of Classical medical treatments of the mad. Foucault does insist that confinement was not practiced for therapeutic purposes and that the distinctive Classical experience of madness associated with confinement did not see the mad as ill. But he also insists on the ineliminable role of Classical medical treatment of madness and in fact poses the relation between non-medical confinement and medical therapy as a major problem for understanding madness in the Classical Age.

As to Foucault's claim that reformers such as Pinel introduced a fundamentally new conception of madness as mental illness, Midel-fort responds that "recent scholarship . . . documents Pinel's explicit debt to earlier English theoreticians and to classical antiquity. Far from standing in a new environment governed by new rules . . . , Pinel clearly felt himself in continuous dialogue with the Hippocratic-Galenic tradition."[22] But this response is quite beside the point unless we falsely assume that conceptual innovation re-quires complete independence from all intellectual influences.[23] The question is whether Pinel transformed the ideas of those to whom he was "indebted" and "in dialogue with" into a fundamen-tally new conception. Midelfort's pointing out that, like everyone else, Pinel had intellectual ancestors has no bearing on this issue.

Midelfort's critique of Foucault's third contention – about the place of confinement in the Classical Age – is much more to the point. Foucault's claims about confinement are absolutely central to his position. He maintains that the isolation of the mad (along with various other people whose behavior involved a rejection of reason) in houses of internment was a practice that took on central signifi-cance during the Classical Age and is essentially connected with the age's fundamental experience of madness. If Foucault is wrong about Classical confinement, then the foundation of his account of mad-ness in the Classical Age is undermined.

Roy Porter has developed this crucial criticism of Foucault in some detail. Foucault, he notes, insists that large-scale confinement was a western-European phenomenon, occuring, if in somewhat dif-ferent ways and at different rates, in France, Germany, England, Spain, and Italy. But at least for England during the "long eighteenth century" (from the Restoration to the Regency), Porter maintains, Foucault is very much off the mark. Although there was some con-finement of the mad and other deviants in workhouses, "the vast majority of the poor and the troublesome were not interned within institutions, remaining at large in society, under the administrative aegis of the Old Poor Law." In particular, studies of the treatment of the mad in specific regions of England show "that lunatics typically remained at large, the responsibility of their family under the eye of the parish."[24] Although some of the mad were confined, the num-bers were quite small: perhaps as little as 5000 and surely no more than 10,000 by early in the nineteenth century, compared with the almost 100,000 confined in 1900. Confinement, Porter suggests, was much more a nineteenth-century phenomenon; during Foucault's Classical Age, "the growth in the practice of excluding the mad was gradual, localized, and piecemeal."[25]

Porter also raises important questions about Foucault's claim that in confinement the mad were homogeneously mixed with a wide variety of other sorts of deviants (prostitutes, free-thinkers, vagabonds, etc.) who violated the Classical Age's ideal of reason. "This picture of indiscriminate confinement does not seem accurately to match what actually happened in England. Few lunatics were kept in gaols, and workhouse superintendents resisted their admission." This tendency "not to lump but to split" was, Porter urges, particularly evident in London, where "scrupulous care was taken to reserve Bethlem for lunatics and Bridewell for the disorderly."[26]

Finally, Porter challenges two of Foucault's key claims about the way the Classical Age conceived madness (its "experience" of madness). According to Foucault, madness, like all the varieties of unreason, was rejected in the first instance because it violated the Classical Age's morality of work. The mad, being idle, were a threat to the stability of a bourgeois society in which labor was the central value. Further, Foucault held that, within the category of unreason, the mad were distinctive for their animality, which put them in radical opposition to the human domain of reason. Porter finds both claims dubious in light of the English experience. "I do not," he says, "find prominent in eighteenth-century discourse the couplings Foucault emphasizes between sanity and work, madness and sloth. Less still was there any concerted attempt to put the asylum population to work."[27] As to the animality of the mad, Porter acknowledges it as one central image, but maintains that there is an at least as important counterimage that Foucault scarcely recognizes. This is the Lockean view of the mad as not raging animals but people who, through misassociation of ideas, go desperately awry in their reasoning. Porter says that Foucault sees this view of madness as arising only with the moral therapy of Tuke and Pinel early in the nineteenth century, whereas in fact it was a very important dimension of seventeenth- and eighteenth-century conceptions of madness.

If Porter is right, Foucault is fundamentally wrong in his characterization of madness in the Classical Age: confinement is not a practice definitive of the epoch's attitude toward madness, the exclusion of the mad is not an expression of bourgeois morality, and animality is not the essence of Classical madness. Is he right? Is Foucault's history bad? Or are Porter and other critics misunderstanding Foucault's historical claims? Or, finally, is Foucault up to something other than history? As a basis for answering these questions, I offer a fairly close reading of the section of *Histoire de la folie* (Part II, Chapters 2–5) in which Foucault develops the fundamentals of his account of madness in the Classical Age. This will provide grounds for drawing some conclusions about the historical value of his work.

FOUCAULT ON CLASSICAL MADNESS

For all its *annalistes* and structuralist affinities, Foucault's history of madness begins from one great *event:* the confinement, within a few years, of a significant portion of the population of western Europe in special houses of internment. Foucault presents this event as an abrupt and major change. He speaks of it as an "abruptly reached . . . threshold" that occurred "almost overnight" (66; *MC,* 45), and describes it as a "massive phenomenon" (75; *MC,* 46) that, for example, displaced in just six years 1 percent of the population of Paris (5000–6000 people) and similar proportions elsewhere during the Classical Age (59, 66, n.2; *MC,* 38, 49). (See n.2 for explanation of reference schema.)

Foucault, however, is not interested in the event of confinement for its own sake, but in the attitudes toward and perceptions of madness connected with it – what he repeatedly refers to as "the Classical experience of madness." The event of confinement is the sudden manifestation of a long-developing "social sensibility" (66). The goal of his history of madness is to describe exhaustively this experience or sensibility and to show how it provided the basis for the modern psychiatric conception of madness as mental illness.

The experience Foucault is tracking is not, he maintains, simply an experience of madness. Rather, the Classical Age saw madness as one division of a wider category, which Foucault calls "unreason" (*déraison*). This corresponds to the fact that not only the mad but a wide variety of other people were confined. Foucault offers successively deeper analyses of just how those confined were perceived.

On the most immediate level, confinement was an economic policy meant to deal with problems of poverty, particularly begging and unemployment. It was a way of getting a large class of idle, potentially disruptive people off the streets and putting them to work in a controlled environment. In purely economic terms, however, confinement was a failure. It hid but did not eliminate poverty, and any gains in employment due to work requirements on those interned were offset by corresponding losses of employment outside the houses of confinement (82).

But, Foucault maintains, the real significance of internment went beyond this economic surface. Far more than an unsuccessful solution to specific economic problems, it represented a new "ethical consciousness of work, in which the difficulties of the economic mechanisms lost their urgency in favor of an affirmation of value" (82; MC, 55). Foucault cites Calvin and Bossuet to show the religious basis for the ethical centrality of work: since the Fall, a refusal to work manifests an absurd pride, which would presume on the divine generosity to provide what we need with no effort of our own. "This is why idleness is rebellion – the worst form of all, in a sense: it waits for nature to be generous as in the innocence of Eden, and seeks to constrain a Goodness to which man cannot lay claim since Adam. . . . Labor in the houses of confinement thus assumed its ethical meaning: since sloth had become the absolute form of rebellion, the idle would be forced to work, in the endless leisure of a labor without utility or profit" (84; MC, 56–57). On this second level, then, those confined (les déraisonnés) were not regarded as the neutral objects of unfortunate economic processes, but as moral reprobates worthy of society's condemnation and punishment.

Foucault goes on to maintain that implicit in the Classical condemnation of "unreasoning" behavior was a deep restructuring of moral categories. He considers the three major classes of those, other than the mad, who were interned: sexual offenders, those guilty of religious profanation, and free-thinkers (les libertins). In every case, behavior that was previously evaluated in other terms was reduced to a violation of bourgeois morality. For example, those suffering from venereal diseases had at first been treated as merely victims of an illness like any other (97–101). But with the beginning of the Classical Age, their afflictions were seen as punishments for their sexual indiscretions. Another, more interesting, case is the inverse fates of sodomy and homosexuality (102). Previously, sodomy had been violently condemned as a religious profanation and homosexuality tolerated as an amorous equivocation. With the Classical Age, sodomy is treated less severely, being regarded as a mere moral fault, not a religious offense requiring the stake. Conversely, homosexuality is no longer overlooked but is treated like other serious offenses against sexual morality. There is a Classical convergence of diverse attitudes toward deviant behavior to the single level of morality.

Foucault further maintains – with particular illustrations from the Classical attitude toward prostitution and debauchery – that the internment of sexual offenders was primarily designed to protect the bourgeois family. "In a sense, internment and the entire 'police' regime that surrounds it serves to oversee [contrôler] a certain order in familial structure. . . . The family with its demands becomes one of the essential requirements of reason; and it is it that above all demands and obtains internment. . . . This period sees the great confiscation of sexual ethics by the morality of the family" (104).

Similarly, such things as blasphemy, suicide, and magical practices, previously regarded as outrageous profanations of religion, are reduced to offenses against the monotone morality of the bourgeoisie. Magic, for example, once violently suppressed as an objectively powerful challenge to religion through its evocation of evil powers, now is regarded as merely a personal delusion that threatens the secular social order. In the same way, free-thinking (libertinage) is no longer a perverse but rational assault on religion's holy truth. It is merely the pathetic consequence of a licentious way of life.

Foucault's first fundamental thesis about Classical madness, then, is that it is assimilated to the broader category of unreason. This is a very puzzling category to us, since it seems to be trying to occupy a nonexistent middle ground between freely chosen criminality and naturally caused illness. If the mad and their partners in unreason have acted freely against the social order, why, we ask, are they merely confined and not punished like other offenders? If they are not sufficiently responsible to merit punishment, why are they not treated like the ill, as innocent victims of natural forces? Foucault acknowledges our difficulty in grasping the conception, but he insists that this is not due to any intrinsic incoherence, but to fundamental disparities between Classical and modern modes of experience.

Foucault does not, however, think we can stop with this simple, if puzzling, account of Classical madness. In some ways the mad were not treated like others who were interned. There were hospitals

(such as the Hôtel de Dieu in Paris, Bethlem in London) where special provision was made for the medical treatment of the mad. True,
such provision is the exception, and Foucault emphasizes that the
internment of the mad (apart from the special hospitals) had no
medical intention. Physicians were assigned to houses of internment only to treat whatever illnesses the inhabitants might come
down with, not as part of a program of medical treatment for madness as such. But even though the medical view of madness is the
less prominent (there were only eighty madmen in the Hôtel de
Dieu compared to the hundreds – perhaps even a thousand – in the
Hôpital Général), it cannot be ignored: "these two experiences each
have their own individuality. The experience of madness as illness,
as restricted as it is, cannot be denied" (131). The problem is to
understand the juxtaposition of these two very different experiences.

Foucault vehemently rejects the Whiggish temptation to see Classical medical treatment of the mad as the first stirrings of progress
toward an enlightened realization (fully blooming in the nineteenth
century) that madness is mental illness. He notes that in fact a
medical approach to madness developed at the end of the Middle
Ages, beginning – possibly under Arab influence – in Spain early in
the fifteenth century. During this period there were increasing num-
bers of institutions (or sections of them) specifically reserved for the
mad. What is striking about the Classical Age is its relative regression in the recognition of the mad, who became less distinct and
more part of the undifferentiated mass of the interned. In this process, the mad became much less the object of medical attention.
Some of them were treated as hospital patients in the Classical Age,
but, according to Foucault, this was mainly a holdover from earlier
periods. It is internment rather than treatment of the mad that is
characteristically Classical. He supports his claim by citing examples of important institutions (such as Bethlem) that increasingly
became mere houses of confinement in the course of the Classical
Age. So Foucault by no means claims that medical treatment of the
mad (and hospitals designed for this purpose) did not exist in the
Classical Age. He does not even claim that the period represents a
regression in the medical knowledge of madness: "the medical texts
of the seventeenth and eighteenth centuries suffice to prove the
contrary" (138). Even though the viewpoints of medical therapy and
of internment are by no means on a par in the Classical Age, both are

present and need to be accounted for. This shows, he says, how "polymorphic and varied the experience of madness could be in the epoch of classicism" (147).

The fact remains that the specifically medical awareness of madness was neither autonomous nor fundamental. Classical madness is, at root, regarded as a disorder of the will, like other forms of unreason. There is, accordingly, "an obscure connection between madness and evil" that passes "through the individual power of man that is his will. Thus, madness is rooted in the moral world" (155).

Even within the realm of unreason, however, madness has a distinctive status. Foucault traces the special status of madness from the striking Classical practice of exhibiting the mad to a curious public. The standard explicit justification of confinement during the Classical Age was the need to avoid scandal. Unreason is hidden away to prevent imitation, to safeguard the reputation of the Church, to preserve the honor of families. But madness is a paradoxical exception: it was during the Classical Age that the practice of displaying the mad to public view (most famously, at Bethlem and Bicêtre) was most prominent.

Foucault finds the explanation of this exception in the peculiar and essential relation of madness to animality in the Classical conception. Like most historians of the period, Foucault does not resist the temptation to cite some of the more vivid reports of how the Classical Age treated the mad like animals. To some extent, he admits, this is (as the Classical Age would have urged) a matter of security against the violence of the insane. But Foucault thinks that there was a more specific and much deeper Classical meaning to the animality of madness.

The animal in man no longer has any value as the sign of a Beyond [as it did in, for example, the Renaissance]; it has become his madness, without relation to anything but itself: his madness in the state of nature. The animality that rages in madness dispossesses man of what is specifically human in him; not in order to deliver him over to other powers, but simply to establish him at the zero degree of his own nature. For classicism, madness in its ultimate form is man in immediate relation to his animality. (166; MC, 73–74).

The mad are animals in the precise sense that they have totally rejected their human nature and put themselves outside the community of reasonable persons.

But why should the Classical Age consider this sort of animality a legitimate object of spectacle? Foucault thinks the answer lies in the new role of madness in Christian thought. Previously there was a reverence and awe before madness based on the idea that Christian faith, as a scandal to reason, was a glorified form of madness. With the Classical Age, this idea is abandoned. Christian wisdom is unequivocally on the side of reason; faith involves no sacrifice of the intellect. Madness, with its choice of animality, is mankind's farthest remove from the truth; the mad are those who have reached the lowest human depths. But this is precisely why madness can function as the unique sign of the extent of divine mercy and the power of grace. The fact that Christ, in taking on human life, allowed himself to be perceived as mad and that his gracious solicitude extended to lunatics shows that salvation is available even to those who have fallen the farthest from the light. Thus the exhibition of the mad served the dual salutary purpose of reminding men how far they might fall and that God's mercy extended even this far.

Here, then, we have the essence of the Classical experience of madness, as Foucault explicates it in Part I of *Histoire de la folie*. There is much more to his story. While Part I extracted the Classical experience from the event of confinement, Part II provides a complementary account of the experience from the standpoint of Classical medical theory and practice, arguing, however, that the two forms of the experience share the same fundamental structure.[28] The essence of this structure is a paradoxical unity of moral guilt and animal innocence. To us, the Classical Age's interning the mad along with those belonging to other categories of unreason is a confusion, a blurring of the distinctive psychology of madness. But Foucault thinks that there is the positive structure of a perception, not the negativity of confusion. Madness is understood by the Classical Age precisely through its place on the horizon of unreason. At one point, Foucault marks this place by a striking religious metaphor: "What the Fall is to the diverse forms of sin, madness is to the other faces of unreason" (176). It is the principle, the model of all the others. More fully, madness "flows through the entire domain of unreason, connecting its two opposed banks: that of moral choice . . . and that of animal rage. . . . Madness is, gathered into a single point, the whole of unreason: the guilty day and the innocent night" (176). This is the "major paradox" involved in the Classical experience of madness: it is equally connected to the moral evaluation of ethical faults and to the "monstrous innocence" of animality. Madness is experienced as "founded on an ethical choice and, at the same time, thoroughly inclined toward animal fury" (177). Such an experience is far removed from (Classical and modern) legal definitions of madness, which seek a division of responsibility (fault) and innocence (external determinism), and from (Classical and modern) medical analyses, which treat madness as a natural phenomenon. Nonetheless, this experience is the key to understanding the Classical view of madness in both thought and practice.

Foucault's ultimate goal in writing his history of madness in the Classical Age was to illuminate (or expose) the true nature of modern (nineteenth century to the present) psychiatry. He repeatedly asserts his view that the modern conception of mental illness and the corresponding institution of the asylum have been unknowingly constructed out of elements of the Classical experience of madness.[29] In particular, he maintains that the theme of innocent animality becomes a "theory of mental alienation as pathological mechanism of nature," and that, by maintaining the practice of internment invented by the Classical Age, psychiatry has preserved (without admitting it) the moral constraint of madness. Both "the positivist psychiatry of the nineteenth century" and that of our own age "have thought that they speak of madness solely in terms of its pathological objectivity; in spite of themselves, they dealt with a madness still entirely imbued with the ethics of unreason and the scandal of animality" (177). These Classical residues in the modern period are the basis of Foucault's analysis and critique (in Part III of *Histoire de la folie*) of modern psychiatry.

FOUCAULT AMONG THE HISTORIANS – PART II

We are now in a position to appreciate in a deeper way the difficulties that historians find in Foucault's work on madness, to see why Porter, for example, for all his praise of Foucault, says he came away from reading *Madness and Civilization* "bewitched, bothered, and begrudging."[30] The central issue of confinement is a good starting point. Porter, as we have seen, has serious objections to the existence of any "great confinement," at least in England, during the Classical Age. Most of the mad simply weren't confined. Those who contrary to Foucault, were carefully separated from other deviants. How should Foucault respond? He has no hope of refuting Porter on the level of the empirical facts. Porter's claim, incorporating numerous careful studies done since Foucault's book, has a decisive advantage here. Foucault might try a tactical retreat: Porter is right for England; but France, in which Foucault is mainly interested, is (as even Porter seems to admit)[31] a different story. Perhaps, then, confinement is a French – or even a continental – phenomenon, with the English, as so often, following a different drummer. But such a retreat puts Foucault into an impossible position, since he purports to be describing not the practices and beliefs of individuals, which might well differ from country to country, but the experience of a culture. He is interested in the fundamental categories in terms of which people perceive, think, and act, not the specific sensations, beliefs, and actions falling under these categories. To allow that the English experience of madness was informed by a different set of fundamental categories would require viewing English and French (or Continental) culture as radically different to an extent that seems indefensible – and is certainly never defended by Foucault.

But perhaps Foucault's concern with fundamental experiential categories rather than with specific perceptions, beliefs, and actions is itself the key to a response to Porter. For, after all, Porter's critique is based on just the sort of specific beliefs and actions that are not Foucault's primary concern. Foucault is not making empirical generalizations about what people in various countries thought or did; he is trying to construct the categorical system that lay behind what was no doubt a very diverse range of beliefs and practices. Confinement, then, is a fact, perhaps most striking in France, but, as Porter admits, also present in England and the rest of Europe. Foucault is concerned with the categorical conditions of possibility for this fact. He wants to know what in the way the Classical Age experienced madness made the sort of confinement it practiced possible. Of course there were, as Foucault admits and even emphasizes, other dimensions of Classical practice, most notably medical therapy, that involved integration rather than isolation of the mad from the community. In some cases this may have meant that, as Porter finds for England, the progress of confinement was slow and piecemeal. But such empirical divergences do not refute Foucault's categorical analysis of the Classical experience of madness.

I think the above is a properly Foucaultian response to Porter. But I also think that accepting it alters the terms of Foucault's confrontation with historical criticism. The crux is this: Given that Foucault's categorical analysis is not refuted by the empirical deviations Porter points out, just what would refute the analysis and, even more important, what would support it?

Here there is a crucial, though easily unnoticed, difference between Foucault and standard historians like Porter. At the outset of his study of madness in the long eighteenth century, Porter formulates his project in a way that seems entirely congruous with Foucault's history of madness. He says that he is "attempting principally to recover the internal coherence of now unfamiliar beliefs about the mind and madness, and to set them in their wider frames of meaning."[32] Further, like Foucault's book, Porter's is filled with facts: names, dates, anecdotes, and quotations from primary sources. Nonetheless, the books are poles apart, and the difference is in the way factual details are related to the overall project of understanding how madness was perceived and treated from 1650 to 1800.

On one level, the difference is that for Porter the facts are primarily *supports* for the interpretative schema, whereas for Foucault they are primarily *illustrations* of it. The opening of Foucault's chapter on confinement is a good example. He begins (57–8) with an analysis of Descartes's rejection of madness as grounds for philosophical doubt, from which he extracts his basic idea of a Classical exclusion of madness from the realm of human existence. Surely he does not regard a single passage from one author as proof of an epoch's conception of madness; the passage from Descartes can only be an illustration of his assertion. He then discusses confinement as a practical expression of this exclusion. The development of confinement is discussed in some detail for France (59–64), but only two brief paragraphs, one on England and the other on the rest of Europe, are deemed enough to show that confinement had "European dimensions" (64; *MC*, 43). Neither paragraph offers much beyond a list of houses of confinement and the dates of their founding. Foucault says nothing about other ways of treating the mad (although, as we have seen, he later pays considerable attention to medical treatment). Most important, he never (here or elsewhere) discusses the extent of confinement relative to other practices and provides no data establishing his view that confinement is the typical Classical reaction to madness. Porter, as we have seen, has substantial evidence that confinement was relatively uncommon in England and, given the strong influence of the Lockean conception of madness, was by no means the distinctively Classical way of dealing with it.

Foucault's procedure is similar throughout the book. His claim that a religious view about the role of work in our postlapsarian world underlies the Classical moral condemnation of madness is supported by brief citations from Calvin, Bossuet, and Bourdaloue (83–4). He bases his claim that there was a "great confiscation of sexual ethics by the morality of the family" (104) on two cases of internment, a few quotations from Molière, and two citations from Classical legal documents (104–5). His "proof" (138) that confinement expressed the fundamental Classical experience of madness and that medical treatment was a marginal holdover of previous practices is that, after Bethlem was opened to the non-mad, there was soon no notable difference between it and the French *hôpitaux généraux;* and that St. Luke's included both the mad and the non-mad from its founding in 1751. With regard to his striking claim that the Classical Age saw unreason as the result of a voluntary choice, he admits that "this awareness is obviously not expressed in an explicit manner in the practices of internment or in their justifications" (156). But he maintains that such a choice can be inferred from Descartes's remarks on madness and that the point is entirely explicit in Spinoza (156–8).

Foucault's penchant for using facts as illustration rather than support does not mean that, as Midelfort suggests, he is "simply indulg[ing] in a whim for arbitrary and witty assertion." It is rather a sign of what I will call his idealist (as opposed to empiricist) approach to history. A characterization of Foucault's history of madness as idealist is apt for a variety of reasons. It is primarily not a history of events or institutions but of an experience, the experience of madness. Also, this experience is not understood in terms of the perceptions or thoughts of individuals; rather, its subject is the anonymous consciousness of an age. (Foucault himself later criticized *Histoire de la folie* because it "accorded far too great a place, and a very enigmatic one too, to what I called an 'experience,' thus showing to what extent one was still close to admitting an anonymous and general subject of history.")[33] Further, Foucault's history exhibits the tense Hegelian combination of anarchic and totalitarian tendencies:

a fascination with conflicting complexities (so that every thought is almost limitlessly qualified and complemented), along with an ultimately triumphant compulsion for unity (so that all the complexity is relentlessly organized). Finally, in typical idealist fashion, the operative justification of Foucault's historical construction is its interpretative coherence rather than its correspondence with independently given external data.

This idealistic cast makes professional historians very uneasy with Foucault's work. They think that, in his insistence on a single unified interpretation, Foucault ignores the messy loose ends that close empirical scrutiny seems to find everywhere in history. David Rothman, for example, complains that "for all the sweep of the analysis, the categories seem rigid (are reason and unreason mutually exclusive?), and there remains too little room for other considerations." He goes on to remark that Foucault's "explanation is so caught up with ideas that their base in events is practically forgotten."[34] Likewise Ian Dowbiggin, while acknowledging the debt of his account of nineteenth-century psychiatry to Foucault, remarks that "there is a seamless quality to Foucault's model that . . . fits historical reality poorly."[35]

As an idealist historian, Foucault could well respond that he is not after an account gerrymandered to fit every recalcitrant fact, an impossible project in any case. What he wants is a comprehensive, unifying interpretation that will give intelligible order to an otherwise meaningless jumble of individual historical truths. The facts are not irrelevant for Foucault, but the primary support for his position is not its demonstrable correspondence with them but its logical and imaginative power to organize them into intelligible configurations. The idea that the Classical Age was one of confinement is an immensely powerful instrument for connecting themes in the theology, literature, philosophy, and medicine of the Classical Age with one another and with the age's political, religious, social, and economic practices. Once we begin to think in terms of confinement as a fundamental category, we are, as Foucault shows, able to develop an extensive and subtle interpretative framework that both raises provocative questions and gives them intriguing answers. Other interpretations may "fit" the facts as well or better than Foucault's, but his provides a perspective with distinctive advantages in unifying power and intellectual fruitfulness. From this standpoint,

although the facts that illustrate Foucault's claims about confinement are not decisive empirical evidence, they are compelling examples of the power of his interpretative framework.

To distinguish between idealist and empiricist history is, of
course, only to specify the opposite ends of a continuum. No system
of interpretation can have historical significance if it is not supported by some significant body of corresponding facts, and no factual data can be formulated independent of some prior interpretative
system. Consequently, even though most standard historical practice is nowadays much closer to the empirical end of the continuum
than Foucault's, my characterization of his work as idealist does not
mean that it is, as Goldstein and Megill suggest, outside the discipline of history. Every historical study must balance idealist interpretation with empiricist fact-gathering, and Foucault's work does not
cease to be history because it is at the currently less-favored end of
the continuum.

Moreover, the reasons Goldstein and Megill offer for thinking Foucault is not an historian seem unpersuasive. Goldstein says that
Foucault is unhistorical because "he questioned the necessary continuity of history."[36] The issue, however, is whether the continuity
Goldstein has in mind is essential for history as such or is just the
defining characteristic of one sort of history. Foucault himself, in
responding to Sartrean claims that his approach eliminates history,
insisted that he eliminated only that history for which "there is an
absolute subject of history, ... who assures its continuity."[37] That
such an elimination is consistent with the historical nature of Foucault's enterprise is supported by the fact that his approach remains
firmly rooted in the central historical category of the event.[38] It is
also relevant to recall that, whatever the role of discontinuity between historical periods in his subsequent works, *Histoire de la folie*
frequently insists on important continuities between Classical and
modern conceptions of madness (see the passages cited in n. 29).[39]

Megill argues that *Histoire de la folie* lies outside of history (and
of all academic disciplines) because it is ambiguous in a way appropriate to literature, rather than an academic discipline: "there is
something central to the disciplinary project that seems thwarted in
Foucault. It is as if, through his love of ambiguity, he has thrown a
monkey wrench into the disciplinary machinery."[40] I agree that the
antidisciplinary rhetoric of ambiguity Megill emphasizes is an im-

portant element in *Histoire de la folie*. But this shows only that it is not exclusively a historical analysis. What basis is there for thinking that, for example, Foucault's elaborate interpretation of the Classical experience of madness, sketched in the middle section of this essay, is not an historical account, evaluable by the disciplinary canons of history? It may well be that, even if such evaluation resulted in the total rejection of the account as accurate history, there would still be literary (and, perhaps, some sort of philosophical) merit in what Foucault wrote. But the fact remains that, whatever else may be going on, *Histoire de la folie* does offer a very detailed history of madness in the Classical Age. My own view is that the book shows an antihistorical character primarily in Foucault's intermittent efforts to evoke madness as it is experienced by the mad themselves. This experience he tends to present as an absolute transcending the history of changing social constructions of madness. (The theme is most apparent in the Preface to the first edition, which Foucault later dropped.) Contrary to Megill, I think this theme is clearly outside the main thrust of the book.[41]

What, then, should we conclude about what we might now, not entirely facetiously, describe as Foucault's *Die Phänomenologie des kranken Geistes*?[42] Granted, as I have just been arguing, that it *is* history, is it good or bad history? The easy answer is that it is good idealist history but bad empiricist history. That, however, is too easy, since a schema of historical interpretation may be so empirically deficient that even its most ingenious and exciting speculations are not worth pursuing. (In the same way, an empirically impeccable account may be so devoid of interpretative interest as to be hardly worth an historian's yawn.)

This, I think, is as far as philosophical kibitzing can take the discussion of Foucault's history of madness. I have argued that there is no good reason to place *Histoire de la folie* entirely outside the domain of history, immune to the critical norms of historiography. I have also maintained that neither of the two most important historical critiques of Foucault shows that his work is bad history. Midelfort's apparently decisive criticisms are mostly based on misunderstandings of Foucault's views. Porter's critique of Foucault's central views on confinement raises an important empirical challenge, but does not, in itself, undermine the interpretative power of Foucault's idealist history. So far there have been no decisive tests of the fruitfulness of Foucault's complex interpretative framework. What is still needed, it seems to me, is an assessment of his overall picture of Classical madness through detailed deployments of its specific interpretative categories. Is, for example, Jan Goldstein right in her suggestion that historians of the Enlightenment should pay more attention to Foucault's idea of a tension in the Classical experience of madness between man as a juridical subject and man as a social being?[43] How much explanatory power is there in his claim that Classical confinement involved a reduction of all sexual offenses to the norms of bourgeois morality? What level of understanding can we reach by developing his account of the religious significance of Classical madness? To what extent is the nature of nineteenth-century psychiatry illuminated by thinking of it as constructed from the polar Classical conceptions of madness as innocent animality and as moral fault? The issue of Foucault's status as a historian of madness should remain open until historians have posed and answered questions such as these.

NOTES

1 Comment at the University of Vermont, October 27, 1982. Cited by Allan Megill, "The Reception of Foucault by Historians," 117.

2 Title of second edition, published in Paris (Gallimard, 1972), to which all references will be given in parentheses in the main test. The English translation, *Madness and Civilization*, trans. Richard Howard is of a drastically abridged French edition. Cited passages that appear in *Madness and Civilization* (*MC*) will be given in Howard's version, other passages in my own translation. For more details on various French editions of *Histoire de la folie*, see Gary Gutting, *Michel Foucault's Archaeology of Scientific Reason*, 70, n.6. Colin Gordon has rightly emphasized the need to consult the full French text; see his "*Histoire de la folie:* An Unknown Book by Michel Foucault," 3–26. Also see the responses to Gordon's article by a variety of writers (among others, Robert Castel, Roy Porter, Andrew Scull, H. C. Eric Midelfort, Jan Goldstein, Dominick La Capra, and Alan Megill) and Gordon's reply, "History, Madness and Other Errors: A Response," in the same volume. An English translation by Anthony Pugh of the full French text is scheduled to appear from Routledge.

3 This essay will focus on *Histoire de la folie*, which is Foucault's only full-scale discussion of madness and, so far, the work of his most influential on historians of psychiatry. Mention should also be made of his

earlier, mainly nonhistorical, discussions, *Maladie mentale et person-nalité*, and the long introduction to a French translation of Ludwig Binswanger's *Traum and Existenz: Le rêve et l'existence* (English transla-tion: "Dream, Imagination, and Existence," trans. F. Williams, *Review of Existential Psychology and Psychiatry* 19 [1984–5]: 29–78.) A second edition of the former work, greatly revised, mostly in accord with the views of *Histoire de la folie*, appeared as *Maladie mentale et psy-chologie* (1962). (English translation: *Mental Illness and Psychology*, trans. A Sheridan). For a discussion of these early works and their rela-tion to *Histoire de la folie*, see Gutting, *Michel Foucault's Archaeology of Scientific Reason*, 55–69.

Foucault's later work on the history of the prison (*Discipline and Punish*, trans. Alan Sheridan, 1978) and on nineteenth-century sexuality (*The History of Sexuality, Vol. I: An Introduction*, trans. Robert Hurley, 1978) have also had an important influence on historians of psychiatry. Their challenging views on the inextricable connections of power and knowledge and on the deep functional similarities of modern institu-tions such as asylums, prisons, factories, and schools may in the long run be more important for historians of psychiatry than even the *History of Madness*. In this connection, see Robert Nye's *Crime, Madness, and Politics in Modern France* (Princeton: Princeton University Press, 1984).

4 "Trois clefs pour comprendre la folie à l'époque classique," *Annales: Economics, Sociétés, Civilisations* (1962): 761–72.

5 *Mystical Bedlam: Madness, Anxiety, and Healing in Seventeenth-Century England* (Cambridge: Cambridge University Press, 1981), xi.

6 Jan Goldstein, *Console and Classify: The French Psychiatric Profession in the Nineteenth Century* (Cambridge: Cambridge University Press, 1987), 396.

7 Roy Porter, "Foucault's Great Confinement," 47.

8 Patricia O'Brien, "Foucault's History of Culture," in Hunt, ed., *The New Cultural History*, 25–46.

9 "Madness and Civilization in Early Modern Europe: A Reappraisal of Michel Foucault," in Malament, ed., *After the Reformation: Essays in Honor of J.H. Hexter*, 259.

10 Peter Sedgwick, *Psycho Politics*, 132, n. 22; Lawrence Stone, "Madness," 36ff. (also see Foucault's reply, 42–44); Ian Hacking, "The Archaeology of Foucault," in Hoy, ed., *Foucault: A Critical Reader*, 29; Dominick LaCapra, "Foucault, History, and Madness," 32–34.

11 Cf., for example, Roy Porter, *Mind Forg'd Manacles* (Cambridge: Har-vard University Press, 1987), xi, 33; Michael MacDonald, *Mystical Bed-lam*, 1; Andrew Scull, *Museums of Madness* (New York: St. Martin's Press, 1979, 70; and the "Introduction" to W.F. Bynum, Roy Porter,

Michael Shepherd, eds., *The Anatomy of Madness*, Vol. I (London: Tavistock, 1985), 3–4.

12 "Michel Foucault's History of Madness," *History of the Human Sciences* 3 (1990): 57.

13 "Foucault's History of Culture," 31.

14 Goldstein, *Console and Classify*, 3.

15 *Journal of Modern History* 51 (1979): 117.

16 "The Reception of Foucault by Historians," 133–4.

17 See Gordon, "History, Madness and Other Errors: A Response," 381.

18 "Madness and Civilization in Early Modern Europe," 249–51.

19 Ibid., 253.

20 Colin Gordon points out that Midelfort seems to be misled by a mistranslation in *Madness and Civilization*, which has Foucault speaking of the "easy wandering life" of the mad in the Middle Ages and Renaissance. See "*Histoire de la folie:* An unknown book by Michel Foucault," 17. For Midelfort's response to Gordon (on this and other points), see "Comments on Colin Gordon," *History of the Human Sciences* 3 (1990): 41–46.

21 I hesitate to add to the already overextended controversy about Midelfort's contention that Foucault is wrong in his belief that the "ship of fools," so prominent in medieval literature and painting, actually existed. Let me say merely that Foucault's use of the ship is almost entirely concerned with its literary and artistic significance and that it is central to his argument only as a striking (and rich) *symbol* of what he thinks was the status of medieval madness. Depriving him of the assumption that such ships actually existed has a nugatory effect on the evidence for his view.

22 "Madness and Civilization in Early Modern Europe," 258–9.

23 Midelfort also takes Foucault to task for accepting as fact the myth of Pinel's liberation of the mad from their chains at Bicêtre. This is a blatant misreading, since Foucault is not only well aware of the lack of factual basis for the anecdote but explicitly treats the story as a myth. For further details, see Gordon, "*Histoire de la folie:* An unknown book by Michel Foucault," 15–16.

24 "Foucault's Great Confinement," 48.

25 Ibid.

26 Ibid., 49.

27 Ibid.

28 On the other hand, Foucault's discussion in Part II importantly refines and deepens his view, particularly by relating the experience of madness to Classical conceptions of imagination, passion, the mind-body union, and language. For a full analysis of Foucault's view of Classical madness

(and of the entire project of *Histoire de la folie*), see Chapter 2 of my *Michel Foucault's Archaeology of Scientific Reason*.

29 See, for example, *Histoire de la folie*, 97, 100–101, 103, 116, 139, 146–9, 177.

30 "Foucault's Great Confinement," 47.

31 *Mind Forg'd Manacles*, 7.

32 Ibid., x.

33 *The Archaeology of Knowledge*, 16, translation modified.

34 *The Discovery of the Asylum* (Boston: Little, Brown & Company, 1971), xviii.

35 *Inheriting Madness: Professionalization and Psychiatric Knowledge in Nineteenth-Century France* (Berkeley: University of California Press, 1991), 170.

36 *Console and Classify*, 3.

37 "Michel Foucault explique son dernier livre," interview with J-J. Brochier, *Magazine littéraire* 28 (1969): 24.

38 Cf. Foucault's remarks on this point in Colin Gordon, ed., *Power/ Knowledge*, 114.

39 For more on Foucault's attitude toward continuity, see Robert Nye, *Crime, Madness, and Politics in Modern France*, 11–12, and Patrick Hutton, "The History of Mentalities: The New Map of Cultural History," *History and Theory* 20 (1981): 254.

40 "Foucault, Ambiguity, and the Rhetoric of Historiography," 358.

41 See ibid., 350–56. For further discussion of Foucault and the experience of madness, see Gutting, *Michel Foucault's Archaeology of Scientific Reason*, 263–65.

42 In comparing Foucault as a historian of madness to Hegel, I am not saying that Foucault endorsed the metaphysics of the Absolute that underlies Hegel's own histories. Foucault's idealism is much more methodological than metaphysical, and primarily derives from the strong influence of phenomenology on his earlier writings. (This influence is most prominent in the essay on Binswanger cited in n. 3 above.) Foucault's penchant for idealistic as opposed to empirical history decreased over the years, but I would argue that it remains strong at least through *Les mots et les choses* and never entirely disappears from his work. Foucault was well aware of his Hegelian tendencies: "We have to determine the extent to which our anti-Hegelianism is possibly one of his tricks directed against us, at the end of which he stands, motionless, waiting for us" ("The Discourse on Language," appendix to *The Archaeology of Knowledge*, 235).

43 " 'The lively sensibility of the Frenchman': Some Reflections on the Place of France in Foucault's *Histoire de la folie*," 336.

GEORGE CANGUILHEM.

TRANSLATED BY CATHERINE PORTER

3   The death of man, or exhaustion of the cogito?

The philosophers who have considered Cervantes's *Don Quixote* to be a major philosophical event can be counted on the fingers of one hand. Indeed, to my knowledge only two have done so: Auguste Comte and Michel Foucault. If Comte had written a history of madness – and he could have – he would have made room for Cervantes, for he referred to *Don Quixote* more than once in defining madness as an excess of subjectivity and as a passion for countering the contradictions of experience by endlessly complicating the interpretations that experience can have. Yet the author of *L'Histoire de la folie* turned to Descartes, not Cervantes, for help in presenting the Classical era's idea of madness.[1] Conversely, in *Les Mots et les choses*,[2] Cervantes and Don Quixote are honored with four brilliant pages, and Descartes is mentioned just two or three times. The single Cartesian text cited, a short passage from the *Regulae*, comes up only by virtue of the manifest subordination of the notion of measure to the notion of order in the idea of *mathesis*. And probably also by virtue of the precocious use of the *Regulae* in *La Logique de Port-Royal*, Foucault elevates that hitherto neglected account of the logic of signs and grammar to the status of a seventeenth-century masterwork. By this striking displacement of the sites where they might have been expected to be invoked as witnesses, Descartes and Cervantes come to be invested with adjudicative or critical power. Descartes is one of the artisans who set out the standards that resulted in the relegation of madness to the asylum space, where nineteenth-century pathologists found it as an object of knowledge. Cervantes is one of the artisans who wrenched words from the prose of the world and wove them together in the warp of signs and the woof of representation.

Les Mots et les choses took a text by Borges as its starting point

71

(xv), and it looked to Velasquez and Cervantes for the keys to a reading of the Classical philosophers. The year it appeared, a printed invitation to the Fourth World Congress of Psychiatry was adorned with the effigy of Don Quixote, and a Picasso exhibit in Paris recalled the still contemporary enigma of the message entrusted to Las Meninas. Let us utilize Henri Brulard's term *espagnolisme*, then, to characterize the philosophical cast of Foucault's mind. For Stendhal, who detested Racine in his youth and trusted no one but Cervantes and Ariosto, *espagnolisme* meant hatred for preachiness and platitudes. To judge by the moralizing reproaches, the outrage, and the indignation aroused in many quarters by Foucault's work, he seems to take direct, if not always deliberate, aim at a type of mind that is as flourishing today as it was during the Bourbon Restoration.

The time seems to have passed when a Kant could write that nothing must escape criticism. In a century in which laws and religion have long since ceased to stave off criticism with their majesty and holiness, respectively, are we going to be forbidden, in the name of philosophy, to challenge the grounding that certain philosophies think they find in the essence or the existence of man? Because, in the concluding pages of Foucault's book, the king's place becomes the place of a dead – or at least a dying – humanity, humanity as close to its end as to its beginning, or better yet to its "recent invention," because we are told that "man is neither the oldest nor the most constant problem that has been posed for human knowledge" (386), must we lose all our composure, as some of those we had counted among the best minds of the day seem to have done? Having refused to live according to the routines of the academy, must one behave like an academician embittered by the imminence of his replacement in the position of mastery? Are we going to witness the creation of a League of the Rights of Man to Be the Subject and Object of Philosophy, under the motto "Humanists of All Parties, Unite!"?

Rather than anathematizing what in a cursory amalgamation is termed "structuralism" or the "structural method," and rather than interpreting the success of a work as proof of its lack of originality, it would be more useful to reflect on the following. In 1943, in *Servius et la Fortune*,[3] Georges Dumézil wrote that he had come across his problem "at the intersection of four paths." We know today, after the reception afforded *La Religion romaine archaïque*[4] in 1967, that by virtue of their meeting at the Dumézil intersection, these four paths have become roads. Along these roads the former detractors of the intersection method, the champions of historical Roman history, would be very happy to accompany Mr. Dumézil today, if their age had left them the time and the strength. Undertakings like those of Dumézil, Lévi-Strauss, and Martinet have determined, without premeditation and by a virtual triangulation, the point where a philosopher would need to situate himself in order to justify these undertakings and their results – by comparing but not amalgamating them. Foucault's success can be fairly taken as a reward for the lucidity that allowed him to perceive this point, to which others were blind.

One fact is striking. Almost all the reviews and commentaries provoked until now by *Les Mots et les choses* single out the term "archaeology" in the subtitle for special – sometimes rather negative – emphasis, and skirt the signifying bloc constituted by the phrase "archaeology of the human sciences." Those who proceed in this way do seem to lose sight of the thesis, in the strict sense of the term, that the ninth and tenth chapters bring together. So far as this thesis is concerned, everything is played out around language – more precisely, around the situation of language today. In the nineteenth century, the substitution of biology for natural history, or the substitution of a theory of production for the analysis of wealth, resulted in the constitution of a unified object of study: life or work. In contrast, the unity of the old general grammar was shattered (303–304) without being replaced by any sort of unique and unifying renewal. Language became the business of philologists and linguists, of symbolic logicians, exegetes and, finally, pure writers, poets. At the end of the nineteenth century when Nietzsche was teaching that the meaning of words has to refer back to whoever provides it (but just who does provide it?), Mallarmé was effacing himself from his own poem:

> Then the phrase came back again in virtual form; for it had freed itself of that first touch of the wing or palm-branch; henceforth it would be heard through the voice. Finally, it came to be uttered of itself and lived through its own personality.[5]

To the traditional question "What does it mean to think?," Michel Foucault substitutes the question "What does it mean to speak?" – or at least deems that the substitution has been made. To that question, he acknowledges (307) that he does not yet know how to respond, whether to regard the question as an effect of our delay in recognizing its loss of relevance or whether to assume that it anticipates future concepts that will enable us to answer it. These days, when so many "thinkers" make bold to offer answers to questions whose relevance and formulation they have not bothered to justify, we do not often have the opportunity to encounter a man who needs some three hundred pages to set forth a question, while reflecting that "perhaps labour begins again," and confessing: "It is true that I do not know what to reply to such questions. . . . I cannot even guess whether I shall ever be able to answer them, or whether the day will come when I shall have reasons enough to make any such choice" (ibid.).

As for the concept of archaeology, most of Foucault's principal critics have latched onto the term only to challenge it and replace it with "geology." It is quite true that Foucault borrows words from the vocabulary of geology and seismology, such as "erosion," (50), "squares" (Fr. *plages*, beaches) and "expanse" (Fr. *nappe*, layer) (217), "shocks" (ibid), and "strata" (221). The end of the preface seems to come from a new discourse on the revolutions of the globe: "I am restoring to our silent and apparently immobile soil its rifts, its instability, its flaws; and it is the same ground that is once more stirring under our feet" (xxiv). But it is no less true that what Foucault is trying to bring back to light is not the analogue of a stratum of the terrestrial shell that has been hidden from sight by a natural phenomenon of rupture and collapse, but rather "the deepest strata of Western culture," that is, a "threshold" (xxiv). Notwithstanding the use of the term "habitat" by geography and ecology, man inhabits a culture, not a planet. Geology deals with sediments, archaeology with monuments. Thus we can readily understand why those who deprecate the structural method (supposing that there is such a thing, properly speaking) in order to defend the rights of history, dialectical or not, are determined to try to substitute geology for archaeology. They do so to shore up their claim to represent humanism. Depicting Foucault as a kind of geologist amounts to saying that he naturalizes culture by withdrawing it from history. The naive children of existentialism can then charge him with positivism – the supreme insult.

Thinkers had installed themselves within dialectics. They had gone beyond what had come before (of necessity, according to some; by choice, according to others), but they remained convinced that they understood what they had left behind. Suddenly along came someone who talked about an "essential rupture," who worried about "no longer being able to think a certain thought," who wondered "how [thought] contrives to escape from itself," and who invited us simply to "accept these discontinuities in the simultaneously manifest and obscure empirical order wherever they posit themselves" (50–51). The archaeologist of knowledge discovered, between the eighteenth and the nineteenth centuries, as between the sixteenth and the seventeenth, an "enigmatic discontinuity" (217) that he can only describe, without pretending to explain it, as a mutation, a "radical event" (ibid.), a "fundamental event" (229), "a minuscule but absolutely essential displacement" (238). Of these discontinuities, these radical events beneath the apparent continuity of a discourse that upset human perception and practice, Michel Foucault's earlier work gave two examples. L'Histoire de la folie identified the break that occured between Montaigne and Descartes in the representation of madness. La Naissance de la clinique[6] identified the break that occurred between Pinel and Bichat in the representation of illness.

We can hardly avoid wondering what has led critics, most of them no doubt in good faith, to denounce the danger that threatens History here. In a sense, what more can be asked, with respect to historicity, of someone who writes: "Since it is the mode of being of all that is given us in experience, History has become the unavoidable element in our thought" (219)? But because this emergence of history, on the one hand as discourse and on the other hand as the mode of being of empiricity, is taken as the sign of a rupture, one is led to conclude that some other rupture – perhaps already under way – will render the historical mode of thinking foreign to us, or even – who knows? – unthinkable. This is just what Michel Foucault seems to conclude: "By revealing the law of time as the external boundary of the human sciences, History shows that everything that has been thought will be thought again by a thought that does not yet exist" (372). In any event, why refuse, in the interim, to apply the qualifier "historical" to a discourse that reports the raw, undeducible, unpredictable succession of the conceptual configurations of systems of thought? The reason is that a sequential arrangement of this sort excludes the idea of progress. And Foucault specifies: "I am not concerned, therefore, to describe the progress of knowledge towards an objectivity in which today's science can finally be recognized" (xxii). In other words, nineteenth-century History is eighteenth-century Progress, which replaced seventeenth-century Order, but this emergence of Progress must not be considered, with respect to History, as an instance of progress. And if the face of Man were to be obliterated from knowledge, "like a face drawn in sand at the edge of the sea" (387), nothing in Foucault's writing allows us to suppose that he would view that possibility as a step backward. We are dealing with an explorer here, not a missionary of modern culture.

It is difficult to be the first to give a name to a thing or, at the very least, to list the distinctive features of the thing one is proposing to name. That is why the concept of *episteme*, which Foucault devoted his work to clarifying, is not immediately transparent. A culture is a code that orders human experience in three respects – linguistic, perceptual, practical; a science or a philosophy is a theory or an interpretation of that ordering. But the theories and interpretations in question do not apply directly to human experience. Science and philosophy presuppose the existence of a network or configuration of forms through which cultural productions are perceived. These forms already constitute, with respect to that culture, *knowledge* different from the knowledge constituted by sciences and philosophies. This network is invariant and unique to a given epoch, and thus identifiable through reference to it (168). Failing to recognize it entails, in the history of ideas as in the history of the sciences, misunderstandings that are as serious as they are persistent.

The history of ideas in the seventeenth century, as it is ritually described, is a case in point: "one might say, if one's mind is filled with ready-made concepts, that the seventeenth century marks the disappearance of the old superstitious or magical beliefs and the entry of nature, at long last, into the scientific order. But what we must grasp and attempt to reconstitute are the modifications that affected knowledge itself, at that archaic level which makes possible both knowledge itself and the mode of being of what is to be known" (54). These modifications are summed up in a retreat of language with respect to the world. Language is no longer, as it was in the Renaissance, the signature or mark of things. It becomes the instrument for manipulating, mobilizing, juxtaposing, and comparing things; the organ allowing them to be composed in a universal tableau of identities and differences; a means not for revealing order, but for dispensing it.

The history of ideas and sciences in the seventeenth century thus cannot be confined to the history of the mechanization, or even the mathematization, of the various empirical domains (56). Moreover, in speaking of mathematization, one ordinarily thinks about measuring things. Yet it is their ordering that ought to strike us as primordial. Otherwise, how can we understand the appearance, during the same period, of theories like that of general grammar, or the naturalists' taxonomy, or the analysis of wealth? Everything becomes clear, and the classical unity emerges, if we suppose that all these domains "rely for their foundation upon a possible science of order" and that "the ordering of things by means of signs constitutes all empirical forms of knowledge as knowledge based upon identity and difference" (37).

This basis of a possible science is what Foucault calls an *episteme*. As such, it is no longer the primary code of Western culture, and it is not yet a science like Huygens's optics nor a philosophy like Malebranche's system. It is what is required for us even to imagine the possibility of that optics in Huygens's day or that philosophy in Malebranche's, rather than three-quarters of a century earlier. It is what is required for us to comprehend the various attempts to construct the sciences as kinds of analyses that are able to reach elements of reality and kinds of calculations or combinations that make it possible to match, through the ordered combination of elements, the universality of nature. To know nature is no longer to decipher it, but to represent it.

For Descartes, as for Leibniz, if the theory of physics is presented as an attempt at decoding, the certainty to which it gives rise is only moral, based on the probability that the true theory is the system of signs that is most complete, most coherent, most open to the complements to come. There is no getting around it: when all is said and done, it is not Michel Foucault who wrote the concluding lines of *Principles of Philosophy*, or Leibniz's letter to Conring of March 19, 1678. It seems to me quite difficult to challenge the contention that bringing to light the "archaeological network that provides Classical thought with its laws" (85) offers a productive renewal of the way the chronological contours of the period and the intellectual kin-

ships or affinities within the field of that *episteme* have been conceptualized. But I also think that such a stimulating indication of renewal, if it succeeded in provoking numerous and rigorous studies
designed to take a fresh look at the doxology of the Classical era,
might lead to modifications in Foucault's thesis, according to which
the discontinuous and autonomous succession of networks of fundamental utterances precludes any effort to reconstitute the past we
have left behind.

Let us read the following sentence attentively: "No doubt it is
because Classical thought about representation excludes any analysis of signification that we today, who conceive of signs only upon
the basis of such an analysis, have so much trouble, despite the
evidence, in recognizing that Classical philosophy, from Malebranche to Ideology, was through and through a philosophy of the
sign" (80). To whom does that evidence appear?

Certainly not to *us*, who have so much trouble in recognizing –
without, however, let us note, being totally incapable of recognizing.
The evidence certainly appears to Michel Foucault. But then, while
the *episteme* of a given era cannot be fully grasped via the intellectual history of that era, which is subtended by the *episteme* of a
different era, the two are not entirely foreign to one another. If they
were, how should we understand the appearance today, within an
epistemological field without precedent, of a work like *Les Mots et
les choses?* Perhaps this remark has already been made. It is inevitable that it should be made. It is not certain, moreover, that the
paradox such a remark exposes is really a paradox. When Foucault,
taking up the question of Classical knowledge (303–4), resumes the
archaeological demonstration that he had undertaken earlier (56–
71), he goes on to invoke a "slow and laborious technique" that
would allow the reconstitution of a network; he recognizes that it is
"difficult today to rediscover how that structure was able to function"; he declares that Classical thought has ceased to be "directly
accessible to us" (303–4). What remains, then, is the fact that pains-
takingly, slowly, laboriously, indirectly, we can dive deep down from
our own epistemic shores and reach a submerged *episteme*.

In the same way, the prohibition on lifting the seven seals that
close the book of the past, applied to a certain sort of history, perhaps
amounts to an invitation to proceed with elaborating a different sort
of history: "If the natural history of Tournefort, Linnaeus, and Buf-

fon can be related to anything at all other than itself, it is not to biology, to Cuvier's comparative anatomy, or to Darwin's theory of evolution, but to Bauzée's general grammar, to the analysis of money and wealth as found in the works of Law, or Verón de Fortbonnais, or Turgot" (xxiii). It would be no trivial achievement if Foucault's reading were to inject a generalized fear of anachronism into the heart of the history of science. The historian of science unwittingly takes from the science whose historian he has made himself the idea of a progressively constituted truth. An example of a conscience at ease within anachronism is found in a text by Emile Guyénot, *Les Sciences de la vie aux XVIIe et XVIIIe siècles: l'idée d'évolution.*[7]

Despite what most of Foucault's critics have claimed, the term "archaeology" says just what he wants it to say. It is the condition of an *other history*, in which the concept of event is retained, but in which events affect concepts and not men. Such a history must in its turn recognize breaks, like any history, but breaks that are situated differently. There are few historians of biology and still fewer historians of ideas who do not describe a continuity of thought between Buffon or Maupertuis and Darwin, and who do not claim a discontinuity between Darwin and Cuvier – that Cuvier who is so often presented as the evil genius of biology at the beginning of the nineteenth century. Foucault, for his part, locates the discontinuity between Buffon and Cuvier – more precisely, between Buffon and Antoine-Laurent de Jussieu – and he makes Cuvier's work the condition of historical possibility of Darwin's work. We can leave that question on the table, open to argument. It is certainly worth arguing about. Even if one does not think Foucault is right on this point – and I personally think he is right – is that reason enough for accusing him of tossing History out the window? Buffon did not understand how Aldrovandi could have written the history of snakes the way he did. Foucault thinks he understands: "Aldrovandi was neither a better or a worse observer than Buffon; he was neither more credulous than he, nor less attached to the faithfulness of the observing eye or to the rationality of things. His observation was simply not linked to things in accordance with the same system or by the same arrangement of the *episteme*" (40). Buffon, on the other hand, was linked to things by the same arrangement of the *episteme* as Linnaeus: "Buffon and Linnaeus employ the same grid" (135). Foucault thus proposes nothing less than a systematic program for turning the working methods of most historians of biology inside out (123–28).

Why then does he cause a scandal? Because history today is a kind of magical field in which, for many philosophers, existence is identified with discourse, and the actors of history are identified with the authors of histories, even histories garnished with ideological presuppositions. This is why a program for turning historical discourse inside out is denounced as a manifesto calling for the subversion of the course of history. The subversion of a progressivist discourse cannot be anything but a conservative project. And that is why your structure is neo-capitalist. The critics forget, or more precisely ignore, the fact that Foucault – and he does not hide this – found substantial encouragement for denying the preexistence of evolutionist concepts in the eighteenth century in Henri Daudin's remarkable theses, published in 1926, on the methods of classification developed by Linnaeus, Lamarck, and Cuvier.

Henri Daudin, a professor of philosophy at the University of Bordeaux, gave those who knew him no reason to think that it is a betrayal of humanity or the populace to affirm, in opposition to those who amalgamate biological evolutionism and political and social progressism, that Darwin the biologist owes more to Cuvier than to Lamarck. Foucault is right to say that Lamarck is more a contemporary of A.-L. de Jussieu than of Cuvier (275), and his reading of Cuvier's *Leçons d'anatomie comparée*[8] warrants close attention, especially for the thesis according to which "evolutionism is a biological theory, of which the condition of possibility was a biology without evolution – that of Cuvier" (294). In the eighteenth century the theory of the continuous scale of life forms did more to prevent the conception of a history of life than to encourage it. Transitional forms and intermediate species were required for the composition of an unbroken tableau; they did not contradict the simultaneity of relationships. The history of living beings on the globe was the history of the progressive clarification of a schema, not the history of its sequential accomplishment. "Continuity is not the visible wake of a fundamental history in which one same living principle struggles with a variable environment. For continuity precedes time. It is its condition. And history can play no more than a negative role in relation to it: it either picks out an entity and allows it to survive, or ignores it and allows it to disappear" (155). It is thus not overstating the case to conclude that natural history cannot possibly conceive of the history of nature (157).

I have restricted my attempt to understand what Foucault means when he speaks of *episteme* to that aspect of his demonstration in which, rightly or wrongly. I see myself as having a long-standing interest if not a certain competence. We still have to wonder whether the well-constructed sketches in the history of language, life, and work that are based on this concept of *episteme* suffice to assure us that we are dealing with something more than a simple word here. Is the *episteme*, the reason for conceiving of a program for overturning history, something more than an intellectual construct? And, first, what kind of object is it, for what kind of discourse? A science is an object for the history of science, for the philosophy of science. It is a paradox that the *episteme* is not an object for epistemology. For the time being, and for Michel Foucault, the *episteme* is *that for which* a discursive status is sought throughout *Les Mots et les choses*. For the time being, the object is what the person talking about it says it is.

What sort of verification can be applied to such a discourse? It cannot be a matter of referring, in the name of verification, to an object given in advance to be constituted according to a rule. Cuvier's comparative anatomy sustained a relationship with living or fossil organisms, but those organisms were perceived or reconstructed according to an idea of organisms and of organization that, through the principle of the correlation of forms, overturned eighteenth-century continuist taxonomy. Darwin threw out the chart of the species and traced the succession of living forms with no preordained plan. Daudin wrote a nonconformist history of the dispute between Cuvier and Lamarck. In that history, the archaeologist discovers the traces of an epistemic network. Why? Because he has taken up a position both inside and outside the history of biology. Because, having adopted the tactic of reversible overturning, he has superimposed two sets of readings – the ones offered by theories of language and the one provided by economic theories – on the reading of living beings.

The verification of the discourse on the *episteme* depends upon the variety of domains in which the invariant is discovered. In order to perceive the *episteme*, it was necessary to exit from a given science and from the history of a given science; it was necessary to defy

the specialization of specialists, and to try to become a specialist not
of generality, but of interregionality. To paraphrase one of Foucault's
critics, a man as intelligent as he is severe,[9] it was necessary to rise
with the larks and go to bed with the owls. The archaeologist has to
have read a great number of things that the others have not read.
Here is one of the reasons for the astonishment that Foucault's text
has aroused in several of his sternest critics. Foucault cites none of
the historians in a given discipline; he refers only to original texts
that slumber in libraries. People have talked about "dust." Fair
enough. But just as a layer of dust on furniture is a measure of the
housekeeper's negligence, so a layer of dust on books is a measure of
the carelessness of their custodians.

The *episteme* is an object that has not been the object of any book
up to now, but that has encompassed – because at bottom it had
constituted them – all the books of a given period. Yet if those books
have finally been read, is it not through Foucault's "grid"? Would
not a different grid produce a different reading harvest? Let us examine the objection. It is certain that Foucault does not read the eighteenth century quite the way Ernst Cassirer does in *La Philosophie
des Lumières*,[10] and still less the way Paul Hazard does in his two
studies of European thought. It is revealing to compare the chapter
on the natural sciences in *La Pensée européenne au XVIIIe siècle*[11]
with the fifth chapter of Foucault's book. It is also revealing to
compare the bibliographic references. Foucault cites only original
texts. Which of the two scholars is reading by means of a grid?
Conversely, a reader like Cassirer who knows how to make his way
to the texts, and to little-read texts, proposes a reading of the eighteenth century that is not unrelated to Foucault's, and he too discovers a network of themes that constitute a ground on which Kant will
one day sprout, without our knowing how.

Undeniably it is Foucault himself who speaks of grids. And to the
extent that an allusion to cryptography is involved, readers believe
they are justified in trying to find out who is the inventor of the grid.
But it may be that Foucault has no grid of his own, only his own
particular use of the grid. The idea that language is a grid for experience is not new. But the idea that the grid itself calls for decoding
still had to be formulated. Foucault spotted the enigma of language
at the point where pure poetry, formal mathematics, psychoanalysis,
and linguistics converge. "What is language, how can we find a way

round it in order to make it appear in itself, in all its plenitude?" (306). It is in the shock of the return of language (303) as a thing calling for a grid that we encounter the break with the period in which language itself was the grid for things, after having been, even earlier, their signature. In order for the *episteme* of the Classical era to appear as an object, one had to situate oneself at the point where, participating in the *episteme* of the nineteenth century, one was far enough away from its birth to *see* the rupture with the eighteenth century, and close enough to what was being announced as its end to imagine that one was going to *experience* another rupture, the break after which Man, like Order at an earlier moment, would appear as an object. In order to discover that before calling for the application of a grid itself, language, the grid of grids, founded the knowledge of nature by constituting a representative schema of identities and differences from which man, the master of theoretical discourse, is absent, it sufficed, one would like to say, for Foucault to situate himself at a crossroads of disciplines. But to do this he was obliged to follow each discipline's separate path. There was nothing to invent except the simultaneous use of the philosophical and philological inventions of the nineteenth century. This is what could be called objective originality. Still, to find the point where one encounters this originality as the reward for one's work, one must have the impetus of subjective originality that is not given to all.

This situation of objective originality explains why Michel Foucault found himself constrained, as it were, to introduce within the diachrony of a given culture a concept or function of intelligibility that appears analogous at first glance to the one that American cultural analysts have introduced into the synchronic tableau of cultures. The concept of basic personality is what makes it possible, when one is considering the coexistence of cultures, to discern the invariant factor that anchors the integration of the individual into the social whole proper to each particular culture. The basic *episteme*, for a given culture, is in a way its universal system of reference to a given period, the only relation that it maintains with the *episteme* that follows being one of difference. In the case of the basic personality, the function of intelligibility it assumes is thought to imply a refusal to put the schema of cultures into perspective from the privileged vantage point of one particular culture. And it is fairly common knowledge that American cultural analysts have provided the policies of

their own government with conscience-soothing arguments necessary for taking to task, in a way economically profitable to its authors,
the colonial powers of the old Continent. But Foucault holds that if
the colonizing situation is not indispensable to ethnology (377), the
latter discipline nevertheless "can assume its proper dimensions only
within the historical sovereignty – always restrained, but always
present – of European thought and the relation that can bring it face
to face with all other cultures as well as with itself" (ibid.). So that the
existence of a culturalist ethnology, having contributed, in its own
way, to the liquidation of European colonialism, appears, owing to its
inscription within the framework of Western *ratio*, as the symptom of
a naive American obliviousness to a cultural ethnocentrism that is
illusorily anticolonialist. This is because the concept of basic personality and the concept of *episteme* differ radically in their uses. The
first concept is at once that of a given and of a norm that a social whole
imposes on its component parts in order to judge them, in order to
define normalcy and deviance. The concept of *episteme* is that of a
humus on which only certain forms of discursive organization can
grow, and for which the confrontation with other forms cannot arise
from a value judgment. No philosophy today is less normative than
Foucault's, none is more alien to the distinction between the normal
and the pathological. What characterizes modern thought, according
to him, is that it is neither willing nor able to propose a morality (328).
Here again humanists, invited to forego their sermonizing, respond
with indignation.

There is nevertheless a question, even more than an objection, that
it seems to me impossible to ignore. Where theoretical *knowledge* is
concerned, can that knowledge be elaborated in the specificity of its
concept without reference to some norm? Among the theoretical
discourses produced in conformity with the epistemic system of the
seventeenth and eighteenth centuries, certain ones, such as that of
natural history, were rejected by the nineteenth-century *episteme*,
but others were integrated. Even though it served as a model for the
eighteenth-century physiologists of animal economy, Newton's physics did not go down with them. Buffon is refuted by Darwin, if not by
Etienne Geoffroy Saint-Hilaire. But Newton is no more refuted by
Einstein than by Maxwell. Darwin is not refuted by Mendel or Mor-
gan. The succession from Galileo to Newton to Einstein does not
present ruptures similar to those that can be identified in the succes-

sion from Tournefort to Linnaeus to Engler in systematic botany. This objection, which Foucault anticipates (xxii–xxiii), does not seem to me to be answered by the decision not to take it into account on the grounds that it belongs to a different sort of study. Foucault in fact did not rule out all allusions to mathematics and physics in his exploration of the *episteme* of the nineteenth century, but he considers them only as models of formalization for the human sciences, that is, only as a language. This is not a mistaken approach, at least for mathematics, but it is questionable for physics, where theories, when they succeed one another by generalization and integration, have the effect of detaching and separating, on the one hand, the changing discourse and the concepts it uses, and on the other hand, what has to be called, and this time in a strict sense, the resistant mathematical structure. To which Foucault can reply that he is not interested in the truth of discourse, but rather in its positive reality. Still, should we overlook the fact that certain discourses, like the discourse of mathematical physics, have no positive reality beyond what is provided by their norm and that that norm stubbornly conquers the purity of its rigor by depositing in the epistemic succession discourses whose vocabulary appears, from one *episteme* to another, devoid of meaning? At the end of the nineteenth century people had ceased to understand what physicists meant when they spoke about the ether, but they had nevertheless not ceased to grasp the mathematic apodicticity of Fresnel's theories; and no error of anachronism is committed if we seek in Huygens not the origin of a melodic history, but the beginning of a progress.

After this discussion of inevitable questions having to do with the *episteme*, it is time to recall that Michel Foucault sought to write not the general theory (that will come later) of an archaeology of knowledge, but its application to the human sciences, and that he set out to show when and how man could have become an object for science, as nature had been in the seventeenth and eighteenth centuries. It is not possible to be more radical than he in the refusal to recognize as meaningful any attempt to locate the origins or the premises of our contemporary, so-called human sciences in the Classical era (312). As long as people believed in the possibility of a single, common discourse of representation and of things (311), it was not possible to take man as an object of science, that is, as an existence to be treated as a problem.

In the Classical era, man coincided with his own consciousness of a power to contemplate or to produce the ideas of all beings, among which man defined himself as living, speaking, and tool-making; this power was experienced as deficient or defective in the eyes of an infinite power that was thought to base the phenomenon of human power on its concession or delegation of some part of that same infinite power. The Cartesian *cogito* was for a long time viewed as the canonical form of the relation of the thinker to thought – for as long as people failed to understand that there was no alternative to the Cartesian *cogito*, no *cogito* at all but the one that has as its subject an I that can say "Myself." But at the end of the eighteenth century and the beginning of the nineteenth, Kantian philosophy, on the one hand, and the constitution of biology, economy, and linguistics, on the other, raised the question *What is man?* From the moment when life, work, and language ceased to be attributes of a nature and became natures themselves, rooted in their own specific history, natures at whose intersection man discovers himself natured, that is, both supported and contained, then empirical sciences of all natures are constituted as specific sciences of the product of these natures, thus of man. One of the difficult points in Foucault's demonstration is its exposure of the unpremeditated connivance between Kantianism and the work of Cuvier, Ricardo, and Bopp in the manifestation of the nineteenth-century *episteme.*

In a sense, Descartes's invention of the *cogito* is not what constituted, for more than a century, the essential achievement of its inventor's philosophy. Kant had to prosecute the *cogito* before the critical tribunal of the *I think* and deny it all substantialist import before modern philosophy could adopt the habit of referring to the *cogito* as the philosophic event that inaugurated it. The Kantian *I think,* a vehicle for the concepts of understanding, is a light that opens experience to its intelligibility. But this light comes from behind us, and we cannot turn around to face it. The transcendental subject of thoughts, like the transcendental object of experience, is an unknown. The originally synthetic unity of apperception constitutes, in ante-representative fashion, a restricted representation in the sense that it cannot have access to the ground in which it originates. Thus, unlike the Cartesian *cogito,* the *I think* is posited as an in-itself, without being able to grasp itself for itself. The *I* cannot know itself as *Myself.*

From this point on, in philosophy, the concept of the function of the *cogito* without a functioning subject becomes possible. The Kantian *I think*, since it always remains on the hither side of the consciousness that is achieved of the effects of its power, does not prohibit efforts to find out whether the founding function, the legitimation of the content of our knowledge by the structure of their forms, could not be assured by functions or structures that science itself would determine to be at work in the elaboration of this knowledge. In his analysis of the relations between the empirical and the transcendental (318), Foucault summarizes quite clearly the procedures by which the nonreflexive philosophies of the nineteenth century attempted to reduce "the proper dimension of criticism to the contents of an empirical knowledge" without being able to avoid recourse to a certain criticism, without being able to avoid bringing about a split not between the true and the false, in this case, or between the legitimate and the illusory, but between the normal and the abnormal as indicated, it was believed, by man's nature or history.

Foucault cited Comte only once (320). It would have been worth his while to deal with Comte's case in greater depth, however. Comte often thought that he was the true Kant, through a substitution of the scientific relation between organism and environment for the metaphysical relation between subject and object. Gall and Condorcet supplied Comte with the means for succeeding where Kant had failed: Gall, through cerebral physiology, which gave Comte the idea of a table of functions that would play the role of the Kantian table of categories; Condorcet, through his theory of the progress of the human spirit. The physiological *a priori* and the historical *a priori* could be summed up by saying that humanity is what thinks in man. But for Comte, the biological *a priori* is an *a priori* for the historical *a priori*. History cannot denature nature. From the beginning, and not only toward the end, Comte's thought, by proposing to found a science of society, that is, of the collective and historical subject of human activities, understood philosophy as a synthesis "presided over by the human viewpoint," that is, as a subjective synthesis. Comte's philosophy is the exemplary case of an empirical treatment of the unrelinquished transcendental project. This empirical treatment seeks its principal instrument in biology, remaining dismissive or ignorant of economy and linguistics. Thus this philosophy for which geneses are never anything but developments of living structures does not recognize in the mathematics and the grammar of its day the disciplines that will bring the concept of structure into philosophy, where it will take over from the *cogito*, which positivism abandons sarcastically to eclecticism.

Far be it from me to criticize Foucault for comparing phenomenology and positivism (320–22) in a way many find paradoxical and some find scandalous. The analysis of lived experience seems to him to be an attempt, only a more demanding and thus a more rigorous one, to "make the empirical . . . stand for the transcendental" (321). When Husserl tried to be more radical than Descartes and a better transcendentalist than Kant, the times – by which we can understand the *episteme* – had changed. The *cogito* had ceased to appear to be the most venerable ancestor of the transcendental function, and the extension of the transcendentalist enterprise had ceased to be confused with the philosophical function itself. The Husserlian interrogation was thus to concern science more than nature, and the question that man poses for being more than the question of the foundation of man's being in the *cogito*. "The phenomenological project continually resolves itself, before our eyes, into a description – empirical despite itself – of actual experience, and into an ontology of the unthought that automatically short-circuits the primacy of the 'I think' " (326).

Twenty years ago, the final pages and especially the closing lines of the posthumous work of Jean Cavaillès, *Sur la logique et la théorie de la science*[12] posited the necessity, for a theory of science, to substitute concepts for consciousness. The philosopher-mathematician who, in a letter to his mentor Léon Brunschvicg, had reproached Husserl for his exorbitant utilization of the *cogito*, also took his leave, philosophically speaking, of his mentor when he wrote: "It is not a philosophy of consciousness but a philosophy of concepts that can provide a doctrine for science. The generative necessity is not that of an activity but that of a dialectic." These words struck many readers, at the time, as enigmatic. Today we can appreciate the predictive value of the enigma. Cavaillès assigned the phenomenological enterprise its limits even before that enterprise had exhibited its unlimited ambitions – even in France itself, which is to say, with a certain lag – and he assigned, twenty years in advance, the task that philosophy is in the process of accepting today – the task of substituting for the primacy of experienced or reflexive consciousness the primacy of concepts, systems, or structures. That is not all. Shot by the Nazis for his Resistance activity, Cavaillès, who called himself a Spinozist and did not believe in history in the existential sense, refuted in advance – by the action he felt himself impelled to undertake, by his participation in the history that he lived out tragically until his death – the argument of those who seek to discredit what they call structuralism by condemning it to generate, among other misdeeds, passivity in the face of reality.

When he wrote the short section called "The 'Cogito' and the Unthought" (322–28), Michel Foucault no doubt had the feeling that he was not speaking for himself alone; that he was not only indicating the obscure though hardly secret point on the basis of which the rigorous and sometimes difficult discourse proffered in *Les Mots et les Choses* was deployed; but also that he was pointing to the question that, distinct from all traditional preoccupations, constitutes the task of philosophy. The modern cogito is no longer the intuitive grasp of the identity, in the activity of thinking, of thinking thought with its being; it is "the constantly renewed interrogation as to how thought can reside elsewhere than here, and yet so very close to itself, how it can be in can *be* in the forms of non-thinking" (324). In *Le Nouvel Esprit scientifique*,[13] Gaston Bachelard had undertaken to distinguish the norms of a non-Cartesian epistemology in the new theories of physics, and he had wondered (on p. 168) what the subject of knowledge becomes when one puts the *cogito* in the passive (*cogitatur ergo est*). In *La Philosophie du non*,[14] he had sketched out, with regard to the new theories of chemistry, the tasks of a non-Kantian analytics. Whether he is working in Bachelard's wake or not, Michel Foucault extends the obligation of non-Cartesianism and non-Kantianism to philosophical reflection itself (325). "The whole of modern thought is imbued with the necessity of thinking the unthought" (327). But to think this unthought is not only, according to Foucault, to think in the theoretical or speculative sense of the term; it is to produce oneself while running the risk of astonishing oneself and even taking fright at oneself. "Thought, at the level of its existence, in its very dawning, is in itself an action – a perilous act" (328). It is hard to understand – unless we suppose that they reacted before they had read him carefully – how certain of Foucault's critics could speak, with respect to his work, of Cartesianism or positivism.

Designating under the general heading of anthropology the set of sciences that was constituted in the nineteenth century not as a legacy from the eighteenth century, but as "an event in the order of knowledge" (345), Foucault uses the term "anthropological sleep" for the tranquil assurance with which the contemporary promoters of the human sciences take for granted, as a preordained object for their progressive studies, what was initially only the project of constituting that object. In this respect, *Les Mots et les choses* might play for a future Kant, as yet unknown as such, the awakening role that Kant attributed to Hume. In such a case we would have skipped a step in the nonrepetitive reproduction of epistemic history by saying of this work that it is to the sciences of man what the *Critique of Pure Reason* was to the sciences of nature. Unless – as it is no longer a question of nature and things, but of an adventure that creates its own norms, an adventure for which the empirico-metaphysical concept of man, if not the word itself, might one day cease to be suitable – unless, then, there is no difference to be made between the call to philosophical vigilance and the bringing to light – to a light even more crude than it is cruel – of its *practical* conditions of possibility.

NOTES

1 *Histoire de la folie à l'âge classique* (Paris: Plon, 1961). In English, *Madness and Civilization: A History of Insanity in the Age of Reason*, trans. Richard Howard, (New York: New American Library, 1967).
2 Translated as *The Order of Things* (London: Tavistock, 1970; New York: Pantheon, 1971; reprinted New York: Vintage Books, 1973). All citations are from the 1973 reprint edition.
3 Paris: Gallimard.
4 Paris: Payot, 1966. In English, *Archaic Roman Religion* trans. Philip Krapp (Chicago: University of Chicago Press, 1970).
5 "The Demon of Analogy," in *Mallarmé: Selected Prose Poems. Essays, and Letters*, trans. Bradford Cook (Baltimore: The Johns Hopkins Press, 1956), p. 3. On Mallarmé and language, see Philippe Sollers, "Littérature et totalité," in *Tel Quel* 26 (Summer 1966): 81–95.
6 Paris: Presses Universitaires de France, 1963. In English, *The Birth of the Clinic: An Archaeology of Medical Perception*, trans. A. M. Sheridan Smith (London: Tavistock, 1973).
7 Paris: Albin Michel, 1941.

8 Paris: Baudoin, 1800–1805; vols. 1–2 in English, *Lectures on Comparative Anatomy*, trans. William Ross (London: Longman and Ries, 1802).

9 Michel Amiot, "Le Relativisme culturaliste de Michel Foucault," *Les Temps modernes* (January 1967): 1271–98.

10 *Die Philosophie der Aufklärung* (Tübingen: Mohr, 1932). In English, *The Philosophy of the Enlightenment*, trans. Fritz C. A. Koelln and James P. Pettegrove (Boston: Beacon Press, 1955).

11 Paris: Boivin, 1946. In English, *European Thought in the Eighteenth Century, from Montesquieu to Lessing*, trans. J. Lewis May (New Haven: Yale University Press, 1959).

12 Paris: Presses Universitaires de France, 1947.

13 Paris: Félix Alcan, 1934, 1937; Presses Universitaires de France, 1941. In English, *The New Scientific Spirit*, trans. Arthur Goldhammer (Boston: Beacon Press, 1984).

14 Paris: Presses Universitaires de France, 1940. In English, *The Philosophy of No; A Philosophy of the New Scientific Mind*, trans. G. C. Waterston (New York: Orion Press, 1968).

4 Power/Knowledge

Michel Foucault wrote extensively about historical reconfigurations of knowledge in what would now be called the human sciences. During the 1970s, however, he argued (most notably in *Discipline and Punish* and the first volume of *The History of Sexuality*) that these reorganizations of knowledge also constituted new forms of power and domination. Foucault's works from this period have often generated contradictory responses from readers. His detailed historical remarks on the emergence of disciplinary and regulatory bio-power have been widely influential. Yet these detailed studies are connected to a more general conception of power, and of the epistemic and political positioning of the criticism of power, which many critics have found less satisfactory. Foucault's discussions of the relation between truth and power have similarly provoked concerns about their reflexive implications for his own analysis.

The principal purpose of this essay is to offer a sympathetic interpretation of the understanding of power and of knowledge that informs Foucault's historical studies of prisons and of the construction of a scientific discourse about sexuality. Since Foucault discussed power in this period rather more thematically than he did knowledge, my discussion of knowledge will build extensively upon his remarks about power. The essay will proceed in three parts. First I will briefly recapitulate Foucault's account of the intertwined emergence of new forms of power and knowledge in the eighteenth and nineteenth centuries. The second part will initiate my reflections upon the concepts of "power" and "knowledge" with a critical discussion of political and epistemic sovereignty. Foucault framed his investigations as an alternative to the preoccupation of political thought with questions about sovereignty and legitimacy. Many of his readers have found this critical concern troubling, because they worry that it undercuts any possible stance from which Foucault might be able to criticize the modern forms of knowledge and power that he has described. I will argue in the third part of the essay that this worry is plausible only if one ignores Foucault's understanding of both power and knowledge as *dynamic*. Foucault explicitly sketched a dynamics of power; I will show that his account also suggests a similarly dynamic interpretation of knowledge. In both cases, Foucault's account provides ample possibilities for reasoned critical response.

I. DISCIPLINES AND NORMS

Foucault had been writing about the history of knowledge in the human sciences long before he ever explicitly raised questions about power. What had interested Foucault was not the specific bodies of knowledge compiled through disciplined investigation at various times. Instead, Foucault had written about the epistemic context within which those bodies of knowledge became intelligible and authoritative. He argued that particular investigations were structured by which concepts and statements were intelligible together, how those statements were organized thematically, which of those statements counted as "serious,"[1] who was empowered to speak seriously, and what questions and procedures were relevant to assess the credibility of those statements that were taken seriously.[2] These historically situated fields of knowledge (which Foucault in *The Archaeology of Knowledge* called "discursive formations") also included the *objects* under discussion. Foucault was thus committed to a strong nominalism in the human sciences: the types of objects in their domains were not already demarcated, but came into existence only contemporaneous with the discursive formations that made it possible to talk about them.

What made Foucault's inquiry into the structure of such discursive formations interesting was the possibility that there might be significant changes in the organization of such a discursive field. Thus, it might be that what counts as a serious and important claim at one time will not (perhaps cannot) even be entertained as a candidate for truth at another. Statements can be dismissed (or never even be considered) not because they are thought to be false, but because it is not clear what it would amount to for them to be either true or false.

Foucault's earlier studies were in fact directed toward significant changes in the "discursive formations" that governed the serious possibilities for talking about things. He proposed that there were important shifts in what counted as serious discussion of madness, disease, wealth, language, or life, shifts that were evident in the historical archives. His aim was not to explain those shifts, but rather to display the structural differences they embody, and to some extent to document the parallels between contemporary shifts in several discursive formations. Foucault was especially concerned to demonstrate the parallel shifts in several discursive fields in the eighteenth and nineteenth centuries, through which the modern sciences of "man" replaced the classical tables of representation that displayed the order of things.

Discipline and Punish expanded the scope of Foucault's inquiries into this modern reconfiguration of knowledge. His earlier studies had often associated the reconfiguration of discursive fields with the organization of new institutions, for example, asylums, clinics, and hospitals. Nevertheless, his emphasis had always been the structure of *discourse*.[3] In *Discipline and Punish*, however, the eighteenth–nineteenth century transformation of the human sciences was explicitly set in the context of practices of discipline, surveillance, and constraint, which made possible new kinds of knowledge of human beings even as they created new forms of social control.

Perhaps the most important transformation that Foucault described was in the scale and continuity of the exercise of power, which also involved much greater knowledge of detail. Foucault was interested in the difference between massive but infrequent exercises of destructive force (public executions, military occupations, the violent suppression of insurrections) and the uninterrupted constraints imposed in practices of discipline and training: "It was a question not of treating the body, *en masse,* 'wholesale,' as if it were an indissociable unity, but of working it 'retail,' individually; of exercising upon it a subtle coercion, of obtaining holds upon it at the level of the mechanism itself – movements, gestures, attitudes, rapidity: an infinitesimal power over the active body" (*DP,* 136–37). Other ways of exercising force can only coerce or destroy their tar-

get. Discipline and training can reconstruct it to produce new gestures, actions, habits and skills, and ultimately new kinds of people.

The human body was entering a machinery of power that explores it, breaks
it down and rearranges it. . . . It defined how one may have a hold over
others' bodies, not only so that they may do what one wishes, but so that
they may operate as one wishes, with the techniques, the speed and the
efficiency that one determines. Thus discipline produces subjected and practiced bodies, "docile" bodies (DP, 138).

Often these practices of subjection worked indirectly, by reconstructing the spaces and reorganizing the timing within which people
functioned. The enclosure, partitioning, and functional distribution
of activities enabled an inconspicuous direction of activity:

Disciplinary space tends to be divided into as many sections as there are
bodies or elements to be distributed. . . . Its aim was to establish presences
and absences, to know where and how to locate individuals, to set up useful
communications, to interrupt others, to be able at each moment to super-
vise the conduct of each individual, to assess it, to judge it, to calculate its
qualities or merits. It was a procedure, therefore, aimed at knowing, master-
ing, and using (DP, 143).

Similarly, schedules, programmed movements, and exercises correlated with developmental stages "served to economize the time of
life, to accumulate it in a useful form and to exercise power over
men through the mediation of time" (DP, 162).

These forms of detailed intervention also reversed the prevailing
relationships between power and visibility or "audibility." Foucault
documented a shift in political practice from the display of power as
spectacle to the exercise of power through making its target more
thoroughly visible and audible. There was a gradual development of
techniques of surveillance, whose function was far more complex
and subtle than massive and spectacular displays of force:

Hierarchized, continuous and functional surveillance . . . was organized as a
multiple, automatic, and anonymous power. . . . This enables the disciplinary power to be both absolutely indiscreet, since it is everywhere and always
alert, since by its very principle it leaves no zone of shade and constantly
supervises the very individuals who are entrusted with the task of supervis-
ing; and absolutely "discreet," for it functions permanently and largely in
silence (DP, 176–77).

Surveillance was often built into the physical structures of institutions that were organized to enhance visibility within them; here especially there was a new architecture of power ("stones can make people docile and knowable," *DP,* 172). Surveillance was also manifest in the creation or extension of rituals, such as the proliferating practices of examination: scholastic tests but also medical or psychiatric examinations and histories, employment interviews, prison musters, and military reviews (in which the commander no longer heads the procession, but instead stands aside to examine its passing).

Previously inconspicuous people became more audible as well as visible. In *The History of Sexuality,* Foucault extended his argument to show how

We have become a singularly confessing society. . . . [The confession] plays a part in justice, medicine, education, family relationships, and love relations, in the most ordinary affairs of everyday life, and in the most solemn rites: one confesses one's crimes, one's sins, one's thoughts and desires, one's illnesses and troubles; one goes about telling, with the greatest precision, whatever is most difficult to tell. . . . One confesses – or is forced to confess (*HS,* 59).

What is thereby seen and heard is then documented, as a resource for further examination and constraint.

Among the fundamental conditions of a good medical "discipline," in both senses of the word, one must include the procedures of writing that made it possible to integrate individual data into cumulative systems in such a way that they were not lost; so to arrange things that an individual could be located in the general register and that, conversely, each datum of the individual examination might affect overall calculations (*DP,* 190).

These practices of surveillance, elicitation, and documentation constrain behavior precisely by making it more thoroughly knowable or known. But these new forms of knowledge also presuppose new kinds of constraint, which make people's actions visible and constrain them to speak. It is in this sense primarily that Foucault spoke of "power/knowledge." A more extensive and finer-grained knowledge enables a more continuous and pervasive control of what people do, which in turn offers further possibilities for more intrusive inquiry and disclosure.

Foucault saw these techniques of power and knowledge as undergoing a two-stage development. They were instituted initially as means of control or neutralization of dangerous social elements, and evolved into techniques for enhancing the utility and productivity of those subjected to them. They were also initially cultivated within isolated institutions (most notably prisons, hospitals, army camps, schools, and factories), but then were gradually adapted into techniques that could be applied in various other contexts. Foucault called this broadening of their scope of application the "swarming" of disciplinary mechanisms:

the mechanisms [of the disciplinary establishments] have a certain tendency to become "de-institutionalized," to emerge from the closed fortresses in which they once functioned and to circulate in a "free" state; the massive, compact disciplines are broken down into flexible methods of control, which may be transferred and adapted.... One can [therefore] speak of the formation of a disciplinary society in this movement that stretches from the enclosed disciplines, a sort of social "quarantine," to an indefinitely generalizable mechanism of "panopticism" (DP, 211, 216).

Foucault did not see these new techniques as simply superimposed upon a preexisting social order. His nominalism remained prominent in his studies of power/knowledge, as he took these politico-epistemic practices to constitute new kinds of object for knowledge to be about: "biographical unities" (DP, 254) like delinquency, homosexuality, or hyperactivity; developmental structures, such as reading grade-levels or appropriate age-group attainments; significant distributions, as in a family history of heart disease, a low-income household, or an "advanced maternal age pregnancy"; and signs of a condition of life, such as cholesterol level or T-cell counts. Ultimately, these practices produced new kinds of human subjects. But they also produced new *kinds* of knowledge along with new objects to know, and new modalities of power.

Foucault often spoke of the correlative constitution of two levels of knowledge through the politico-epistemic practices he had been describing. On the one hand, there was the emergence of a systematic knowledge of individuals, through connected practices of surveillance, confession, and documentation:

the constitution of the individual as a describable, analyzable object, not in order to reduce him to "specific" features, as did the naturalists in relation to living beings, but in order to maintain him in his individual features, in his particular evolution, in his particular evolution, in his own aptitudes and abilities, under the gaze of a permanent corpus of knowledge (*DP*, 190).

But Foucault thought that this individuating knowledge was connected in important ways to the

emergence of "population" as an economic and political problem: population as wealth, population as manpower or labor capacity, population balanced between its own growth and the resources it commanded. Governments perceived that they were not dealing simply with subjects, or even with a "people," but with a "population," with its specific phenomena and its peculiar variables: birth and death rates, life expectancy, fertility, state of health, frequency of illnesses, patterns of diet and habitation (*HS*, 25).

What connected these two levels of epistemic analysis and political regulation was the practice of "normalizing judgment" and the construction of norms as a field of possible knowledge. Norms seem to have their place primarily in the knowledge of populations, since they demarcate distributions. We are all familiar with the "normal curve" as a representation of a distribution of traits around a mean. And as Ian Hacking (1990) has recently described,[4] this conception of a normal distribution has a nineteenth-century origin in the attempts to understand/impute statistical stability to the "avalanche of printed numbers" created by European statistical bureaus to survey their populations. Yet norms were also indispensable to the new knowledges of individuals. For how else was one to produce *knowledge* of individuals that did not simply subsume their individuality under a type? A normalizing distribution enables one to locate the individual within an epistemic field, without reducing the individual to the typical. Foucault most often discussed normalization as a technique of power, but its epistemic implications emerged clearly in his account. Normalizing judgment produced

a whole range of degrees of normality indicating membership of a homogeneous social body but also playing a part in classification, hierarchization and the distribution of rank. In a sense, the power of normalization imposes homogeneity; but it individualizes by making it possible to measure gaps, to determine levels, to fix specialities and to render the differences useful by fitting them one to another (*DP*, 184).

The stories Foucault told about the emergence together of these new forms of knowledge and power have an ironic side. They are intended as counterpoint to the familiar stories of the enlightened humanization of punishment and the liberation from sexual repression. Foucault's irony works by portraying the very practices of humane penal reform and sexual liberation as instead further enmeshing us in a "carceral society" and an enforced regimen of truth. Yet for many readers his irony is troubling.⁵ The tone of Foucault's portrayal suggests that these new forms of power/knowledge ought to be resisted. Yet he resolutely rejects the idea that there is any ground or standpoint from which such a call to resistance could be legitimated. The connection he proposes between power and knowledge is not just a particular institutional *use* of knowledge as a means to domination. Foucault objects to the very idea of a knowledge or a truth outside of networks of power relations. The scope of his objection thus also encompasses the possibility of a critical knowledge that would speak the truth to power, exposing domination for what it is, and thereby enabling or encouraging effective resistance to it.

To see how Foucault's discussion of power/knowledge took him in this direction, and what its consequences are for the political and epistemic positioning of his own work, we need to consider his discussion of the problem of sovereignty. This in turn will enable us to assess the implications of his insistence on a situated dynamics of power and, I will argue, of knowledge as well.

II. POWER (AND KNOWLEDGE) WITHOUT SOVEREIGNTY

Foucault did not often explicitly address the relation between his discussions of power/knowledge and more traditional ways of conceptualizing knowledge. He had more to say about how his understanding of power differs from its treatment in mainstream political theories. Foucault repeatedly situated his own reflections as an attempt to break free of the orientation of political thought toward questions of sovereign power and its legitimacy: "At bottom, despite the differences in epochs and objectives, the representation of power has remained under the spell of monarchy. In political thought and analysis, we still have not cut off the head of the king" (*HS*, 88).

Hobbes's *Leviathan*, and the social contract tradition more generally, had posed the scope and the legitimacy of the power of the sovereign as the original and fundamental questions of politics. But

Foucault argued that both the underlying conception of power as sovereign power, and the questions of law and right with which it is engaged, have a historical location in the formation of European monarchy.

The great institutions of power that developed in the Middle Ages – monarchy, the state with its apparatus – rose up on the basis of a multiplicity of prior powers, and to a certain extent in opposition to them: dense, entangled, conflicting powers, powers tied to the direct or indirect dominion over the land, to the possession of arms, to serfdom, to bonds of suzerainty and vassalage. If these institutions were able to implant themselves, if, by profiting from a whole series of tactical alliances, they were able to gain acceptance, this was because they presented themselves as agencies of regulation, arbitration, and demarcation, as a way of introducing order in the midst of these powers, of establishing a principle that would temper them and distribute them according to boundaries and a fixed hierarchy (*HS*, 86–87).

The conception of sovereignty that emerges from this historical moment has three crucial aspects for Foucault. First, sovereignty is a standpoint above or outside particular conflicts that resolves their competing claims into a *unified* and coherent system. Second, the dividing question in terms of which these claims are resolved is that of legitimacy (often framed in terms of law or rights): Which powers can be *rightfully* exercised, which actions are *lawful*, which regimes are *legitimate?* Together, these two points present the sovereign as the protector of peace in the war of all against all, and the embodiment of justice in the settling of competing claims.

The third point concerns the specific conception of power entailed by this understanding of sovereignty as the embodiment of law or legitimacy. Although there are no limits to the *scope* of sovereign power (everyone and everything is, in principle, subject to the sovereign), the actual exercise of that power must always be discontinuous and negative. Sovereign power comes into play only at specific points where law or rights have been violated, and can only act to punish or restrain the violation. Thus, Foucault suggested that "power in this instance was essentially a right of seizure: of things, time, bodies, and ultimately life itself" (*HS*, 136). Sovereign power prohibits, confiscates, or destroys what sovereign judgment pronounces illegitimate. Foucault therefore speaks interchangably of "sovereign power" and "juridical power."

Although Foucault claimed that this conception of sovereignty and of sovereign power arose in response to the consolidation of the European monarchies, it would be a mistake to equate sovereignty in his sense with the state, ₁ ɹr two reasons. First, power is conceived and exercised in terms of sovereignty in other social locations, wherever power is deployed to restrain or punish what escapes the bounds of a unified scheme of what is right. "Whether one attributes to it the form of the prince who formulates rights, of the father who forbids, of the censor who enforces silence, or of the master who states the law, in any case one schematizes power in a juridical form, and one defines its effects as obedience" (HS, 85).

Second, although sovereignty was conceived as a standpoint of judgment above all particular conflicts, no actual sovereign could realize this conception in practice. Thus, political theory increasingly deployed this conception of the sovereign's role against its nominal occupant.

Criticism of the eighteenth-century monarchic institution in France was not directed against the juridico-monarchic sphere as such, but was made on behalf of a pure and rigorous juridical system to which all the mechanisms of power could conform, with no excesses or irregularities, as opposed to a monarchy which, notwithstanding its own assertions, continuously overstepped its legal framework and set itself above the laws (HS, 88).

This separation of the principle of sovereignty from its embodiment in any actual sovereign is crucial to understanding Foucault's position. Sovereignty in this sense has been removed from any real political location, and is instead a theoretical construction with respect to which political practice is to be assessed. Foucault, however, suggested in several places that such assessments dangerously misconceive both their target and their own critical practices. Consequently, he objected to the very conception of a sovereign standpoint from which the legitimacy of particular political struggles could be ascertained. His own criticism of this conception of sovereignty should therefore not be seen as another such attempt to hold a sovereign power to account to a higher principle of legitimacy.

That political criticism invoking principles of sovereignty and right misunderstands its targets is a claim that Foucault took to follow from his account of the emergence of disciplinary and regulatory power relations. He claimed that although many of the politi-

102 THE CAMBRIDGE COMPANION TO FOUCAULT

cal forms and practices of sovereign power remained in place, they were gradually taken over and ultimately sustained on the basis of power relations that functioned at a different location and scale. Increasingly, the sovereign apparatus (such as courts, prisons, the army) became both dependent upon and productive of disciplinary and regulatory power. These power relations were disseminated through more extensive social networks, and did not transmit power in only one direction. They did not simply impose sanctions that might be amenable to a binary classification as legitimate or not. They were instrumental to the production or enhancement of various "goods," such as knowledge, health, wealth, or social cohesion. Thus, political theories of sovereignty failed to recognize the many ways in which power nominally deployed through the state apparatus (or, for Marxists, through the class ownership of capital) was more complexly mediated. Foucault concluded from this failure that the traditional concerns for rights and justice provided an inadequate framework for political criticism of the modern nexus of power/knowledge.

When today one wants to object in some way to the disciplines and all the effects of power and knowledge that are linked to them, what is it that one does . . . if not precisely appeal to this canon of right, this famous, formal right, that is said to be bourgeois, and which in reality is the right of sovereignty? But I believe that we find ourselves here in a kind of blind alley: it is not through recourse to sovereignty against discipline that the effects of disciplinary power can be limited, because sovereignty and disciplinary mechanisms are two absolutely integral components of the general mechanism of power in our society (PK, 108).

But Foucault was more fundamentally concerned that political criticism in terms of sovereignty, right, and law dangerously misunderstands its own positioning. Here we find perhaps his most basic reason for juxtaposing knowledge and truth with power. It is one thing to articulate and take up a stance on the political struggles in the midst of which one finds oneself situated historically. It is another thing altogether to seek an epistemic standpoint outside those ongoing conflicts from which that stance can be validated. The move to which Foucault objected is therefore that of identifying one's own political and epistemic position with the standpoint of sovereignty. In the French intellectual context especially, the aspiration for such a position of *epistemic* sovereignty was designated by the quest for the status of *science*. Foucault's response to that aspiration was withering:

Which theoretical-political *avant garde* do you want to enthrone in order to isolate it from all the discontinuous forms of knowledge that circulate about it? When I see you straining to establish the scientificity of Marxism I do not really think that you are demonstrating once and for all that Marxism has a rational structure and that therefore its propositions are the outcome of verifiable procedures; for me you are doing something altogether different, you are investing Marxist discourses and those who uphold them with the effects of a power which the West since Medieval times has attributed to science and has reserved for those engaged in scientific discourse (*PK*, 85).

Although Foucault does not use the term "epistemic sovereignty," it is not hard to see that there is a close parallel within epistemology to the preoccupation of political reflection with sovereignty as Foucault construes it. Recall the crucial constituents of political sovereignty: a unitary regime, representing legitimacy through law, established from an impartial standpoint above particular conflicts, and enforced through discontinuous interventions which aim to suppress illegitimacy. Just as a sovereign power stands above and adjudicates conflicts among its subject powers, epistemic sovereignty is the standpoint above disputes among competing truth-claims. Epistemic sovereignty constitutes knowledge as the unified (or consistently unifiable) network of truths that can be extracted from the circulation of conflicting statements. They are legitimated as truths by the precepts of rational method, the epistemic surrogate for law. Yet this legitimation does not *produce* knowledge, in the sense of producing new possibilities for truth. Rather, it allows truth to stand forth by suppressing error and irrationality, that is, those statements that do not conform to method and cohere with the regime it establishes. Foucault has the same dual objection to this conception of epistemic sovereignty as to that of political sovereignty. On the one hand, this conception of knowledge overlooks the micropractices through which particular candidates for knowledge and their objects are produced (this network of micropractices is the parallel in Foucault's later work to what he had earlier called a "discursive formation"). Both knowing subjects and truths known are the product of relations of power and knowledge. On the other hand, it demarcates an aspiration to power, to the suppression of all conflicting voices and lives, which Foucault saw as one of the chief dangers confronting us.

Consequently, just as Foucault aimed to "break free ... of the theoretical privilege of law and sovereignty" (*HS*, 90) in the analysis of power, his conception of a genealogical investigation "should be seen as a kind of attempt to emancipate historical knowledges from subjection [to the hierarchical order of power associated with science], to render them, that is, capable of opposition and of struggle against the coercion of a theoretical, unitary, formal, and scientific discourse" (*PK*, 85). It is precisely this aim that has troubled many of Foucault's readers and critics. Charles Taylor and Richard Rorty have between them expressed this worry with particular cogency. Taylor concludes that on Foucault's account, "There can be no such thing as a truth independent of its regime, unless it be that of another. So that liberation in the name of 'truth' could only be the substitution of another system of power for this one."[6] Foucault, for Taylor, gives us no reason to think that the succeeding system of power will be any better than the present one, and hence no *justification* for a struggle to change it.

Rorty sees a resulting hopelessness in Foucault's vision, "a remoteness which reminds one of the conservative who pours cold water on hopes for reform, who affects to look at the problems of his fellow-citizens with the eye of the future historian ... rather than suggest[ing] how our children might inhabit a better world in the future."[7] Taylor's and Rorty's criticisms suggest a multiple incoherence in Foucault's rejection of any standpoint of political or epistemic sovereignty: he makes truth-claims while denying that they could have any claim upon us; he objects to domination while denying that there can be anything like liberation from it; and he portrays dangers (Taylor even uses the word "evils") while insisting that any attempt to avert or ameliorate them would inevitably reproduce them in new guise.

III. THE DYNAMICS OF POWER AND KNOWLEDGE

There is nevertheless something unsatisfying about these criticisms. Rorty's and Taylor's criticisms (and others' as well) depend upon crucial disjunctions: either a critique of power in the name of legitimacy, or an acceptance that power makes right; either the validation of one's claims from a standpoint of science/epistemic sovereignty, or an acceptance that all claims to truth are of equivalent standing. Yet these disjunctions themselves presuppose a standpoint of epistemic sovereignty, and to invoke them may beg the question. Even the positions that in the end are attributed to Foucault (epistemological relativism and/or a reduction of truth to domination and legitimacy to forced acceptance) are positions that claim sovereignty by standing outside epistemic and political conflicts to adjudicate the claims competing parties can legitimately make upon us. My point is not to dismiss these criticisms out of hand for question-begging, but instead to pose a question. Foucault's critics take attempted rejection of the problematic of sovereignty to reduce to some position within that problematic, which suggests that they cannot (yet) conceive what power or knowledge without sovereignty could mean. So the question that needs to be posed is how Foucault thought his account might successfully go beyond sovereignty.

To this end, I will argue that Foucault accomplished this aim by conceiving of power dynamically. Although once again he did not discuss this explicitly, I believe that his account also requires a dynamical understanding of knowledge. Together, these accounts suggest an engaged political and epistemic criticism that does not project itself into either the standpoint of the sovereign who adjudicates all political struggles in the name of right or the standpoint of a science that would resolve disputes in the name of truth.

Foucault's more general understanding of power as dynamic begins with his rejection of any reification of power. He insists that "power is not something that is acquired, seized, or shared, something that one holds on to or allows to slip away" (*HS*, 94) or that "power is employed through a net-like organization" (*PK*, 98). Thomas Wartenburg's discussion of power as always mediated by "social alignments" may help us make sense of Foucault's claim. As Wartenburg uses the term,

A field of social agents can constitute an alignment in regard to a social agent if and only if, first of all, their actions in regard to that agent are coordinated in a specific manner. To be an alignment, however, the coordinated practices of these social agents need to be comprehensive enough that the social agent facing the alignment encounters that alignment as having control over certain things that she might either need or desire. . . . The concept of a social alignment thus provides a way of understanding the "field" that constitutes a situated power relationship *as* a power relationship.[8]

Wartenburg's point is that even in situations in which we might characteristically describe one person as having or exercising power over another, that power depends upon other persons or groups acting in concert with what the first person does. In Wartenburg's examples, when teachers grade students or employers discipline or fire employees, they exercise power only when others (the school admissions officers, or possible future employers) act, or are prepared to act, in ways oriented by their own actions. Agents may thereby also exercise power unbeknownst to themselves, or even contrary to their own intentions, if other agents orient their actions in response to what the first agents do.

It is in this context that we can understand Foucault's assertion that "power is everywhere not because it embraces everything, but because it comes from everywhere" (*HS*, 93). Power is not possessed by a dominant agent, nor located in that agent's relations to those dominated, but is instead distributed throughout complex social networks. The actions of the peripheral agents in these networks are often what establish or enforce the connections between what a dominant agent does and the fulfillment or frustration of a subordinate agent's desires. Certainly this must be true of a power exercised discreetly through surveillance and documentation. Such practices can embody power only as far as and insofar as a significant alignment of agents orients their actions to what is thereby disclosed and recorded. Indeed, Foucault would go on to emphasize the heterogeneity of the alignments (*dispositifs*) that dispose power. They include not just agents but also the instruments of power (buildings, documents, tools, etc.) and the practices and rituals through which it is deployed.

This sense of power as dispersed emphasizes the importance of what Foucault called the "swarming" of the disciplinary mechanisms; those mechanisms were thereby transformed from a local exercise of force within the confines of a particular institution into far-reaching relationships of power. Indeed, as Wartenburg has pointed out, these practices exert power only to the extent that they reach far enough to affect the availability or absence of alternative access to the goods that the exercise of power would enable or prevent.[9]

These networks through which power is exercised are not static. Foucault speaks of power as "something that circulates" (*PK*, 98) and as being "produced from one moment to the next" (*HS*, 93). Wartenburg points out that such a dynamic account is inherent in the recognition that power is always mediated by social alignments. In exercising power through a coordinated social alignment, "the *present* actions of a dominant agent count on the *future* actions of the aligned agents being similar to their *past* actions. But this faith in a future whose path can be charted entails that the dominant agent not act in a way that challenges the allegiance of his aligned agents, for only through their actions can that future be made actual."[10] Power can thus never be simply present, as one action forcibly constraining or modifying another. Its constitution as a *power relation* depends upon its reenactment or reproduction over time as a sustained power *relationship*.

Foucault does not conceive of such relationships as being imposed from the top down. The configuration of power relations emerges instead from "the support which force relations find in one another, thus forming a chain or a system, or on the contrary, the disjunction and contradictions which isolate them from one another" (*HS*, 92). Foucault therefore does not deny that there are large-scale structures of power. He claims only that they are the dynamic outcome of the ways in which "infinitesimal mechanisms of power have been – and continue to be – invested, colonized, utilized, involuted, transformed, displaced, extended, etc., by ever more general mechanisms and by forms of global domination" (*PK*, 99).

This conception of power as constituted by the reenactment or reproduction of social alignments explains why Foucault is drawn toward conceiving power in terms of war or struggle, and its intelligibility in terms of strategy and tactics. Foucault makes two different contrasts when he says he wants to conceive of politics as "war continued by other means" (*PK*, 90). On the one hand, the military metaphor is an alternative to "the great model of language and signs" (*PK*, 114). On the other hand, he sees it as perhaps the only alternative to an *economic* model of power, either as itself a form of exchange or contract, or as subordinate to the functioning of the economy (*PK*, 88–90).

The contrst between war and language may seem surprising at first, until one recalls the structuralist conception of language as a system of signs governed by rules. Foucault seems to be making two connected points in proposing to model power relations upon war. First, war is senseless. Likewise, the totality of power relations cannot be understood as a *meaningful* system (Foucault explicitly refers to Hegelian-Marxist dialectic and to semiotics as examples of what the model of war is opposed to). Without doubt, meaningful actions and situations do occur within specific alignments of power, but these have only local intelligibility, which Foucault understands as tactical. That is, they make sense only as responses to a particular configuration of forces within an ongoing conflict. Second, war is not governed by *rules*. Proponents of just-war theory have of course attempted to specify rules adjudicating when and how it is legitimate to wage war, but Foucault is not talking about such attempts to constrain war within the forms and strictures of constitutional politics. In practice war is governed only by the actual play of forces within an ongoing struggle (which may of course make some conformity to accepted norms of conduct strategically advisable).

It is in this context that we can understand Foucault's insistence on a close connection between power and resistance. Resistance cannot be external to power, because power is not a system of domination with an inside or an outside. Here, once again, Wartenburg's conception of power as mediated by dynamic social alignments can help us understand Foucault. Power is exercised through an agent's actions only to the extent that other agents' actions remain appropriately aligned with them. The actions of dominant agents are therefore constrained by the need to sustain that alignment in the future; but, simultaneously, subordinate agents may seek ways of challenging or evading that alignment. Wartenburg concludes that a

subordinate agent is never absolutely disempowered, but only relatively so. . . . just as the dominant agent's actions are subject to the problematic of maintaining power by maintaining the allegiance of the aligned agents, the subordinate agent is always in the position of being able to challenge the aligned agents' complicity in her disempowerment."[11]

Foucault's conception of power relations in terms of war elevates this sense that resistance to specific alignments of power is alway possible to a conception of power as itself the outcome of ongoing struggles to sustain or undermine networks of domination: "the strictly relational character of power relationships [is such that t]heir existence depends on a multiplicity of points of resistance: these play the role of adversary, target, support, or handle in power relations. These points of resistance are present everywhere in the power network" (*HS*, 95). Power is not something possessed or wielded by powerful agents, because it is co-constituted by those who support and resist it. It is not a system of domination that imposes its rules upon all those it governs, because any such rule is always at issue in ongoing struggles.

The classic form in which power relations have been thought to be rule-governed is that of the contract. Hobbes's war of all against all is constrained by the cession of power to the sovereign in exchange for protection of life and property. We have already seen that Foucault rejects Hobbes's project and its successors. But neither is Foucault's modeling of power relations upon war a return in theory to Hobbes's state of nature. Foucault pictures a *society* shaped by militant conflicts:

one is dealing with mobile and transitory points of resistance, producing cleavages in a society that shift about, fracturing unities and effecting regroupings, furrowing across individuals themselves. . . . Just as the network of power relations ends by forming a dense web that passes through apparatuses and institutions, without being exactly localized in them, so too the swarm of points of resistance traverses social stratifications and individual unities (*HS*, 96).

In any case, we can now see the connection between Foucault's two contrasts to the model of war: the form in which politics has most typically been taken to be a rule-governed system is that of a system of economic relations. Even Marxism, which rejects the idea of a social contract, models power on the economy, which contemporary French Marxists in turn frequently model on structural linguistics.

We now have a picture of Foucault's dynamics of power: power is dispersed across complicated and heterogeneous social networks marked by ongoing struggle. Power is not something present at specific locations within those networks, but is instead always at issue in ongoing attempts to (re)produce effective social alignments, and conversely to avoid or erode their effects, often by producing various counteralignments. But what could it mean to conceive similarly of a dynamics of knowledge? This notion may seem initially very strange, because the conception of knowledge as a body of warranted true beliefs has such a strong hold upon us.

Foucault had taken a first step toward such a dynamic conception of knowledge even before *Discipline and Punish*, when he distinguished the formation of a discursive field of knowledge (*savoir*) from the specific statements held true at specific points within that field (*connaissances*). Knowledge (*savoir*) in this sense is dispersed across the entire field, rather than located in particular statements or groups of statements. Foucault spoke in this way to indicate that the "seriousness," sense, and possible truth of any particular *connaissances* were determined by their place within a larger field. What was missing from this earlier conception, however, was a sense of the heterogeneity of epistemic fields, and of their temporal dimension shaped by ongoing epistemic conflict.

Knowledge is established not only in relation to a field of statements but also of objects, instruments, practices, research programs, skills, social networks, and institutions. Some elements of such an epistemic field reinforce and strengthen one another, and are taken up, extended, and reproduced in other contexts; others remain isolated from, or conflict with, these emergent "strategies" and eventually become forgotten curiosities. The configuration of knowledge requires that these heterogeneous elements be adequately adapted to one another, and that their mutual alignment be sustained over time.

The temporality of these epistemic fields is evident in the construction of such epistemic alignments and in the conflicts and resistances they engender. Taken by itself, a statement, a technique or skill, a practice, or a machine cannot count as knowledge. Only in the ways it is used, and thereby increasingly connected to other elements over time, does it become (and remain) epistemically significant. But these uses and alignments encounter snags and generate conflicts with other emerging epistemic practices. These conflicts have a particular configuration that arises historically from the development of competing epistemic alignments and from the specific respects in which they come into conflict. Such conflict, however, spurs further investigations, articulations, and technical refinements. Conflict thus becomes the locus for the continuing development and reorganization of knowledge. It is ironic that where knowledge does not encounter resistance, it is likely to receive little or no further articulation, and to risk becoming isolated and inconsequential. Foucault used the term "strategies" for the multiple ways in which heterogeneous elements align or conflict with one another to constitute power relations. Once we recognize the complex and contested dynamics of knowledge production, we might say of knowledge as well as of power that "it is the name that one attributes to a complex strategical situation in a particular society" (HS, 93).

What relation between the strategical alignments that constitute knowledge and those that form a configuration of power is Foucault describing? Foucault noted that

Relations of power are not in a position of exteriority with respect to other types of relationships (economic processes, knowledge relationships, sexual relations), but are immanent in the latter; they are the immediate effects of the divisions, inequalities, and disequilibriums which occur in the latter, and conversely they are the internal conditions of these differentiations (HS, 94).

Foucault is thus not identifying knowledge and power, but he is recognizing that the strategic alignments that constitute each contain many of the same elements and relations. Indeed, their alignment as relationships of power is part of the makeup of an epistemic field, and vice versa. *How* knowledge and power come together is historically specific and may vary significantly in different domains. Foucault proposed these remarks about knowledge and power first and foremost as an interpretation of his particular historical studies. They were put forward to make sense of how the observation, documentation, and classification of individuals and populations contributed to newly emerging strategies of domination, which themselves were part of the complex social field within which those techniques and their applications came to constitute knowledge.

We can now approach the crucial question. Even supposing we grant everything I have said about Foucault's insistence upon the interrelated dynamics of knowledge and power, how would that respond to Taylor's or Rorty's concerns about the epistemic coherence and political significance of Foucault's work? Their worry was that Foucault could not coherently make truth-claims, criticize power, or offer hope for a better world. I suggest instead that Foucault has offered a different sense of what it is to make truth-claims, criticize power, or offer hope. Foucault's critics presuppose a conception of epistemic and political sovereignty: to claim truth or to criticize power is to try to stand outside an epistemic or political conflict in order to *settle* it. Truth and right are conceived as the unified structures from which conflict, struggle, and difference are banned, as all competing assertions and all conflicting agents receive their due.

Foucault suggests a different image in which conflict and struggle are always present and inescapable. To make truth-claims is to try to strengthen some epistemic alignments, and to challenge, undermine, or evade others. To criticize power is to participate in counteralignments to resist or evade its effects. The question Foucault's critics insistently raise is, Why engage in *these* struggles rather than others? Why take *this* side rather than an opposing one? Their concern is that without some legitimating standpoint to provide reasons for them, these choices will always be arbitrary or dictated from "without." But Foucault was perfectly prepared to offer reasons for his choices of struggles and sides. He was equally prepared to offer reasons and evidence for the statements he made.

What Foucault was not prepared to do was to see these choices, statements, and reasons as more than a situated response to a particular political and epistemic configuration. Thus, he remarked in an interview that

I am not looking for an alternative. . . . You see, what I want to do is not the history of solutions, and that's the reason why I don't accept the word "alternative." I would like to do genealogy of problems, of *problematiques.* My point is not that everything is bad, but that everything is dangerous, which is not exactly the same as bad. If everything is dangerous, then we always have something to do. So my position leads not to apathy but to a hyper- and pessimistic activism. I think that the ethico-political choice we have to make every day is to determine which is the main danger.[12]

Presumably such a choice requires a considered and informed judgment, but cannot be further legitimated by any appeal to a science or a principle of right. Foucault was in any case suspicious of the charges of arbitrariness or "external" determination, which are the often alleged consequences of doing without such sovereign legitimation. Political criticism is not arbitrary if it can be historically situated as a response to specific institutions and practices. "The theoretical and practical experience that we have of our [historical] limits and of the possibility of moving beyond them is always limited and determined; thus we are always in the position of beginning again. But that does not mean that no work can be done except in disorder and contingency"[13]. Rather, it means that such work must always be reflective about its historical limits, and experimental in spirit.

I will conclude with two brief critical reflections. The first concerns Foucault's frequent appeal to images of war, conflict, and resistance. I have argued above that he explicitly proposed a martial imagery in order to emphasize the dynamics and non-systematicity of power and knowledge. Yet feminist theorists have often reminded us of the epistemological and political dangers of building militarism and violence into our very tools of theoretical analysis and political criticism.[14] So one important question to be raised about Foucault's work is to what extent his sense of the dynamics of power and knowledge remains tied to his Nietzschean imagery of war, and the related notions of strategy and tactics.

A second question concerns the scope of Foucault's argument. He repeatedly insisted that his arguments were of quite restricted generality, both historically and epistemologically. He wrote extensively about the interconnected disciplines of psychiatry, criminology, pedagogy, and clinical medicine, but was reluctant to extend his arguments beyond what he once called these "dubious" disciplines (PK, 109). Yet his more general remarks about power and knowledge are more difficult to constrain in this fashion. I have argued elsewhere that the natural sciences offer important analogues to detailed aspects of Foucault's historical studies of power and knowledge.[15] Whether or not these analogies can be sustained, however, Foucault's insistence that power and knowledge be understood as dynamic relationships rather than things possessed must have more general import. There are undoubtedly important structural differences in the ways that alignments of power and of knowledge are organized and deployed in different fields and historical periods. Nor would one expect always to find the same patterns of interaction between knowledge and other kinds of relationship among us and the world. But if I am right in attributing to Foucault an account of the dynamics of knowledge, this should have important consequences still to be worked out for epistemology and the philosophy of science.

NOTES

1 Herbert Dreyfus and Paul Rabinow, *Michel Foucault: Beyond Structuralism and Hermeneutics*, 45–56, offer an extensive and useful discussion of what it means for a statement to be a "serious act" in Foucault's earlier work.

2 Undoubtedly the best discussion in English of Foucault's work in this period is Gary Gutting, *Michel Foucault's Archaeology of Scientific Reason.*

3 Gutting (ibid.) and Dreyfus and Rabinow (*Michel Foucault*) each provide a useful and interesting discussion of the nature and significance of this emphasis on discourse, although their accounts are not mutually consistent.

4 Hacking, *The Taming of Chance* (Cambridge: Cambridge University Press, 1990).

5 Among the more prominent and sophisticated expressions of this concern are Charles Taylor, "Foucault on Freedom and Truth," in David Hoy, ed., *Foucault: A Critical Reader*, 69–102; Nancy Fraser, *Unruly Practices: Power, Discourse, and Gender in Contemporary Social Theory;* and Jürgen Habermas, *The Philosophical Discourse of Modernity: Twelve Lectures*, trans. Frederick Lawrence (Cambridge: MIT Press, 1987).

6 Taylor, ":Foucault on Freedom and Truth," 94.

7 Richard Rorty, "Habermas and Lyotard on Postmodernity," in Richard Bernstein, ed., *Habermas and Modernity* (Cambridge: MIT Press, 1985), 172.

8 Thomas Wartenburg, *The Forms of Power: From Domination to Transformation* (Philadelphia: Temple University Press, 1990), 150.

9 Ibid., 149–61.

10 Ibid., 170.

11 Ibid., 173.

12 Dreyfus and Rabinow, *Michel Foucault*, 231–32.

13 Paul Rabinow, ed., *The Foucault Reader*, 47.

14 Two excellent examples of such feminist reflection are Nancy Hartsock, *Money, Sex, and Power: Toward a Feminist Historical Materialism* (Boston: Northeastern University Press, 1985); and Donna Haraway, "Situated Knowledges: The Science Question in Feminism and the Privilege of Partial Perspective," in Donna Haraway, ed., *Simians, Cyborgs, and Women* (New York: Routledge, Chapman, and Hall, 1990), 183–201.

15 Joseph Rouse, *Knowledge and Power: Toward a Political Philosophy of Science* (Ithaca: Cornell University Press, 1987), esp. chap. 7, and "Foucault and the Natural Sciences," in J. Caputo and M. Yount, eds., *Institutions, Normalization, and Power* (State College: Pennsylvania State University Press, 1993).

5   Ethics as ascetics:
Foucault, the history of ethics,
and ancient thought

In presenting the topic of Michel Foucault's significance as a writer of the history of ethics, I have two main goals. First, I hope to be able to elucidate Foucault's own aims in shifting his attention, in his last writings, to what he himself called "ethics." These aims, in my opinion, have been widely misinterpreted and even more widely ignored, and the result has been a failure to come to terms with the conceptual and philosophical distinctiveness of Foucault's last works. Volumes 2 and 3 of *The History of Sexuality* are about sex in roughly the way that *Discipline and Punish* is about the prison. As the modern prison serves as a reference point for Foucault to work out his analytics of power, so ancient sex functions as the material around which Foucault elaborates his conception of ethics. Although the history of sex is, obviously, sexier than the history of ethics, it is this latter history that oriented Foucault's last writings. Foucault once remarked to me, as he had to others, that "sex is so boring." He used this remark in different ways on different occasions, but one thing he meant by it was that what made sex so interesting to him had little to do with sex itself. His focus on the history of ancient sex, its interest for him, was part of his interest in the history of ancient ethics.

   Whatever one's disagreements with Foucault's interpretation of specific ancient texts, his conceptualization of ethics, the framework in which he placed these interpretations, is as potentially transformative for writing the history of ethics as, to take the strongest comparison I can think of, John Rawls's *A Theory of Justice* is, in its cultural context, for articulating the aims of political philosophy. But this transformative potential has been obscured for philosophy by a way of thinking about and writing the history of ethics that passes over the very domain that Foucault demarcated as ethics, as if

Reprinted from *Foucault and the Writing of History*, edited by Jan Goldstein and published by Basil Blackwell, Oxford, UK and Cambridge, MA, 1994. It is reprinted with the permission of Blackwell.

whatever Foucault wrote about in these works, it could not have been ethics. And this potential has been further darkened in the discussions of some classicists who, to give only a partial caricature, have been so taken with tired and tiresome debates about whether Foucault knew enough Greek and Latin to legitimize his readings of the texts of classical and late antiquity that they have lost sight of his most basic aims. By giving an interpretation of Foucault's work that attempts to clarify these aims, and to show how they affected his readings of particular texts, I hope to reorient discussions of his last works toward what I think is genuinely at stake in them – how to conceptualize ethics and how to write its history.

My second goal, not unrelated to my first, is to place Foucault's work in the context of writings by historians of ancient thought: Paul Veyne, Georges Dumézil, and especially Pierre Hadot, with whom Foucault was engaged in intense, if sometimes submerged, intellectual exchange. These writers, as well as others such as Jean-Pierre Vernant, in turn discussed Foucault's work in terms that help us to see how it can be elaborated and criticized in philosophically fruitful ways. The reception of Foucault's last writings by French ancient historians and philosophers is markedly disjoint from its Anglo-American reception, not, as some people seem to believe, because of the dynamics of French fads, but rather because the manner in which Foucault conceptualized issues showed clear resonances with work that had been and continues to be undertaken by the most significant historians of ancient thought in France. Setting the proper intellectual context will help us to understand better the contours and emplacement of Foucault's own writing on ancient thought, and thus help us to see how his conceptualization of ethics relates to, derives from, and modifies a set of considerations that were not his alone.

One of my ultimate interests in Foucault's interpretation of ethics stems from the way in which I think it can be used to transform our understanding of texts and historical periods that he himself did not discuss. In other parts of this project to reassess Foucault's history of ethics, I will show how his *conceptualization* of ethics provides a compelling interpretative framework for understanding the genre of early Christian virginity treatises. Less predictably, I also argue that Old Testament texts on abominations can be rethought, and certain long-standing problems resolved, by sifting these texts through the specific conception of ethics rooted in Foucault's work. But this interest in using Foucault requires a positioning of his thought centered around the history of ethics, and it is to this philosophical positioning, and to its concepts, its sources, and consequences, that I shall restrict myself here.

The first volume of Michel Foucault's *The History of Sexuality* was published in 1976. The back cover of that volume announced the titles of the five forthcoming volumes that would complete Foucault's project. Volume 2 was to be called *The Flesh and the Body* and would concern the prehistory of our modern experience of sexuality, concentrating on the problematization of sex in early Christianity. Volumes 3 through 5 were to focus on some of the major figures (of the eighteenth and nineteenth centuries) around which problems, themes, and questions of sex had come to circle. Volume 3, *The Children's Crusade*, would discuss the sexuality of children, especially the problem of childhood masturbation; volume 4, *Woman, Mother, Hysteric*, would discuss the specific ways in which sexuality had been invested in the female body; volume 5, *Perverts*, was planned to investigate exactly what the title named, the person of the pervert, an ever-present target of nineteenth-century thought. Finally, volume 6, *Population and Races*, was to examine the way in which treatises, both theoretical and practical, on the topics of population and race were linked to the history of what Foucault had called "biopolitics."[1]

In 1984, when volumes 2 and 3 of *The History of Sexuality* were finally published, some years after they had been expected, many of Foucault's readers must have been bewildered by their content, to say the least. This bewilderment was occasioned, most immediately, by the profound chronological reorientation of these two volumes. Volume 2, *The Use of Pleasure*, studied problems of sex in classical Greek thought, while volume 3, *The Care of the Self*, analyzed theses problems as they appeared in Greek and Latin texts of the first and second centuries A.D. Moreover, in the introduction to volume 2, which served as an introduction to his new project, Foucault reconceptualized the entire aim of his history of sexuality and introduced a set of concepts that had been absent from volume 1. The most significant philosophical consequence of this reorientation was Foucault's conceptualization of ethics, his theoretical elaboration of ethics as a framework for interpreting these Greek and Roman problematizations of sex. I shall leave aside here many of the general features of Foucault's conceptualization of ethics, since I have discussed them at length elsewhere.[2] But given the way this essay will proceed, I should remind you that Foucault thought of ethics as that component of morality that concerns the self's relationship to itself. Foucault argued that our histories of morality should not be exclusively focused on the history of codes of moral behavior, and that we must also pay careful attention to the history of the forms of moral subjectivation, to how we constitute ourselves as moral subjects of our own actions. Foucault thought of ethics proper, of the self's relationship to itself, as having four main aspects: the ethical substance, that part of oneself that is taken to be the relevant domain for ethical judgment; the mode of subjection, the way in which the individual establishes his or her relation to moral obligations and rules; the self-forming activity or ethical work that one performs on oneself in order to transform oneself into an ethical subject; and, finally, the *telos*, the mode of being at which one aims in behaving ethically.[3]

Another way of understanding Foucault's new concern with the self's relationship to itself is to think of it, as Foucault himself explicitly did in 1980–1981, as at the intersection of two themes that he had previously treated, namely, a history of subjectivity and an analysis of the forms of governmentality. Foucault claimed that he had undertaken to study the history of subjectivity by studying the divisions carried out in society in the name of madness, illness, and delinquency, and by studying the effects of these divisions on the constitution of the subject. In addition, his history of subjectivity attempted to locate the "modes of objectivation" of the subject in scientific knowledge, for example, knowledge concerning language (linguistics), work (economics), and life (biology). As for the analysis of forms of "governmentality," a crucial concept for Foucault's work beginning around 1977, this analysis responded to a "double objective." On the one hand, Foucault wanted to criticize current conceptions of power that, in one way or another, perceived power as a unitary system, a critique undertaken most thoroughly in *Discipline and Punish* and volume 1 of *The History of Sexuality*. On the other hand, Foucault wanted to analyze power as a domain of strategic relations between individuals and groups, relations whose strategies were to govern the conduct of these individuals.[4] Thus Foucault's new concern with the self would be

a way of doing the history of subjectivity: no longer, however, by way of the divisions between the mad and those who are not mad, the ill and those who are not ill, delinquents and those who are not delinquents; no longer by way of the constitution of the field of scientific objectivity giving rise to the living, speaking, working subject. But rather by the putting into place and the transformations, in our culture, of the "relations to oneself," with their technical armature and their effects of knowledge. And one could thus take up, under another aspect, the question of "governmentality": the government of the self by the self in its articulation with relations to others (as one finds it in pedagogy, advice for conduct, spiritual direction, the prescription of models of life, etc.).[5]

As I would interpret Foucault, ethics, or the self's relation to itself, is therefore part of both the history of subjectivity and the history of governmentality. Our "technologies of the self," the ways in which we relate ourselves to ourselves, contribute to the forms in which our subjectivity is constituted and experienced, as well as to the forms in which we govern our thought and conduct.[6] We relate to ourselves as specific kinds of subjects who govern themselves in particular ways. In response to the questions "What kinds of subjects should we be?" and "How should we govern ourselves?", Foucault offered his history of ethics.

In addition to the concepts I have already mentioned, Foucault's last works introduced other related notions, most prominent that of the esthetics of existence and styles of existence. These notions are, in my opinion, far more complex and multilayered than most commentators have acknowledged. One central aspect of these notions has been lucidly described by Paul Veyne:

The idea of styles of existence played a major role in Foucault's conversations and doubtless in his inner life during the final months of a life that only he knew to be in danger. *Style* does not mean distinction here; the word is to be taken in the sense of the Greeks, for whom an artist was first of all an artisan and a work of art was first of all a work. Greek ethics is quite dead and Foucault judged it as undesirable as it would be impossible to resuscitate this ethics; but he considered one of its elements, namely the idea of a work of the self on the self, to be capable of reacquiring a contemporary meaning, in the manner of one of those pagan temple columns that are occasionally reutilized in more recent structures. We can guess at what might emerge from this diagnosis: the self, taking itself as a work to be accomplished, could sustain an ethics that is no longer supported by either tradition or reason; as an artist of itself, the self would enjoy that autonomy that modernity can no longer do without. "Everything has disappeared," said Medea, "but I have one thing left: myself."[7]

This aspect of Foucault's idea of the esthetics of existence reaches its apogee in *The Care of the Self*, especially in the chapter entitled "The Cultivation of the Self." In this chapter, Foucault argues that in the texts of the first two centuries A.D. with which he is concerned, there is an "insistence on the attention that must be brought to bear on oneself," and that the added emphasis on sexual austerity in these texts should not be interpreted in terms of a tightening of the moral code and its prohibitions, but rather in terms of "an intensification of the relation to oneself by which one constituted oneself as the subject of one's acts."[8] More specifically, he argues that the practices of the self in late antiquity are characterized by the general principle of conversion to self – *epistrophé eis heauton*.[9] This conversion to self requires that one change one's activities and shift one's attention so as to constantly take care of oneself. One result of this conversion, claims Foucault, is the "experience of a pleasure that one takes in oneself. The individual who has finally succeeded in gaining access to himself is, for himself, an object of pleasure."[10] And Foucault quotes Seneca:

"*Disce gaudere*, learn how to feel joy," says Seneca to Lucilius: "I do not wish you ever to be deprived of gladness. I would have it born in your house; and it is born there, if only it is inside of you . . . for it will never fail you when once you have found its source . . . look toward the true good, and rejoice only in that which comes from your own store [*de tuo*]. But what do I mean by 'your own store'? I mean your very self and the best part of you."[11]

These texts certainly appear to advocate an esthetics of existence, a cultivation of the self, that culminates, to quote Veyne's words again, in "that autonomy that modernity cannot do without," and that is symbolized by the pleasure that one takes in oneself, a pleasure of which one cannot be deprived. But, as Pierre Hadot has convincingly argued, Seneca opposes pleasure and joy – *voluptas* and *gaudium* – and it is misleading for Foucault to speak of the joy described by Seneca as "a form of pleasure."[12] More important, as Hadot indicates, Seneca finds his joy not in his self *per se*, but in that "best part of the self" that Seneca identifies with perfect reason and, ultimately, with divine reason:

The 'best part' of oneself, then, is ultimately a transcendent self. Seneca does not find his joy in "Seneca," but by transcending Seneca; by discovering that he has in him a reason that is part of universal Reason, that is within all human beings and within the cosmos itself.[13]

Hadot has argued that an essential element of the psychic content of the spiritual exercises of ancient philosophy is "the feeling of belonging to a Whole," what he often describes as a cosmic consciousness, a consciousness of being part of the cosmic whole.[14] This consciousness is summarized in Seneca's four words: *Toti se inserens mundo* ("Plunging oneself into the totality of the world").[15] Adjacent to the cultivation of the self, that movement of interiorization in which "one seeks to be master of oneself, to possess oneself, to find one's happiness in freedom and inner independence," emphasized by Foucault, there is "another movement, in which one raises oneself to a higher psychic level . . . which consists in becoming aware of oneself as part of Nature, as a portion of universal Reason."[16] Indeed, I would claim, following Hadot, that one of the most distinctive features of that care of the self studied by Foucault in volume 3 of *The History of Sexuality* is its indissociable link with this cosmic consciousness; one philosophical aim of this care of the self is to transform oneself so that one places oneself in the perspective of the cosmic Whole. The care of the self receives its distinctive philosophical tint in late antiquity through those practices that raise the self to a universal level, that place the self within a cosmic dimension that at the same time transforms the self, even to the point, as Hadot writes, of surpassing the self:

In Platonism, but in Epicureanism and Stoicism as well, freedom from anxiety is thus achieved by a movement in which one passes from individual and impassioned subjectivity to the objectivity of the universal perspective. It is a question, not of a construction of a self as a work of art, but, on the contrary, of a surpassing of the self, or, at the least, of an exercise by which the self situates itself in the totality and experiences itself as part of this totality.[17]

As Foucault himself made clear in his 1981–1982 course at the Collège de France, the care of the self has a very long history.[18] In trying to recapture the different forms in which the care of the self has appeared, it is essential to understand not only the ways in which the self became an object of concern but also the ways in which one went beyond oneself, relating the self to something grander than itself. The spiritual exercises of ancient philosophy, that philosophical *askésis* so central to Foucault's last works, could, at one and the same time, result in an intense preoccupation with the self and in a sort of dilation of the self that realized the true magnitude of the soul.[19] Hadot is concerned that by focusing too exclusively on the cultivation of the self and by linking his ethical model too closely to an aesthetics of existence, Foucault was suggesting "a culture of the self that is too purely aesthetic."[20] In other words, writes Hadot, "I fear a new form of dandyism, a version for the end of the twentieth century."[21] Without taking up Foucault's discussion, in his essay "What Is Enlightenment?," of dandyism in Baudelaire,[22] I do think that there is a use of the concept of styles of existence to be found in Foucault's last works that can and ought to be preserved, one, moreover, that aligns Foucault's writings more closely with Hadot's own interpretation of ancient thought. Although I believe that Foucault's interpretation of the culture of the self in late antiquity is sometimes too narrow and therefore misleading, I think that this is *a defect of interpretation, not of conceptualization.*[23] Foucault's conceptualization of ethics as the self's relationship to itself provides us with a framework of enormous depth and subtlety, and it is this framework – of ethical substance, mode of subjection, self-forming activity, and telos – that allows us to grasp aspects of ancient thought that would otherwise remain occluded. I have argued elsewhere that Foucault's conception of ethics is, in fact, indebted to Hadot's work in *Exercices spirituels et philosophie antique,* to Hadot's history of ancient philosophy as a history of spiritual exercises.[24] Nevertheless, by giving detailed conceptual content to the idea of the self's relationship to itself, by analyzing this relationship in terms of four distinct components, Foucault makes it possible for us to see precisely how to write a history of ethics that will not collapse into a history of moral codes. Furthermore, his conceptualization allows us to examine the connections, the kinds of dependence and independence, among these four aspects of ethics, thus showing us the various ways in which continuities, modifications, and ruptures can occur in one or more of these four dimensions of our relation to ourselves. In some historical periods, for example, the ethical substance may remain constant, while the mode of subjection gradually alters; or the telos may stay continuous, while the self-forming activity is modified. In other periods, the ethical substance, mode of subjection, self-forming activity, and telos may be so inextricably intertwined that they undergo change together, thereby resulting in an entirely new form of the self's relationship to itself.

Pierre Hadot has brilliantly shown that one of the fundamental aspects of philosophy in the Greek, Hellenistic, and Roman eras is that philosophy "is a way of life, which does not mean only that it is a certain moral conduct . . . but that it is a way of existing in the world, which should be practiced at each instant and which should transform all of life."[25] A sense of philosophy as a way of life is also expressed by Foucault when he explains his own motivation in writing the second and third volumes of *The History of Sexuality*. After claiming that for him philosophical activity consists in "the endeavor to know how and to what extent it might be possible to think differently,"[26] Foucault writes

The "essay" – which should be understood as the assay or test by which, in the game of truth, one undergoes changes, and not as the simplistic appropriation of others for the purpose of communication – is the living substance of philosophy, at least if we assume that philosophy is still what it was in times past, i.e., an ascesis, *askésis*, an exercise of oneself in the activity of thought.[27]

For Foucault himself philosophy was a spiritual exercise, an exercise of oneself in which one submitted oneself to modifications and tests, underwent changes, in order to learn to think differently. This idea of philosophy as a way of life and, I shall argue, of ethics as proposing styles of life is one of the most forceful and provocative directions of Foucault's later thought.

In approaching these ideas, I want first to distinguish between the notions of a way of life and a style of life.[28] In the ancient world *philosophy itself* was a way of life, a way of life that was distinct from everyday life, and that was perceived as strange and even dangerous. In conveying this fact about philosophy, I can do no better here than to quote Hadot's marvelous description:

to be a philosopher implies a rupture with what the skeptics called *bios*, that is, daily life . . .

This very rupture between the philosopher and the conduct of everyday life is strongly felt by nonphilosophers . . . philosophers are strange, a race apart. Strange indeed are those Epicureans, who lead a frugal life, practicing a total equality between the men and the women inside their philosophical circle – and even between married women and courtesans; strange, too, those Roman Stoics who disinterestedly administer the provinces of the Empire entrusted to them and are the only ones to take seriously the laws promulgated against excess; strange as well this Roman Platonist, the Senator Rogatianus, a disciple of Plotinus, who on the very day he is to assume his functions as praetor gives up his possessions, frees his slaves, and eats only every other day. Strange indeed all those philosophers whose behavior, without being inspired by religion, nonetheless completely breaks with the customs and habits of most mortals.

By the time of the Platonic dialogues Socrates was called *atopos*, that is, "unclassifiable". What makes him *atopos* is precisely the fact that he is a "philo-sopher" in the etymological sense of the word; that is, he is in love with wisdom. For wisdom, says Diotima in Plato's *Symposium*, is not a human state, it is a state of perfection of being and knowledge that can only be divine. It is the love of this wisdom, which is foreign to the world, that makes the philosopher a stranger in it.[29]

Stoics, Epicureans, Platonists, Cynics, and even Skeptics each embodied the philosophical *way of life*, a way of life whose peculiarity, whatever its particular guises, was everywhere recognized. And early Christianity, itself conceived of as a way of life, namely living in conformity with the divine Logos, was also presented as a philosophy.[30] Socrates attempted to convert his interlocutors from the unexamined way of life to the philosophical way of life. It was this experience of philosophy as a way of life, and not simply as a theoretical doctrine, that brought Socrates into deadly conflict with the authorities.

Given this basic characteristic of philosophy itself as a way of life, there were, of course, different philosophies, what I shall call different *styles of life*, different styles of living philosophically. Each philosophical school – Stoic, Epicurean, Platonist, and so on – represented a style of life that had a corresponding fundamental inner attitude.[31] As Hadot says, "In this period, to philosophize is to choose a school, convert to its way of life, and accept its dogmas."[32] I propose that we take each particular conceptual combination of ethical substance, mode of subjection, self-forming activity,

and telos as representing a style of life. One's style of life, as speci-
fied by a determinate content and mesh of each of these four components, gives expression to the self's relationship to itself. To indicate what part of oneself one judges, how one relates oneself to
moral obligations, what one does to transform oneself into an ethical subject, and what mode of being one aims to realize is to indicate how one lives, is to characterize one's style of life. Although
Foucault does not explicitly use the notion of style of life in exactly
this way, this usage is, I believe, consistent with his interpretation
of ancient philosophy. As we read the last volumes of *The History
of Sexuality*, it is evident that the idea of the care of the self is part
of a broader conceptual matrix, and that a history of the care of the
self must be written in terms of a history of ethics.[33] In every
historical period the care of the self is expressed in particular relationships of the self to itself, particular styles of life. As the self's
relationship to itself undergoes modification, as the way in which
one cares for oneself changes, one's style of life will change. And
when Foucault says that the problem of an ethics is the problem of
"a form [I would say "style" here] to be given to one's conduct and
one's life," he does in fact link the notions of ethics and style of life
in a conceptually intimate way.[34]

Some of Foucault's most suggestive, and philosophically revealing, invocations of the notions of *askésis* and style of life can be
found in his discussions of his own attitude to homosexuality. Foucault claims that one goal of homosexuality today is "to advance
into a homosexual *askésis* that would make us work on ourselves
and invent, I do not say discover, a manner of being that is still
improbable."[35] Let me underline, in this quotation, the connection
between *askésis* and manner of being, a connection that is, I would
claim, also to be uncovered in Foucault's discussion of ancient male/
male sexual practices. He insists that the notion of a homosexual
mode or style of life, with its new forms of relationship, is what is
most significant about contemporary gay practices:

Is it possible to create a homosexual mode of life? This notion of mode of life
seems important to me ... It seems to me that a way of life can yield a
culture and an ethics. To be "gay", I think, is not to identify with the
psychological traits and the visible marks of the homosexual, but to try to
define and develop a way of life.[36]

Just as Foucault argued that ancient thought was not primarily concerned with the morphology of the sexual act,[37] so he too was interested not in the nature of the sexual act itself, its morphology or shape, but in the style of life, and the corresponding art of life, of which these sexual acts are part.[38] Even in his most explicit discussion of gay male sexual practices – *"les pratiques physiques de type fist-fucking"* – Foucault insists on relating these practices to a style of life that expresses a new sense of masculinity, a sense that is devirilised, even desexualised (*"devirilisées, voire désexuées"*).[39] So it is these "new forms of relationship, new forms of love, new forms of creation" that most captured Foucault's attention and interest.[40] Foucault believed that "what most bothers those who are not gay about gayness is the gay lifestyle, not sex acts themselves."[41] As strange as it may sound at first, Foucault pointed to homosexuality as one resource for answering the question of how to practice spiritual exercises in the twentieth century. Ultimately, for Foucault, one link between the ancient practices of self-mastery and contemporary homosexuality is that both require an ethics or ascetics of the self tied to a particular, and particularly threatening, way of life. I know it would have given Foucault genuine pleasure to think that the threat to everyday life posed by ancient philosophy had a contemporary analogue in the fears and disturbances that derive from the self-formation and style of life of being gay.[42]

Although Foucault's famous declaration that he is interested in writing the history of the present[43] must certainly be acknowledged as at play in his interpretation of ancient texts, and in the linkages that can be found in his emphases on ancient philosophical *askesis* and contemporary homosexual *askésis*, such a concern with the history of the present, which I share with Foucault, need not, and should not, lead us to transform the ancient intensification of the relation to the self into the modern estheticization of the self. The ancient experience of the self ought to retain its distinctiveness, not simply for reasons of historical accuracy but especially if it is to provide a philosophical standpoint from which we can begin to learn how to think differently. In "The Individual within the City-State", Jean-Pierre Vernant has reminded us how conceptually specific is the ancient notion of *psuché*, and how distinct it is from the modern intimacy of the self. Vernant makes analytically useful distinctions between the individual, the subject, and the ego. The history of the individual, in the strict sense, concerns "his place and role in his group or groups; the value accorded him; the margin of movement left to him; his relative autonomy with respect to his institutional framework."[44] Vernant marks out the subject as appearing "when the individual uses the first person to express himself and, speaking in his own name, enunciates certain features that make him a unique being."[45] Finally, the ego is

the ensemble of psychological practices and attitudes that give an interior dimension and a sense of wholeness to the subject. These practices and attitudes constitute him within himself as a unique being, real and original, whose authentic nature resides entirely in the secrecy of his interior life. It resides at the very heart of an intimacy to which no one except him can have access because it is defined as self-consciousness.[46]

Vernant compares these three levels to three literary genres: the individual corresponds to biography, a genre based on the life of a single character, in contrast to epic or historical narrative; the subject corresponds to autobiography or memoirs, where the individual tells his own life story; and the ego corresponds to confessions or a diary "in which the inner life, the unique subject of a private life – in all its psychological complexity and richness, and its relative opacity or incommunicability – provides the material for what is written."[47] Following Arnaldo Momigliano and others, Vernant stresses that, although the Greeks produced some forms of biography and autobiography, both the classical and Hellenistic periods lacked confessions and diaries; moreover, "the characterization of the individual in Greek autobiography allows no 'intimacy of the self.' "[48]

After charting the evolution from the Homeric to Platonic conceptions of *psuché*, a transformation that takes us from the soul as "a ghostly double of the body" to the body "as a ghostly reflection of the soul,"[49] Vernant insists on the importance of the fact that the Platonic *psuché* is "a *daimón* in us, a divine being, a supernatural force whose place and function in the universe goes beyond our single person."[50] This *psuché*, as impersonal or superpersonal force, is "*the* soul in me and not *my* soul."[51] Thus Vernant claims that the Greek experience of the self could not have given rise to a *cogito ergo sum*, since my *psuché* is not my psychological ego. Citing Bernard Groethuysen's formula, he maintains that the ancient consciousness of self consists in the apprehension of the self in a *he*, and not yet in an *I*. There is no Cartesian, or even Augustinian, self-consciousness in the ancient preoccupation with the self.[52]

Can we reconcile Foucault's emphasis on the ancient care of the self with Vernant's historically nuanced argument that this *psuché* is a *superpersonal* force? How is the Greek and Roman "intensity of the relations to self" to be placed alongside the fact that this self is but a "simulacrum of the divine"?[53] The philosophical ideal that allows us to put together the care of the self and the *psuché* as *daimón* is the figure of the sage or wise man. The figure of the sage is notably absent from Foucault's writings on ancient philosophy, and it is precisely this absence that sometimes permits him to pass too smoothly from ancient to modern experiences of the self. By anchoring the ideal of the sage at the basis of ancient ethics, we can better see the abyss that separates *psuché* from any possible estheticization of the self.

The figure of the wise man, although described in different terms in different philosophical schools, was, according to Hadot, the "transcendent model that inspired all of philosophy" and that, moreover, was the basis for constructing the two other regulative models of ancient thought, the figure of the ideal king and the idea of God.[54] Of the many aspects of this figure that were crucial to ancient thought, I want to focus on what Hadot, in his brilliant essay "La figure du sage dans l'Antiquité gréco-latine," describes as a

fundamental theme . . . wisdom is the state in which man is at the same time essentially man and beyond man, as if the essence of man consisted in being beyond himself.[55]

Or, as Paul Veyne puts a similar, if more specific, claim, in his introduction to the French translation of Seneca's *De Tranquillitate animi*, Stoic eudamonianism is an "ethics of the ideal" that aims to imitate the figure of the sage, "a dream situated beyond human capacities."[56] Michelet differently stressed this aspect of the ideal in his formulation, "Greek religion culminated with its true God: the sage."[57]

Despite their contrasting concrete ideals of wisdom, all of the ancient philosophical schools conceived of philosophy and the philosopher as oriented toward this "transcendent and almost inaccessible ideal."[58] Even if, as Cicero claimed, the true sage is born perhaps once every five hundred years, nevertheless, the philosopher can attain at least a certain relative perfection. He can hope to become, if not the ideal and divine sage, "a sage among men, conscious of the distance that separates him from the gods," a relative sage.[59] But this achievement can only be attained through the arduous path of spiritual exercises that require nothing less than a transformation of one's way of life. It is this self-transforming, life-transforming *askēsis* that makes Socrates, and every other true philosopher, *atopos*.

In his interpretation of Seneca, Hadot draws out a series of equivalences that takes one from the true good to the best part of the self to perfect or divine reason. Thus on this reading, as I have already indicated, Seneca's true good, which is the best part of his self, is also a transcendent self; it is the sage or *daimón* in Seneca.[60] So in Letter 23 when Seneca urges the turning of one's attention toward the true good, he is urging a conversion to self that is at the same time a conversion to the *deus* in each one of us.[61] To be a philosopher, a lover of wisdom, is to exert a constant care of the self that, proceeding by way of spiritual exercises, culminates in the surpassing of the self, brings one to an identification with universal Reason, the god, the sage that both is and is beyond one's self. The joy obtained when one achieves this identification requires struggle and combat with oneself, since we are "too readily satisfied with ourselves," substituting pleasurable delights for real joy.[62] Real joy, writes Seneca, "is a stern matter" (*verum gaudium severa est*), and it demands that we go "deep below the surface" in order to take up the perspective of the god that is within us.[63] We can acquire this real joy from within ourselves, provided that we surpass ourselves, transforming ourselves. The ancient spiritual progress that aims at wisdom, the life of the sage, confronts the apparent paradox, as formulated again by Hadot, that "man appears, in that which is most his own, as something that is more than man, or, to speak more precisely, the true self of each individual transcends each individual."[64]

Foucault is absolutely correct to emphasize the ancient care of the self, for conversion to self is a precondition of the spiritual transformation that constitutes philosophy. Such a conversion is, however, not to be confused with the kind of psychologization or estheticization that shrinks the world to the size of oneself. Rather, this conversion, dilating the self beyond itself, brings about that cosmic consciousness in which one sees the human world "from above."[65] The care of the self does not take the form of a pose or posture, of the fashioning of oneself into a dramatic character. To invoke Plotinus' formulation, it is, instead, the sculpting of oneself as a statue, the scraping away of what is superfluous and extraneous to oneself. The art of living required by the realization of the self is not compared, by Plotinus, to painting, which was considered an art of addition, but rather to sculpture, an art of taking away. Since the statue already exists in the block of marble, it is sufficient to take away what is superfluous in order to make the statue appear. So when Plotinus tells us that if we do not yet see our own beauty we should sculpt our own beautiful statue of ourselves, far from urging any estheticization of the self, he is enjoining a purification, an exercise that liberates us from our passions and that returns us to our self, ultimately identified by Plotinus with the One.[66] The beauty of this sculpting is not independent from the reality of the Good;[67] it is not an estheticization of morality, but a spiritual transfiguration in which we scrape away at ourselves, identifying with the Good beyond ourselves so that we can see our own beauty, that is, so that the "divine glory of virtue" will shine upon us.[68] So, as Plotinus maintains, "it is right to say that the soul's becoming something good and beautiful is its being made like to God . . ."[69]

Although underlining the cosmic consciousness of the ancient sage, Hadot does acknowledge that the figure of the sage in ancient thought corresponds to a more acute consciousness of the self, of the personality, of interiority.[70] But the internal freedom recognized by all the philosophical schools, "this inexpungible core of the personality," is located in the faculty of judgment, not in some psychologically thick form of introspection.[71] When Epictetus and Marcus Aurelius distinguish between the things themselves and the judgments we form of those things, they are insisting on the fundamental distinction between that which depends on us (our judgments) and that which does not depend on us (the things themselves) in order to make us conscious of the power we have to be independent, to choose the judgments and representations we will have of things and not to be concerned with the things themselves.[72] Internal freedom of judgment leads to *autarkeia*, self-sufficiency, that assures the sage *ataraxia*, tranquility of the soul. The dimension of interiority in ancient thought, constituted by vigilance and attention to the self, by self-examination, and exertions of the will, memory, imagination and reason, is in service of a freedom to judge that will guarantee one the independence of wisdom.[73] It is an internal life ultimately concentrated around the sage or *daimón* in one, therefore allowing the philosopher to separate himself from passions and desires that do not depend on him. This is a kind of interiorization that aims at transcendence, and if Foucault's interpretation of ancient ethics seems sometimes to border on an estheticization of the self, Hadot's interpretation insists on the divinization of the self.

This is not the occasion on which to sketch further the history of ethics as the history of the self's relationship to itself, the history of ethics as ascetics. Foucault has pointed to homosexual *askésis* and the homosexual style of life as exemplifications of this history. Hadot has himself indicated that certain experiences of the modern artist partake of the cosmic consciousness of the ancient sage; as Klee wrote, "His progress in the observation and the vision of nature makes him accede little by little to a philosophical vision of the universe that allows him freely to create abstract forms. . . . The artist thus creates works, or participates in the creation of works that are in the image of the work of God."[74] If most of modern moral philosophy finds the idea of ethics as a spiritual exercise, to say the least, strange, it would be false to conclude that these ethical problematizations disappear from the history of philosophy after the ancients. The thematics that Stanley Cavell identifies as moral perfectionism constitutes one continuation of this history of ethics. When Cavell portrays Emersonian self-reliance as "the mode of the self's relation to itself"[75] or when he describes Wittgenstein's *Philosophical Investigations* as exhibiting, "as purely as any work I know, philosophizing as a spiritual struggle,"[76] he is working toward a conceptualization of ethics that shares with Foucault and Hadot the idea that what is at issue is not only a code of good conduct but a way of being that involves every aspect of one's soul.[77] And as Cavell follows out Emerson's remark in "History" ("So all that is said of the wise man by stoic or oriental or modern essayist, describes to each man his own idea, describes his unattained but attainable self"), he is pursuing the ancient conception of the sage or *daimón* in us, that self-reliance both within and beyond one's self.[78]

Paul Veyne has described the Nietzschean *Übermensch* as the modernized version of the ancient sage.[79] If the *Übermensch* is such a modernized version, obviously it is not identical with the ancient figure. But there are points of comparison so startling that it would be perverse to overlook them. Hadot's interpretation of ancient philosophy lays great emphasis on the representation of philosophy as an exercise and training for death, and as a meditation upon death.[80] In his 1981–82 course at the Collège de France, Foucault devoted detailed descriptions to those ancient "exercises of thought" known as *praemeditatio malorum*, meditation on future evils, and *melete thanatou*, meditation on or exercise for death.[81] He interprets the latter as "a way of rendering death present in life," an exercise by which the sage effects spiritual transformation.[82] Such a dimension seems to me to capture precisely the force of Nietzsche's introduction of the idea of the eternal recurrence in section 341 of *The Gay Science*. I quote this section in full:

> What if some day or night a demon were to steal after you into your loneliest loneliness and say to you: "This life as you now live it and have lived it, you will have to live once more and innumerable times more; and there will be nothing new in it, but every pain and every joy and every thought and sign and everything unutterably small or great in your life will have to return to you, all in the same succession and sequence – even this spider and this moonlight between the trees, and even this moment and I myself. The eternal hourglass of existence is turned upside down again and again, and you with it, speck of dust!"
>
> Would you not throw yourself down and gnash your teeth and curse the demon who spoke thus? Or have you once experienced a tremendous moment when you would have answered him: "You are a god and never have I heard anything more divine." If this thought gained possession of you, it would change you as you are or perhaps crush you. The question in each and every thing, "Do you desire this once more and innumerable times more?" would lie upon your actions as the greatest weight. Or how well disposed would you have to become to yourself and to life to *crave nothing more fervently* than this ultimate eternal confirmation and seal?[83]

How could one fail to see that this is a modern meditation that effects spiritual transformation; that is, problematizes one's way of life through a series of questions with ancient reverberations? This is from Seneca's fifty-ninth Letter:

> I shall now show you how you may know that you are not wise. The wise man is joyful, happy and calm, unshaken; he lives on a plane with the gods.

Now go, question yourself; if you are never downcast, if your mind is not harassed by any apprehension, through anticipations of what is to come, if day and night your soul keeps on its even and unswerving course, upright and content with itself, then you have attained to the greatest good that mortals can possess.[84]

If this thought gained possession of you, so Seneca believed, it would change you as you are.

In concentrating on questions of interpretation of ancient texts, I hope to have shown, first, that Foucault's conceptualization of ethics as the self's relation to itself does *not depend on* any modern understanding of subjectivity. Writing this history of ethics is part of writing a history of the self. Second, Foucault's conceptualization does not entail a narrowing of the domain of ethics, as if this history were threatened with a collapse into a history of the varieties of egoism. The demarcation of the self's relation to itself as the central arena of ethical problematization is inextricably tied to the theme of the proper way of life. The self's relation to itself manifests one's style of life, and the philosophical way of life forces a transformed relation to oneself. In his extraordinary interpretation of the *Apology, Crito,* and *Phaedo* in his last lectures at the Collège de France, as well as in his 1983 seminar at the University of California at Berkeley, Foucault argued that Socratic *parrhésia,* the Socratic practice of truth-telling, is a specifically ethical practice and is distinguished from other kinds of truth-telling, and especially from political truth-telling, by its objective – to incite each person to occupy himself with himself. Thus the essential theme of ethical *parrhésia* is the care of the self.[85] It is evident in listening to these lectures that Foucault wanted to link the theme of the care of the self to that of the peculiarly philosophical way of life, a link that, although perhaps not explicit, is present in his discussion of Socrates' last words in the *Phaedo.* Taking up Georges Dumézil's remarkable "Divertissement sur les dernières paroles de Socrate," Foucault follows Dumézil in arguing that one cannot interpret Socrates' last words – "Crito, we owe a cock to Asclepius" – as acknowledging a debt to Asclepius (the god to whom the Greeks offered a sacrifice when a cure was at issue) for having cured Socrates of the illness that is life.[86] Despite this traditional and often-repeated interpretation, Dumézil and Foucault attempt to show that it is completely at odds with Socratic teaching to impute to Socrates the claim that life is an illness and that death thus cures us of life. But Asclepius is the god one thanks for a cure, and so, following a complicated philological and philosophical path that I will not attempt to reconstruct here, Dumézil and Foucault argue that the illness that Socrates is cured of is that corruption of the soul which results from following the general, ordinary opinion of mankind. Socrates is not concerned with the opinion of the masses, appealed to in the *Crito* in an attempt to convince him to escape from prison; he is rather concerned with himself and with his own relation to truth, and he has courageously learned to free himself from the soul-sickness of common opinion.[87] Socrates' ethical *parrhésia*, divorced from the opinion of the public, is his style of life. It is this style of life that he ceaselessly presents to others, for which others put him to death. Foucault says that it is the principle of concerning oneself with oneself that Socrates bequeaths to others;[88] he might have equally underscored the figure of Socrates that endures for us as a constantly irritating and inspiring reminder of the philosophical way of life. Socrates reminds us of nothing less than the fact that, for the practitioners of ancient philosophy, philosophy itself was a way of life.[89] Ethical problems were not resolved by producing a list of required, permitted, and forbidden actions, but were centered around one's attitude to oneself, and so to others and the world – one's style of living.

In his last writings Foucault expressed concern that the ancient principle "Know thyself" had obscured, at least for us moderns, the similarly ancient requirement that we occupy ourselves with ourselves, that we care for ourselves. He insisted that we not forget that the demand to know oneself was "regularly associated with the theme of the care of the self."[90] It is in this spirit that I have urged that the care of the self must itself be placed in the context of a style of life, that in order to make sense of the care of the self we must widen our vision to include the style of life that gives form and direction to the self's relation to itself. Classical Greek, Hellenistic, and Roman thought, early Christianity, and even the Old Testament[91] all prescribe the care of the self; but the styles of life in which this care is embedded are so different that it affects the notion of care, the notion of the self, and the notions of how and why we are to bear this relation of care to ourselves. One of the great virtues of ancient thought is that knowledge of oneself, care of oneself, and one's style of life are everywhere so woven together that one cannot, without distortion, isolate any of these issues from the entire philosophical thematics of which they form part. If we ignore these dimensions of the moral life, we shall be able to do justice neither to history nor philosophy. And, without doubt worse, we shall not be able to take account of ourselves, of who we have become, of how we might become different.

NOTES

1 My understanding of these unpublished volumes is derived both from remarks made by Foucault in Volume 1 of *The History of Sexuality* and from conversations with him in 1976 just after the publication of that volume.

2 Arnold I. Davidson, "Archaeology, Genealogy, Ethics," in *Foucault: A Critical Reader*, ed. David Couzens Hoy (Oxford: Basil Blackwell, 1986).

3 Michel Foucault, *The Use of Pleasure* (New York: Pantheon Books, 1985), 26–32. See also "On the Genealogy of Ethics: An Overview of Work in Progress," in *The Foucault Reader*, ed. Paul Rabinow (New York: Pantheon Books).

4 Michel Foucault, "Subjectivité et verité, 1980–81," in *Résumé des Cours, 1970–1982* (Paris: Julliard, 1989), 134–35.

5 Ibid., 135–36.

6 The quoted phrase is from ibid., 134.

7 Paul Veyne, "The Final Foucault and His Ethics," *Critical Inquiry* 20, no. 1 (Autumn 1993), 7.

8 Michel Foucault, *The Care of the Self* (New York: Pantheon Books, 1986), 41.

9 Ibid., 64.

10 Ibid., 66.

11 Ibid., 66–67. The quotation from Seneca is from "Epistle XXIII" of Seneca, *The Epistles of Seneca* (Cambridge: Harvard University Press, 1917).

12 Foucault, *The Care of the Self*, 66. Pierre Haddot, "Refléxions sur la notion de 'culture de soi,'" in *Michel Foucault, Philosophe* (Paris: Éditions du Seuil, 1989), 262.

13 Pierre Hadot, ibid., 262.

14 Ibid., 263, and Pierre Hadot, *Exercices spirituels et philosophie antique, Deuxième édition revue et augmentée* (Paris: Études Augustiniennes, 1987), 218–19, 231.

15 Hadot, "Refléxions sur la notion de 'culture de soi,' " 263. See also Pierre Hadot, "Le Sage et le monde," in *Le Temps de la refléxion*, Vol. X (Paris: Gallimard, 1989), 176–77.

16 Hadot, "Refléxions sur la notion de 'culture de soi,' " 267.

17 Hadot, *Exercices spirituels et philosophie antique*, 232.

18 Michel Foucault, "L'herméneutique du sujet, 1981–82," in *Résumé des cours, 1970–1982*, 145–49.

19 On the notion of the dilation of the self, see Hadot, *Exercices spirituels et philosophie antique*, 231.

20 Hadot, "Refléxions sur la notion de 'culture de soi,' " 267. See also Hadot, "Le Sage et le monde," 176.

21 Ibid., 267.

22 For Foucault's discussion of Baudelaire and dandyism, see "What is Enlightenment?" in *The Foucault Reader*, 39–42.

23 I do think that Hadot's interpretation of these ancient texts is the historically accurate interpretation. Foucault's interpretations are, I believe, motivated, at least in part, by his specific interest in the history of the present, by, for example, his interest in the notion of homosexual *askésis* (which I discuss later in this essay) and by his insistence, in discussing dandyism in "What Is Enlightenment?" (41–42), on linking the ascetic and the aesthetic. For Hadot the relation between beauty and moral value, or the good, is quite different (see *Exercices spirituels et philosophie antique*, 231). As Hadot recognizes, what is ultimately at stake is not just differences of interpretation but basic philosophical choices ("Refléxions sur la notion de 'culture de soi,' " 261).

24 Arnold I. Davidson, "Spiritual Exercises and Ancient Philosophy: An Introduction to Pierre Hadot," *Critical Inquiry* 16, no. 3 (Spring 1990).

25 Pierre Hadot, *Exercices spirituels et philosophie antique*, 218. For more discussion, see my "Spiritual Exercises and Ancient Philosophy: An Introduction to Pierre Hadot."

26 Foucault, *The Use of Pleasure*, 9.

27 Ibid.

28 In what follows, I say nothing about the Wittgensteinian idea (which is distinct from that of a way of life and a style of life) of forms of life. My understanding of the latter idea follows Stanley Cavell, *This New Yet Unapproachable America* (Albuquerque, New Mexico: Living Batch Press, 1989), 40–52.

29 Pierre Hadot, "Forms of Life and Forms of Discourse in Ancient Philosophy" *Critical Inquiry* 16, no. 3 (Spring 1990), 491–92.

30 Hadot, *Exercices spirituels et philosophie antique*, Chapter 2.

31 Ibid., 51–52, 57, 225. For more discussion of this point, see my "Spiri-

tual Exercises and Ancient Philosophy: An Introduction to Pierre Hadot," 477–478.

32 Hadot, "Forms of Life and Forms of Discourse in Ancient Philosphy," 495.

33 Foucault, "L'herméneutique du sujet, 1981–1982," 148–49.

34 Michel Foucault, "The Concern for Truth," in *Foucault Live (Interviews, 1966–84)* (New York: Semiotext[e], 1989), 302.

35 Michel Foucault, "Friendship as a Way of Life," in *Foucault Live (Interviews, 1966–84)*, 206.

36 Ibid., 206–207.

37 Foucault, *The Use of Pleasure*, 50.

38 Foucault, "Friendship as a Way of Life," in *Foucault Live*, 205–207; "Sexual Choice, Sexual Act," in *Foucault Live*, 228; and "Michel Foucault. An Interview: Sex, power and the Politics of Identity," in *Advocate* (August 7, 1984).

39 Michel Foucault, "Michel Foucault. Le gai savoir," in *Mec Magazine* (June 1988), 34. See also "Michel Foucault. An Interview: Sex, Power and the Politics of Identity," in *Advocate*, 27.

40 Foucault, "Michel Foucault. An Interview: Sex, Power and the Politics of Identity," in *Advocate*, 27.

41 Foucault, "Sexual Choice, Sexual Act," in *Foucault Live*, 228.

42 Discussions with Pierre Hadot have made it clear to me that my claims here depend on the view, which I believe was Foucault's view, that homosexuality, as he wanted to understand it, could involve a style of life in the sense of a philosophical ethics. It is such an understanding that allows one to link ancient philosophical *askésis* and contemporary homosexual *askésis*.

43 The notion of the history of the present appears at the end of Chapter One of Michel Foucault, *Discipline and Punish: The Birth of the Prison* (New York: Vintage Books, 1979).

44 Jean-Pierre Vernant, "The Individual within the City-State," in *Mortals and Immortals, Collected Essays*, ed. Froma I. Zeitlin (Princeton: Princeton University Press, 1991), 321.

45 Ibid.

46 Ibid.

47 Ibid.

48 Ibid., 332. See Arnaldo Momigliano, "Marcel Mauss e il problema della persona nella biografia greca," in *Ottavo contributo alla storia degli studi classici e del mondo antico* (Roma: Edizioni di storia e letteratura, 1987). For related issues, see Paul Veyne, *Roman Erotic Elegy* (Chicago: University of Chicago Press, 1988).

49 Jean-Pierre Vernant, "Psuché: Simulacrum of the Body or Image of the Divine," in *Mortals and Immortals*. The quotation is from 190.

50 Vernant, "The Individual within the City-State," 330.

51 Ibid.

52 Ibid., 328–29, 332.

53 The first quotation is from Foucault, *The Care of the Self*, 42. The second quotation is from Vernant, "Psuché: Simulacrum of the Body or Image of the Divine," 192.

54 Pierre Hadot, *Titres et Travaux de Pierre Hadot*. Privately printed by the Collège de France, 28.

55 Pierre Hadot, "Le figure du sage dans l'Antiquité gréco-latine" in *Les sagesses du monde*, ed. Gilbert Gadoffre (Paris: Editions Universitaires, 1991), 13.

56 Paul Veyne, "La medication interminable" in Seneca, *De la tranquilité de l'âme* (Paris: Editions Rivages, 1988), 56.

57 Cited by Hadot in "La figure du sage dans l'Antiquité gréco-latine," 13.

58 Ibid., 11.

59 Ibid., 18, 12.

60 I shall not take up here the complicated question of the precise relation between the ideas of the *daimón* and the sage. Each of them corresponds, in a certain way, to a transcendent norm. But the *daimón*, which derives from religious psychology, is perceived as an active presence in the soul, while the sage is conceived of as an almost inaccessible ideal that orients and guides one's life. I am indebted to Pierre Hadot for discussion on this point. See Hadot, *Exercices spirituels et philosophie antique*, 102–103, 105–106; *La Citadelle intérieure. Introduction aux "Pensées" de Marc Aurèle* (Paris: Fayard, 1992), 92–93, 139–41, 176–77; and "La figure du sage dans l'Antiquité gréco-latine," especially p. 20.

61 See also Seneca, "Epistle XLI" and "Epistle CXXIV" in *The Epistles of Seneca*.

62 Seneca, "Epistle LIX" in *The Epistles of Seneca*. The quotation is from 417.

63 The first quotation is from "Epistle XXIII" in *The Epistles of Seneca*, 161; the second quotation is from "Epistle LIX" in *The Epistles of Seneca*, 417. See also "Epistle XLI" in *The Epistles of Seneca*.

64 Hadot, "La figure du sage dans l'Antiquité gréco-latine," 20.

65 See Pierre Hadot, "La terre vue d'en haut et le voyage cosmique. Le point de vue du poète, du philosophe et de l'historien," in *Frontiers and Space Conquest*, ed. J. Schneider and M. Léger-Orine (The Netherlands: Kluwer Academic Publishers, 1988); "Histoire de la pensée hellénistique et romaine: La physique comme exercise spirituel et le regard d'en haut," in

Annuaire du Collège de France, 1987–1988: Resumé des cours et travaux (Paris: Collège de France, 1988); and *La Citadelle intérieure*, 188–93.

66 Pierre Hadot, *Exercices spirituels et philosophie antique*, 46–47, 48–49. The relevant text of Plotinus is *Ennead* I, 6, 9. I discuss this passage and Hadot's interpretation of it at length in my introduction to Pierre Hadot, *Plotinus or the Simplicity of Vision* (Chicago: The University of Chicago Press, 1993). See also Jean-Pierre Vernant, "Psuché: Simulacrum of the Body or Image of the Divine," 192.

67 Hadot, *Exercices spirituels et philosophie antique*, 231.

68 Plotinus, *Enneads*, trans A. H. Armstrong (Cambridge: Harvard University Press, 1966); *Ennead*, I, 6, 9, 259.

69 Plotinus, *Enneads*, ibid. *Ennead*, I, 6, 6, 251.

70 Hadot, "La figure du sage dans l'Antiquité gréco-latine," 19–20.

71 Ibid., p. 19. See also Pierre Hadot, "Histoire de la pensée hellenistique et romaine: Interiorité et liberté chez Marc Aurèle," in *Annuaire du Collège de France, 1989–90: Resumé des cours et travaux* (Paris: Collège de France, 1990).

72 See, for example, Epictetus, *Manual*, 5 and Marcus Aurelius, *Meditations*, XI, 16.

73 Hadot, "La figure du sage dans l'Antiquité gréco-latine," 19–20.

74 Hadot, "Le Sage et le monde," 181.

75 Stanley Cavell, "Thinking of Emerson," in *The Senses of Walden* (San Francisco: North Point Press, 1981), 134.

76 Stanley Cavell, *This New Yet Unapproachable America*, 37.

77 Foucault, *The Use of Pleasure*, 28–32; Hadot, *Exercices spirituels et philosophie antique*, 13–14, 59–60. I bring together Cavell's and Hadot's work in "La découverte de Thoreau et d'Emerson par Stanley Cavell ou les exercices spirituels de la philosophie," forthcoming in *Lire Cavell*, ed. Sandra Laugier (Éditions de l'éclat).

78 Stanley Cavell, *Conditions Handsome and Unhandsome. The Constitution of Emersonian Perfectionism* (Chicago: The University of Chicago Press, 1990), 8–10.

79 Paul Veyne, "La medication interminable," 27.

80 Hadot, *Exercices spirituels et philosophie antique*, 37–47; "Forms of Life and Forms of Discourse in Ancient Philosophy," 494–495.

81 Foucault, "L'herméneutique du sujet," 160–166.

82 Ibid., 164.

83 Friedrich Nietzsche, *The Gay Science* (New York: Vintage Books, 1974), 273–74. I am indebted to Jim Conant for discussion of this point.

84 Seneca, "Epistle LIX" in *The Epistles of Seneca*, 419.

85 Foucault's seminar at the University of California, Berkeley, 1983, was

on the theme of *parrhésia*. His 1984 lectures at the Collège de France were also on this theme. In my characterization here, I follow Foucault's lecture of February 15, 1984, Collège de France.

86 Georges Dumézil, "Divertissement sur les dernières paroles de Socrate," in "*. . . Le Moyne noir en gris dedans Varennes*" (Paris: Gallimard, 1984); Foucault, Lecture of February 15, 1984, Collège de France. See also Eliane Allo's conversation with Dumézil, "Entretien avec Georges Dumézil à propos de l'interprétation de Michel Foucault, juin 1985," in *Actes de la recherche en sciences sociales* 61 (March 1986). The text from Plato's *Phaedo* occurs at 118.

87 For a brief statement of Dumézil's interpretation, see Eliane Allo, "Entretien avec Georges Dumézil à propos de l'interprétation de Michel Foucault, juin, 1985," 87. Foucault discusses the relevant texts at length in his lectures of February 15, February 22, and February 29, 1984, Collège de France.

88 This remark occurs at the end of Foucault's lecture, February 15, 1984, Collège de France.

89 On this topic, see Hadot, *Exercices spirituels et philosophie antique*, Chapter 3.

90 Foucault, "L'herméneutique du sujet," 145. On the history of the theme "know thyself", see Pierre Courcelle, *Connais-toi toi-même; de Socrate à saint Bernard* (Paris: Études Augustiniennes, 1974–1975).

91 Among the Old Testament texts I have in mind is Deuteronomy 4:9.

I am indebted to Diane Brentari, Stanley Cavell, Jim Conant, Jan Goldstein, Pierre Hadot, and David Halperin for comments on and discussions of earlier versions of this paper. This essay is dedicated to Pierre Hadot on his seventieth birthday.

JAMES W. BERNAUER

MICHAEL MAHON

6 The ethics of Michel Foucault

A recent ethics textbook aimed at university-level students, in listing the presuppositions of any ethical system, begins, "Singular
moral judgments are never merely singular." By their very nature
moral judgments are implicitly universalizable, and only "a peculiar
kind of irrationality" that "has come to infect contemporary thinking" could allow one to dispute this self-evident truth.[1] Aristotle
was mystified by those who claimed that a characteristic function
could be found for an eye, a hand, a foot, a carpenter, or a tanner, but
that none could be found for human beings in general. An ethical
principle, according to Kant, must be universally applicable if it is to
be considered as having any validity whatsoever.

Foucault, however, disconcerts. By claiming that there are no universally applicable principles, no normative standards, "no order of
human life, or way we are, or human nature, that one can appeal to
in order to judge or evaluate between ways of life," Foucault, according to Charles Taylor, relinquishes any critical power that his historical analyses might have.[2] Without such a "normative yardstick,"
according to Jürgen Habermas, Foucault's historical analyses cannot
be genuinely critical.[3] Indeed, Foucault's skepticism with regard to
the notions of universal human nature or universal rationality is
clear. He associates universal human nature with the Enlightenment doctrine of humanism, which provides a vision of the human
essence with which men and women are expected to conform, thus
offering a universal criterion of moral judgment. Humanism, however, has been so diverse in history that it fails to provide such a
universal, or even a coherent, doctrine for philosophical analysis:
Christianity, the critique of Christianity, science, anti-science, Marxism, existentialism, personalism, National Socialism, and Stalinism

141

have each worn the label "humanism" for a time. Enlightenment humanism borrows its conception of the human from religion, science, or politics, and imposes it upon all men and women, but this conception is tainted by the parochialism of its source. Foucault offers no alternative and refuses any surrogate, as Ian Hacking ironically phrased it, "for whatever it is that springs eternal in the human breast."[4] Each of these "humanisms," moreover, was intertwined with a distinctive type of rationality. "[I]t was on the basis of the flamboyant rationality of social Darwinism," for example, "that racism was formulated, becoming one of the most enduring and powerful ingredients of Nazism. This was, of course, an irrationality, but an irrationality that was at the same time, after all, a certain form of rationality."[5] Although he recognizes the necessity and indispensability of rationality, Foucault, with Kant, wants to analyze its limits, dangers, and historical effects: "How can we exist as rational beings, fortunately committed to practicing a rationality that is unfortunately crisscrossed by intrinsic dangers?" In opposition to any universal system of ethics founded on humanism or a monolithic conception of rationality, Foucault boldly proclaims that the quest for a morality to which everyone must submit would be "catastrophic."[6] But even though he questions humanism and rationality, Foucault never abandons ethical inquiry. Only through such an inquiry can we appreciate the contingency and inadequacy of our modern moral identity. Only through such an inquiry will the emancipatory resources of our specific historical situation be excavated.

The explicit ethical voice that sounds in Foucault's last writings possesses new accents, but his moral interest is certainly not novel.[7] In one of his earliest works, a meditation on the psychoanalytic theory of Ludwig Binswanger, Foucault claimed that dreams reveal "radical liberty" as the human essence, the matrix within which self and world, subject and object, appear. This experience of the dream is inseparable from its ethical content, "not because it may release the whole flock of instincts," but because it "restores the movement of freedom in its authentic meaning, showing how it establishes itself or alienates itself, how it constitutes itself as radical responsibility in the world, or how it forgets itself and abandons itself to its plunge into causality."[8] Psychology's proper goal, according to Foucault, is the person's victory over whatever alienates him or her from the reality of liberty, which the human person is essentially, over whatever alienates him or her from the historical drama that is the stage for human fulfillment.[9] In the light of his later examination of power-knowledge relations, Foucault corrected his description of the human person as radical liberty because a person "does not begin with liberty but with the limit."[10] A recognition of the limit, however, need not entail the abandonment of ethics; the encounter with the limit creates the opportunity for its transgression.

It would have to be a very critical transgression, for Foucault's ensuing work is a fierce criticism of the modern myths of and routes for the achievement of freedom: the liberation of the mentally ill in the asylum, the march of enlightenment in the human sciences, the reform of the imprisoned in the penitentiary, the liberation of the self in the overcoming of sexual repressions. In each of these movements of emancipation, Foucault discovered a process that he came to call "normalization," a narrowing and impoverishment of human possibilities. Although a primary effect of the institutions he analyzed throughout his writings is the social exclusion of certain individuals in asylums, prisons, and categories of deviance, the primary end of these institutions is to bind men and women to an apparatus of normalization.[11] The purpose of Foucault's genealogical analyses was to reveal that, despite their apparent necessity and naturalness, these institutions arose from quite contingent historical circumstances. He showed that they are not the only possible ways of dealing with social conflict, and opened the possibility of new modes of human interaction.

Although Foucault's passion for freedom in his last works, then, is not novel, it does speak with a new accent. In these last works on the history of sexuality he probes a new axis of intellectual responsibility: in addition to the domains of power-knowledge relations, he excavates a specific axis of the relationship to oneself, the ways we fashion our subjectivity. He recognizes techniques for an even deeper penetration of normalization and greater possibilities for transgression of these limits. This axis of subjectivity refers to the set of practices we perform on ourselves, and for Foucault ethics is essentially a mode of self-formation, the way we fashion our freedom. Ethics is the "process in which the individual delimits that part of himself that will form the object of his moral practice, defines his position relative to the precept he will follow, and decides on a certain mode of being that will serve as his moral goal. And this requires him to act upon him-

self, to monitor, test, improve, and transform himself."[12] Within this
dense formulation is Foucault's vision of ethical practice and its contrast with any ethics that would define itself as an abstract normative
code or customary conduct. This view led him to ask new questions
of himself and of the cultures he studied. How have individuals been
invited or incited to apply techniques to themselves that enable them
to recognize themselves as ethical subjects? What aspect of oneself or
one's behavior is relevant for ethical attention and judgment (the
ethical substance)? Under what rule of conduct do people subject
themselves, and how do they establish their relationship with this
rule (the mode of subjection)? In what type of activities do people
engage in order to form themselves, to moderate their behavior, to
decipher what they are, to eradicate their desires (the ascetics)? What
type of being is one attempting to become by means of these ascetical
practices (the *telos*)?[13]

Two moments are operative in Foucault's genealogies. The first
critical moment is a historical questioning of our existence, a historical investigation into the events that have led us to constitute
ourselves and to recognize ourselves as subjects of what we are
doing, thinking, saying. Second, genealogy separates out, from the
contingent circumstances that have made us what we are, the possibility of no longer being, doing, or thinking what we are, do, or
think. Corresponding to these two genealogical moments, this essay has two specific objectives: first, to understand how Foucault's exploration of the ethical aimed to undermine contemporary power-knowledge-subjectivity relations and why it aspired to
be a political ethic; second, to appreciate the fundamental structure of his positive ethic of self-formation. Before turning to these,
however, we will examine the immediate context for Foucault's
turn to the subject and ethical life.

The specific focus of Foucault's ethical concern is comprehensible
only in the context of his project for the history of sexuality, but he
was also motivated by two events in the political realm. The first was
the Iranian Revolution of 1978–1979. When he was criticized for his
initial sympathetic analysis of the revolution, Foucault refused to
dismiss the moral achievement of those who made the revolution
when it resulted in new political repression. He spoke of his ethics as
"anti-strategic," as irreducible to the question of political success.[14]

This acknowlegment of the specifically ethical was strengthened by his support of the Solidarity movement in Poland, where he had lived in 1958. When the movement was temporarily suppressed in 1982, Foucault was critical of the passive response made by Western governments. Although he recognized that military action was unacceptable, Foucault called for a clear attitude of protest, of ethical rejection that could itself become a political force.[15]

This orientation to an explicitly ethical perspective was decisively determined by his study of the Christian experience of sexuality, which he took up as part of his history of sexuality. Foucault's original 1976 plan for the series of additional volumes which was to make up the history opened with a volume, *Flesh and Body*, which was to present the establishment in Christianity of a sexuality centered on the notion of "flesh" as opposed to the modern understanding of the body. Although he never published the volume on Christian sexuality, the interpretation of Christian experience, as he worked it out in his courses, lectures, and articles, led him to a close interrogation of subjectivity.[16] Early Christian writers put forward a program that embraced not only relations of power and knowledge but also subtle relations of oneself to oneself. Since desires became the ethical substance for the Christian, that dimension of the self most relevant for ethical concern, the Christian was required to decipher these desires, to exercise a "permanent hermeneutics of oneself" demanding "very strict truth obligations."[17] More than merely knowing the truth of the moral life, the Christian needed to scrutinize himself or herself constantly as a desiring subject. In the monasteries of the fourth and fifth centuries, rigorous techniques of self-examination had been invented in response to this need: "Detailed techniques were elaborated for use in seminaries and monasteries, techniques of discursive rendition of daily life, of self-examination, confession, direction of conscience and regulation of the relationship between director and directed."[18] This self-surveillance, once reserved for monks, permeated Christian society as a whole by the sixteenth century. The importance Christianity accorded to this "pastoral power," this permanent concern with the total well-being of religious subjects, emphasized obedience as a paramount virtue and, thus, generated a struggle with one's desires, with oneself. This obedience was pledged, however, on the basis of a pastoral knowledge of oneself that was made up of each person's specific truths. Christianity encouraged a search for the truth of one's self, and this search was served by sophisticated practices of examination of conscience and confession.

These practices produced a unique form of subjectivization in the human being. The self is constituted as a hermeneutical reality, as an obscure text requiring permanent decipherment. Paradoxically, however, the purpose of the hermeneutic was to facilitate the renunciation of the self who had been deciphered. At the heart of religious life was the spirit of mortification, a unique ascetical relation to the self. Foucault's reading of the Christian experience of subjectivity and its embeddedness in power-knowledge relations prepared him for the realization that, in the modern period, no political issue is more significant than how the person is defined and how one's relationship to one's self is organized.

I. FOUCAULT'S POLITICAL ETHIC

Foucault planned his multivolume history of sexuality as an investigation of modern bio-politics, which he designated as those forces which "brought life and its mechanisms into the realm of explicit calculations and made knowledge-power an agent of transformation of human life."[19] Sexuality was the crucial field of operation for this bio-politics because it was located at the pivot of the two axes along which Foucault saw the power over life developing: access to both the individual and the social bodies. The most striking example he gives of how this power operated on an individual's life was Herculine Barbin, a nineteenth-century hermaphrodite. Born and baptized in 1838, Barbin was raised and lived as a girl for the next twenty years. Because of the development in her time of new and precise categories of a single, true sexual identity, a civil court intervened in her life and declared a change of gender status and name: on June 22, 1860, Mademoiselle Herculine became Monsieur Abel. Her neighbors were shocked by the transformation of their schoolmistress, and local newspapers published sensational reports; but in general people sympathized with Barbin, for, as the newspapers pointed out, she had "lived piously and modestly until today in ignorance of herself."[20] The sympathy failed to sustain Barbin. Eight years later he/she committed suicide, the victim, according to Foucault, of a new passion for the truth of sexual identity.

This passion presented a modern transformation of the Christian experience. Political treatises of the sixteenth to the eighteenth centuries tended to emphasize the immanence of the art of government; that is, governing political society is a pastoral matter, analogous to and continuous with the caring for "a household, souls, children, a province, a convent, a religious order, or a family."[21] This pastoral power "is essentially concerned with answering the question of how to introduce oeconomy, that is the correct manner of managing individuals, goods and wealth within the family (which a good father is expected to do in relation to his wife, children and servants) and of making it thrive – how to introduce this meticulous attention of the father toward his family, into the management of the State."[22] Later, in the eighteenth century, Rousseau advises introducing techniques for governing families into the art of state government, establishing "a form of surveillance, of control, which is as watchful as that of the head of a family over his household and his goods."[23]

Although pastoral power's aims may have become secular, the effect of its modern version is to fashion a type of individuality with which one's desire is incited to identify. Foucault articulates a political ethic in response to this modern operation. In addition to resistance against forms of domination and exploitation, a political ethic necessarily entails combat with a pastoral power that "categorizes the individual, marks him by his own individuality, attaches him to his own identity, imposes a law of truth on him which he must recognize," and that "makes individuals subjects." Because of the pastoral functioning of state power, present political struggles must "revolve around the question: Who are we? They are a refusal of these abstractions, of economic and ideological state violence that ignores who we are individually, and also a refusal of a scientific or administrative inquistion which determines who one is." If one side of this resistance is to "refuse what we are," the other side is to invent, not discover, who we are by promoting "new forms of subjectivity."[24]

As a result of this conception of the political struggle as a "politics of ourselves," the ethical perspective becomes central to Foucault's last work: How should one develop a form of subjectivity that could be the source of effective resistance to a widespread type of power? This is why he is able to speak of his final concerns in terms of "politics as an ethics."[25] The practice of a politically effective ethics requires as its prelude a defamiliarization of the "desiring man" who lies at the root of our willingness to identify with the form of subjectivity constructed for us in the modern period. This requires a genealogy of the modern subject, a historical analysis of the emergence of this form of subjectivity, in order to achieve a critical distance from our sedimented self-understanding. Genealogy reveals the contingency, even arbitrariness, of our apparently natural and necessary understanding of ourselves. A central enterprise of the second and third volumes in Foucault's history of sexuality, then, is to "investigate how individuals were led to practice, on themselves and on others, a hermeneutics of desire."[26] Such a genealogy constitutes a "historical ontology of ourselves," an investigation of how we have been fashioned and have fashioned ourselves as ethical subjects. While ethics is the domain of such an analysis, its aim is to provoke and sustain a form of resistance to newly recognized political forces.[27]

The significance and form of Foucault's genealogy of the subject of desire are best grasped if understood as a contribution to his "archaeology of psychoanalysis," the objective of which is to undermine modern anthropology and the notion of the self that is one of its firmest supports and expressions.[28] Freud offers the model of this notion of the self and thus is the principal target of Foucault's attempt to render the self freshly problematic. Taking Foucault's own consideration of Sophocles's *Oedipus* as a clue, we can see how his history of the subject of desire is the last campaign in his subversion of the psychoanalytic vision of the person.

Freud's interpretation of the tragedy of Oedipus is familiar. Oedipus's search for the truth "can be likened to the work of a psychoanalysis." He relentlessly pursues the truth of his identity, which is hidden far from his conscious awareness and shows itself tied to the dimension of desire and sexuality. The story possesses perennial appeal because we recognize ourselves in Oedipus. As Freud points out, "His destiny moves us – because the oracle laid the same curse upon us before our birth as upon him."[29] Perhaps the story attracted Foucault's attention because it portrays the major concerns of his own work: an examination of the branches of knowledge that constitute us as knowable beings and that offer us routes in our quest for self-knowledge; an analysis of the power relations generated by these branches of knowledge and the systems of dependence to which we subject ourselves in our search for the truth about ourselves; a study of how our subjectivity became intertwined with sexuality, how the truth of our sexuality became the hallmark of our true selves. In Foucault's earlier writings, especially *The Birth of the Clinic* and *The Order of Things*, the archaeology of psychoanalysis involved an identification of its power-knowledge relations, especially its dependence upon a medical model and its notion of the unconscious. In the first volume of his history of sexuality, the archaeology of psychoanalysis entailed a critique of the role psychoanalysis plays in the modern deployment of sexuality. Foucault's genealogy of the subject of desire, finally, excavates Freudian thought and the types of relationships of the self to the self operative there.

The Oedipal triangle of father-mother-son, according to Freud, is the dominant metaphor for understanding oneself and is, according to Foucault, the psychoanalyst's key instrument for governing individuals. The story of Oedipus, for Foucault, is not essentially a deep truth about ourselves "but an instrument of limitation and compulsion that psychoanalysts, since Freud, utilize in order to calculate desire and to make it enter into a familial structure which our society defined at a determined moment." Rather than the deeply hidden content of the unconscious, as Freud would have it, Oedipus is "the form of compulsion which psychoanalysis wants to impose on our desire and our unconscious." Rather than the fundamental structure of human existence, as Freud maintains, Oedipus is an instrument of power, "a certain type of constraint, a relation of power which society, the family, political power establishes over individuals."[30] This is not a distortion of the psychiatric establishment's role; from the very beginning, psychiatry's "true vocation," "its climate," "its horizon of birth," "its fundamental project," has been to be "a permanent function of social order."[31] Rooted in early Christian confessional practices, psychoanalysis is our modern theory and practice, moreover, which continues to fortify the priority of the subject established in western thought since Descartes.[32]

The logic of sex is the key to personal identity in our time. Our sexuality reveals us to ourselves, and our desire to have this secret self-knowledge revealed drives us to engage in discourse on our sexuality. How else can we explain the fact that modern men and women "would purchase so dearly the bi-weekly right to laboriously formulate the truth of their desire, and to wait patiently for the benefits of the interpretation?"[33] An immense strategy for producing truth has been constituted around sexuality: "We demand that sex speak the truth . . . , and we demand that it tell us our truth, or rather, the deeply buried truth of that truth about ourselves which we think we possess in our immediate consciousness."[34] Two ideas intersect in our time, according to Foucault: "that we must not deceive ourselves concerning our sex, and that our sex harbors what is most true in ourselves"; and at this intersection "psychoanalysis has rooted its cultural vigor."[35]

The greatest support for the psychoanalytic project as a normative discipline is the notion that sexuality is the index of one's subjectivity, of one's true self. The capacity of sexual desire to become the most revealing sign of our truest, deepest selves depends upon a long historical formation through which we were constituted as subjects in a special relation to truth and sex. Traditional Christian confessional practices were reconstituted in scientific terms. Psychoanalysis developed from the institutionalized confessional procedures of the time of the Inquisition and brought about a "medicalisation of sexuality . . . , as though it were an area of particular pathological fragility in human existence."[36] Postulated as the cause of numerous maladies, sex was subjected to interrogation whose full truth required authoritative interpretation: "Spoken in time, to the proper party, and by the person who was both the bearer of it and the one responsible for it, the truth healed."[37] This modern medical management of sexuality resides "at the heart of the society of normalization."[38]

While the historical fusion of subjectivity, sexuality, and truth is a legacy of Christian experience, that experience was the last of three moments in early western culture's constitution of this kinship. Foucault's final two volumes in the history of sexuality study the first two moments in the constitution of western subjectivity, the cultures of Classical Greece and the later Graeco-Roman period. The initial interrogation of the subject of desire grew from the soil of Greek ethics. The central problematic of this pre-Platonic ethic was the proper use of pleasures so that one could achieve the mastery over oneself that made one fit to be a free citizen worthy to exercise authority over others. Plato's examination of this question turned it into an ontological consideration of desire itself and its objects, and thus opened an inquiry into desiring man that would lead in time to the Christian hermeneutics of the self. Foucault briefly examines the transition to the latter in the third volume, discussing the formation of a culture of the self in the reflections of the moralists, philosophers, and doctors in the first two centuries of our era. Christianity brought this culture of the self to an integration that then became a partial model for the modern quest for self-knowledge.

Freud's interpretation of the Oedipus myth exemplifies this model of self-knowledge. Although he solved the riddle of the Sphinx with the answer "man," Oedipus remained ignorant of his own identity. This ignorance could be erased, however, for a knowledge exists that could reveal him to himself once he took responsibility to seek his secret self and to become subject to a master of truth. In our modern culture the program for self-knowledge, embraced as a vehicle for discovering one's uniqueness, merely reenacts power-knowledge-subjectivity relations. The quest for freedom is diverted into a series of illusory liberations from repression. Along with its appropriation of an earlier technology of the self that includes rigorous self-examination and confession, the modern age also fundamentally changed the relation to the subject that that earlier age produced. For Christians the truth of the self was always precarious because it always depended on the soul's continual struggle with the evil within it. There could be no firm allegiance to a positive self because there was no truth about the self that could not be used as a device for misleading the soul. Modern knowledge and technologies of the self aim, however, to foster the emergence of a positive self; one recognizes and attaches oneself to a self presented through the normative categories of psychological and psychoanalytic science and through the normative disciplines consistent with them. Thus, like Oedipus, we become victims of our own self-knowledge. For Foucault, this is an event of supreme political importance because this victimization fashions the potentially transgressive dimension of the person into yet another element of the disciplinary matrix that *Discipline and Punish* described as the carceral archipelago. If the struggle with this modern power-knowledge-subjectivity formation is a politics of our selves, the key campaign in that struggle will be a new mode of fashioning an ethical way of being a self.

2. FOUCAULT'S ETHICS OF FREEDOM FROM THE MODERN SELF

The task of self-formation that Foucault proposes has a specificity that reflects his own commitments as an intellectual. He seeks to develop not a normative ethics applicable to all, but a particular style that emerges from his own personal history of freedom and thought.[39] Even though his ethics extracts significant elements from both classical and Christian moralities, this recourse represents neither an idealization nor a return to the premodern. The elements he derives from earlier periods are integrated into a uniquely personal context, Foucault's effort to articulate himself as a moral thinker. Foucault's ethics is the practice of an intellectual freedom that is transgressive of modern knowledge-power-subjectivity relations. He embraced Kant's definition of Enlightenment as an *Ausgang*, an exit or way out, because it corresponded to the central concern of his own work, the need to escape those prisons of thought and action that shape our politics, our ethics, our relations to ourselves.[40] Embracing a transgressive experiment beyond Kant, his last writings declare the need to escape our inherited relation to the self, a declaration that complements and intensifies his earlier announcement of the "death of man." "What can be the ethic of an intellectual – I accept the title of intellectual which seems at present to nauseate some people – if not that: to render oneself permanently capable of getting free of oneself?" A special curiosity motivates his final works, the curiosity that "enables one to get free of oneself."[41] How is this desire to be understood?

It emerges largely as Foucault's response to reading Georges Bataille and Maurice Blanchot. Both saw that Nietzsche's proclamation of the death of God did not provide a "mandate for a redefinition of man," but rather revealed the absence of absolute boundaries. A morality after the death of God, according to Bataille, is one "not centered on the guarantee of social and individual life given us by the 'main precepts' but on mystical passion leading man to die to himself in order to inherit eternal life. What it condemns is the dragging weight of attachment to the self, in the guise of pride and mediocrity and self-satisfaction."[42] "The man-subject, the subject of his own freedom, conscious of his own freedom, is at bottom a sort of image correlative to God," Foucault argued in an exchange with Jean-Paul Sartre. "There has been a sort of theologization of man, the redescent of God on earth which in some fashion made the man of the nineteenth century theologized."[43] The death of man calls forth a similar mystical passion, a transgression of the self that seeks to establish itself as the ultimate reality in place of an Absent Absolute. Sartre tried to avoid reliance upon any positive conception of the self, but by introducing the notion of authenticity with its moral connotations, he affirms the requirement to conform with some notion of the true self. In place of Sartre's moral notion of authenticity, Foucault proposes the practice of creativity; "we have to create ourselves as a work of art."[44] Not to be confused with absolute emancipation, Foucault's ethics is thoroughly historically rooted; he subverts any otherworldly ideal of contemplative self-possession and insists that one's relation to the self be defined in terms of its movement within history. His ethics invites a series of critiques in the context of one's concrete historical circumstances and experimental transgressions of the self as these circumstances present it. The force of resistance, of revolt against modern power-knowledge-subjectivity relations, expresses Foucaultian spirituality: "It is through revolt that subjectivity (not that of great men but that of whomever) introduces itself into history and gives it the breath of life. A delinquent puts his life into the balance against absurd punishments; a madman can no longer accept confinement and the forfeiture of his rights; a people refuses the regime which oppresses it."[45] This breath of life manifests the human capacity to transcend any product of history that claims necessity.

To create oneself as a work of art requires an esthetics of existence, a task of stylization. Such expressions have been the source of grave misunderstandings of Foucault's ethics, misunderstandings that perceive him as calling for a return to a morality modeled on that of the ancient Greeks or, worse, as an invitation to an amoral estheticism. Having elevated the quest for beauty over all other virtues, it is claimed, the "*self* rather than the *world* and its inhabitants becomes the central focus of aesthetic enhancement" for Foucault. Thus, "Foucault's standpoint favors either an attitude of narcissistic self-absorption or one of outwardly directed, aggressive self-aggrandizement."[46] The notion of stylization does remove ethics from the quest for universal standards of behavior that legislate conformity and normalization, reducing men and women to a mode of existence in accordance with a least common denominator. It focuses upon the dimension of freedom distinctive of an individual's place or role in life. The liberty to transgress modern power-knowledge-subjectivity relations differs for the philosopher, the head of state, or the bureaucrat, and an ethics of stylization invites one to engage in struggle according to one's unique rootedness in the world and history. Rather than promoting self-absorption, moreover, Foucault deprives the self of the illusion that it can separate itself from the world. Medical, economic, political, and erotic dimensions of life shape the moral experience of the self, as his last works show; thus, Foucault always presents his notion of self-formation as a struggle for freedom within the confines of a historical situation. The subject for Foucault is an "agonism," a "permanent provocation" to the knowledge-power-subjectivity relations presented to us.[47] This agonistic self is "not the decontextualized self of inwardness, but a self that becomes autonomous through a stylization of the concrete possibilities that present themselves to us."[48] Foucault's ethics is an invitation to a practice of liberty, to struggle and transgression, which seeks to open possibilities for new relations to self and events in the world.

What is the necessity of these new relations? What are the stakes? The crucial but overlooked final section of Foucault's first volume on the history of sexuality, "Right of Death and Power over Life," reveals how high the stakes are: "wars were never as bloody as they have been since the nineteenth century, and all things being equal, never did regimes visit such holocausts on their own populations." The motivating force behind Foucault's attempt to subvert the Freudian linkage of truth-sexuality-subjectivity is the prevalence of the corresponding Freudian tendency to understand human existence as a struggle of life against death, eros against thanatos. Our souls have been fashioned as mirrors of our modern political terrain in which massacres are vital, in which there is a right to kill those who are perceived as representing a biological danger, in which political choice is governed by the sole option between survival or suicide.[49] Ethics for Foucault is a stylization, a mode of self-formation, that struggles against this perverse relation between life and death. In praise of Gilles Deleuze and Felix Guattari, Foucault calls their work "a book of ethics, the first book of ethics to be written in France in quite a long time," and by ethics he means a stylization, "a life style, a way of thinking and living." The distinctiveness of Deleuze and Guattari's ethics of stylization at our peculiar juncture in history is to incite us to struggle against fascism – certainly fascism of the historical variety which so successfully moved so many, "but also the fascism in us all, in our heads and in our everyday behavior, the fascism that causes us to love power, to desire the very thing that dominates and exploits us." As the Christian was provoked to drive sin from the soul, our distinctive task, our modern ethical task, is to "ferret out the fascism."[50] If *Discipline and Punish* shows that philosophical thought must struggle with the power-knowledge relations that would transform the human soul and existence into a mechanism, Foucault's history of sexuality points to the ethical task of detaching ourselves from those forces that would subordinate human existence (the Greek "bios," which Foucault employs) to biological life (the Greek "zoë"). An "esthetics of existence" resists a "science of life." To think human existence in esthetic categories releases it from the realm of scientific knowledge. It liberates us from endless self-decipherment and from subjecting ourselves to psychological norms. If psychology obliges human beings to decipher our truth in our sexuality, it is because psychology is rooted in biology and its identification of sexuality with life itself, thus binding us to the struggle with death. Modern biology's articulation of life in terms of the murderous laws of evolution engages our identity with our destiny of death. Human existence and civilization, since Freud, is essentially the contest of life against death (*Eros und Tod, Lebenstrieb und Destruktionstrieb*). Foucault's genealogy of the desiring subject is an act of transgression against the life and death struggle that bio-power has made the horizon of human existence.

Foucault's ethics, then, is not Nietzsche's "beyond good and evil" but is beyond life and death. Nor does it constitute a Nietzschean leap beyond common morality into a splendid isolation cut off from ethical and political solidarity.[51] Foucault committed himself to the cause of human rights, to the transformation of the plight of prisoners, mental patients, and other victims in both his theory and his practice.[52] He identified with Pierre Rivière and Herculine Barbin, in whose memoirs "one feels, under words polished like stone, the relentlessness and the ruin."[53] His thought moved toward an ever-expanding embrace of otherness, the condition for any community of moral action. Foucault's last writings put forward an ethical interrogation, an impatience for liberty, for a freedom that does not surrender to the pursuit of some messianic future but is an engagement with the numberless potential transgressions of those forces that war against our self-creation. The commitment to that task will inaugurate new experiences of self and human solidarity, experiences that will renounce the ambition of any abstract principle to name itself the human essence.

NOTES

1 Robert B. Ashmore, *Building a Moral System* (Englewood Cliffs, NJ: Prentice-Hall, 1987), 155.

2 Charles Taylor, "Foucault on Freedom and Truth," *Foucault: A Critical Reader*, ed. David Couzens Hoy (New York: Basil Blackwell, 1986), 93.

3 Jürgen Habermas, "Taking Aim at the Heart of the Present," *Foucault: A Critical Reader*, 108.

4 Ian Hacking, "The Archaeology of Foucault," *Foucault: A Critical Reader*, 40.

5 Foucault, "Space, Knowledge, and Power," *The Foucault Reader*, ed. Paul Rabinow (New York: Pantheon Books, 1984), 249.

6 Foucault, "Final Interview," *Raritan* 5, 1 (Summer 1985): 12.

7 The major texts for an understanding of Foucault's ethics are the three published volumes in the history of sexuality series: *The History of Sexuality I: An Introduction; II: The Use of Pleasure; III: The Care of the Self.* In addition to these are his scattered publications on Christian sexuality (see note 16 below).

8 Foucault, "Dream, Imagination and Existence," *Review of Existential Psychology and Psychiatry* 19, 1 (1984–85); 51–52.

9 Foucault, *Maladie mentale et personnalité* (Paris: PUF, 1954), 109–10.

10 "La folie, l'absence d'oeuvre" (1964), published as appendix to the 1972 edition of *Histoire de la folie à l'âge classique* (Paris: Gallimard), 578.

11 Foucault, *La Verdad y las Formas Jurídicas* (Barcelona: Gedisa, 1980), 127–28. This is a Spanish translation of five lectures Foucault delivered in 1973 at Pontificia Universidade Católica do Rio de Janeiro.

12 *The Use of Pleasure*, 28.

13 *The Use of Pleasure*, 26–28.

14 "Is it useless to revolt?" *Philosophy and Social Criticism* 8 (Spring 1981): 5.

15 "Politics and Ethics: An Interview" (with Foucault), *The Foucault Reader*. For Foucault's viewpoint on Poland and the crisis generated by Solidarity, see "En Abandonnant les Polonais, nous renonçons à part de nous-mêmes," *Le Nouvel Observateur* 935 (October 9, 1982): 36.

16 See Foucault's summary of his 1980 course in the *Annuaire du Collège de France* 80 (1980): 449–52. Also, "Omnes et Singulatim: Towards a Criticism of 'Political Reason,' " in *The Tanner Lectures on Human Values* 2 (Salt Lake City: University of Utah Press, 1981), 225–54; "Sexu-

ality and Solitude," *Humanities in Review* 1 (1982), ed. David Rieff (New York: Cambridge University Press, 1982); "The Battle for Chastity," *Western Sexuality: Practice and Precept in Past and Present Times*, ed. Philippe Ariès and André Béjin (Oxford: Basil Blackwell, 1985), 14–25; "L'écriture de soi," *Corps écrit* 5 (1983), 3–23. In addition, there are several discussions: "On the Genealogy of Ethics," in H. Dreyfus and P. Rabinow, *Michel Foucault: Beyond Structuralism and Hermeneutics*, 229–52; "The Regard for Truth," *Art and Text* 16 (Summer 1984): 320–31; "The Confession of the Flesh" in *Power/Knowledge*; and "Final Interview," *Raritan* 5, 1 (Summer 1985): 1–13.

17 "Sexuality and Solitude," 15.

18 "Confession of the Flesh," 200.

19 *The History of Sexuality I*, 143.

20 *Herculine Barbin, Being the Recently Discovered Memoirs of a Nineteenth Century Hermaphrodite*, 144. See also Foucault's introduction to the English translation of this book, vii–xvii.

21 "Governmentality," *Ideology and Consciousness* 6 (Autumn, 1979), 8.

22 Ibid., 10.

23 Ibid.

24 Foucault, "The Subject and Power" in Dreyfus and Rabinow, *Beyond Structuralism and Hermeneutics*, 212, 216.

25 The expression "politics of ourselves" comes from the lecture "Christianity and Confession" that Foucault delivered at Dartmouth College in November 1980; "politics as an ethics" comes from the interview "Politics and Ethics," *The Foucault Reader*, 375.

26 *The Use of Pleasure*, 5.

27 Foucault, "What Is Enlightenment?" *The Foucault Reader*, 46.

28 *The History of Sexuality I*, 130.

29 Foucault took a political approach to the Oedipus legend in three lectures at the Collège de France (January 16, 23, 30, 1980). Also see *La Verdad y las Formas Jurídicas*, 91. For Freud's interpretation, see Sigmund Freud, *The Interpretation of Dreams* in *The Standard Edition* 4, ed. James Strachey (London: Hogarth, 1973), 262.

30 *La Verdad y las Formas Jurídicas*, 37, 147.

31 "Confinement, Psychiatry, Prison" in *Politics, Philosophy, Culture*, 180–81, translation modified: "C'est la vraie vocation de la psychiatrie. Et c'est son climat, et c'est son horizon de naissance."

32 *La Verdad y las Formas Jurídicas*, 15. Cf. also *The History of Sexuality I:*, 45.

33 "The West and the Truth of Sex," 7.

34 *The History of Sexuality I:*, 69.

35 Ibid., and "Introduction" to *Herculine Barbin*, x.

36 "The History of Sexuality," an interview with Lucette Finas in *Power/Knowledge*, 191. Cf. also "The Confession of the Flesh," Power/Knowledge, 211.

37 *The History of Sexuality I*, 67.

38 "L'extension sociale de la norme," 213.

39 "Final Interview," 12.

40 "What Is Englightenment?," 34.

41 "The Regard for Truth," 29; *The Use of Pleasure*, 8.

42 Allan Stoekl, *Politics, Writing, Mutilation* (Minneapolis: University of Minnesota Press, 1985), 109; Georges Bataille, *Death and Sensuality* (New York: Walker and Company, 1962), 229–30.

43 "Foucault répond à Sartre," *La Quinzaine Littéraire* 46 (March 1–15, 1968), 20.

44 "On the Genealogy of Ethics," in Dreyfus and Rainbow, *Beyond Structuralism and Hermeneutics*, 237.

45 "Is it useless to revolt?," 8.

46 Richard Wolin, "Foucault's Aesthetic Decisionism." *Telos* 67 (Spring 1986): 84, 85.

47 "The Subject and Power," 222.

48 Reiner Schürmann, "What Can I Do? in an Archaeological-Genealogical History," *The Journal of Philosophy* 82, 10 (October 1985): 545.

49 For an important statement on this theme, see the last lecture of Foucault's 1976 course, which was recently published as "Faire vivre et laisser mourir: La naissance du racisme," *Les Temps Modernes* 535 (February 1991): 37–61. For general discussions of the theme, see Maurice Blanchot, "Michel Foucault as I Imagine Him" in *Foucault/Blanchot*, ed. J. Mehlman (New York: Zone Books, 1987); and Bernauer, "Beyond Life and Death: On Foucault's Post-Auschwitz Ethic," *Philosophy Today* 32, 2 (Summer 1988): 128–42.

50 Foucault, "Preface" to Gilles Deleuze and Felix Guattari, *Anti-Oedipus, Capitalism and Schizophrenia* (Minneapolis: University of Minnesota Press, 1983), xiii.

51 For an example of this view, see Stephen White, "Foucault's Challenge to Critical Theory," *American Political Science Review* 80, 21 (June 1986): 428–30.

52 For accounts of Foucault's political work, see Claude Mauriac, *Le temps immobile 3: Et comme l'espérance est violente*, especially 261–591; Bernard Kouchmer, "Un vrai samourai," in *Michel Foucault: Une histoire de la vérité* (Paris: Syros, 1985), 85–89; and Didier Eribon, *Michel Foucault* (Paris: Flammarion, 1989).

53 Foucault, "The Life of Infamous Men," *Power, Truth, Strategy*, ed. Meaghan Morris and Paul Patton (Sydney: Feral, 1979), 77.

7 "What is enlightenment?": Kant according to Foucault

I

Many commentators have noted a marked change of emphasis in Foucault's later thinking about issues of truth, ethics, and social responsibility. For some, this change was characterized chiefly by a certain relaxation of the skeptical rigor – the attitude of extreme Nietzschean suspicion with regard to truth-claims or ethical values of whatever kind – that had hitherto played a prominent role in his work. Thus, according to Roy Boyne, the shift can be located with a fair degree of precision as occurring between Volume One of *The History of Sexuality* (where Foucault's genealogies of power/knowledge seem to exclude all notions of truth, enlightenment, self-understanding or effective political agency) and the later, posthumous volumes where this doctrine gives way to a sense of renewed ethical and social engagement.[1] In this work, as Boyne reads it,

there is . . . the suggestion of a certain Utopian residue. It pertains to the exercise of discipline, but this time it is not so much a question of an alienating imposition, rather one of normatively reinforced self-regulation. . . . The stake in this contest is freedom. A self ruled by the desires is unfree. Therefore moderation equals freedom. Thus the exercise of self-mastery is closely connected to the state of freedom.[2]

This is not to deny that there remain great problems – especially from the standpoint of present-day cultural and gender politics – with Foucault's appeal to those techniques of self-fashioning that he finds best embodied in the ethos of Classical (Graeco-Roman) sexual mores. Although it offers an escape-route of sorts from his earlier outlook of cognitive and ethical skepticism, it still leaves certain crucial questions unanswered. Most important of these, Boyne points out, is the

159

question that has preoccupied thinkers from Plato to Kant and beyond: the relation between those various faculties of knowledge, practical reason, and esthetic taste whose claims philosophy has sought to
adjudicate. What is at issue here – especially since Kant – is the status of the subject (the knowing, willing, and judging subject) as pos-
sessor of a certain strenuously argued autonomy, a freedom of reflective or self-willed choice that finds no place in the phenomenal realm
of determinate causes and effects.

These difficulties are by no means peculiar to Foucault's project
or the wider post-structuralist enterprise. In fact, they are at the
heart of much current debate about the limits of moral philosophy
as traditionally conceived, the antinomies of Kantian ("formalist")
ethics, and the need for an approach that would take more account
of the contingent, historical, or situated character of real-world
ethical issues.³ But they are pushed to an extreme by Foucault's
insistence – still present in his later writings – that subjectivity is
constructed through and through by the various discourses, conventions, or regulative codes that alone provide a means of "esthetic"
self-fashioning in the absence of any other normative standard. For
on this account the subject is indeed nothing more than a localized
point of intersection, a product of the various contending forces
that define its very conditions of possibility. In the early Foucault –
the self-styled "archaeologist" of discourses, knowledges, and signifying systems – there is no real attempt to avoid this bleakly deter-
minist conclusion. What analysis uncovers as it digs down into the
stratified history of the present is a sequence of rifts in the order of
discursive relations, a sequence that reveals the diversity of truth-
claims from one epoch to the next, the utter lack of grounds – or
validity-conditions – for judging between these incommensurable
paradigms, and the fact that "man" (or the transcendental subject
of humanist discourse) has arrived very late on the cultural scene
and is even now heading for oblivion.⁴

In Foucault's middle-period texts this structuralist approach gives
way to a Nietzschean-Deleuzean rhetoric of forces, affects, and
power/knowledge differentials that would seem – on the face of it –
more amenable to notions of practical agency and will.⁵ But this
appearance is deceptive since he still operates with a minimalist
(indeed purely nominal) concept of the "subject" that gives no hold
for the treatment of substantive ethical or socio-political questions.

And the problem persists, as I have argued, even in those writings of his final decade where Foucault has a great deal to say concerning the self and its various formative mechanisms. What emerges is not as much a radical re-thinking of these issues as a shift in rhetorical strategy, one that allows him to place more emphasis on the active, self-shaping, volitional aspects of human conduct and thought, but that signally fails to explain how such impulses could ever arise, given the self's inescapable subjection to a range of preexisting disciplinary codes and imperatives that between them determine the very shape and limits of its "freedom." In this respect at least – with regard to its ethical bearings – Foucault's work continues to generate the same kinds of deep-laid philosophical perplexity.

Of course Foucault was alert to such criticisms and addressed them repeatedly in the essays and interviews of his last years. One response was his distinction between "morality" and "ethics," the latter conceived as an activity of disciplined self-knowledge in accordance with certain shared or communal norms, the former as a discourse of rule-bound abstract generalities with no real claim upon the self and its modes of jointly private and social fulfilment. Thus, "Care for the self is ethical in itself, but it implies complex relations with others, in the measure that this *ethos* of freedom is also a way of caring for others."[6] And again: "*Ethos* implies a relation with others to the extent that care for self renders one competent to occupy a place in the city, in the community ... whether it be to exercise a magistracy or to have friendly relationships."[7] For it is the greatest virtue of such ethical (as opposed to moralizing) thought that it places questions of value and human obligation where they belong in the context of a flourishing communal way of life, and thus helps to dissolve those sterile antinomies that have for so long plagued the axiology of Western (post-Classical) reason.

There is a parallel here with the argument of philosophers like Bernard Williams, who also put the case for a different way of thinking about ethical issues, one that would break with Kantian or other such "formalist" approaches, and would take more account of those contextual factors – the variety of culture-specific values, motives, and interests – by which we make sense of our day-to-day lives as moral agents.[8] And this is part of a wider movement of thought among liberals of various color who reject what they see as the overweening claims – the prescriptivist appeal to universal values or abstract principles – bound up with the philosophic discourse of Enlightenment. In its place they suggest a return to the alternative tradition that stresses the essentially communal nature of our ethical commitments and priorities, the fact that such values can only be realized through a project of shared endeavor. Some – like Alasdair MacIntyre – conceive this project in Aristotelian terms as a doctrine of the practical virtues that would find its highest good in a life devoted to the exercise of civic, domestic, and private self-perfection.[9] For others (among them thinkers of a liberal-pluralist persuasion like Michael Walzer) it is a matter of respecting the variety of values, moral viewpoints, or cultural "forms of life" that will always coexist in any genuine participant democracy.[10] And in support of such claims – as far as they are taken to require philosophical support – most often there is some reference to Wittgenstein or another proponent of an anti-foundationalist view, to the effect (roughly speaking) that those "forms of life" go all the way down, so that there is no way to justify one's beliefs, values, or ethical priorities other than by simply remarking that they make good sense for members of a given cultural community.

When this line of argument is pushed through, as by current neo-pragmatists like Richard Rorty, the upshot is to render "philosophy" pretty much redundant, along with any version of "enlightened" thinking – or critique of in-place consensus values – that claims to distinguish reason or truth from what is presently and contingently "good in the way of belief."[11] For, on their view, there is simply no point in appealing to grounds, principles, validity-conditions, precepts of "practical reason," or whatever, since the only thing that counts is the performative power to carry conviction with this or that "interpretive community."[12] And in the end such conviction will always be relative to the values and beliefs held in common by at least some significant proportion of the community concerned. That is to say, one can only be deluded in thinking to criticize "false" or "ideological" consensus beliefs if those beliefs make up the very background of tacit presupposition – the cultural "horizon of intelligibility" – against which such arguments have to be assessed. And in this case (as Rorty cheerfully concludes) we might as well give up the whole vain enterprise and acknowledge that, for all practical purposes, there is *simply no difference* – no difference that makes any difference – between truth and what presently counts as such by our own, albeit contingent and self-interested, cultural lights.

My point about Foucault can be put most simply by remarking that Rorty can recruit him with relative ease as yet another thinker who has been traveling this road toward something like a postmodern-pragmatist endpoint. Thus Rorty sees no great problem in playing down Foucault's more "radical" claims – his Nietzschean rhetoric, his activist injunctions, his heady talk of "power/knowledge," etc. – and playing up the theme of esthetic self-invention that supposedly aligns him with the liberal ironists and debunkers of Enlightenment wisdom. On this view, Foucault worked his way around to a position that was largely disabused of those old-fashioned ideas about truth, knowledge, emancipatory critique, or the "political responsibility of the intellectuals." Insofar as he cut these pretensions down to size – as by advocating the role of "specific intellectuals" in contrast to the "universal" types of an earlier (superannuated) epoch – Foucault wins Rorty's full approval. Where he lapses on occasion is in tending to suggest that the resultant "micropolitics" of localized struggle can effectively generate a dissident ethos that would run strongly counter to the currency of received (that is, "postmodern bourgeois liberal") values and beliefs. To this extent Foucault has failed to take his own best lessons to heart; chief among them is the fact that there is no secure vantage-point, no "sky-hook" (as Rorty engagingly puts it) on which to hang one's arguments, judgments, and criticisms, apart from the various kinds of suasive appeal that happen to work in some given cultural context. But of course Foucault knows this perfectly well, having always maintained an attitude of healthy skepticism with regard to the truth-claims of Enlightenment critique and their lack of any possible justification – least of all any transcendental grounding – except within the discourse (or the "final vocabulary") of an outworn philosophic culture. In other words, Rorty can read Foucault – along with Heidegger, Habermas, Derrida, Rawls, and a good many more – as basically a kind of half-way pragmatist, one who might as well complete the journey by dumping all that pointless "philosophical" baggage and easing himself back into the communal fold. For it is Rorty's belief that all these thinkers have been heading toward a pragmatist conclusion, despite their various unfortunate hold-ups along the way. And in Foucault's case (Rorty suggests) the problem can be got around easily enough by discounting his more grandiose or dramatic claims – those that would tend to disrupt the ongoing "cultural conversation" – and valuing his work for what it yields in the way of new vocabularies, metaphors, or styles of inventive self-description.

I am not suggesting for a moment that Rorty is right about Foucault, or that pragmatism is indeed where his arguments were always heading, give or take a few lapses into Nietzschean genealogy and suchlike frivolous pursuits. Indeed, one could instance numerous passages – early and late – where Foucault affirms just the opposite: that his researches into the history of penal institutions, of psychiatric practices, or gender-role construction should all be viewed primarily as active attempts to reshape the collective self-image and memory of Western culture, and thus to bring about desirable changes in the way we live now.[13] Certainly he showed small patience with interviewers who naively raised questions about the "relevance" of theory to practice, or who assumed that this relevance should somehow consist in a matching-up – a proven correspondence – between the themes of his writing and the activist concerns of his life as a public intellectual. From the Nietzschean standpoint such questions appeared strictly unintelligible, assuming as they did that theory or scholarship could exist in some realm of pure, disinterested knowledge, immune to the effects of institutional power or the motivating will to subvert or contest such power. On the contrary, he argued: these discourses were *performative* through and through, their truth-claims bound up with forms of disciplinary surveillance and control – or structures of instituted power/knowledge – that could be challenged only by a counter-discourse with its own performative efficacy, its own rhetorical power to redefine what counted as a relevant contribution to debate. All of which suggests that Rorty is absurdly wide of the mark in his effort to talk Foucault down to the level of an easygoing pragmatist exchange of views between like-minded partners in the cultural conversation.

On the other hand there is a sense in which Foucault lays himself open to just such a reading through his avowal of a Nietzschean-relativist stance in matters of interpretive validity or truth. Thus Rorty could argue that he has, after all, respected the spirit, if not the letter, of Foucault's texts; that it is the interpreter's prerogative to practice a form of strong-revisionist reading responsive to present-day cultural needs; and that Foucault was in any case a thoroughgoing skeptic as regards the claims of authorial intention or scholarly objectivity. More than that, he could answer – again with some show of Foucaultian warrant – that we miss the whole point of these texts if we think that they are in any way concerned to offer arguments, reasons, or justifying principles for the stance they adopt on various questions of an ethical or socio-political nature. For, in Rorty's view, this is just another relic of the old foundationalist paradigm, the assumption that anyone with a case to argue – or a new scheme of values to promote – will need to offer more by way of philosophical back-up than a mere appeal to consensus ideas of what is "good in the way of belief." But since Foucault is not a "philosopher" – since he labors under no such delusory burden – we should therefore read him as he asks to be read, that is to say, as a Nietzschean, strong self-inventor and source of new-found rhetorical strategies whose meaning is whatever we choose to make of it in pursuit of our own pet projects. "Such a reply would sound less shocking," Rorty remarks,

if one substituted "poet" for "philosopher". For as opposed to poets, philosophers are traditionally supposed to offer a "basis" for our moral obligations to others. . . . Unlike poets, they are supposed to be "rational", and rationality is supposed to consist in being able to exhibit the "universal validity" of one's position. Foucault, like Nietzsche, was a philosopher who claimed a poet's privileges. One of these privileges is to rejoin "What has universal validity to do with *me?*" I think that philosophers are as entitled to this privilege as poets, so I think this rejoinder sufficient.[14]

Such, according to Rorty, is the pragmatist outcome of the "ancient quarrel" between poetry and philosophy that Plato was the first to articulate, and whose latter-day offshoot is the long-running feud between continental and analytic schools. The issue has been resolved pretty much by default, he thinks, since we can now recognize (after Nietzsche, Heidegger, Derrida, et al.) that philosophy was always just another "kind of writing," a discourse peculiarly prone to denying its own poetic or literary character, but none the less rhetorical for that. In which case it is the merit of Foucault's later work to have taken this message to heart and come up with a strong revisionist line – a poetics of endless metaphorical self-fashioning – that simply collapses the notional difference between philosophy and its old antagonist.

I have taken this detour via Rorty's essay because it shows the extent to which Foucault can be misread by a well-disposed liberal commentator and also the way that such a reading can latch onto problems with Foucault's work – philosophical, ethical, and political problems – that tend to be ignored by other more devoted or *echt*-Foucaultian types. For in one respect Rorty is undoubtedly right: if you follow Foucault's skeptical genealogies to a point where the subject – the knowing, willing, and judging subject – becomes nothing more than a transient illusion, a "face drawn in sand at the edge of the sea," soon to be erased by the incoming tide, then this does give rise to some stark alternatives in the ethico-political realm. More specifically, it opens the way to Rorty's private-estheticist reading of Foucault by reducing the subject to a nominal entity – a vanishing-point or *tabula rasa* – with no scope for moral agency and choice unless through an act of pure, poetic self-invention.

It seems to me that Foucault found himself in the awkward position of one who sought to maintain a strongly oppositional or counter-hegemonic stance, yet whose outlook of extreme epistemological and ethical skepticism left him at the last with no ground on which to stand in advancing these dissident claims. This is nowhere more apparent than in the record of Foucault's repeated encounters with Kant, from *The Order of Things* (where Kant's philosophy figures as the merest of transient discursive paradigms) to the later writings where Foucault is engaged in what amounts to a full-scale revisionist reading of Kantian ethical themes. To pursue the often-complex and circuitous course of these encounters is, I think, the best way to grasp what is at stake in the current postmodernist turn against the discourse of Enlightenment values and beliefs.

II

The most crucial text here is Foucault's essay "What Is Enlightenment?," which took its cue (and its title) from a piece that Kant published in November 1784 in response to a call for disquisitions on this topic by the liberal *Berliner Monatschrift*.[15] Up to a point Foucault offers what could well be taken as a summary account, a faithful exposition of the various claims that Kant advances on behalf of Enlightenment and its ethico-political bearings. Thus: "Kant

indicates right away that the 'way out' that characterizes Enlightenment is a process that releases us from the status of 'immaturity.' "
By "immaturity" Kant means "a certain state of our will that makes
us accept someone else's authority to lead us in areas where the use
of reason is called for" (WIE 34). So Enlightenment is defined, in
Foucault's scrupulously Kantian terms, as a certain "modification of
the preexisting relation linking will, authority and the use of reason" (35). Its motto is Aude sapere ("Dare to know!"), and it must
therefore be construed "both as a process in which men participate
collectively and as an act of courage to be accomplished personally"
(35). But in presenting these claims in the mode of paraphrase or
shorthand synopsis, Foucault finds room for misgivings as regards
their "ambiguous" status, and in particular their failure – as he sees
it – to resolve certain issues in the realm of practical agency and
will. These doubts become steadily more prominent to the point
where commentary leans over into overt dissent or a form of immanent critique.

Thus Enlightenment is characterized by Kant on the one hand as
"a phenomenon, an ongoing process" and on the other as "a task and
an obligation." In which case there clearly is an issue – one confronted by numerous latter-day schools of thought, among them Al-
thusserian Marxism and the structuralist "sciences of man" – as to
how these two perspectives could ever be reconciled. "Are we to
understand," Foucault asks,

that the entire human race is caught up in the process of Enlightenment?
Then we must imagine Enlightenment as a historical change that affects the
political and social existence of all people on the face of the earth. Or are we
to understand that it involves a change affecting what constitutes the humanity of human beings? But the question then arises of knowing what this
change is. Here again, Kant's answer is not without a certain ambiguity. In
any case, beneath its appearance of simplicity, it is really rather complex
(WIE 35).

From this point his essay goes on to remark some of the further
problems – the antinomies, Foucault all but names them – that
emerge in the course of Kant's reflections on Enlightenment as "process" and "phenomenon." His treatment preserves an attitude of
qualified respect, at least when compared with those pages of arch-
skeptical commentary in The Order of Things where the Kantian

project appears as nothing more than a species of transcendental illusion, a mirage created, and soon to be erased, by the imperious order of
"discourse." Thus Foucault now acknowledges that "this little text is
located in a sense at the crossroads of critical reflection and reflection
on history" (38). Moreover, it marks the first occasion on which "a
philosopher has connected in this way, closely and from the inside,
the significance of his work with respect to knowledge, a reflection on
history and a particular analysis of the specific moment at which he is
writing and because of which he is writing" (ibid.).[16]

But these tributes have a double-edged character that emerges
more clearly as Foucault expounds what he takes to be the crucial
and unresolved tension within Kant's philosophical project. This
results from Kant's commitment to a notion of critique that, on the
one hand, takes rise in response to certain highly specific historical
conditions, while on the other hand claiming to transcend those
conditions through an exercise of the human faculties – of understanding, reason, and judgment – deduced a priori as a matter of
timeless, self-evident truth. On Foucault's reading, this latter must
be seen as a form of residual anthropomorphism, a humanist or
subject-centered philosophy that fails to take the point of its own
best insights as regards the radically contingent or historically situated character of all such truth-claims.

Thus Kant still figures – here as in *The Order of Things* – as one of
those thinkers whose will to contest and problematize existing relations of power/knowledge was itself the product of a finally un-self-
questioning drive to establish its own "enlightened" credentials.
And this despite the fact, which Foucault readily concedes, that any
competent, good-faith discussion of these issues will have to go by
way of a critical encounter whose terms always largely have been set
in advance by that same legacy of thought. In short, "We must try to
proceed with the analysis of ourselves as beings who are historically
determined, to a certain extent, by the Enlightenment" (*WIE* 43).
But to this extent, precisely, we shall have to acknowledge – unlike
Kant – that the Enlightenment project is (and always was) just one of
those manifold discursive paradigms, those shifting orders of language or representation that make up the structural genealogy of
Western reason. So the process of enquiring-back into this history of
thought will not – in Foucault's words – "be oriented retrospec-

tively toward 'the essential kernel of rationality' that can be found in the Enlightenment and that would have to be preserved in any event" (ibid.). On the contrary, such thinking "will be oriented toward 'the contemporary limits of the necessary,' that is, toward what is not or is no longer indispensable for the constitution of ourselves as autonomous subjects" (ibid.). Clearly this amounts to something more than a mildly revisionist reading of Kant, a modest proposal – in the history-of-ideas vein – that we take some account of social or circumstantial factors as well as substantive philosophical arguments. For Foucault's contention goes far beyond this amicable parceling-out of disciplinary domains. What it requires, in effect, is that we read Kant's philosophy as marked *through and through* by this error of mistaking culture-specific for a priori valid truth-claims, or "contemporary limits of the necessary" for limits intrinsic to our very constitution as thinking and willing subjects.

Thus it might well seem, on the evidence of "What Is Enlightenment?," that Foucault has scarcely altered his skeptical stance with regard to the agenda and entire axiology of Kantian critique. But this appearance is deceptive, as soon becomes clear as one reads further into the essay. For it is now Foucault's central concern to articulate an ethics premised on the values of autonomy, freedom, and self-determination attained though an exercise of practical will. And when he comes to describe this project in more detail, it turns out remarkably akin to Kant's own, as expressed in the famous threefold question "What can I know?, What should I will?, and What may I reasonably hope for?" The crucial difference in Foucault's way of posing these questions is that he treats them – in genealogical fashion – as belonging to a certain historically delimited configuration of knowledge, discourse, or the will-to-truth. That is to say, he rejects any version of the strong universalist premise that would hold such values to be more than contingent, more than just a product of our own (now waning) cultural attachment to the philosophic discourse of modernity. What remains of that delusory Enlightenment project is not so much "a theory, a doctrine, or . . . a permanent body of knowledge that is accumulating," but rather – in Foucault's carefully chosen words – "an ethos, a philosophical life in which the critique of what we are is at one and the same time the historical analysis of the limits that are imposed on us and an experiment with the possibility of going beyond them" (*WIE*, 50). And again, taking aim at the heart of Kant's distinction between reason in its "public" (critical) and "private" (doxastic or opinionative) modes:

criticism is no longer going to be practised in the search for formal structures with universal value, but rather as an historical investigation into the events that have led us to constitute ourselves and to recognize ourselves as subjects of what we are doing, thinking, saying. In that sense, this criticism is not transcendental. . . . it is genealogical in its design and archaeological in its method (45–46).

In fact, Foucault precisely inverts Kant's order of priorities. On the one hand, he demotes the claims of "transcendental" reason (or critique) to the status of a merely localized episode in the recent history of thought. On the other, he identifies truth – for all practical purposes – with the level of contingent events or shifts in the order of power/knowledge relations that can best be revealed through a jointly "archaeological" and "genealogical" approach. Insofar as the Enlightenment project survives, it does so in a sharply delimited or relativized form, as an impetus to the kind of investigative thinking – the enquiring-back into its own genesis and historical conditions of emergence – that can offer no hold for the truth-telling claims of old-style "universal" reason. To adapt Karl Krauss's famous remark about Freudian psychoanalysis: Enlightenment now shows up as a symptom of the condition for which it once professed to be the cure.

And yet, as Foucault very pointedly remarks, there is no question of simply having done with that entire heritage of thought, no way of jumping outside it (so to speak) into some alternative – maybe postmodern – terrain of disabused skeptical hindsight. Such, after all, had been the attitude evinced in those pages on Kant in *The Order of Things* where Foucault proclaimed the imminent demise of "man" as the specular figment of a discourse premised on obsolete (Enlightenment) truth-claims and values. If he is now less inclined to adopt this style of heady post-structuralist talk, it is because he perceives the risk it entails, that of "letting ourselves be determined by more general structures of which we may not be conscious, and over which we may have no control" (*WIE*, 47). In short, Foucault's wager is that we can in some sense keep faith with the project of enlightened critique, while acknowledging that in another sense – on the strong universalist or transcendental reading – that project has long since run its course and relinquished all claims to validity or truth. Thus "the thread that may connect us with the Enlightenment," he writes, "is not faithfulness to doctrinal elements, but rather the permanent reactivation of an attitude – that is, of a philosophical ethos that could be described as a permanent critique of our historical era" (42).

What this amounts to is an argument for decoupling ethics from any version of the old foundationalist paradigm, the idea on the one hand that self-knowledge comes about through an exercise of autonomous practical reason, and on the other that this involves a critical reflection on the powers and capacities – as well as the constitutive limits – of human knowledge in general. Of course Kant's philosophy goes a long and sometimes tortuous way around to establish the relation between knowing and willing, or the complex "architectonic" of the faculties within which the various orders of truth-claim find their legitimate place.[17] Moreover, he lays great stress on the need to respect these distinctions, especially that between phenomenal cognition and judgments in the ethico-political realm, since otherwise such judgments would ultimately fall under the laws of natural necessity, and would thus be deprived of their autonomous character, their standing as freely willed acts of assent to the requirements of morality and justice. In this sense it might be argued that Foucault – along with postmodernist skeptics like Lyotard – is merely following out the logic of Kant's own position when he seeks to drive a wedge between the truth-claims of Enlightenment reason and the project of ethical self-fashioning that survives the eclipse or demise of those claims.[18] Thus, "rather than seeking to distinguish the 'modern era' from the 'premodern' or 'postmodern,' I think it would be more useful to try to find out how the attitude of modernity, ever since its formation, has found itself struggling with attitudes of 'countermodernity' " (WIE, 39). In which case Foucault's revisionist reading would in fact be no more than a faithful rendition, an attempt to conserve this liberating impulse, or "to bring some measure of clarity to the consciousness that we have of ourselves and our past" (45).

So the Kantian questions still have a pertinence, a capacity to provoke critical reflection on the ways and means of enlightened self-knowledge that exist for us now as subjects inscribed within a certain culture-specific discourse. But on Foucault's account they need to be framed rather differently, re-cast in such a form as to exclude any notion of truth or critique as values transcending this localized context of utterance. Thus: "How are we constituted as subjects of our own knowledge? How are we constituted as subjects who exercise or submit to power relations? How are we constituted as subjects of our own actions?" (49). These are still recognizably the same kinds of question that have occupied thinkers in the modern or critical-enlightenment tradition, from Kant to Habermas.¹⁹ But they differ in respect of the one crucial point: that for Foucault self-knowledge can come about only through the exercise of a freedom – a space of individual autonomy – created in the margins or interstices of an otherwise ubiquitous will-to-power whose watchwords are "reason," "enlightenment," and "truth." Hence the single most important question for Foucault: "how can the growth of capabilities be disconnected from the intensification of power relations?" (48). And his answer – to this extent in common with Lyotard and other postmodernizing critics of Kant – is to shift the main burden of enquiry from the relationship between knowledge and ethics (as developed chiefly in the first two *Critiques*) to the relationship between ethics and esthetics (as taken up in the *Critique of Judgment* with reference to the beautiful and the sublime).²⁰ For it then becomes possible to re-write the history of the present in terms of an elective genealogy that downplays the critical-enlightenment aspects of the modern, and that instead stresses the esthetic dimension – the very different "modernity" of a poet like Baudelaire – by way of contesting that other line of descent.

What is at issue here is an ambivalence that inhabits the key-word *modern* – almost, one could say, an elaborate pun on the meanings of that term – whereby it comes to signal the passage from philosophy to poetry, or from Kantian critique to the symbolist project of autonomous self-creation through esthetic means. "For the attitude of modernity," Foucault writes,

the high value of the present is indissociable from a desperate eagerness to imagine it, to imagine it otherwise than it is. . . . Baudelairean modernity is an exercise in which extreme attention to what is real is confronted with the practice of a liberty that simultaneously respects this reality and violates it (*WIE*, 41).

Hence the great difference between Kant's and Foucault's ways of answering the question "What Is Enlightenment?" For Kant, it is a matter of attaining intellectual and moral maturity through the exercise of criticism in its various modes, whether applied to issues of theoretical understanding (where intuitions must be "brought under" adequate concepts), to questions of an ethical or political order (where practical reason supplies the rule), or to issues in the sphere of esthetic judgment where the relevant tribunal can only be that of an intersubjective community of taste appealing to shared principles or criteria of value. For Foucault, on the contrary, this doctrine of the faculties is the merest of "transcendental" illusions, an elective self-image whose hold upon the discourse of Enlightenment was soon to be eclipsed by an advent of a "counter-modernism," a primarily artistic and literary ethos possessed of no such grandiose philosophical ideas. So it is that the esthetic moves to center stage as the focal point for everything that challenges, eludes, or subverts the truth-claims of Enlightenment critique.

Thus, "modern man, for Baudelaire, is not the man who goes off to discover himself, his secrets and his hidden truth; he is the man who tries to invent himself" (*WIE*, 42). It is here, midway through his essay, that Foucault abruptly switches over from discussing modernity as a project of enlightened or truth-seeking thought to a sequence of reflections on Baudelaire, estheticism, and the ethos of poetic self-fashioning conceived as the hallmark of the authentically modern. His main text is Baudelaire's well-known essay on the painter Constantin Guys, an artist of the everyday, of fleeting impressions, of humdrum realities that are somehow "transfigured" into something more profound and revealing.[21] Thus Guys,

"in appearance a spectator, a collector of curiosities," should rather be seen (in Baudelaire's words) as "the last to linger wherever there can be a glow of light, an echo of poetry, a quiver of life or a chord of music; wherever a passion can *pose* before him, wherever natural man and conventional man display themselves in a strange beauty, wherever the sun lights up the swift joys of the *depraved animal*" (41).

What Foucault seeks to emphasize by citing these and similar observations from Baudelaire's essay is the passage, as he sees it, from a discourse of modernity premised on outmoded (Enlightenment) ideas of knowledge, reason, and truth, to a modernism that not only accepts its condition as a localized, ephemeral state of awareness but also turns this predicament into a source of new-found imaginative strength by ironically "heroizing" the present moment and the scope it offers for esthetic self-creation. In short, "this deliberate, difficult attitude consists in recapturing something eternal that is not beyond the present instant, nor behind it, but within it" (39).

For Baudelaire, as indeed for Kant, modernity is characterized as a break with tradition, a sense of the "discontinuity of time" and the lack of those taken-for-granted certitudes – those items of received commonsense knowledge – that had once seemed to offer enough in the way of ontological or ethical assurance.[22] But where Kant conceived this break as a coming-to-maturity through the exercise of autonomous critical reason, Baudelaire imagines it – in high Romantic fashion – as the discovery of ever more-inventive variations on the theme of esthetic self-invention. And Foucault follows Baudelaire, rather than Kant, in equating modernity with that spirit of perpetual transformation, the "feeling of novelty, of vertigo in the face of the passing moment" that alone enables us to grasp what is authentic in our experience of contemporary art-forms and life-styles alike. For it is precisely in "the ephemeral, the fleeting, the contingent" that consciousness discovers its true vocation as a register of novel modes and intensities of feeling, such as cannot be perceived, much less theorized, by a philosophy still wedded to Enlightenment notions of reason, truth, and critique. What this amounts to, on Foucault's interpretation, is a decisive break with those humanist motifs that attached themselves to the discourse of Kantian critical philosophy, and that prevented it – so he argues – from moving beyond its subject-centered or anthropological orgins. "Humanism serves to colour and to justify the conception of man to which it is, after all, obliged to take recourse" (WIE, 44). But with Baudelaire and the ethos of esthetic self-fashioning, there enters an alternative notion of modernity, one that renounces any such appeal to man as transcendental subject or constitutive source of knowledge and truth. Humanism can thus be opposed, as Foucault now thinks, "by the principle of a permanent critique and a permanent creation of ourselves in our autonomy: that is, a principle that is at the heart of the historical consciousness that the Enlightenment has of itself" (44).

The word critique has here acquired a meaning very different from that assigned to it by Kant, or indeed by any of those thinkers, including Marxists, who took it to imply some determinate relation to matters of epistemological warrant, or to issues of truth and falsehood conceived as something more than what is "good in the way of belief." It has undergone much the same kind of semantic shift as emerges in Foucault's revisionist usage of the terms *modernity* and *enlightenment.* That is to say, these words are no longer construed as signaling a decisive difference in the way that criticism bears upon the currency of commonsense or taken-for-granted knowledge. Now it is a matter of perpetual self-transformation, a process carried on in the absence of truth-claims or validating grounds, and aimed, very much as Rorty conceives it, toward an ethos of "private" (esthetic) fulfillment that would render such notions altogether otiose. This is why Foucault reads Kant with Baudelaire: in order to facilitate the otherwise dubious (not to say sophistical) move that redefines *modernity, enlightenment,* and *critique* on his own preferential terms. "This ironic heroization of the present, this transfiguring play of freedom with reality, this ascetic elaboration of the self – Baudelaire does not imagine that these have any place in society itself, or in the body politic. They can only be produced in another, a different place, which Baudelaire calls art" (*WIE,* 42).

As we have seen, this is just the line that Rorty adopts in debunking the upholders of a public, that is, a politically engaged or civic, morality that would amount to something more than an attitude of benign disregard for whatever goes on in the private-individual sphere. Thus it does lend a certain prima facie plausibility to Rorty's claim that Foucault was a good neo-pragmatist at heart, despite his occasional lapses into other, more "radical" (and hence self-deluding) styles of talk. For the upshot of Foucault's revisionist reading of Kant is to *estheticize* issues of politics, morality, and social justice to the point where they become, in his own words, a "transfiguring play of freedom with reality," an "ascetic elaboration of the self" worked out by the Nietzschean strong individual in pursuit of his or her own desires, or in accordance with that mode of private self-fashioning, that "ironic heroization of the present . . . which Baudelaire calls art."

It is largely by means of this semantic slide, this elision of the difference between *ascesis* and *aesthesis,* that Foucault so adroitly negotiates the passage from Kant to Baudelaire. That is to say, it enables him to move – with at least some show of textual and historical warrant – from an ethics grounded in the maxims and postulates of enlightened practical reason to an ethics premised on the Nietzschean will to treat existence as "justified" solely to the extent that we can view it "as an esthetic phenomenon." And it is for this reason also – as I have argued above – that Foucault's late texts can so easily be appropriated by a postmodern-pragmatist thinker such as Rorty. For those texts undoubtedly lend credence to Rorty's view that "Foucault, like Nietzsche, was a philosopher who claimed a poet's privileges," and that "one of these privileges is to rejoin 'What has universal validity to do with *me?' "*[23] From this point Rorty, having set up the Kantian "universal" moralist as a target for the usual range of knock-down arguments, then proceeds to enlist Foucault as an ally in what he takes to be the only viable alternative, a project of "esthetic" self-fashioning that renounces any claim to normative validity beyond the individual or private domain. In short, there is no reason why a strong revisionist or poet-philosopher like Foucault should feel himself obliged to answer such questions as "Where do you stand?" or "What are your values?" And if he does so answer, then the best response is, "I stand with you as fellow-citizens, but as a philosopher, I stand off by myself, pursuing projects of self-invention which are none of your concern."[24] All of which follows, as can hardly be denied, from the estheticizing impulse – the strain of high romantic or counter-Enlightenment thought – that motivates Foucault to read Kant *avec* Baudelaire, thereby constructing his own (decidedly inventive) "history of the present."

III

No doubt it will be said, with some justice, that when Rorty welcomes Foucault as a convert to this way of thinking, he is obliged to discount the whole dimension of Foucault's work that bore very directly on issues of a wider (socio-political) import. There is no denying his record of involvement with pressure-groups and activist campaigns concerned with (for instance) racial discrimination, abuses of psychiatric medicine, the persecution of "deviant" minorities, sexual transgressors, victims of the French penal system. Moreover, these concerns also found expression in a series of powerfully argued works (from *Madness and Civilization* and *The Birth of the Clinic* to *Discipline and Punish, Pierre Rivière,* and the three-volume *History of Sexuality*) that leave no doubt as to Foucault's belief that scholarship and "theory" cannot be divorced from real-world issues of moral and political conscience. In this respect he clearly belongs to that company of left-dissident intellectuals – Noam Chomsky and Edward Said among them – who, whatever their differences, stand worlds apart from the self-engrossed frivolities of current postmodernist fashion.[25] All this I would willingly concede, along with the fact that Foucault's writings have undoubtedly done more than most to sustain the existence of a genuine oppositional culture – a "counter-public-sphere," in Habermasian parlance – during these past two decades of concerted right-wing ideological offensives. My point is not to detract from this achievement, which in any case speaks for itself through the range and vitality of debates sparked off by Foucault's various interventions. What interests me more is the odd disjunction – the lack of theoretical fit – between Foucault's highly effective practice as a critical intellectual and the way that he persistently (not to say perversely) deploys every means, in his more speculative writings, to render such a practice untenable. For those writings could be seen to undermine the very ground – the very conditions of possibility for critical discourse – on which he nonetheless and *necessarily* claimed to stand when pursuing his other (historically and politically oriented) lines of research.

In short: there is a near-schizophrenic splitting of roles between (a) Foucault the "public" intellectual, thinking and writing on behalf of those subjects oppressed by the discourses of instituted power/knowledge, and (b) Foucault the avowed esthete, avatar of Nietzsche and Baudelaire, who espouses an ethos of private self-fashioning and an attitude of sovereign disdain toward the principles and values of enlightened critique. That he managed to negotiate the tensions of this dual identity, although not without visible signs of strain, is I think one of the more remarkable aspects of Foucault's life and work. For Rorty, of course, this is simply not a problem, or not one that a strong revisionist like Foucault ever needed to confront, having thought his way through and beyond all those tedious old debates about truth, enlightenment, ethical responsibility, the "political role of the intellectuals," and so forth. Thus we ought to be content, Rorty urges, with a reading of Foucault that honors him, like Freud, for "helping us to see ourselves as centerless, as random assemblages of contingent and idiosyncratic needs" and for thereby opening up "new possibilities for the aesthetic life."²⁶ But the signs of tension are there, as I have argued, in Foucault's protracted series of engagements with Kant, in the talk of "truth" – however elusively defined – that figures so often in his late essays and interviews, and above all in his growing resistance to that strain of facile ultra-relativist talk that forms such a prominent (and depressing) feature of the avant-garde cultural scene. All of which suggests that he cannot be so easily recruited to a postmodern-pragmatist or counter-enlightenment ethos whose watchwords are the "end of philosophy," the demise of Enlightenment critique, and the eclipse of the subject – the Kantian knowing, willing, and judging subject – as a phantom entity whose lineaments have now dissolved into a "random assemblage [of] contingent and idiosyncratic needs." For this is simply to say – whether wittingly or not – that we should look back to Hume, rather than Kant, as an elective precursor for the "new possibilities" that arise with the postmodern passage to a discourse relieved of those old, subject-centered concepts and values. But in Foucault's later writings this idea meets up with a good deal of principled resistance, whatever his attraction – as detailed above – to that wholesale estheticizing impulse that would otherwise bring him out squarely in accord with the Hume-Nietzsche-Rorty line of argument.

What is at issue in these texts is the notion that truth can be relativized to the point where it becomes nothing more than a reflex product of the epistemic will-to-power, a symptom – as thinkers like Lyotard would have it – of the old meta-narrative drive to transcendence bound up with the philosophic discourse of modernity.²⁷ Such had no doubt been Foucault's position in his early "archaeologies" of knowledge, including those remarkable (if also highly questionable) pages on Kant in *The Order of Things*. And it emerges again – yet more emphatically – in his middle-period essays (such as "Nietzsche, Genealogy, History") where truth-claims are exposed to all the skeptical rigors of a thoroughgoing relativist creed, a Nietzschean "transvaluation of values" pushed to the very limits (and beyond) of rational intelligibility. But what Foucault came to recognize as his work went on – notably his detailed researches into ethics, sexuality, and the modes of self-knowledge entailed by these emergent disciplines of conduct and thought – was that they made sense only from a critical viewpoint informed by certain distinctively "enlightenment" values and presuppositions. Hence his remark that "thought is not what inhabits a certain conduct and gives it its meaning," but is rather "what allows one to step back from this way of acting or reacting, to present it to oneself as an object of thought and question it as to its meaning, its conditions, and its goals."[28] This passage is Kantian not only in the minimal sense that it raises certain questions – of agency, autonomy, ethical conduct, reflective self-knowledge etc. – which were also some of Kant's most important concerns throughout the three *Critiques*. My point is rather that it views them as standing in a complex *but accountable* order of relationship, an order whose specific modalities (like the relations between "acting" and "reacting," "conduct" and "thought," the "meaning" of action and its "conditions" or "goals") are described in terms that suggest a very close resemblance to Kant's project of thought.

Not that one could plausibly interpret Foucault as engaged in a covert campaign to resuscitate the Kantian doctrine of faculties in anything like its original form. What can be said, on the evidence of this and similar passages, is that Foucault came around to a viewpoint strikingly at odds with his earlier (skeptical-genealogical) approach, and that one major consequence – manifest in all his later work – was a radical re-thinking of the subject's role in relation to issues of truth, critique, self-knowledge, and practical reason. The following reflections from a 1984 interview are so clearly indicative in this regard that they merit lengthy citation.

To say that the study of thought is the analysis of a freedom does not mean one is dealing with a formal system that has reference to itself. Actually, for a domain of action, a behavior, to enter the field of thought, it is necessary for a certain number of factors to have made it uncertain, to have made it lose its familiarity, or to have provoked a certain number of difficulties around it. These elements result from social, economic, or political processes. But here their only role is that of instigation. They can exist and perform their action for a very long time, before there is effective problematization by thought. And when thought intervenes, it doesn't assume a unique form that is the direct result or the necessary expression of those difficulties; it is an original or specific response – often taking many forms, sometimes even contradictory in its different aspects – to these difficulties, which are defined for it by a situation or a context and which hold true as a possible question.[29]

Again, this passage goes beyond the mere rehearsal of vaguely Kantian themes and issues. What it raises most crucially is the question – much debated by present-day exegetes – as to how far Kant's dictates of "practical reason" must be seen as just a set of empty abstractions, a universalist morality devoid of ethical substance, or (in Foucault's words) as "a formal system that has reference [only] to itself." Such had, I think, been Foucault's view when he composed those pages in *The Order of Things* where man, or the Kantian "transcendental subject," figures in precisely that negative role, as delusory figment of a discourse premised on its own purely circular or self-confirming "system" of quasi-universal concepts and categories. And in his subsequent work – notably *The History of Sexuality* – he remained committed to a genealogical approach that stressed the specificities of context, the social and historical conditions of emergence for various ethical codes, rather than anything remotely akin to Kant's universalist maxims. Yet it is also the case, as the above passage makes clear, that Foucault came to think of these conditions as intelligible only from the critical standpoint of an ethics that "problematized" past or present modes of conduct and belief, which thus allowed thought to intervene with the effect of "provoking difficulties" around them. And it is by virtue of this thinking intervention, he argues, that discourse transcends its confinement to the currency of in-place consensus values – those that belong to a given "situation" or "context" – and attains a more properly ethical perspective.

This is not to deny that Foucault comes out in favor of a heterodox reading of Kant, one that treats ethics as primarily a matter of fashioning the self in accordance with techniques – or inventive variations on the strong individualist *rapport-à-soi* – analogous to those of the symbolist poet. As he puts it in a 1983 interview: "What strikes me is the fact that in our society, art has become something which is related only to objects and not to individuals, or to life. That art is something which is specialized or is done by experts who are artists. But couldn't everyone's life become a work of art? Why should the lamp or the house be an art object, but not our lives?"[30]

What such an attitude promotes, as I have argued elsewhere, is a wholesale estheticization of ethics and politics that typically seizes upon certain passages in Kant, most often passages that work by way of analogy or figural comparison, and treats them as a pretext for maximizing the gulf between issues of knowledge or truth, on the one hand, and issues of ethical accountability, on the other.[31] Of course this reading finds warrant – up to a point – in Kant's appeal to the tribunal of taste (in particular, to our judgments of the beautiful) as a means of suggesting how ethical judgments can claim intersubjective warrant without the recourse to determinate concepts that would render such judgments otiose. And it is further borne out (as postmodernist commentators often remark) by those passages from the third *Critique* where Kant invokes the sublime as an analogue for that which absolutely exceeds our powers of cognitive or phenomenal grasp, and which thus – through an inward or reflective movement of thought – gives access to the realm of "suprasensible" ideas. Such passages undoubtedly justify the claim that, for Kant, there exists a certain affinity between issues of esthetic judgment and questions in the realm of ethics (or practical reason). But it is equally clear to any attentive reader that Kant never seeks to conflate these realms in the current postmodernist fashion. Nor does he argue, like Lyotard, for a drastically antinomian version of the Kantian sublime, one that would enforce the radical "heterogeneity" of cognitive and evaluative phrase-regimes, and thus (in effect) create an insuperable gulf between matters of factual understanding and questions of ethical judgment.[32] To be sure, Kant goes a long way around – and deploys a variety of oblique or analogical arguments – in his address to this most problematical of boundary-disputes in the three *Critiques*. But he nowhere endorses the kind of postmodernist (or estheticist) reading that would treat ethical issues as wholly divorced from questions of circumstantial warrant.

Such readings can be seen as the most extreme variant of that objection to the supposed "formalism" of Kantian ethics that Hegel was the first to articulate, and that is nowadays taken up by critics of a liberal-communitarian persuasion. From this point of view, it is a matter of choice between, on the one hand, an abstract, rule-based morality of generalized precepts or maxims and, on the other, an ethics that would sensibly renounce such presumptive universalist claims and take account of the contingencies – the range of social, cultural, political and other such irreducibly context-specific factors – that people have to cope with in their everyday lives as situated moral agents. And from here it is no great distance to Rorty's postmodern-neopragmatist outlook, that is to say, his suggestion that we give up the misguided quest for reasons, principles, ideas of justice, validating grounds or whatever, and view ourselves rather as creatures whose identity consists in nothing more than a "random assemblage" of "contingent and idiosyncratic needs." For in this way, he thinks, we can best learn to live without those old (henceforth obsolete) ideas, while also enjoying a new-found sense of open-ended creative possibility, a freedom to devise all manner of novel "vocabularies" in the quest for better, more adventurous modes of self-description.

Such is the private-estheticist ethos that Rorty proposes as an antidote to Kant, an escape-route from the "formalist" rigors that he, like the liberal-communitarians, finds so objectionable in Kantian ethics. For Foucault, likewise, it appears to offer an alternative to the whole tradition of Enlightenment ethical discourse, a means of conceiving the autonomous self and its actions, thoughts, and desires in such a way that it would no longer be subject to the vexing antinomies of Kantian practical reason. It would rather be a question of promoting, in Foucault's words, "the reflective and voluntary practices by which men not only fix the rules of their conduct, but seek to transform themselves, to modify themselves in their singular being, and to make of their life a work which bears certain aesthetic values and obeys certain stylistic rules."[33] These *values* and *rules* must therefore be thought of as somehow intrinsic to the self, as belonging to that range of voluntary practices (or self-willed disciplinary techniques) by which subjects are "modified in their singular being" and thereby achieve, like Baudelaire's "man of modernity," the greatest measure of autonomy in conduct and thought. Indeed, one is mistaking the import of Foucault's argument if one uses (as I did just now) these two distinct terms – subject and self – as if they were more-or-less synonymous or simply interchangeable. For it is precisely his point that the *subject* as conceived within an ethical discourse like Kant's is always a product of that imaginary, specular mode of self-relation that generates the various endemic conflicts and antinomies of humanist thought. What is required is therefore a non-subject-centered discourse, one that views the self "in [its] singular being" as the locus of those various practices and rules by which the process of self-transformation somehow comes about. Only thus, so it seems, can thinking regain that long-lost ethical vocation that had not yet suffered the fatal swerve toward forms of internalized conflict or imaginary misrecognition.

Hence Foucault's main purpose in the later volumes of *The His-*

tory of Sexuality: to show how it was that the Classical ethos of disciplined, esthetic self-fashioning gave way to a range of ethical standpoints – whether Stoic, Christian, Kantian, Freudian or whatever – that envisaged the subject as a site of conflict between opposed principles or value-systems. But one can see very clearly from the above-cited passage, as well as from my tortuous commentary upon it, that Foucault fails to articulate this cardinal distinction with anything like the consistency or rigor that his argument requires. What are we to make of those "reflective and voluntary practices" that seemingly take rise within a "singular being" whose selfhood is integral and as yet untouched by the alienating ethos, the unhappy conciousness of modernity? What exactly can it mean for this unitary being to enter upon a process of voluntary "self-transformation" whereby its constitutive "practices" or "rules of conduct" are viewed (so to speak) as the raw material for its own esthetic elaboration? Far from providing an answer to these questions, the passage breaks down into two contradictory lines of argument: one premised on a notional appeal to the self as a unified, autonomous locus of agency and will; the other enmeshed in a subject-centered language of "reflection," non-self-identity, and, as Foucault would have it, specular misrecognition. The antinomies persist, that is to say, despite all Foucault's strenuous efforts to think his way through and beyond them. Nor are these problems effectively resolved by invoking the esthetic as an alternative terrain, a realm wherein the self might achieve true autonomy by shaping its life in accordance with those "values" and "rules" that characterize the discipline of artistic creation. For one still has to ask what relationship exists between the "reflective and voluntary practices" that go toward this project of esthetic self-fashioning, and the "singular being" whose life is thus subject to a process of willed transformation. In short, Foucault's argument is deeply confused, not least when he claims to have annulled or overcome the antinomies of Kantian ethical discourse.

IV

In Foucault's later writings there are many indications that he had come to recognize this troubling liability in his own work. They include those passages where he broaches a markedly different relationship to Kant and the heritage of Enlightenment critique. Even at the time of *The Order of Things*, his period of greatest resistance, there is an undertow of grudging acknowledgment that the Kantian project in some sense defines the very conditions of possibility for present-day critical thought, and thus cannot (despite all his programmatic claims to the contrary) be treated as just another episode in the history of bygone discursive formations. This acknowledgment becomes more explicit in his later work to the point where, with his essay "What Is Enlightenment?," Foucault seems embarked upon a reading of Kant that is also a kind of belated self-reckoning, a renegotiation of problems bequeathed by his own project to date. What marks this protracted encounter, as I have argued, is a complex pattern of ambivalent (sometimes contradictory) responses, a pattern that repeats itself with singular insistence in the writings and interviews of his final decade. It is a tension that results on the one hand from Foucault's espousal of a Nietzschean or private-estheticist creed, and on the other from his growing recognition that the truth-values of enlightened thought – of reason in its jointly epistemo-critical and ethico-political modes – cannot be abandoned without at the same time renouncing any claim to promote or articulate the interests of justice, autonomy, and human emancipation. Foucault is thus faced with a genuine dilemma, but not the kind of self-delighting paradox or wished-for aporia that figures so predictably as the upshot of readings in the postmodern-textualist mode.

Often this conflict is inscribed within the compass of a single sentence, as when Foucault declares (*contra* Kant) that criticism will henceforth "not deduce from the form of what we are what it is impossible for us to know and to do," but should rather seek to "separate out, from the contingency that has made us what we are, the possibility of no longer being, doing, or thinking what we are, do, or think" (*WIE* 46). On the face of it such comments are directed squarely against the residual humanist or anthropological elements that Foucault still detects in Kantian thought. They would then have to be construed as supporting his claim that an ethics (or esthetics) of radical self-invention is the only kind of project that merits our allegiance in an epoch of postmodern, post-Enlightenment thought. Yet it is equally clear that the above sentence corresponds *at every point* to Kant's own claims in the original text "What Is

Enlightenment?." Once again it is a question – quite as much for
Foucault as for Kant – of thinking our way through and beyond
those limits, those various forms of self-imposed tutelage or servi-
tude, which will show up as merely "contingent" (i.e., as socially
conditioned or historically produced) only insofar as we exercise our
powers of autonomous critical reason. And "autonomy" in this context can hardly be understood as involving nothing more than the
private dedication to a mode of being – a *rapport à soi* – which affords the greatest possible scope for the project of esthetic self-
fashioning. Thus it may well be the case, according to Foucault, that
we must henceforth conceive this indispensable "work of thought"
not so much as attempting (in Kantian fashion) "to make possible a
metaphysics that has finally become a science" but rather as seeking
"to give new impetus, as far and wide as possible, to the undefined
work of freedom" (46). But we then have to ask what such claims
could amount to in the absence of a public or critical sphere – a
tribunal of "autonomous" judgment, in the Kantian sense – that
would serve to evaluate their various orders of truth-telling warrant
or ethical accountability. For freedom is not merely undefined, but
strictly *inconceivable* if located – as Foucault often seems to locate
it – in a private realm quite apart from the interests of emancipatory
critique. What beckons from the end of this particular road is a
postmodern variant of the Kantian sublime that nonsensically counsels us to "judge without criteria," and whose appeal, as with
Lyotard, lies in its offering an escape-route from other, more pressing
issues of ethical and political conscience.

So Foucault had good reason for shifting ground with regard to post-
structuralism and kindred forms of modish ultra-relativist doctrine.
The nearest he came to rejecting these ideas outright was in the
interview with Paul Rabinow, conducted in May 1984 just a few
weeks before his death.[34] Most significant here is the way that Foucault moves on directly from questions of ethics and politics to issues
of truth, language, and representation, in each case adopting a clearly
marked critical distance from the attitudes and assumptions that had
characterized his earlier work. Thus to Rabinow's question "What is
a history of problematics?" Foucault responds by defining those respects in which the "work of thought" differs from the kinds of
analysis – among them, presumably, post-structuralist approaches –
that take it for granted that language (or discourse) is the ultimate

horizon of intelligibility. Such thinking is now conceived as "something quite different from the set of representations that underlies a certain behavior" and also as "something quite different from the domain of attitudes that can determine this behavior." On the contrary, the work of thought becomes possible only insofar as it enables the thinker "to step back from [a certain] way of acting or reacting, to present it to oneself as an object of thought and question it as to its meaning, its conditions, and its goals."[35] For it is precisely at the point where "a given" is translated into "a question," or some present mode of conduct into an issue concerning that conduct and its ethical implications, that thinking can begin to problematize the grounds of its own more habitual or taken-for-granted beliefs. And if this means abandoning the main tenet of post-structuralist doctrine (i.e., the claim that thought is constituted through and through by the codes, conventions, language-games or discourses that make up a given cultural order), then Foucault seems ready to do just that. Thus: "The work of philosophical and historical reflection is put back into the field of the work of thought only on condition that one clearly grasps problematization not as an arrangement of representations but as a work of thought."[36] As it happens this is the closing sentence of the last text collected in Rabinow's *Foucault Reader.* One could hardly wish for a firmer declaration of the distance that Foucault had traveled from the reading of Kant that affords such a brilliant (if negative) climax to *The Order of Things.*

When I cited these passages previously it was in order to suggest the deep-laid ambivalence – the unresolved conflicts or tensions – that resulted from Foucault's *Ausseinandersetzung* with the truth-claims of Enlightenment critique. We can now see how much was at stake in this contest of interpretations, this attempt (at the outset) to represent Kantian philosophy as one passing episode in the history of an error, and then – as the issues posed themselves more sharply – to define his own project in uneasy relation to that same much-disputed heritage. No doubt this change of mind came about for various reasons, among them Foucault's growing opposition to "structuralism" and its various offshoots, not least on account of their failure to afford any adequate grasp of the complex relations between truth, knowledge, and the ethical "work of thought." But there was, I think, another, more urgent motive in the problems that Foucault encountered, especially during the late 1960s and early 1970s, when called upon to offer some principled justification of his own current stance on moral and ethico-political questions. For it is clear from some of his essays and interviews at the time (notably those translated in the volume *Power/Knowledge*) that Foucault very often came close to endorsing an attitude that resembled Lyotard's postmodernist notion of "judging without criteria." That is to say, he briefly went along with what amounted to a private-decisionist creed, one that in principle rejected any form of reasoned, enlightened, or "abstract" morality, and that staked all its claims to ethical good faith on a direct appeal to individual conscience as the sole arbiter of action and choice in this or that particular context. After all, this was the heady period before and after *les événements* of 1968, when French dissident or leftist intellectuals were required to take their stand on numerous issues and to choose between a range of competing positions – Marxist, Trotskyist, Marxist-Leninist, Marxist-Leninist-Maoist, anarchist, incipient "post-Marxist," etc. – that could hardly be treated as a matter of straightforward deduction from first principles. At the time it must have seemed that there were as many groupings (or short-lived activist "groupuscules") as there were local issues and day-to-day turns in the course of political events. In this situation one can fully understand why Foucault should have registered the appeal of a "micro-politics" that seemed most responsive to these momentary shifts of tactical alliance, these unpredictable "conjunctures" brought about by the absence of any large-scale unifying movement.

What the times thus required was a flexible attitude, a readiness to abandon high-sounding talk of "truth," "principles," "justice," "emancipatory interests," or whatever, and a corresponding will to bend all one's energies to various short-term "specific" projects of localized resistance and critique. Insofar as such projects stood in need of justification, it could only be a matter of pointing out their strategic usefulness in pursuit of some goal whose desirability was simply self-evident to those pursuing it, but whose ultimate good could never be determined with reference to higher ("universal" or "transcendent") grounds of ethical judgment. For to fall back on such Kantian precepts was a hopelessly obsolete gesture, an evasion of issues that at the time presented themselves entirely in specific, conjunctural, or local-interventionist terms. Thus, for ex-

ample, when asked to offer some thoughts on "revolutionary justice" by the members of a Maoist collective, Foucault in effect took
the line of least resistance by denying that such questions could
possibly be answered, or answered with the kind of principled, self-
validating argument that his interlocutors apparently expected.³⁷
At this point, as I say, there was little to distinguish Foucault's
situationist attitude to issues of ethics, politics, and justice from
Lyotard's postmodernist treatment of such issues as belonging to a
realm of "sublimely" incommensurable truth-claims, and hence as
allowing no appeal to shared standards or criteria of judgment. For
this appeal could work only – could carry some degree of argumen-
tative conviction – insofar as there existed a communal sense of
what should count as valid, legitimate reasoning in any given case.
And therefore, since agreement was so evidently lacking, one had
no choice (as Foucault then saw it) but to give up the quest for
justifying grounds and respond to each new situation as need or
opportunity arose.

In an interview with Rabinow et al., one finds him looking back
on these episodes from his earlier career with a mixture of impatience and wry self-criticism. "There were Marxists," he recalls,

who said I was a danger to Western democracy . . . there was a socialist who
wrote that the thinker who resembled me most closely was Adolf Hitler in
Mein Kampf. I have been considered by liberals as a technocrat, an agent of
the Gaullist government; I have been considered by people on the right,
Gaullists or otherwise, as a dangerous left-wing anarchist; there was an
American professor who asked why a crypto-Marxist like me, manifestly a
KGB agent, was invited to American universities, and so on.³⁸

From which Foucault would appear to draw a lesson very much in line
with both Lyotard's doctrine of plural, incommensurable "phrase-
regimes" and Rorty's advice that we give up on the quest for any
ethics or politics that would bridge the gulf between our private and
public spheres of existence. Thus: "The key to the personal poetic
attitude of a philosopher is not to be sought in his ideas, as if it could
be deduced from them, but rather in his philosophy-as-life, in his
philosophical life, his ethos."³⁹ And this ethos presents itself mainly
in esthetic terms, that is to say, as a project of "poetic" self-invention
that has more to do with "personal" attitudes, beliefs, and predilec-

tions than with anything in the nature of arguments, principles, or philosophical "ideas."

Yet once again there are signs, in the same interview, of Foucault's not wishing to go all the way with this postmodern-pragmatist-estheticist line, and indeed of his adopting a stance more akin to the opposed ("Enlightenment") view. For it is, as he remarks, "not at all a matter of making a particular issue of my own situation; but, if you like, I think that by asking this sort of ethico-epistemologico-political question, one is not taking up a position on a chessboard."[40] In other words, there are issues that can (and should) be raised beyond the private estheticist sphere, and that cannot be reduced, as he sometimes suggests, to an argument for the merely contingent relation between matters of personal ethos or life-style and questions of a wider (socio-political) concern. Insofar as one takes a stand on such issues, one is *not* just adopting some set-piece "position on a chessboard" ("socialist," "liberal," "Gaullist," "left-wing anarchist," "crypto-Marxist," or whatever), but arguing a case whose validity-conditions will always involve both factual truth-claims and the appeal to certain standards – certain stated criteria – of right and wrong. Hence the resistance that Foucault puts up to any account, like Rorty's, that would treat him as traveling a long way around to basically postmodern-pragmatist conclusions. For such thinking comes down to a form of inert consensus-ideology, an apologia for existing values and beliefs that would place them beyond reach of counter-argument or effective oppositional critique.

One last example, also from the interview with Rabinow et al., may help to define more exactly where the difference lies between Foucault and the proponents of a postmodern ethics that exploits the sublime (or its own strong-revisionist reading thereof) as an analogue for the radical "heterogeneity" that supposedly inhabits (or inhibits) all forms of determinate ethical judgment. Its significance can best be grasped through the contrast with Lyotard's shuffling and evasive response on the question of terrorist "morality" vis-à-vis the claims of legal obligation or citizenly virtue. The example is that of Poland, one that Foucault, speaking in 1984, regards as indisputably "touching us all" and therefore as presenting a decisive test-case for anyone who seeks to address these issues in a real-world, practical context. "If we raise the question of Poland in strictly political terms," he remarks,

> it is clear that we quickly reach the point of saying that there is nothing we can do. We can't dispatch a team of paratroopers, and we can't send armoured cars to liberate Warsaw. I think that, politically, we have to recognize this, but I think we have to agree that, for ethical reasons, we have to raise the problem of Poland in the form of a non-acceptance of what is happening there, and a non-acceptance of the passivity of our own governments. I think this attitude is an ethical one, but it is also political; it does not consist in saying merely 'I protest', but in making of that attitude a political phenomenon that is as substantial as possible, and one which those who govern, here or there, will sooner or later be obliged to take into account.[41]

My point is that Foucault, unlike Lyotard, acknowledges the claims of certain moral imperatives that *necessarily* hold for any conscientious subject in possession of the relevant facts, and whose validity cannot be relativized to this or that "phrase-regime," "discourse," or cultural "form of life." Nor can this be merely a matter of one's private attitude, a position arrived at on no firmer basis than Lyotard's fall-back gesture, his voluntarist or decisionist notion of ethics as a leap of faith beyond any standard of reasoned accountability. For as Foucault describes it, the posture of "non-acceptance" is one that follows from a critical review of the best available evidence, a commitment made "as substantial as possible" by giving due weight to all those factors – historical, political, socio-economic, etc. – that enable one to reach an informed judgment. So it is not so much a question of "judging without criteria" (in Lyotard's oxymoronic phrase) as of asking which criteria properly apply in some particular set of circumstances, and then – on those grounds – deciding what should count as a consequent, good-faith, or ethically warranted response.

Thus "politics" is secondary to "ethics" only in the sense that ethics confronts such issues at the crucial point where an adequate knowledge of the given situation passes over into a *reasoned and justified* commitment on moral-evaluative grounds. Thus, in Foucault's words,

> When thought intervenes, it doesn't assume a unique form that is the direct result or the necessary expression of these difficulties; it is an original or specific response – often taking many forms, sometimes even contradictory

in its different aspects – to these difficulties, which are defined for it by a situation or a context, and which hold true as a possible question.[42]

This passage brings out Foucault's eminently Kantian concern to explain how ethical judgment is, on the one hand, a matter of autonomous, freely willed choice – since always to some extent underdetermined by the factual evidence – and, on the other, obliged to take account of such evidence in order to justify its actions, commitments, or evaluative priorities. By this time he had advanced a long way toward abandoning the extreme nominalist position – the attitude of cognitive skepticism linked to a relativist philosophy of meaning and value – that had marked his writings from *The Order of Things* to the period of Nietzsche-inspired "genealogical" thought. Such ideas had been enlisted in the service of a fashionable "end-of-ideology" creed that rejected all truth-claims as a matter of course, and that cheerfully embraced the postmodern prospect of a "cultural conversation" of plural, heterogeneous discourses henceforth given over to judging in the absence of factual or ethical criteria. Whatever their erstwhile appeal for Foucault, or his own central role in promoting them, these ideas now struck him (it is reasonable to infer) as philosophically incoherent and as possessing nothing like the "radical" charge that their adherents claimed for them.

V

Had Foucault lived longer, this resistance might have taken a more overt and polemical form, a challenge to many of the orthodox notions now canvassed in his name. As it is, one can see from the late essays and interviews, especially those that pursue his engagement with Kant, how far he had come in the process of re-thinking his relation to the project of Enlightenment critique. Of course there is no question of claiming Foucault as a good Kantian at heart, a prodigal son who once ventured forth among the vanities and snares of post-structuralist fashion but finally acknowledged the error of his ways and embraced the family creed. Such an argument would ignore those numerous points of tension – "aporias" in the strict, not the current all-purpose rhetorical, sense of that term – that continue to vex Foucault's later dealings with Kant. Yet very often it is precisely at the moment when Foucault is asserting his distance from this legacy of thought that he also bears witness to its present-day significance, its capacity for raising the right kinds of question with regard to matters of ethical, social, and political conscience. Thus "the thread that may connect us to the Enlightenment is not faithfulness to its doctrinal elements, but rather the permanent reactivation of an attitude – that is, of a philosophical ethos that could be described as a permanent critique of our historical era" (WIE 42). We shall misread this and other passages like it if we take them as signaling a postmodern break with all the values of Enlightenment thought. For what could be more in keeping with Kant's critical imperative than this requirement that philosophy take nothing on trust – its own "doctrinal elements" included – but persist in the kind of self-questioning activity that allows of no privileged exemptions, no truth-claims (epistemic or ethical) that cannot be justified on reasoned or principled grounds? Such, after all, is Foucault's ways of linking the "work of thought" with the maintenance of a distinctive "philosophical ethos," one that involves the "permanent critique" of naturalized attitudes and values. If this is no simple "return" to Kant, still less can it be thought of, following the current doxa, as a flat repudiation of Kantian ideas in the wisdom of postmodern hindsight.

When Foucault denounces what he calls the "blackmail of the Enlightenment," his phrase can best be taken as referring to the mythical and demonized view of that tradition adopted, with little in the way of corroborative evidence, by doctrinaire postmodernists like Lyotard. And yet one also finds him, just a few sentences later, declaring that "as an enterprise for linking the progress of truth and the history of liberty in a bond of direct relation, it [the Enlightenment] formulated a philosophical question that remains for us to consider" (43). This affirmative characterization is demonstrably nearer the mark, both as a matter of adequate description (on philosophic and historical grounds) and as regards the motivating interests of Foucault's own engagement with Kant and the discourse of Enlightenment critique. It explains why he continued to treat such questions as a "privileged domain for analysis," a "set of political, economic, social, institutional, and cultural events on which we still depend in large part" (42). Where the conflict arose was in Foucault's uncertainty, still present in his last writings, as to whether those events were historically contingent at bottom and should therefore be treated as just another (albeit *for us* a uniquely "privileged") episode in the structural genealogy of Western thought, or whether, on the contrary, they marked the passage to a new and henceforth indispensable mode of socio-cultural analysis. The former reading is undoubtedly borne out by his work from *The Order of Things* to the late 1960s. Thereafter one can find evidence for both interpretations, often – as I have argued – within the same text and in response to the same sorts of question. But the fact that this remained an issue for Foucault, and the more so through successive encounters with Kant, is evidence enough that he never espoused that line of least resistance (or retreat into postures of private-estheticist whimsy) enjoined by the postmodern skeptics.

In this respect Foucault indeed kept faith with what he saw as the enduring value of Enlightenment thought: its capacity to "separate out, from the contingency that has made us what we are, the possibility of no longer being, doing, or thinking what we are, do, or think." On Rorty's account this would simply be a matter of exchanging one life-style or "final vocabulary" for another, a process that occurs for no good reason save that of momentarily relieving our boredom and providing some new, equally "contingent" set of topics for the ongoing cultural conversation. One could, if so disposed, read Foucault's sentence as a straightforward endorsement of the postmodern-pragmatist line. Thus it might plausibly be construed as urging that "enlightenment" is a thing of the past, that truth is just a matter of what is (currently and contingently) "good in the way of belief," and that value-commitments make sense only insofar as they carry weight – or possess some measure of suasive appeal – for members of an existing interpretive community. But there could then be no accounting for the logic of Foucault's sentence, as opposed to its vaguely rhetorical drift. That is to say, one would be at a loss to understand his assertion that criticism can "separate out" those contingent factors that have "made us what we are" from those other "possibilities" that remain at present unfulfilled, but which yet provide a standard – in Kantian terms, a regulative idea – for the ethical "work of thought." These are not just options that offer themselves randomly according to the current conversational state of play, or within the presently existing range of language-games, discourses, elective self-images, etc. Rather, they are conceived as *conditions of possibility* for that attitude of "permanent critique" that Foucault identifies with the Enlightenment ethos in its authentic, self-questioning form.

It is here that Foucault implicitly takes issue with the facile strain of counter-Enlightenment rhetoric that has often laid claim to his own work, early and late, as a principal source of inspiration. Small wonder that he became increasingly disposed to assert his distance from post-structuralism and its various offshoots on the Francophile cultural scene. For there is nothing more alien to Foucault's thought than the kind of ultra-relativist orthodoxy that erects its own lack of critical and ethical resources into a quasi-universal "postmodern condition," a terminal indifference with regard to issues of truth and falsehood or, to paraphrase Jonathan Swift, that state of perfected self-assurance that comes of being blissfully well deceived. And conversely, there was no question more central to the evolving project of Foucault's life and work than the one taken up in Kant's inaugural essay on the theme "What Is Enlightenment?" Any reading that manages to sidestep this question, or that returns a confidently negative response, is bound to misconstrue that project at numerous points.

NOTES

1 Michel Foucault, *The History of Sexuality*, Vol. I: *An Introduction*, trans. Robert Hurley; *The Use of Pleasure*, trans. Robert Hurley; *The Care of the Self*, trans. Robert Hurley.

2 Roy Boyne, *Foucault and Derrida: The Other Side of Reason*, 144.

3 See, for instance, Michael Sandel, *Liberalism and the Limits of Justice* (Cambridge: Cambridge University Press, 1982); Michael Walzer, *Spheres of Justice: A Defence of Pluralism and Equality* (Oxford: Basil Blackwell, 1983); Walzer, *Interpretation and Social Criticism* (Cambridge: Harvard University Press, 1987); Bernard Williams, *Ethics and the Limits of Philosophy* (London: Fontana, 1985).

4 Foucault, *The Order of Things*, trans. A. Sheridan.

5 See especially the essays collected in Foucault, *Language, Counter-Memory, Practice*, trans. D.F. Bouchard and Sherry Simon.

6 Foucault, "The Ethics of Care of the Self as a Practice of Freedom" (interview), in *The Final Foucault*, ed. James Bernauer and David Rasmussen (Cambridge: M.I.T. Press, 1988), 7.

7 Ibid.

8 Bernard Williams, *Ethics and the Limits of Philosophy* (London: Fontana, 1985).

9 Alasdair MacIntyre, *After Virtue: A Study in Moral Theory* (London: Duckworth, 1985)

10 Michael Walzer, *Spheres of Justice.*

11 See, for instance, Richard Rorty, *Contingency, Irony, and Solidarity* (Cambridge: Cambridge University Press, 1989); *Objectivity, Relativism, and Truth* (C.U.P., 1991); and *Essays on Heidegger and Others* (C.U.P., 1991).

12 For some ingenious variations on this postmodern-pragmatist theme, see Stanley Fish, *Doing What Comes Naturally: Change, Rhetoric, and the Practice of Theory in Literary and Legal Studies* (Durham, N.C.: Duke University Press, 1989).

13 See especially Foucault, *Power/Knowledge*, ed. C. Gordon.

14 Rorty, "Moral Identity and Private Autonomy," 198.

15 Foucault, "What Is Enlightenment?" trans. Catherine Porter, in Rabinow (ed.), *The Foucault Reader*, 32–50. Hereafter cited as *WIE* with page-number in the text. See also Kant, "What Is Enlightenment,?" in L.W. Beck, ed., *Kant: On History* (Indianapolis: Bobbs-Merrill, 1963). For further commentary on Foucault's reading of Kant, see Jürgen Habermas, "Taking Aim at the Heart of the Present," Hubert L. Dreyfus and Paul Rabinow, "What Is Maturity: Habermas and Foucault on "What is Enlightenment?" and Ian Hacking, "Self-Improvement," all in Hoy, ed., *Foucault, A Critical Reader.*

16 See also Foucault, "Kant on Enlightenment and Revolution," trans. Colin Gordon, *Economy and Society* 15 (February 1986): 88–96.

17 See Gilles Deleuze, *Kant's Critical Philosophy: The Doctrine of the Faculties*, trans. Hugh Tomlinson and Barbara Habberjam (London: Athlone Press, 1984) for an incisive treatment that takes full account of these complexities in the Kantian project of thought.

18 See, for instance, Jean-Francois Lyotard, *The Differend: Phrases in Dispute*, trans. Georges van den Abbeele (Manchester: Manchester University Press, 1988).

19 See especially Jürgen Habermas, *Knowledge and Human Interests*, trans. Jeremy Shapiro (London: Heinemann, 1971).

20 Kant, *Critique of Judgement*, trans. J.C. Meredith (Oxford: Oxford University Press, 1978).

21 Charles Baudelaire, "Le peintre de la vie moderne," in F.F. Gautier, ed., *L'Art romantique* (*Oeuvres complètes* IV (Paris, 1923).

22 For a differently angled though pertinent commentary on these same texts of Baudelaire, see Paul de Man, "Literary History and Literary Modernity," in *Blindness and Insight: Essays in the Rhetoric of Contemporary Criticism* (London: Methuen, 1983), 142–65.

23 Richard Rorty, "Moral Identity and Private Autonomy: The Case of

Foucault," in *Essays on Heidegger and Others* (Cambridge: Cambridge University Press, 1991), 198.

24 Ibid.

25 For their respective (and sharply differing) views on the role of the critical intellectual, see "Noam Chomsky and Michel Foucault: Human Nature, Justice *versus* Power" (transcript of televised dialogue) in Fons Elders, ed., *Reflexive Waters: The Basic Concerns of Mankind* (London: Souvenir Press, 1974), 133–97. See also Norris, *Uncritical Theory: Postmodernism, Intellectuals, and the Gulf of War* (London: Lawrence and Wishart, 1992) for further discussion of the issues raised by Foucault's refusal to play the role of so-called "universal intellectual" in the typecast Enlightenment mould.

26 Richard Rorty, "Freud and Moral Reflection" in *Essays on Heidegger and Others* (Cambridge: Cambridge University Press, 1991).

27 Jean-Francois Lyotard, *The Postmodern Condition: A Report on Knowledge*, trans. Geoff Bennington and Brian Massumi (Manchester: Manchester University Press, 1986).

28 Foucault, "Polemics, Politics, and Problematizations," interview with Paul Robinow in *The Foucault Reader*, 388.

29 Ibid., 388–89.

30 Foucault, "On the Genealogy of Ethics: An Overview of Work in Progress" (interview), in Rabinow, ed. *The Foucault Reader*, 340–72; 350

31 See Norris, *What's Wrong with Postmodernism.*

32 Lyotard, *The Differend; Phrases in Dispute.*

33 Foucault, "On the Genealogy of Ethics," 350.

34 Foucault, "Polemics, Politics, and Problematizations,"

35 Ibid, 388.

36 Ibid, 390.

37 Foucault, "On Popular Justice: A Discussion with Maoists," trans. John Mepham, in *Power/Knowledge*, ed. C. Gordon, 1–36.

38 Foucault, "Politics and Ethics: An Interview," 376.

39 Ibid., 374.

40 Ibid., 376.

41 Ibid., 377.

42 Foucault, "Polemics, Politics, and Problematizations," 388–89.

8   Modern and counter-modern: Ethos and epoch in Heidegger and Foucault

In one of his last essays, one that is uncharacteristic in its positive and programmatic format, Michel Foucault asked: "What is modern philosophy? . . . modern philosophy is the philosophy that is attempting to answer the question raised by Kant two centuries ago: What is Enlightenment?"[1] Foucault, echoing Kant, answered that Enlightenment is not the name of an epoch but the exit from immaturity to maturity. The possibility of that exit lies in the relationship the philosopher establishes with the use of reason at the present historical moment. Such a philosopher is not searching for origins and uncovering totalities, nor sculpting utopias. A modern philosopher, one who is curious about the specificity of the present moment, is someone seeking to find out what difference it makes to be thinking today. This is a critical task in the Kantian sense of an exploration of limits. The task is to inquire into the conditions in which the use of reason is legitimate "in order to determine what can be known, what must be done, and what may be hoped."[2] Such an inquiry entails reflection on the limits of the individual's free use of reason, the political conditions under which that use is possible, and a diagnosis of the current state of affairs. It sits at the crossroads of "critical reflection and reflection on history." As we will see, it requires an understanding of thought as a practice and critical thought as a specific kind of situated testing and reflection on the results of that testing which is thoroughly active.

Today one domain of the field of thought that has been increasingly problematized is the question of modernity, witness the extraordinary proliferation of texts on post-modernity. I follow Foucault, however, in casting the question somewhat differently; not by opposing modernity to post-modernity, but by opposing modernity to

197

counter-modernity. While there are many ways of taking up these issues, I have chosen to frame this essay in part as a comparison of the understanding of modernity in two thinkers, Martin Heidegger and Michel Foucault. Without more background preparation such a comparison contains a certain awkwardness, as there is no essential reason to compare the two since their problems and approaches are in important ways quite disparate. But there are conjunctural reasons for attempting such a comparison as well as broader historical ones, which I intend to explore in a larger project on modernity and counter-modernity that will include more developed accounts of these themes in Weber, Heidegger, Foucault, and Habermas.

There are two conjunctural reasons for exploring the issue of modernity and counter-modernity. First, the return of the "Heidegger debate," the re-presentation of Heidegger's relation with the Nazis, this time with archival research demonstrating beyond any doubt Heidegger's pervasive and enduring connection to the National Socialists, has removed the possibility of legitimately denying the question of the meaning of this connection, as had generally been the case previously for Heidegger's disciples. The documentation by Victor Farias and Hugo Ott of Heidegger's involvement has led, particularly in France, to a major re-interpretation of Heidegger's thought as well as an important new debate on the question of the relations of philosophy, ethics, and politics in general.[3] Not entirely coincidentally, the debate took place within a new cultural and political context occasioned by the rise of post-modernism and the fall of Communism. Defenders of Heidegger such as Jacques Derrida and Philippe Lacoue-Labarthe have presented what could be called a "post-modern" Heidegger who erred briefly before understanding that modernity as humanism was the problem.[4] Others, especially Pierre Bourdieu, have presented a portrait of Heidegger as a "conservative-revolutionary" in politics and an anti-humanist in philosophy whose importance was to invent a philosophic language linking the two domains.[5] The German debate has been less passionate because Heidegger is taken less seriously by the leading philosophers there, and any resurrection or recuperation of his politics is unlikely to attain legitimacy. Jürgen Habermas, among others, has linked Heidegger's condemnation of modernity with his philosophic project. Habermas has also attempted to show Heidegger's influence on French post-modernists and post-structuralists, including Foucault.[6] Foucault's essay, "What Is Enlightenment?" is, in part, a response to Habermas.

Second, in the United States, Hubert Dreyfus is defending a postion that sees deep connections between Heidegger's understanding of Being and Foucault's understanding of power. In this view, ethics and politics, on which the two thinkers obviously differ, are fundamentally separate from philosophy and therefore can be ignored.[7] Neither Heidegger nor Foucault held this position although, as we will see, Foucault thought that the relations between politics, ethics, and truth were contingent ones. While I am convinced that Dreyfus's interpretion is misleading, it does offer a challenge. There are complicated links between dimensions of Heidegger's work and Foucault's early work. Gilles Deleuze indicates the importance of Heidegger and Merleau-Ponty for Foucault's approach to "seeing" and "speaking" as appearing together in a linguistic and cultural "clearing," rather than as products of intentionality or objects present in some brute state. Deleuze shows how Foucault went on to separate what Heidegger collapsed and to add, from Nietzsche, a concept of "force" as will-to-power. Deleuze concludes "Heidegger is Nietzsche's potential, but not the other way round, and Nietzsche did not see his potential fulfilled."[8]

Although no one would contest that Being and its "history" are central to Heidegger's project, many would contest that Foucault's project has power at its center. Foremost among those who would deny this equation is Foucault himself. In an essay Foucault gave to Dreyfus and me to publish in our joint book, Foucault began by saying "I would like to say, first of all, what has been the goal of my work during the last twenty years. It has not been to analyze the phenomena of power, nor to elaborate the foundations of such an analysis. My objective, instead, has been to create a history of the different modes by which, in our culture, human beings are made subjects."[9] As he said elsewhere: "I am no theoretician of power. The question of power in itself does not interest me."[10] Such quotations could easily be multiplied. Therefore it seems more interesting to pursue the simultaneously broader, and more specific, question of "modernity" as a problematization of the place of thinking in the work of these two thinkers.

Critical thinking entails a diagnostic relationship to the present. "It is a reflection on 'today' as difference in history and as a motive for a particular philosophical task."[11] Of course, throughout Western history philosophers have frequently interrogated the present. Foucault identified three other ways the relationship of the philosopher to the present had been taken up. All three involved the positing of an objective totality that oriented the task of thinking.

(1) The present may . . . be analyzed as a point of transition toward the dawning of a new world. [**An Achievement**]
(2) The present may be represented as belonging to a certain era of the world, distinct from the others through some inherent characteristics, or separated from the others by some dramatic event. [**An Age**]
(3) The present may be interrogated in an attempt to decipher it in the heralding signs of a forthcoming event. [**A Threshold**][12]

Foucault's challenge was to develop a different relationship to the present than any of these. He takes up Kant's challenge of understanding what difference it makes to be thinking today.

Whatever these three types of objective totalities formerly meant in the history of Western thought, they were not epochs. Epoch, understood as one of several distinctive, historical periods, is a contemporary idea. In fact Hans Blumenburg argues, in *The Legitimacy of the Modern Age*, epochal self-understanding is one of the linchpins of modern self-consciousness. Blumenberg demonstrates that it was roughly at the time of Napoleon – Goethe's time, Cuvier's time – that the concept of epoch underwent a reversal from a term that designates an event in the present to one that designates an extended period of time of which the event is only an indicator. The etymology of the word indicates its primary meaning as punctuate.

The Greek word "epoche" signifies a pause [*Innehalten*] in a movement, and then also the point at which a halt is made or a reversal of direction takes place. For ancient Skepticism, this root meaning gave rise to the application that commanded restraint in the movement of cognition and judgement. . . . For the technical language of astronomy, the epoche was a special point at which to observe a heavenly body, its transit through its zenith or its greatest proximity to or distance from another star.[13]

Blumenberg's etymology provides the elements for a genealogy of Foucault's modern ethos; the emphasis on a point in time, the pause to look out, the "commanded restraint," even the viewpoint "as if from afar" Foucault adopted from Nietzsche.[14] The contemporary position is perspectival and nominalist in that, as opposed to the Greeks or the Skeptics or astronomers, one is looking out not at a fixed cosmos; one is pausing to examine the present in its particularity and contingency.

This punctuate, positional view began to give way in Western philosophical self-understanding in the period following the French Revolution to historical epochs understood as complex unities, states, configurations. For Goethe, Napoleon revealed the end of one epoch and the dawning of another. Blumenberg argues that eventually a choice between the real or nominalistic characteristics of the criteria chosen to pick out and define these periods of time comes into prominence. He argues that the realist's decision to choose definite starting points always leads to irresolvable problems. Detailed historical examination dissolves the sharp breaks, revealing precursors and continuities: Descartes was not possible without Nicolas of Cusa. Blumenberg reminds us that "It is not history but this contemplator of history who halts at a resting place so as to survey what happens before and after." As a nominalist, Foucault would likely agree with Blumenberg that "Man does indeed make history, but he does not make epochs."[15] Although Heidegger presumably holds that man makes neither history nor epochs and that both simply come to presence in the mystery of "the clearing," he seems to be a realist about epochs of Being.

HEIDEGGER: COUNTER-MODERN

Martin Heidegger's diagnosis of modernity is epochal, in Blumenberg's sense of history as real periods. Heidegger held three views of modernity as an epoch of the understanding of Being, which correspond to the three types Foucault proposed.[16] Stripped of the apologetics or hermeneutic gymnastics so adroitly performed by contemporary interpreters, Heidegger's positions are surprisingly straightforward. Foucault's term "counter-modern" captures all three of Heidegger's diagnoses of modern times.

1. In his infamous 1933 Rectorate speech, Heidegger saw the present as an **achievement:** the transition to the dawning of a new world, which the resolute will of the German students had in fact already accomplished. The task of the philosopher was to recognize this achievement by analyzing its essence and showing how the German people, science, and the German university shared a common destiny.

2. In his 1938 essay "Age of the World Picture," Heidegger diagnosed the present as an **age:** the metaphysical essence of modernity was humanism, pointing to the thought of Descartes as articulating the distinctive characteristics of modern thought; the task of the philosopher lay in analyzing the essence of the humanist understanding of Being.

3. In Heidegger's 1955 essay "The Question Concerning Technology," modernity was no longer humanism but technicity, the relentless taking up and optimizing of all things for the sake of optimization itself. The history of Being revealed the relentless nihilistic totalizing of the present metaphysics. This genealogical account loosened the grip of this totalizing, opening up the possibility that a receptive thinker could see, if they ever came, **signs of a new age,** a new understanding of Being, hence the significance of Heidegger's famous phrase "only a God can save us now."

Heidegger thought that "technicity" was the greatest danger, not that technology would destroy the world but, to the contrary, that it would succeed in achieving its aims of ordering everything in an efficient manner.

Enframing blocks the shining-forth and holding-sway of truth. The destining that sends into ordering is consequently the extreme danger. What is dangerous is not technology. There is no demonry of technology, but rather there is the mystery of its essence. . . . The rule of Enframing threatens man with the possibility that it could be denied to him to enter into a more original revealing and hence to experience the call of a more primal truth.[17]

Even more mundanely, Heidegger says elsewhere that the greatest danger would be not the collapse but the complete success of the social welfare system.[18] In Heidegger's view, as interpreted at least by Dreyfus, if the Nazis had set about to impose a total welfare system on everyone, it would have been just as "dangerous" as

Auschwitz. This grotesque understanding of things is underlined in a famous letter Heidegger sent to his student Herbert Marcuse, in which he equates mechanized agriculture and the gas chambers.

Genealogy and epochality

Can Michel Foucault be fit into a similar frame? Are his genealogies of the subject and Heidegger's history of Being comparable enterprises? There are some places in which Foucault can legitimately be read as epochal. Michael Donnelly argues that there is a profound ambiguity in Foucault's use of "bio-power," which he identifies as an alternation between "genealogy" and "epochality."[19] Especially in *Discipline and Punish*, Foucault presents a series of analyses of localized and specific mechanisms, events and technologies, while also making general claims about long-term trends. Phrases such as "the carceral society" sound epochal. The distinctions between specific events, historical generalizations, and epochal levels is not always very clear.

Strictly speaking, the genealogical approach is descriptive and conjunctural; it presents a series of discrete elements that, while following their own periodicity and their own dynamics, assemble at the same conjuncture. These processes are complex and contingent, that is why Foucault's descriptions are laden with historical details and are necessarily localized: Nietzsche's famous gray, meticulous, patiently documented, inglorious labor. The link Foucault established between the genealogical dimension and these epochal-sounding claims is a rhetorical one, seeking to exaggerate one group of practices as a means of moving an audience to vigilance. Genealogy focuses on "the moment of arising" not "as the final term of an historical development," but as a diagnosis. Genealogy deals not with the typical but "with events in their most acute manifestations.... The world we know is not this ultimately simple configuration where events are reduced to accentuate their essential traits ... history has a more important task than to be a handmaiden to philosophy."[20] This diagnostic dimension is linked to the "affirmation of knowledge as perspective.... Nietzsche's version of historical sense ... gives equal weight to its own sight and to its objects. Through this historical sense, knowledge is allowed to create its own genealogy in the act of cognition: and 'wirkliche Historie' composes a genealogy of history as the vertical projection of its position."[21] This reading of Nietzsche is surely close to Blumenberg's sense of epochs as punctual and conjunctural.

AN ETHICS OF DANGER

Foucault's genealogical position has a number of distinct characteristics, not least of which is his use of the concept of danger as defining a certain line of thinkers, in which he situates himself. "My point is not that everything is bad, but that everything is dangerous, which is not exactly the same thing. If everything is dangerous, then we always have something to do. So my position leads not to apathy but to a hyper- and pessimistic activism."[22] Foucault's concept of "danger," while provocative and plausible-sounding, nonetheless never seeems very precise. On the one hand, it seemed to have the status of an existential or autobiographical claim, the way Michel Foucault happened to engage the world. On the other hand, his claim has been interpreted to mean something like what Heidegger meant, that in this particular understanding of Being the danger of forgetting other understandings was at its height. Neither view seems adequate. In the first case, the sense of danger would be merely idiosyncratic. In the second, as Foucault's critics have so often complained, if there is an objective danger – if, for example, Being is being covered up, communication is being distorted, hegemonic domination is being exercised – then Foucault owed us a diagnosis as well as some criterion to explain the current danger and our consequent distress in face of it. However, Foucault always refused such moves, to the common irritation of Heideggerians, Habermasians, and Marxists.

How, therefore, did Foucault use the term "danger"? The theme of the place of danger in the philosophic life forms the subject matter of Foucault's last lectures on *parrhesia*, "truth-speaking," "*le franc parler*," different versions of which were presented in Berkeley and Paris. Foucault approached truth-speaking not from the side of formal criteria and logical coherence, but as an activity. Who is able to tell the truth? About what topics is it important to tell the truth? What are the moral, the ethical, and the spiritual conditions that entitle someone to present himself as a truth-speaker? What are the

consequences of telling the truth? What is the relation b
activity of truth-telling and the exercise of power?[23]

The parrhesiast is the one who speaks the truth, b_
truth-speaker is a parrhesiast. The first distinctive element is u_
relationship the parrhesiast establishes with himself: he must be
sincere and pronounce the truth in the most direct form possible.
This stance toward truth distinguishes him from the rhetorician,
who may speak the truth but not believe it. The second element is
the relationship the parrhesiast establishes with an Other. For the
situation to be one of parrhesia it must involve an element of risk or
danger to the speaker. The parrhesiast speaks truth to someone who
is more powerful than he is. While he is free not to speak the truth,
he nonetheless feels an ethical duty to take the risk of doing so. This
is why the school teacher teaching geometry is not a parrhesiast any
more than is a sovereign speaking truths to his ministers. "Parrhesia
is linked to courage in the face of danger: it demands the courage to
speak the truth in spite of some danger."[24] It is an ethical act precisely because the possibility of not speaking the truth is open to the
speaker who chooses to run the risks.

Foucault contrasted the parrhesiast with three other types of
truth-speakers in the Western tradition and intended eventually to
work out the massively complicated historical elaborations this
schema had undergone. The three other types are the prophet, the
sage, and the technician-teacher. All four are characterized by a relationship of truth, power, and ethics as well as an attitude toward
time. The **prophet** is concerned with truth as destiny. He does not
speak in his own name. He attempts to mediate the present and the
future. He does not speak directly but in words that "require a certain interpretation because typically they cover even as they unveil
what is hidden."[25] Prophecy seeks to collapse *aletheia* (truth), *po-
liteia* (civilization), and ethos as it focuses on the production of truth
concerning the future. The **sage** is concerned with truth as being. He
may well hold his wisdom within or speak only in terms of general
principles. Wisdom claims to think their basic unity of truth, power,
and ethics. The **teacher-technician,** possesses *techne*, skill learned
by apprenticeship, which he is expected to transmit clearly and without risk. The teacher-technician seeks to define the irreducibility
and distinctiveness of different domains. The **parrhesiast** focuses on
the present. Parrhesia "seeks the political conditions and the ethical

differences at work in the question of true discourse, in other words, it underscores the impossibility of thinking any one way without thinking all three poles, while insisting on their irreducible distinctness."[26] Clearly and unambiguously, then, Foucault refuses the a priori separation of ethics from politics and each of these from the practices of truth. His task was precisely to re-problematize their relationships in the present.

In this schema Heidegger would seem to combine elements of the prophet and the sage, while Foucault is clearly the parrhesiast with connections to the technician-teacher. It is worth underlining why the parrhesiast's position is different from the "speaker's benefit" of the universal intellectual.[27] The parrhesiast speaks from within the power field; without danger there is no parrhesia. This engaged stance distinguishes the parrhesiast and places him in especially strong contrast to prophets who might first announce the achievement of an accomplishment, later denounce the snares of a new age, and finally retreat from a dangerous present while adopting a receptive attentiveness to signs of a new era.

Danger, then, provides a link between truth, power, and ethics. In his essays on "The Subject and Power" and "How Is Power Exercised?," Foucault presented a view of power and freedom as coextensive. Power relations depend on freedom of action. "Power is exercised only over free subjects, and only so far as they are free."[28] Where freedom is no longer a possibility, relations of force or violence hold sway. Furthermore, this is not an empty Sartrean notion of freedom applicable to all situations, but one that rests on an analysis of the specifics of the historical situation. The truth dimension in the diagnosis of the present is crucial precisely because rational activity is at stake. Foucault warned against overgeneralization. Precisely because power relations entail knowledge relations, they also carry with them the potential for misunderstanding. Precisely because power relations entail freedom, they carry with them the possibility of losing that freedom. Just as power must be exercised to work, so, too, freedom and knowledge are active states. Any new formation of power and knowledge would carry with it multiple dangers. The task of the parrhesiast is to analyze those dangers by putting himself in a situation where he confronts them. This is not a question of speaking truth to power, but of willfully testing how the multiple relations of truth, power, and ethics, within which the thinker acts, have been formed and how much they can be changed.

A PRACTICE OF CRITICAL CURIOSITY

The modern ethos Foucault was exploring has another distinctive dimension to it. It both embodies and is the consequence of a critical curiosity. By "critical" Foucault means limit-testing and limit-setting in the Kantian sense; but what about curiosity? Hans Blumenberg in his *The Legitimacy of the Modern Age* has given us a fascinating history of the "Trial of Theoretical Curiosity." He traces the long trajectory of the idea from the Greeks, through the myriad reactions against it during the Christian Middle Ages, to its re-emergence during the Enlightenment as a dimension of encyclopedic understanding and order, and to its most recent re-articulation as a central element in modern consciousness as a form of "reflected curiosity," endlessly in search of "the new," constantly reflecting on its own restless explorations, until finally the ceaseless appearance of "new things" becomes itself merely expected.

In an interview he gave the newspaper *Le Monde,* which was interviewing French thinkers on the present state of philosophy, Foucault, thinly disguised as "the masked philospher," chose to affirm the present and to affirm it in terms of the greatly expanded possibilities of curiosity. He said:

I don't believe in the refrain of decadence, the absence of great writers, the sterility of thought, the restricted and bleak horizon. I think on the contrary that there is a plethora. And then there is an immense curiosity, a need or desire to know. Curiosity is a vice that has been stigmatized in turn by Christianity, by philosophy, and even by a certain conception of science. The word, however, pleases me. To me it suggests something altogether different: it evokes "concern"; it evokes the care one takes for what exists and could exist; a readiness to find strange and singular what surrounds us; a certain relentlessness to break up the familiarities and to regard otherwise the same things; a fervor to grasp what is happening and what passes; a casualness in regard to traditional hierarchies of the important and the essential. I dream of a new age of curiosity. We have the technical means for it; the desire is there; the things to be known are infinite; the people who can employ themselves in this task exist.[29]

This curiosity is certainly modern in the transformed Baudelairian sense Foucault sketched in "What Is Enlightenment?," but is it critical?

Blumenberg points out, in an extraordinary chapter on the Enlightenment, that while it was curiosity that "appears as the very power that drives through the barriers to setting free the shared activity of nature and man . . . , this curiosity cannot produce from itself any criterion for its restriction."[30] Nietzsche raised the specter of the application of man's theoretical curiosity to himself, without any criterion for its restriction, ultimately as self-sacrifice on the altar of science. Curiosity had become the rancorous "volonté de savoir" that had lost "all sense of limitations and all claim to truth in its unavoidable sacrifice of the subject of knowledge."[31]

Although in "Nietzsche, Genealogy, History" Foucault certainly seemed to be affirming this bleak diagnosis of the will to knowledge, Foucault later claimed that Canguilhem, "at once close to and far from Nietzsche," had found a way to a form of truth, one not based on the subject of knowledge. "Phenomenology could indeed introduce the body, sexuality, death, the perceived world into the field of analysis; the Cogito remained central; neither the rationality of science nor the specificity of the life sciences could compromise its founding role. It is to this philosophy of meaning, subject and the experienced thing that Canguilhem has opposed a philosophy of error, concept and the living being."[32] For the sciences of life, the historian's ethic is constituted by the demarcation of truth and procedures of verification.

Foucault's domain is not that of the life sciences. Hence the guiding norm is not that of *truth* understood as a "history of 'truthful discourses,' that is discourses which rectify, correct themselves and which effect on themselves a whole work of elaboration finalized by the task of 'speaking true' " through the elaboration of concepts. Nor is his object-realm *life*. Rather, in Kantian fashion, Foucault made distinctions between realms; his work was devoted to the practical world. There the guiding norm is *freedom* understood as a capacity and an essential dimension of the *subject*, situated in, traversed by, and active in the field of relations of power and knowledge. "While the historian of science in France busied himself primarily with the problem of the constitution of scientific objects, I asked myself another question. How does it happen that the human subject makes himself into an object of possible knowledge, through which forms of rationality, through what historic necessities, and at what price?"[33] This type of questioning is precisely what Blumenberg calls "self-assertion," a central, legitimate characteristic of modernity.

Of course, at this level of abstraction, these claims remain little more than broad sketches of a critical activity Foucault always carried out at the "merely ontic," ungrounded level in the historical details that fill his books and in the attention to the specifics of political conjunctures that, as in Habermas, frequently form the subject matter of his critical interventions. Deleuze captures this division of labor nicely when he says: "If Foucault's interviews form an integral part of his work, it is because they extend the historical problematization of each of his books into the construction of the present problem, be it madness, punishment or sexuality."[34] Perhaps an example of how Foucault approached a present problem would be helpful.

Social security: capacities and powers, rights and limits

In 1983 Foucault was interviewed by an official of one of France's largest labor unions, the C.F.D.T., on the problems of the social security system. Foucault proposed a conjunctural and diagnostic approach that weighed the system's comparative strengths and weaknesses, its dangers and benefits, its changing institutions and its shifting interfaces with French society. He spoke as an intellectual and as a citizen. His recent work had been on the genealogy of the welfare state, specifically on the concept of "bio-power." He spoke as a citizen-interlocutor in dialogue with a union official whose membership had been engaged for some time in formulating policy concerning specific changes in social security currently under debate in France. The interview contained a clear and unequivocal commitment to the positive value of social security. Foucault says "[T]he objective of an optimal social coverage joined to a maximum of independence is clear enough."[35] The interview contained no talk of Normalization as the greatest danger, nor increasing totalization, nor epochs, nor Gods. To point this out is not merely to underline the obvious ethical and political distance of Heidegger and Foucault, but to underline that, from Foucault's perspective, contempt for matters of the present amounted to contempt for thinking. Said perhaps a bit more precisely: that disdaining, or fleeing from, engagement with matters of the present amounted to disdaining or fleeing from thinking.

Today the welfare state sets the context for important dimensions of "people's sensibilities, their moral choices, their relations to themselves, and, the institutions which surround them (162)." Foucault proposed analyzing the current situation of social security along several axes, indicating the need to recast the conceptual model of social security born around World War I and elaborated to deal with the social conflicts during the interwar period, a model that, through its success in meeting the needs of that period, had produced new circumstances. These circumstances bring into new prominence two major aspects of welfare society: (1) the paradox of capacities and powers and (2) the play of rights and limits.

(1) The positive effects of the welfare state, the provision of social security, are in growing tension with the negative ones, rigid bureaucratic mechanisms and a more generalized situation of dependency. The rationality of the social security system had created a field in which security and dependency were implicitly weighted against each other. The system arose after World War I when the security side of the tandem was pressing and the dependency side was less attended to. There were severe housing shortages, inadequate child care, an archaic medical system, minimal pensions, etc. To a significant degree institutions and policies had been devised to address these problems in France. The price to be paid was the increased dependency on the massive and intrusive bureaucracies that arose to administer the programs and ended up administering their recipients as well. We came to expect that social security should not only free us from the immediate threats to our daily lives but that it should "protect us from situations that tend to debase or to subjugate us (160)." This protection in turn produced new forms of debasement and subjugation. With the success of the system in meeting basic needs, the demand for autonomy rose on the agenda, making dependency a "perverse" effect of the system. There is a range of possible reactions to this situation. Foucault pointed out that simply opposing integration into the welfare system in the name of independence had its own specific dangers, to wit, the massive marginalization of people from the satisfaction of their most elemental needs of housing, health care, and security so evident in the United States today.

This brings us back to "What Is Enlightenment?" in which Foucault introduces what he calls the "paradox of the relations of capacity and power."[36] The great hope of eighteenth-century Enlightenment thinkers was that the spread of reason would enlighten individuals and society alike. The only losers would be superstition, fear, and tyranny. Two centuries later we know that things are not as simple as the eighteenth century hoped they would be. Forms of domination, subjection, and incapacitation have insidiously accompanied all the advances in technical mastery, means of communication, and practices of self-constitution. "What is at stake, then, is this: How can the growth of capabilities be disconnected from the intensification of power relations?"[37] There is, of course, no general answer to this question. It is a question that must be repeatedly answered, and the answers will never be completely satisfactory.

(2) Rights and Limits. With the rise of the social security systems during the interwar period, there was a broad consensus, forged through political struggle and negotiation, about a minimum threshold of health needs. However, the recent expansion of the technical capacities of medicine and growing and more wide-spread prosperity changed the life course, with a corresponding expansion of the demand for health. This dynamic has revealed that the need for health has no internal principle of limitation. Since these needs have no inherent principle of limitation, it follows that asserting such rights as absolutes could have no "conceivable translation into practice (169)." It follows, Foucault asserts, that we should approach health as a condition and not a right. While there may be a right to a safe work environment, to compensation and other such matters, there is no right not to be ill or to live forever. Hence, instead of "rights to health," one could speak of rights to the available means of health. Such an approach brings into play the medical, technical, and economic capacities of the collectivity. Principles of access to these capacities can be defined. But the definitions arrived at will be pragmatic and provisional ones not deducible from either a scientific or legal/philosophical norm, that is, a medical definition of health or a right to health. How to establish such a norm and associated policies is simultaneously a technical, a political, and an ethical question. The problem is that of reconciling "an infinite demand with a finite system." It is a problem with no fixed solution. Like the paradox of

capacities and powers, it is part of a field of political rationality within which we find ourselves. Or, as Foucault puts it, "I would say that social security contributes to an ethic of the human person at least by posing a certain number of problems, and especially by posing the question about the value of life and they way in which we face up to death (176)." It also poses the political question about how we handle everything in between.

Where does Foucault stand in all this? Where does he speak from? His stance as a teacher-technician is clear. He provides an analysis of the present situation and its key diagnostic features (capacities/ powers, rights/limits), which he draws from his on-going scholarly work on the genealogy of bio-power and ethics. This diagnostic work is only a beginning. "There is an enormous amount of work in the way of investigation, experimentation, measure-taking, and intellectual and moral reformulation to be done . . . a rigorous empiricism is required [to] transform the field of social institutions into a field of experimentation (173, 165)." Such experimentation on ourselves, then, has its truth component, its political tasks, and its self-formative ethical dimensions. Foucault seems to be speaking as a citizen-technician. He is speaking with a "specific intellectual," his union interlocutor, who is faced with policy decisions over technical details and union strategy. In such a context Foucault himself is the citizen-technician speaking from a less specifically located, more generalized position; his concern is to foster the best policies whose effects will be felt by all citizens. It is the specific intellectual, not Foucault, who will proceed to articulate those policies.

But where is the risk? It does not come from physical threats of the government or police. Such dangers would be the type those speaking truth to power from the outside would provoke and confront. Rather, to the extent there is any danger involved, it comes from those authorized to produce the truth. On the one hand, the guardians of metaphysics (including the anti-metaphysicians) who argue that Foucault has no theory, no grounds, and hence could not possibly see or speak what he sees and says; on the other hand, those who want to essentialize their lives and their politics by grounding them in pre-established rights and natures. Foucault placed himself in a kind of tenuous liminal zone between speakers of the universal, whose grounds his genealogical works grind down, and social actors speaking in the name of fixed truths, whose shifting foundations

Foucault's archaelogical excavations reveal. Foucault, at the end of his life, was a kind of impossible intellectual-citizen, navigating a free-fire zone. To the extent that he was a technician-parrhesiast, he was voluntarily among the Enlighteners, playing the role of a kind of "technician of general ideas."[38] Perhaps this is what he meant at the end of "What Is Enlightenment?" when he said, "I continue to think that [the critical task] requires work on our limits, that is, a patient labor giving form to our impatience for liberty."[39]

NOTES

1 Michel Foucault, "What Is Enlightenment?" in Paul Rabinow, ed., *The Foucault Reader,* 32. Special thanks to Michael Meranze and James Faubion for on-going discussions on these issues.

2 Ibid., 38.

3 Victor Farias, *Heidegger and Nazism* (Philadelphia: Temple University Press, trans. Paul Burrell, 1989.

4 See a special issue of *Critical Inquiry:* 15, 2 (Winter 1989).

5. Pierre Bourdieu, *L'Ontologie politique de Martin Heidegger* (Paris: Les Editions de Minuit, 1988).

6 Jürgen Habermas, *The Philosophical Discourse of Modernity,* 1987.

7 Hubert Dreyfus, "On the Ordering of Things: Being and Power in Heidegger and Foucault," *Southern Journal of Philosophy,* Supplement 28 (1989), 83–96.

8 Gilles Deleuze, *Foucault,* 113.

9 Foucault, "The Subject and Power," in Dreyfus and Rabinow, *Beyond Structuralism,* 208.

10 Foucault, "How Much Does It Cost for Reason to Tell the Truth," in *FL.* p. 254.

11 "What Is Enlightenment?," 38.

12 Ibid., 33–34.

13 Hans Blumenberg, *The Legitimacy of the Modern Age,* trans. Robert M. Wallace (Cambridge, Mass.: MIT Press, 1983), 460.

14 On the "famous perspective of frogs," see Foucault, "Nietzsche, Genealogy, History," in D. Bouchard, ed. *Language, Counter-Memory, Practice,* 155.

15 Ibid., 460, 478.

16 Heidegger's early philosophy was not epochal and needs to be approached differently.

17 Heidegger, *The Question Concerning Technology and Other Essays,* trans. W. Lovitt (New York: Harper & Row, 1977), 28.

214 THE CAMBRIDGE COMPANION TO FOUCAULT

18 Martin Heidegger, "What Are Poets For?," *Poetry, Language, Thought*, trans. A. Hofstader (New York: Harper & Row, 1971), 116.
19 Michael Donnelly, "Des divers usages de la notion de biopouvoir," *Michel Foucault, Philosophe* (Paris: Editions du Seuil, 1988), 231.
20 Foucault, "Nietzsche, Genealogy, History," 155.
21 Ibid., 157.
22 Micharl Foucault, "The Subject and Power," in Rabinow and Dreyfus, 2nd ed. 231.
23 This list is taken from Foucault's lectures at Berkeley.
24 Ibid.
25 Thomas Flynn, "Foucault as Parrhesiast," in *The Final Foucault*, 109.
26 Ibid., 106.
27 On the "speaker's benefit" see *The History of Sexuality*, Vol. 1. On "universal intellectuals," see "Truth and Power," in Gordon (ed.), *Power/Knowledge*, 126.
28 Foucault, "How Is Power Exercised?" in Dreyfus and Rabinow, *Beyond Structuralism*, 221.
29 "The Masked Philosopher," *Le Monde*, April 6, 1980. Reprinted in *Foucault Live*, ed. Sylvére Lotringer, 198–99. Foucault is clearly using "age" in a colloquial manner.
30 *Legitimacy of the Modern Age*, 412–13.
31 Foucault, "Nietzsche, Genealogy, History," p. 164.
32 Foucault, "Introduction," to George Canguilhem *On the Normal and the Pathological* pp.23–24.
33 Foucault, "How Much Does It Cost . . . for reason to tell the truth," *Foucault Live*, 245.
34 Deleuze, *Foucault*, 115.
35 "Social Security," in Lawrence Kritzman, ed., *Michel Foucault, Politics, Philosophy, Culture*, 165. Further page references are given in the text. Translations have been modified.
36 "What Is Enlightenment?", 47.
37 Ibid., 48.
38 The expression comes from a French colonial general, Hubert Lyautey. For its history see Paul Rabinow, *French Modern: Norms and Forms of the Social Environment* (Cambridge: MIT Press, 1989).
39 "What Is Enlightenment?", 50.

9 Foucault and Habermas on the subject of reason

> But truly to escape Hegel involves an exact appreciation of the price we have to pay to detach ourselves from him. It assumes that we are aware of the extent to which Hegel, insidiously perhaps, is close to us; it implies a knowledge, in that which permits us to think against Hegel, of that which remains Hegelian. We have to determine the extent to which our anti-Hegelianism is possibly one of his tricks directed against us, at the end of which he stands, motionless, waiting for us.[1]
>
> Michel Foucault

Foucault's last attempt to situate his life's work in the Enlightenment tradition presumably laid to rest any lingering doubts about the rational basis of his work.[2] Yet, Habermas and his sympathizers remained skeptical. The rational subject, they argued, was never adequately accounted for in Foucault's work.[3]

Explanation for this discrepancy must be sought in Foucault's original disenchantment with the Enlightenment project – above all, his critique of modern humanism and the kind of subjectivity it entails.[4] For the purposes of this essay, it will suffice to broach this topic by contrasting Foucault's critical method with the critique of ideology undertaken by members of the Frankfurt School (Part I). As we shall see, Foucault's critical method is more radical than theirs

Earlier versions of this paper were presented at the 1989 Central Division meeting of the American Philosophical Association and the 1992 Conference on Enlightenment, Law, and Formation of the Subject sponsored by The Greater Philadelphia Philosophy Consortium. I am especially grateful to Julia Simon-Ingram for her invaluable advice in preparing the final draft of this paper.

215

in that it brackets the emancipatory ideals underwriting reason itself. Stronger still, it allegedly shows the impossibility of the Hegelian categories of reflection in which these ideals are cast.

I shall argue that these categories are not as paradoxical as Foucault thinks. Indeed, I shall show that, *mutatis mutandis*, they inform the very hermeneutic circle in which he himself reformulated his understanding of the rational, self-empowering subject. The road leading to this conclusion must pass through the difficult terrain staked out by Habermas's theory of communicative action (Part II). The latter ostensibly redeems reason from its paradoxes while simultaneously demonstrating the self-referential contradictions attending its wholesale rejection.

Although this strategy has its merits, our inquiry will show that it, too, succumbs to self-referential paradoxes (Part III). Habermas's attempt to avoid the hermeneutic circle that fuels these paradoxes presupposes questionable distinctions between transcendent reason (form) and historical reality (content), on the one hand, and between communicative and strategic types of action, on the other. Foucault may well be right that strategic action *broadly conceived* supervenes on communicative action. If so, then it also supervenes on the self-empowerment of a rational subject who remains subject to the power of others.

It would be hasty to infer the legitimacy of liberal polity – or, for that matter, the illegitimacy of rational subjectivity – from this result. On this point Foucault and Habermas agree. Indeed, once we acknowledge the rational imbrication of ethical intersubjectivity and self-empowering subjectivity, we will have to concede *both* that the freedom of abstract rights and entitlements afforded by the liberal state is a mixed blessing *and* that emancipation born of enlightenment is a conditioned achievement, intersected by the contextual effects of strategic power relations and communicative agreements. Thus, from this perspective, Habermas's disagreement with Foucault over the conditions of rational subjectivity appears somewhat exaggerated (Part IV). Such a conclusion, however, is wholly consistent with the view that the "paradoxical" subject of reason – *ethically self-determined* and *esthetically reconciled to the other* – is more deeply entrenched in critical theory than perhaps either philosopher realizes.

I. THE SUBJECT OF CRITICISM: HUMANISM AND THE CRITIQUE OF IDEOLOGY

Foucault and his counterparts in the Frankfurt School share a mutual concern about subjectivity and its relationship to knowledge. This concern is doubly complicated. On the one hand, they conceive subjectivity as a social construct. They regard as illusory the rational, self-determined unity that Descartes and Kant attribute to the isolated subject. On the other hand, they hold that the *metaphysical* illusion of a self-empowering ego captures a real, *practical* dimension of rational moral agency as it has taken shape in modern, occidental culture.

Here we detect a further complication. The need to know who we really are – a practical need imposed on us by the emancipatory legacy of the Enlightenment – can be satisfied (so it seems) only by the self-objectifying and self-alienating effects of rational discipline. This ambiguity is exemplified in the Enlightenment's appeal to science and natural law as touchstones for dispelling ideological domination. For the thinkers of the Enlightenment, the Rights of Man founded on the universal laws of nature ostensibly represent the real, universal interests of humanity in opposition to the false, partial interests legitimated by religious dogma. Yet, as critical theorists from Marx to Marcuse later observed, these universal ideas are themselves contingent artifacts that reflect and legitimate the abstract subjectivity of contractual exchange.[5] Such laws, they argue, legitimate class domination in the name of emancipation, substituting the right to property, its work ethic, and its consumer ideology for collective self-determination.

A similar paradox threatens the coherence of critical theory. Marx himself had appealed to the rational interests of humanity and its universal historical agent, the proletariat, in criticizing the abstractions of rationalist ideology. Members of the early Frankfurt School did the same, while making explicit, however, the contradiction implicit in such appeal. They invoked reason in criticizing the ideological repression of human instincts, even as they accepted Freud's view that repression itself is rational.

Critical theorists initially sought to avoid this paradox by arguing that repression is irrational only when it extends beyond what is mandated by scarcity. On this reading, class societies, which impose surplus repression disproportionately on the laboring classes, tend to be more irrational on balance than egalitarian societies. The exigencies of consumption under advanced capitalism impose surplus repression on all, however, since the technological exploitation of labor for profit requires universal regimentation and sacrifice, even in the absence of real scarcity. Ultimately, critical theorists resolved the paradox of reason by adopting a theoretical strategy akin to that found in the early writings of Marx; they embraced a dualistic conception of reason that pitted esthetic reconciliation and spontaneity against the diremptions and objectifications of scientific enlightenment.[6]

The above critique resonates with Foucault's on numerous points.[7] Both unmask the universalist pretentions of scientific reason by locating the limits and possibilities of knowing and acting in historically sedimented practices. Both unmask the Cartesian subject, understood as a fixed and universal foundation prior to experience, as incompatible with these practical presuppositions. Both eschew the notion that knowledge is disinterested contemplation of a pregiven object; instead, given the priority of material practice, they assume that knower and knowable mutually constitute one another as meaningful identities. Finally, by *reflecting* on their own practical genealogy, both critiques seek to enlighten individuals about the social conditions under which their identities, needs, and interests are historically constituted.

Both critiques also seem to share an awareness of their own problematic relationship to the Enlightenment. Despite their materialist critique of rationalism, members of the early Frankfurt School never succeeded in eluding the paradox of reason. As Adorno and Horkheimer later observed, since critical theory participates in, and thus reflects, the social reality it criticizes, its own status as theory and practice must remain ambiguous. For Foucault, too, the rational discourses of bourgeois science and morality that inform critical theory only emancipate through domination. By investing the self with dangerous drives and energies requiring constant surveillance (self-examination, interpretation and observation) and rigorous control (technical predictability), they compel the self to subject itself to others as a condition for its own ethical self-empowerment.

The paradox of reason confronts critical theory with the following dilemma: either a wholesale critique of ideology invalidates its own rationale or, lacking any rationale save that of esthetic spontaneity, it ceases to be critical. The former presents us with a theory that undermines the juridical assumptions of the free, ethical subjectivity it wants to redeem; the latter presents us with a theory that wants to affirm, but cannot conceive, the self-determination of an esthetic subjectivity lost in its own immediate nature.

Foucault sought to avoid this dilemma by detaching his critique from the idealistic heritage of the Enlightenment. Critical theorists still shared Marx's and Freud's belief in a single *rational* trajectory along which humanity fulfills its essential nature. This trajectory maps out a logic of emancipation by means of which individuals reappropriate basic capacities (Marx) and inherent dispositions (Freud) that have been externalized, alienated, distorted, and suppressed by social domination. It is assumed that elimination of social domination enables transparent insight into true needs, so that individuals, reconciled with their biological natures, will live freely and harmoniously with one another. In this manner first-generation critical theorists continued to endorse the humanistic goals of enlightenment, which they now located in the reconciliatory powers of esthetic self-realization.

Foucault rejects the humanistic assumptions underlying this critique on empirical and logical grounds. The empirical grounds pertain to the illusoriness of a universal subject striving to realize its essential nature free from the constraints of power.[8] For critical theorists, these constraints emanate from the state, conceived as the legal and ideological instrument of class domination. Thus, by advancing the interests of the few against the interests of the many, the power of the state violates the ideal of universal, democratic inclusion that underwrites its own rational legitimacy.

Arguing that power is more ubiquitous, diffuse, and corporeal than this hierarchical model suggests, Foucault hopes to undermine the legitimating ideology of universal human rights that continues to guide critical theory's exposure of the immanent contradictions of the bourgeois state. According to Foucault, the state has long since dispensed with this ideology. The legitimate exercise of power is a notion that gained currency during the Middle Ages. Based on Roman Law, it provided the technical means for organizing the administrative apparatus of those absolute monarchies that emerged during the sixteenth century. Its scope was territorially defined, its basis was centralized, and its function was linked to the rightful appropriation of goods and wealth (*PK*, 104).

The bourgeois revolutions that sought to limit monarchic authority democratically did not appeal to a different kind of power. Like the Cartesian concept of the self and the Classical model of knowledge with which it was associated, legitimate power *represented* a higher-order truth that descended vertically from the personal integrity of the monarch or the unitary will of the people. Its violation was therefore punished in ways that represented this organic hierarchy derivatively. Torture and dismemberment, for example, served as visible reminders of a sovereign power whose own personal (if not bodily) integrity had been violated (*DP*, 49–56).

In Foucault's opinion, if punishment no longer assumes this tangible form, it is because the exercise of power itself has changed. Today maintenance of law and order depends on a gentler sanction. The remnants of sovereign power may persist in the empty ritual of plebiscitary democracy, but the exercise of civil and political liberties only serves to mask the deeper discipline required of citizens inhabiting modern states. With the advent of a highly differentiated and fragmented society, the pretense of a unitary will evaporates. Liberal democracy fails to represent a legitimate guarantee of the people's freedom. And so the harmony requisite for the functioning of the system must rely on a different kind of power.

Foucault cites Rusche and Kirchheimer's *Punishment and Social Structures* (1939) as an example of critical theory's failure to grasp this new power. While relating historical changes in punishment to broader changes in political economy, it retained the Classical presumption in favor of a vertical distribution of power (in this instance centered on class domination), thereby overlooking the fact that punishment is a general feature of social conditioning that circulates horizontally throughout all areas of life in which the productivity and docility of the body are at stake (*DP*, 24).[9] But if social conditioning is much less a function of inculcating the "dominant ideas of the ruling class" from the top down than it is of engendering the reciprocal confluence of common desires and corporeal dispositions, it is not, Foucault insists, necessarily more repressive. Freud's hypothesis explains only the *exclusionary* function of power, not its *productivity* in constituting subjects as predictable moral agents who act freely with responsibility (*PK*, 59, 91). Indeed, the stress on productivity is itself a defining feature of those human sciences, such as Freudian psychoanalysis, that have emerged since the Classical Age. In tandem with the capillary overlapping of such older microtechniques as the religious confessional, the clinical examination, and the military exercise in strategies of governance, these disciplines increase the economic efficiency of the body politic exponentially. Scientific measurement, classification, and therapy modify strategies of detention, surveillance, conditioning, and spatial partitioning that find increasing deployment in schools and factories, prisons and hospitals. Thus, scientific discipline conspires with strategic technique to create a new hierarchy of knowledge/power that instrumentalizes social relations both vertically and horizontally (*PK*, 92ff).

Foucault does not hesitate to draw what, for a critical theorist, appears to be a damning conclusion: if power insinuates itself into the very discipline constitutive of rational self-identity, then it is impossible to know rationally one's true humanity independent of power's distorting effects (*PK*, 96, 101). Insofar as "ideology" continues to denote a worthy topic of criticism in the Foucaultian agenda, it does so qualifiedly – not as "false consciousness" of genuine emancipatory needs, but as blindness with respect to the irrecusable historicity, conditionality, and otherness of one's own subjectivity (*PK*, 118, 133).

In Foucault's opinion, the logical contradictions associated with humanism are of a different order of magnitude, since it is they, not ideological blindness, that actually motivate the disciplinary rationalization of society. These paradoxes, elaborated in *The Order of Things* (1966), revolve around the "analytic of finitude of man" as "a strange empirico-transcendental doublet" (*OT*, 318).

As Foucault conceives it, the humanism associated with "The Image of Man" is a distinctly modern ideology whose rational impulse Kant first articulated. Kant shattered the classical model of knowledge conceived as passive representation by endowing the knowing subject with new productive powers. "Man" replaced God as the measure and source of all knowledge and action, but only insofar as "He" was conceived dualistically. Subjectivity thus oscillates between two selves: a rational self that thinks its own productive freedom unconditionally, and an empirical self that perceives its own and nature's objective determination through the refracted prism of sensuous (esthetic) intuition.[10]

Kant's claim to have successfully defended objective knowledge by deducing its transcendental conditions in the subject was met with skepticism by his epigones in the German Idealist tradition. They argued that any dualism of thought and unthought contradicted the kind of absolute, transcendental knowledge Kant himself professed to have of the subject. At the same time, however, they endorsed the dualism of subject and object immanent within the reflexive structure of transcendental thought itself.

We can paraphrase this contradiction accordingly: once we concede that object and subject reflect one another, they cease to be opposed. Nevertheless, it is indisputable that the object derives its epistemic sense only in opposition to the subject, who reflexively generates it as a division internal to itself.

For Foucault, the failure of German Idealism to escape this vicious circle is mirrored in its pathetic vacillation between subjectivism and objectivism, esthetic self-reconciliation and ethical self-determination. Fichte, for example, conceived the identity of subject and object as an infinite task of *ethical* striving in which the dual, transcendental-empirical subject is compelled to *practically re*produce "external" reality as a mirror image of its own internal freedom. Schelling, by contrast, rejected the infinite striving of the ethical subject in favor of an *esthetic* reconciliation with self. For him, the "moment" of moral striving retains a residue of self-diremption (or *self-objectification*). Only by returning to itself in immediate intuition could the self reaffirm its original identity as unconditioned spontaneity. Hegel, however, could not endorse the notion of a reflection that produces and transcends its own objective determinations.[11] As he conceived it, the immediate self-identity of esthetic intuition must itself be realized within the ethical compass of the modern state. Indeed, he argued that the identity of esthetic self-reconciliation and ethical duty, subjective spontaneity and objective determination, is logically necessitated by the very incompleteness of each conjunct. Moreover, since he, unlike his predecessors, conceded the inherent historicity of reflection, he could only attribute his own grasp of this identity to what he assumed to be the completion of the past in the present. History, he concluded, shows us that the objective conditions of life, language, and labor, which historically condition individual subjectivity, progressively reveal *and* realize their own universal truth: free *Spirit*, or self-transparent *Reason.*

Foucault cannot abide this dialectic. If it is true that the human spirit aspires to total self-reflection, it is truer still that it always finds its limit in the impenetrable opacity of desire, language, and labor. Comprising the limits to and conditions of possible knowledge, these structures remain unknowable. The same applies to the return to the origin. The attempt by Hegel and critical theorists to define humanity historically only appears to mark an advance beyond Kant's transcendentalism. As Foucault points out, the preservation and realization of previous historical epochs in the modern age is belied by fundamental discontinuities in the archaeological deep structures circumscribing the various fields of knowledge in any given period, hence the futility of hermeneutically recovering (à la Heidegger) a prelapsarian origin unsullied by the history of its continuous representation.

The paradoxes elaborated above explain the "will to knowledge" motivating the human sciences. Impelled by emancipatory striving, yet confronted with its own facticity, this will constitutes a humanity whose progressive self-understanding is as infinite as it is elusive. Attempting to penetrate beneath the uneven surface of ethical life to the pristine uniformity and spontaneity of instinctual nature, it ends up dissolving the most intimate expressions of desire and feeling into the most alien objectifications of nomothetic science. The esthetic redemption of repressed desires, sensibilities, and productive powers sought by Freud and Marx itself contributes to ever greater objectification and repression. Ultimately, hope for a rational reconciliation of ethos and eros unwittingly becomes a pretext for increased domination.

It remains to be seen whether Foucault offers a way out of this dilemma. In the short run he preferred to cut the Gordian knot, thereby dissolving instead of resolving the erotic-ethical subject. Accordingly, Foucault concluded *The Order of Things* by pointing out that some human sciences – especially structuralist psychoanalysis, ethnology, and linguistics – had "overcome man" (in Nietzsche's sense) by taking Kant's transcendentalism to its zero degree: the reduction of the subject to purely formal sign systems.

This fact looms large for understanding the precarious no-man's land in which Foucault situated his own critical theory. Having rejected the inhumanism of humanism as contrary to human liberation, Foucault embraced the anti-humanism of positivism as strangely compatible with it (*AK*, 234). Indeed, after *The Archaeology of Knowledge* (1969), he further radicalized the anti-humanist consequences of structuralism by purging it of any vestige of transcendental idealism. He now began to situate linguistic codes (discourses) in local and historically contingent practices governed by strategic power relations. The genealogy of power complemented the archaeology of knowledge, and both served to debunk the rational subject of progress.

This solution, as we shall see, raises more questions than it answers. Can a happy positivism fill the critical void vacated by humanism? And in whose name – if not the rational subject's – can it be justified?

II. HABERMAS'S DEFENSE OF HUMANISM

Among Foucault's critics, it is Habermas especially who presses these questions. His answer amounts to a resounding affirmation of the rational subject. Not only does he argue that a humanism founded on communication circumvents the paradoxes described by Foucault, but he contends that the archaeological/genealogical alternative proposed by Foucault succumbs to paradoxes of its own.

A. The communicative basis of humanism and the vindication of legitimacy

Habermas is hardly oblivious to the metaphysical deficiencies of the self-contained subject bequeathed to humanism by way of the "philosophy of consciousness" from Descartes on. Indeed, he agrees with Foucault that the practical implications of subjectivism so conceived are incompatible with the emancipatory intentions of humanism. Contrary to Foucault, however, he thinks these intentions can be redeemed.

According to Habermas, philosophy of consciousness departs from the subject-object dualism implicit in Descartes's epistemological problematic. Idealism overcomes the dualism by reducing objectivity to a moment of the reflecting subject. As our discussion of humanism showed, however, this reduction paradoxically entails the rational objectification of the subject. Rational emancipation is narrowly construed to mean the conceptual articulation of subjectivity in the form of explicit, necessary moments. Its rationale is instrumental in that the efficient management of desire is undertaken in the name of self-preservation, or the moral freedom afforded by self-certainty (as Hegel, recounting the lord-servant dialectic of the *Phenomenology*, so felicitously put it).

Instead of departing from philosophy of consciousness and its epistemological problematic, as Foucault and first-generation critical theorists do, Habermas turns his attention to the moral foundations implicit in philosophy of social action.[12] Here he observes that the communicative dynamics underlying interaction call forth a distinctly non-instrumental and non-strategic rationale.

Philosophy of consciousness ignores the fact that the identity of the knowing subject is founded on *intersubjective reciprocity* between free and equal actors. This insight, which forms the cornerstone of Hegel's social thought, is given a peculiar reading by Habermas. Turning to Hegel's early theological writings and the philosophy of spirit contained in the Jena System of 1803–4, Habermas shows how identity is shaped within communicative encounters in which actors mutually exchange the roles of speaker and listener. *Communicative action* foregrounds the internalization of social roles and the acquisition of higher-order competencies for rational argumentation requisite for reflexive forms of learning. Such discourse, Habermas believes, is always an immanent possibility for speakers who hold themselves rationally accountable. They must be prepared to justify their utterances if challenged, and they must do so rationally. This, in turn, implies a commitment to reach an impartial consensus on disputed knowledge claims and moral beliefs – a consensus that can be guaranteed only if each interlocutor has equal opportunities to speak, free from the external and internal constraints that distort communication and frustrate mutual understanding (*PDM*, 294ff).

By retrieving the openness-to-other implicit in communicative rationality, Habermas thinks he has found a locus for reason that precedes and conditions the more abstract and derivative forms of *instrumental* (and strategic) rationality on which Foucault exclusively focuses. In so doing, he also thinks he has located a space for personal and public expression that securely shelters humanism from the objectifications of subjectivism. Hence, he concludes – perhaps too quickly – that it is also safe from the various paradoxes attributed to it by Foucault.

First, a theory of communicative action ostensibly avoids the paradox of Man as a transcendental-empirical doublet. One aspect of this paradox, we noted, involves the reflexive objectification of a subject whose transcendental activity properly precedes (and thus precludes) empirical representation. The theory of communicative action circumvents the subject-object dualism on which this paradox builds by transferring the transcendental framework formerly ensconced in the isolated subject to the pragmatic assumptions underlying communicative intersubjectivity. Instead of the self relating to itself directly as an observable object – the *aporia* associated with the transcendental-empirical doubling of the subject – it relates to itself indirectly "from the angle of vision of a second person."[13] Stated somewhat differently, the self relates to the other in the *participatory* mode of performative reciprocity, not in the objectifying mode of cognitive-instrumental domination.

The theory of communicative action ostensibly avoids the other side of this paradox: the self divided into transcendental and empirical aspects. Habermas denies that his theory *is* a transcendental theory. Hewing closely to the interdisciplinary ideal advocated by Horkheimer in the thirties, he maintains that the rational reconstruction of formal competencies of speech and action must cohere with both the empirical findings of social science and the considered normative intuitions of real, historical agents in a manner not unlike Rawls's procedure for achieving reflective equilibrium. Furthermore, the formal conditions underlying communicative competence are not, strictly speaking, transcendentally constitutive of speech action, as his colleague-in-arms, Karl-Otto Apel, sometimes argues. Being counterfactual, they regulate, without necessitating, actual speech performance. In any case, such pragmatic norms are not transcendental, if one means by "transcendental" conditions whose necessity and universality can be ascertained with reflexive certainty. Since these norms are regulative for public communication, their proper interpretation and confirmation can occur only in actual discourse, not in private introspection. Hence, whatever universality we might be warranted in ascribing to them here and now must be qualified in light of the essential fallibility of *our* critically considered judgments about their meaning and scope (*PDM*, 297).

Habermas claims his theory avoids the other aporias as well. The paradox of a self that is conceived simultaneously as thought and unthought vanishes once we realize that language comprises a *background* and a *foreground* for mutual understanding. On the one hand, speakers draw from a vast fund of stored meanings, competencies, values, and other shared background assumptions that can be thematized only selectively (*PDM*, 299). On the other hand, the most abstract rules regulating communicative competency can be reconstructed in their entirety. Furthermore, contrary to Foucault's pessimistic diagnosis, critical and analytic modes of self-reflection of the sort carried on by psychoanalysis and ideology critique can improve the narrative integrity of an individual's identity. Since biological drives cannot function as motivations apart from being collectively interpreted as socially recognized needs, it no longer makes sense to oppose esthetic and ethical moments of identity. Reason does not suppress nature; it emancipates it expressively. Once we realize that scientific self-reflection articulates the dynamics and interests of communicative interaction rather than instrumental objectification, we can better appreciate how it eliminates the pseudo-nature of hidden motives that divide us from ourselves and others.

Habermas's theory also seems to vanquish the paradox of the return and retreat of the origin and, along with it, that of the self as creator and created. Habermas insists that communication is neither a unitary "process of self-generation (whether of the spirit or of the species)" nor an alien fate to which we must submit. Communication and its evolutionary logic are themselves contingent on external historical forces, so that "even basic concepts that are starkly universalist have a temporal core" (*PDM*, 301). If there remains any vestige of paradox in Habermas's account of the *progressive* potential of reason, it is that the expansion of communicative networks promotes the establishment of juridical institutions whose emancipatory effects are themselves highly ambiguous. These institutions anchor and legitimate self-regulating economic and administrative systems that constrain and otherwise limit the field of communicative interaction. Despite their adverse effects, such strategic power relations, Habermas believes, are susceptible to *some* democratic control to the degree that they are publicly debated.

Doubtless Foucault would query many of the points raised in this defense. Can we assume that subjects possess an identity capable of becoming rationally integrated? Why is the "integration" of eros and ethos effected by psychoanalysis not complicit in the normalization of subjects? And can we speak of a communicative normalization of the subject – including the rational, critical participant of democratic dialogue – free from the constraints of strategic power? Indeed, is rational, moral discourse capable of adequately articulating the erotic and existential dimension of human being apart from esthetic experience?

Space limitations prevent us from pursuing all these questions here. Presently, other questions about Habermas's success in avoiding the paradox of humanism press upon us with greater urgency. In particular, the question arises whether Habermas's communicative grounding of critical theory is not really a transcendental one after all. Does not the postulation – however fallibilistically intended – of an evolutionary moral logic commit him to some variant of Hegel's philosophy of a transhistorical meta-subject? And does this not, in turn, commit him to a closed reading of history wherein the always implicit emancipatory potential of language fully realizes itself with the anticipated completion of modernity?

As pressing as these questions are, they cannot be dealt with adequately until we have examined Habermas's critique of Foucault. Yet if the aforementioned reference to the fallibilistic, *interpretative* nature of rational reconstruction – as an enterprise whose own validity depends on confirmation via *coherence* and *communication* – is at all indicative of the kind of circularity Habermas wishes to avoid, then his charge that Foucault's social theory vacillates between transcendental structuralism and empirical contextualism applies to himself as well. Whether he also succumbs to the other main version of this dialectic – the self as spontaneous eros and lawful ethos – is more problematic and, just possibly, defensible.

I will forego discussing these difficult issues until the conclusion of this paper. But before turning to Habermas's critique of Foucault, we must again broach the subject of power. If, for Habermas, the notion of a legitimate exercise of power retains any currency at all, it will be possible to show how Foucault's own critique tacitly – albeit inconsistently – appeals to it. But can Habermas's retention of this notion withstand Foucault's analysis of the colonization of juridical institutions by disciplinary power?

Foucault tells us that appeal to legal rights against the usurpations of disciplinary power is futile: "if one wants to look for a non-disciplinary form of power, or rather, to struggle against disciplines and disciplinary powers, it is not towards the ancient right of sovereignty that one should turn, but towards the possibility of a new form of right, one which must indeed be anti-disciplinarian, but at the same time liberated from the principle of sovereignty" (PK, 108).

Habermas's response to this challenge is twofold. First, he accepts, up to a point, Foucault's diagnosis of the carceral malignancy of modern society. First, he deplores the extent to which dividing practices and hierarchies of knowledge destroy competencies for critical reflection. The segmentation of the labor process and the splitting-off of specialized forms of technical expertise, he notes, easily lend themselves to the conformist aims of disciplinary power. He even shares Foucault's conviction that the spread of legal regulation in the welfare democracies of the West embodies a kind of paternalism that hinders freedom.[14]

The colonization of the domestic sphere by welfare provisions exemplifies the kind of bureaucratic domination that Habermas especially finds interesting. But here he diverges from Foucault. While it is true, for Habermas, that the pastoral power exercised through welfare law dehumanizes recipients of aid by reducing them to faceless case histories classifiable by type, it is also true that it entitles them to social rights requisite for equal citizenship.

Habermas, then, thinks Foucault underestimates the emancipatory power of a sovereign authority whose efficacy remains linked, however tenuously, to demands for legitimation. How otherwise could one explain the resistance of parents and teachers to the education bureaucracy, of social workers and clients to the welfare bureaucracy, and of nurses, doctors, and patients to the health bureaucracy (PDM, 287)?[15]

The question "Who exercises power over whom and by what authority?" thus retains its importance in Habermas's analysis of power.[16] For him, both the modern welfare state and its forerunner, the liberal democratic state, are progressive attempts to satisfy the implicit conditions legitimating constitutional government. If Foucault is right that consent theories based on natural law doctrines embody an economistic individualism that is less germane to the welfare state than to the bourgeois constitutional state, he is wrong, Habermas claims, in regarding them as mere dysfunctional relics from the period of absolutism.

Indeed, Foucault's own defense of the rights of prisoners, homosexuals, and mental patients transcends the limits of contract law (*PDM*, 290). Civil rights like these are justified, Habermas contends, because, in a democratic forum freed from the constraints of inequality, everyone would accept them as advancing genuine, emancipatory needs (*LC*, 123ff).

We are now in a position to address the other side of Habermas's response to Foucault. Foucault's appeal to a "new form of right," he submits, belies his own old-fashioned, civil libertarian defense of marginalized groups. Furthermore, despite Foucault's disavowal of prescriptive language in favor of cold description, his functional analysis of carceral society is far from value-neutral; it contains rhetorically charged terms whose pejorative significance implicitly condemns the very reality they denote (PDM, 282).[17]

B. The paradoxes of antihumanism: the impossible bracketing of the subject

The *crypto-normativity* of Foucault's rhetoric about a new kind of right provides Habermas with his second line of defense: proof that a wholesale critique of humanistic ideals is itself paradoxical. Habermas frames this defense in the form of a dense commentary on Foucault's work, beginning with *Madness and Civilization* (1961) and concluding with the first volume of the *History of Sexuality* (1978). The defense hinges on the self-referential paradox attached to wholesale criticisms of rationality. Foucault's work is caught in the dilemma mentioned at the outset of this essay: it bases its critique of reason on normative standards that either implicate reason or prescind from it. The former horn of the dilemma entangles his theory in inconsistency; the latter mires it in mute estheticism.

Habermas traces the evolution of Foucault's thought through three major stages. In the existential-phenomenological stage culminating in *Madness and Civilization*, Foucault succumbs to estheticism. In the structuralist stage culminating in *The Archaeology of Knowledge* (1969), he succumbs to inconsistency. And in the post-structuralist, genealogical stage culminating in the *History of Sexuality*, he vacillates between these extremes. In each instance Foucault's difficulties stem from a failure to locate critical reason in communicative presuppositions that lie outside the objectifications of subject-centered rationality.

Madness and Civilization traces the modern understanding of madness back to the rationalization of European society begun in the seventeenth century. Until that time, Foucault argues, madness had been regarded as a special kind of wisdom; it expressed insight into the tragic secret of humanity's archaic past and its fatal link to atavistic passions. This changed with the advent of the modern nation-state. Political absolutism conspired with the nascent medical sciences to create a healthy, productive, well-ordered and uniform citizenry who could truck no relation to madness. The latter was then reconstituted as a mental illness requiring containment and proscription.

If, for Foucault, insanity is now constituted as the diametric antithesis of reason, it is only because reason incarnate – the transparent, self-identical ego – suppresses the unthinkable depths of human existence. This valorization of an esthetic intuition that precedes clear articulation, Habermas notes, is doubly paradoxical. First, as Foucault himself conceded, his own attempt to apprehend and articulate the original meaning of madness "in its unfettered state" is self-contradictory. Second, the desire to return to an original truth is symptomatic of the very humanism Foucault later excoriated.

Foucault sought to resolve these paradoxes by bracketing the subjectivity in which self-interpretation moves. The second and third stages of his thought comprise progressive steps in this direction. The second stage deploys an *archaeological* method that brackets both the intentional meaning and the truth (or falsity) of statements. The third stage supplements this procedure with a *genealogical* method that brackets the moral preferability of practices.

The archaeology of knowledge construes meaning in terms of objective structure. The meaning of a statement is defined by the sequence of statements that precede and follow it. This sequence, in turn, is one possible articulation among many alternatives that are permitted by a system of statements. Such a system is not closed, however. Unlike classical structuralists, Foucault does not believe

that the determination of semantic elements and the rules governing their possible articulation precedes, in some transcendental
sense, their actual articulation.[18] So construed, the system of regularities governing possible speech delimits the range of what can be
accepted as a possible true statement, censors unacceptable themes
and utterances, and silences "unqualified" speakers in a continually
shifting manner.

Foucault principally deploys his archaeological method in analyzing just those performative utterances (*énoncés*) that figure in the
regimented language games of science. His aim is to articulate the
archaeological deep structures that determine the limits and possibilities of knowledge for any given period (*AK*, 191; *OT*, xi–xiv). The
systems of language that comprise these formation rules – what Foucault calls *epistemes* – are historically discontinuous. Their analysis
ostensibly shows that heterogeneous disciplines within a given period have more in common than disciplines sharing the same subject
matter but falling into different periods. Thus, whereas the natural
history, general grammar, and the analysis of wealth formed by the
classical *episteme* of the seventeenth century sought to represent
and analyze a table of elements, their counterparts in the modern
age (biology, philology, and economics) are guided by an altogether
different figure: the genetic explanation of visceral functions and
productive systems.

Habermas argues that the archaeology of knowledge is incapable of
providing a coherent account of its own scientific objectivity. From an
archaeological perspective, the truth of its statements is but a function of its own groundless formation rules. True, *The Order of Things*
suggests otherwise in its assertion that the turn to archaeological
science is itself compelled by the humanism preceding it. But such a
dialectical grounding assumes more continuity between *epistemes*
than the archaeological method will allow. Indeed, as Habermas
notes, the postulation of radical discontinuity makes it difficult to
understand how archaeology – or, indeed, any method – could critically check its own objectivity. For here the achievement of objectivity could occur only if the proponents of one *episteme* (method) could
engage proponents of other *epistemes* (methods) in critical dialogue, a
mutual hermeneutics of self-clarification that archaeology forswears.
Parenthetically, it might be argued in this context that archaeology's
structuralist method seems to bear a stronger resemblance to the

classical *episteme* than to the modern (despite its functionalist vocabulary) and, thus, suffers from a similar defect: failure to account
critically for its own point of view (*PDM*, 262).

Aside from this basic difficulty, Foucault's structuralist account of
meaning cannot explain actual speech. Structuralism at best accounts for the formal conditions of *possible* syntactic and semantic
combinations, transformations, and exclusions at any given time.
Conditions of possibility, however, do not explain the actual selection, or *genesis*, of particular utterances (*AK*, 38, 73, 121).[19] These
still depend on subjective intentions and, more basically still, the
communicative competence embodied in speaker/listener roles.[20]
The latter are learned competencies, acquired through socialization.
They comprise capacities for utilizing a know-how – an application
of rules – that cannot itself be reduced to mere rule-following, without generating an infinite regress. Bluntly stated, the system of language (*langue*) cannot be divorced from practices that generate actual speech-action (*parole*).

The above criticism is related to a deeper problem. As we have
seen, Foucault sometimes talks as if his theory of language is really
post-structuralist. He cannot maintain a rigid dichotomy between
the system of formation rules and actual speech without raising the
spector of a transcendental/empirical dualism of the sort he wants to
avoid. Instead, he collapses the system into the local and shifting
context of speech. This strategy creates two difficulties. First, it is
unclear how the mere factual constellation of dispersed assertoric
events can yield regularities of any kind. Context alone – the open
field of signs externally connected to one another – yields no warrant for distinguishing acceptable from unacceptable sign events.[21]
Second, any statistical regularities that might be adduced from such
an external concatenation would only enable us to predict repeti-
tions of past events. But the rules structuring language games do not
function like stochastic regularities; they permit the regular generation of new and wholly unpredictable utterances that often deviate
markedly from past practice. Linguistic rules are neither discon-
firmed nor violated by such innovations because they themselves
consist of generative competencies rather than mere habits.

Of course, archaeology might avoid this conundrum by simply
acknowledging the prescriptive nature of linguistic rules. In fact,
while speaking of a unity that resides anterior to the "visible, hori-

zontal coherence of the elements formed [in the] system that makes possible and governs this formation" (*AK*, 72), Foucault notes that the rules of formation "lay down [*prescrit*] what must be related, in a particular discursive practice, for such and such an enunciation to be made, for such and such a concept to be used, for such and such a strategy to be organized" (*AK*, 74). The problem with this acknowledgment of prescriptivity is obvious. Prescriptivity is gained at the cost of reintroducing an *anterior unity*, or transcendental structure, that remains untouched by actual practice.

The archaeology of knowledge thus finds itself impaled on the transcendental/empirical, prescriptive/descriptive dialectic of humanism. The genealogy of power that dominates the third stage of Foucault's thought can be understood as an attempt to overcome the dualism that fuels this dialectic.[22] First, it sees linguistic competence as inextricably bound to actual speech performance. The rules of formation are now conceived as aspects of a practice whose normativity is continually contested. In contrast to the relatively static juxtaposition of discontinuous *epistemes* that one finds in archaeology, genealogy traces the genesis of less global institutions, technologies, and practices across periodic divides. In every instance, their normativity and genesis are conceived as a function of power relations.

Whereas archaeology brackets the truth and intentional meaning of linguistic discourse, genealogy brackets the moral preferability of practices. Like Nietzsche's *Genealogy of Morals*, after which it is patterned, genealogy eschews a universal history of progress or decline. As Foucault puts it in "Nietzsche, Genealogy, History" (1971), genealogy shows that "all knowledge rests on injustice (there is no right, even in the act of knowing, no truth or foundation for truth)" (*LCP*, 163).

Given statements like these, one cannot but agree with Habermas that Foucault's genealogical criticism, no less than his archaeology of knowledge, succumbs to self-referential paradox. Aside from this obvious defect, it is less clear whether genealogy resolves the problems it inherits from archaeology. Can power relations explain speech action any better than disembodied linguistic structures?

Habermas thinks not. Indeed, he points out that, "in Foucault's genealogy, 'power' is initially a synonym for this *purely structuralistic activity*; it takes the same place as *différance* does in Derrida.

But this power constitutive of discourse is supposed to be a power of transcendental generativity *and* of empirical self-assertion simultaneously" (*PDM*, 256). Foucault merely resolves his transcendental/ empirical dialectic by conflating these terms in the concept of power.

This conflation is apparent in Foucault's inaugural address, "The Order of Discourse" (1970). The essay distinguishes the peculiar "will to knowledge" characteristic of modern science from "the power of constituting domains of objects" (*AK*, 234). The former is an empirical event traceable to Platonic rationalism and its distinction between true and false, essence and appearance; the latter, a kind of ontological generativity.

The conflation of these distinct notions of power results from Foucault's attribution of features to the one that properly belong to the other. What Foucault calls a *dispositive* captures the way in which the will to knowledge inscribed in the technical apparatus of rational society directly creates the rule-governed normativity constitutive of modern productive subjects. The panoptic objectifications of modern society are thus endowed by him with powers formerly ascribed to transcendental subjectivity. Conversely, power, conceived as a transhistorical condition productive of knowledge and discourse in general, is described in the strategic, objectifying language of the historical *apriori* appertaining to the modern (subjectless) will to knowledge. Thus the categories of disciplinary power reverberate throughout Foucault's description of ontological power and vice versa.

In Habermas's opinion, this last defect vitiates Foucault's account of subjectivity (*PDM*, 242). Foucault misconceives the constitution of subjectivity as a process of objectification and thus misses the connection between socialization and individuation. On Foucault's reading, socialization constitutes subjects as normal types, whose role behavior is little more than conditioned reflex. So little do they exhibit the critical autonomy, creativity, and individuality of modern subjects that one is continually reminded of Durkheim's segmented tribes (or Garfinkel's "judgmental dopes"), who labor under the mechanical determinism of a monolithic, collective consciousness.

It is strange that the image of a unified, functional system that thoroughly dominates its *subjecta membra* is belied by the language of strategic gaming that colors Foucault's characterization of power relations. Instead of the determinism of *habitus,* we are given the anarchism of unregulated clashes between warring forces that – to cite Habermas – "emerge and pop like glittering bubbles from a swamp of anonymous processes of subjugation" (*PDM*, 268).

Foucault's theory thus vacillates between subjectivist (voluntarist) and objectivist (constructivist) conceptions of agency in a manner reminiscent of German Idealism. Either the agent is a wholly determined object, in which case individual autonomy is but an illusory mask concealing coercively programmed ethical roles, or s/he is a strategic subject, whose normatively unbounded gaming creates external relations of domination. The former view predominates in Foucault's "positivistic" writings culminating in *Discipline and Punish* (1976); the latter, in his "romantic" panegyric to the "esthetics of existence" contained in his last interviews and in the second and third volumes of *The History of Sexuality.*[23]

Here, then, we find the rationale underlying Habermas's charge that Foucault is a "young conservative" (*MP*, 13). Foucault's cynicism regarding modern legal ideals undermines the only ground supporting struggles for freedom and justice.[24] This cynicism, we now realize, lies deeper than Foucault's empirical analysis of biopower in modern society. Even if Foucault were right about this analysis – and it is by no means clear that he is – genealogical criticism could hardly abjure the task of justifying its own norms. But the metatheoretical basis of genealogical critique – above all, its defective conceptualization of the rational subject – makes it virtually impossible for him to do so. The normative reciprocity constitutive of a critical subject is simply absent. Either Foucault conceives norms as systemic functions of a disciplinary power that confronts the agent as an external fate to which s/he must passively submit,[25] or he conceives them as coercive effects of unregulated wars between strategic actors seeking their own subjective advantage. In neither case are they conceived as obligations whose peculiar force derives from their *presumed* satisfaction of genuine social needs.

III. FOUCAULT'S HERMENEUTIC TURN AND THE
RESOLUTION OF THE DEBATE

As I shall endeavor to show, Foucault's later turn toward hermeneutic sociology resulted in a major reconceptualization of strategic power relations that meets most of Habermas's objections. It is significant that this reconceptualization provides a certain corrective to Habermas's own theory of communicative action. First, it shows how strategic and communicative action mutually condition one another. Second, it shows how a certain kind of power accompanies any speech action. Together these facts establish a necessary connection between power, strategic action, reason, and subjective agency capable of normatively grounding critical genealogy.

A. Foucault's hermeneutic turn

Foucault's later turn to hermeneutic genealogy can be seen as a belated attempt to provide normative justification for his theory. By the late seventies Foucault was seeking such justification in the unsystematic "subjugated forms of knowledge" that circulate in the contemporary counterdiscourses of everyday life. In so doing, he adopted a strategy that could be found in the writings of critical theorists dating back to Marx. Here the justification for criticism is assumed to be immanent in the ordinary understanding that oppressed groups have of themselves. Alienated from themselves by the objectifying regimen of scientific management, they nonetheless aspire to freedom and happiness.

If Foucault embraces the subject of commonsense reason, it is not because he thinks the latter can be theoretically grounded. This difference from Habermas is insurmountable. Nevertheless, by 1983 he had come to see his own work as a continuation of the Enlightenment ethos he had formerly repudiated. He not only openly acknowledged the kinship between his social theory and Habermas's but, in a late interview, also ironically observed that he was in "a little more agreement" with Habermas than Habermas was with him.[26]

Indeed, the last two volumes of the *History of Sexuality* marked something of a watershed in Foucault's understanding of his life's work. He now admitted that the central preoccupation of his research from the very beginning – the relationship between the subject and truth – could best be approached by way of a hermeneutically enlightened genealogy.[27] Gone is the cold, objective description of functionalist relations. What now occupies center stage in his analysis is ethics or, more precisely, the way in which subjects voluntarily and intentionally subject themselves to technologies of self-control – technologies that are embedded in specific practices and types of knowledge determinant of a way of life, a manner of self-understanding, an identity – in short, an *ethos* (*UP,* 10).

These practices exhibit their own continuity through time. In contrast to Foucault's earlier emphasis on epistemological breaks, his genealogical account of the Christian ethos that has shaped the modern age acknowledges superficial resemblances between its moral codes and those of its Greek and Greco-Roman predecessors. If we think of the moral code as "the set of values and rules of action that are recommended to the individual through the intermediary of various prescriptive agencies," then all three systems are alike in their prescription of sexual abstinence (*UP,* 25).

At the same time, Foucault points out that this continuity conceals deeper shifts in their "ethical substance." The latter refers to "the way in which the individual has to constitute this or that part of himself as the prime material of his moral conduct," that is, the way in which he incorporates the moral code into his conduct (*UP,* 26).[28] Some ethical regimes place greater emphasis on the moral code, its systematicity and inclusiveness. Here adherence to law is decisive in determining the mode of subjection. Others place emphasis on the esthetics of self-transformation. The Christian ethos and especially its modern, secular equivalent tend toward the former; the Greek and Greco-Roman ethic, toward the latter (*UP,* 21, 31). Transposed over the morality of sexual abstinence, the difference between the three is apparent. Whereas the Greek ethos sought to cultivate a moderate use of pleasure for the sake of personal and civic virtue, and the Greco-Roman ethos sought to cultivate a solicitous care over the self for the sake of rationally administering a complex identity, the Christian ethos seeks to cultivate a hermeneutics of desire aimed at discovering the hidden truth of the soul. Its renunciation of a fallen self that is permanently deceived about itself marks the transition to a deontological ethic that privileges dutiful regulation of conduct over esthetic self-realization.

B. Beyond hermeneutics: toward a new theory of the subject

Foucault continued to describe the peculiar *hermeneutics of desire* by which modern agents constitute themselves as dutiful subjects in

terms of self-objectification rather than intersubjective mutuality
(*SP*, 208). It remains to be seen whether, for Foucault, this mode of
self-objectification is essential to modernity. Does the Protestant
Ethic and its Pastoral Power comprise our historical *apriori*, or can
we imagine a more emancipated strain of enlightenment that might
draw freely from the pagan ethos of esthetic self-transformation?

I think the answer to these questions may be found in Foucault's
groping effort to articulate something like a general theory of the
subject. Before discussing this theory, I would like to question the
one-dimensionality of Foucault's ethology from the standpoint of
Carol Gilligan's research on moral development.

If we accept Carol Gilligan's analysis of postconventional moral
development in American society, the modern ethos described by
Foucault is more complicated than he thinks. It divides into two
distinct, *gendered* paths of postconventional self-realization: an
ethic of responsibility and an ethic of care. The former designates
the achievement of ego-centered individuation consonant with ac-
quiring a deontological appreciation of rights and abstract principles of justice. Typically associated with masculine socialization
patterns involving strategies of conflict resolution in competitive
games, it abstracts from concrete associations in which care for self
and others as unique, *associated* persons emerges. By contrast, the
ethic of care designates the achievement of personal integrity consonant with generative attachment to others. Typically associated
with feminine socialization patterns originating in non-competi-
tive games, it focuses on the unique constellation of personal commitments, needs, and situational demands of the "concrete other."
For Gilligan, these paths of moral development, which partially
resonate with Foucault's historical distinction between an ethos of
esthetic care and an ethos of legal autonomy, are complementary.
Seen from the perspective of Foucault's central problematic, they
designate two aspects or types of power: the productive, esthetic
empowering of self and other through mutual caring, and the exclusionary, juridical *power* of self over other through legal agency.[29]

As we shall see, Foucault's general theory of the subject as an
active agent of power explains these different senses of freedom and
reciprocity better than Habermas's, without relinquishing the latter's universalism. At the same time, Foucault's appeal to universal
structures in lieu of historical discourses is more self-consciously

interpretative and historically situated than Habermas's. To cite the original preface to the second volume of the *History of Sexuality:*

"Thought" . . . can and must be analyzed in every manner of speaking, do-ing, or behaving in which the individual appears and acts as subject of learning, as ethical and juridical subject, as subject conscious of himself and other. In this sense. thought is understood as *the very form of action – as action insofar as it implies the play of true and false, the acceptance or refusal of rules, the relation of oneself to others.* . . . Posing the question in this way brings into play certain altogether *general principles.* Singular forms of experience may perfectly well harbor *universal structures;* they may well not be independent from the concrete determinations of social existence . . . [t]his thought has a historicity which is proper to it. That it should have this historicity does not mean that it is deprived of all *universal form,* but instead the putting into play of these universal forms is itself historical (*FR,* 335).

These comments suggest the rudiments of a formal theory of subjec-tivity that acknowledges the universal interplay of cognition, moral intersubjectivity, and expressive relation to self and other while con-ceding its irrecusible historicity.[30] More important, as we shall see below, they also indicate a much deeper entwinement of communica-tive and strategic relations than any of Foucault's critics – Habermas included – seem to realize.

To see this we need only turn to Foucault's important essay "The Subject and Power" (1982), where he expressly follows Habermas in distinguishing power relations (or domination) from communica-tive relations and objective (instrumental) capacities. According to Foucault,

power relations, relationships of communication, objective capacities should not therefore be confused. This is not to say that there is a question of three separate domains. Nor that there is on one hand the field of things, of perfected technique, work, and the transformation of the real; on the other that of signs, communication, reciprocity, and production of meaning; finally that of the domination of the means of constraint, of inequality and the action of men upon men. It is a question of three types of relationships which in fact always overlap one another, support one another reciprocally, and use each other mutually as means to an end (*SP,* 217–18).

It might be objected that the convergence between Foucault and Habermas as regards the interdependence of communication, domination, and objective capacity obscures an important difference. In Foucault's essay, power relations are seamlessly assimilated to domination, which in turn is characterized as a "transcendental" on a par with communicative relationships and instrumental capacities. However, in only one of the possible texts to which Foucault might have been referring does Habermas even remotely suggest that power is a transcendental medium of knowledge and action.[31] In *Knowledge and Human Interests* (1968) and in a somewhat later essay on Hannah Arendt, Habermas describes domination (*Herrschaft*) as a wholly contingent and unjustifiable use of a power (*Macht*) whose meaning eludes transcendental categorization.[32]

This disagreement between Foucault and Habermas would be decisive were it not for the fact that both eventually came to regard power as a permanent, if variable, feature of society. For Habermas, the manifestations of power, ranging from relatively innocuous forms of subtle influence to overt forms of violent domination, vary both structurally and historically. From a structural point of view, power may designate a feature of speech or a mechanism of system integration. As a feature of a speech, it specifies the peculiar sanction of authority backing up commands. Although in the *Theory of Communicative Action* (1981) Habermas categorically distinguished commands backed by mere threat of force from commands backed by rationally binding moral authority, in a more recent reply to critics he conceded that "a continuum obtains between power that is merely a matter of factual custom and power transformed into normative authority."[33] Such a continuum is attested to by the simple fact that *rationally binding* moral platitudes such as "Tell the truth!" are initially learned as commands backed by threat of sanctions.[34]

A similar continuity obtains in the case of power when viewed as a vertical mechanism of social (or systemic) differentiation.[35] Here Habermas notes that in stratified tribal societies the exercise of power in the form of *personal* prestige and influence need not rely on sanctions of any kind. The asymmetrical exercise of power owing to differences in lineage, gender, and/or generation is still interwoven in communicative relations between groups and individuals situated horizontally with respect to one another. Thus the communicative links between groups and individuals remain bound to symmetrical moral expectations. By contrast, the bureaucratic power exercised in modern organizations depends on *impersonal* legal sanction. Here the routine asymmetrical exercise of power is all but sundered from the personal and symmetrical moral consensus critically negotiated in everyday communicative action. Whereas the influence and prestige possessed by technical experts and charismatic leaders in modern society still rely on communicative interaction and, in some sense, condense negotiations with respect to rational and moral accountability, bureaucratic power is exercised *strategically*, without regard to such negotiations (*TCA2*, 181–83, 273–81). Indeed, as we shall see below, the exercise of bureaucratic and economic power represents an extreme – and by no means typical – case of strategic action, according to Habermas. Yet notwithstanding his identification of institutionalized forms of strategic power with the unilateral and hegemonic repression of interests, he insists that power "legitimated" through democratic channels retains a *moral* link – however tenuous and ideologically compromised – to a *productive*, communicative consensus on general interests.[36]

In a manner that invites comparison with Habermas's taxonomy, some of Foucault's late interviews also distinguish between levels, or degrees, of power: strategic relationships, domination, and governance.[37] Whereas domination involves exercising a unilateral and irreversible power over others, governance and strategic relations presuppose reciprocity. Governance implies an unequal relationship that may degenerate into domination under certain circumstances. However, as Gilligan notes, in education or any other kind of nurturing relationship, governance can *empower* the one who is governed, thereby leading to its own transcendence.[38] Strategic relations, by contrast, involve the most reciprocity, since they comprise games in which players use influence to elicit free responses. In all these instances power varies structurally and historically depending on its degree of formal institutionalization. A close examination of Foucault's work would show that he, no less than Habermas, distinguishes overt from covert, strategic (narrowly construed) from communicative, normative from non-normative forms of domination, governance, and strategic relationship.

At this juncture we encounter another obstacle in our attempt to deconstruct the rigid opposition between strategic power and moral reason. Despite the language of reciprocity, many commentators conclude that Foucault's quasi-transcendental notion of strategic relationship is incompatible with Habermas's notion of communicative interaction.[39] In Habermas's lexicon strategic interaction occurs whenever one or more actors pursue personal aims by influencing the behavior of others through threat of force, covert manipulation, or some other instrumental inducement. Instead of implicitly or explicitly orienting himself to obligatory norms or other reasons that ostensibly advance common interests and mutual respect, the strategic actor offers incentives calculated to advance his own interest (*TCA1*, 10, 85, 273–74). Often this requires concealing a primary strategic intent behind the facade of communication oriented toward mutual understanding.

Although Habermas's retention of a real distinction between communicative and strategic types of action is, strictly speaking, incompatible with the Foucaultian scheme of mutually overlapping and conditioning aspects, it is more compatible with the latter than one might expect. Here again, a brief examination of Habermas's distinction reveals structural overlappings and continuities linking strategic and communicative action. For Habermas, the deployment of official power, like the use of money, represents a relatively pure case of strategic action, in that bureaucratic aims can be pursued according to established legal procedure, without regard to moral constraints and communicative rationales circulating in everyday life. However, this *pure* exercise of power represents an atypical case even at the organizational level. As examples of sexual harassment on the job all too frequently attest, superiors are morally accountable to subordinates with regard to personal conduct, if not with regard to choice of policy aims. The situation gets even murkier when we consider strategic pursuits in non-institutional settings. For, in the absence of rigid procedures and sanctions, strategic adversaries (from, say, labor and big business) still need to justify their strategic aims in the communicative vocabulary of public interest.[40]

The convergence between Habermas and Foucault on the issue of overlapping types of action is perhaps better seen from the latter's vantage point. For if it can be said that Foucault interprets communicative action strategically, as a game of power, it can also be argued that he interprets strategic action communicatively, as a game of dialogue. Foucault contests the idea that strategic action – or any action involving game-theoretic calculations aimed at coordinating interaction for purposes of successfully realizing personal goals – is necessarily manipulative, egoistic, or atomistic, as Habermas sometimes suggests. Indeed, egoism and atomism are even less pronounced in his account of strategic relations than in game theories generally, since he repudiates methodological individualism. Indeed, as we shall see below, by emphasizing the normative reciprocity of strategic action, his account of gaming comports with Gadamer's account of the play structure underlying all forms of mutual understanding, in which the action itself conducts the responses of the actors. In both instances we have accounts of communication and non-manipulative exercise of power that seek to influence – through relatively transparent, but literally unannounced – contextual effects.

On the one hand, Foucault says that a strategic power relation is "not simply a relationship between partners, individual or collective; it is a way in which certain actions modify others" (*SP*, 219). This comports with the Gadamerian concept of a free play in which the context (or perlocutionary effect, as Habermas, following Austin refers to it) elicits a response. To this extent, subjective agency remains beholden to actions that have a meaning (power and efficacy) of their own, independent of consciously intended aims – a condition of ego *un*boundedness that comes to the fore in feelings of mutual caring. On the other hand, he insists that it is not a relationship of violence, but requires "that 'the other' (the one over whom power is exercised) be thoroughly recognized and maintained to the very end as a person who acts" (*SP*, 220). This is to say that "power is less a confrontation between two adversaries or the linking of one to the other than a question of government": the structuration of a field of possible responses (*SP*, 221). According to this latter reading, not only are freedom and power not mutually exclusive, but "freedom may well appear as the condition for the exercise of power" (*SP*, 220). Hence the free play of actions and effects is not entirely independent of rational agency, but presupposes a real – and potentially legal – capacity for initiative and counter-initiative.

Speech act theory provides ample confirmation of this strategic/ dialogic interplay in its differentiation between manipulative strategies, which aim at domination, and strategic relations, which aim at reciprocity. In particular, it shows that the success of the former is dependent on the success of the latter. Take the example of promising. As Habermas notes, the freedom of the addressee depends on his or her capacity to refuse the promise. This offer thus presents an opportunity for exercising freedom; that is, it opens up a field of possible responses on the part of the addressee. We might say that, by taking the initiative in opening up a determinate field of possibilities, the speaker's offer constitutes a deployment of power whereby the response of the addressee is conducted. This conducting, however, is not a manipulating. To begin with, the field of possibilities is indirectly communicated by the perlocutionary effects stemming from both illocutionary acts and contexts of speech. Further, this determination of an initial field of response *enables* a potential refusal. Conversely, the freedom of the addressee is conditional for the exercise of power; promise-making would make no sense if the addressee had no choice but to accept the offer. By contrast, promise-breaking is parasitic on (and hence secondary to) a normal practice of promise-making; as Kant showed, without the assumption of reciprocity that accompanies promise-making, the manipulation of the promise-breaker would never succeed.

These remarks are important not only because they suggest that strategic reciprocity is prior to strategic manipulation, but also because they imply that strategic actors – far from being passive bearers of functional roles and internalized norms – actively and freely contribute to the structuration of the field of possible responses. Here we see how Foucault's contextualist account of discourse as strategic action might be vindicated against Habermas's charge of inconsistency. *From a hermeneutic perspective,* the regular and reflexive structuration of a field of possible responses implies that the rules governing language games are continually reinterpreted in every new, situation-bound application.[41]

As we shall see, this circularity of form and content will enable us to resolve the paradox of the subject as ethically determined and esthetically free. For not only is the moral-juridical subject of speech action decentered in a free play in which multiple agencies and contexts mutually interpret and affect one another. So is the moral-esthetic subject of care, whose own creative spontaneity and experience, as Dewey convincingly argued, depends on the emotional and affective features of its social environment.

Before discussing the interplay between ethos and eros, we must see how the concept of strategic relationship impacts upon Habermas's notion of consensual communication. Just as Foucault's account of strategic relations is more complex and concrete than Habermas's, so too is his account of consensual communication. Foucault seems to accept Habermas's general characterization of consensual communication as foundational for the raising of validity claims and the incurring of general obligations in a modern society. This impression is reinforced by his remark that

in the serious play of questions and answers, in the work of reciprocal elucidation, the rights of each person are in some sense immanent in the discussion. . . . The person asking the questions is merely exercising the right that has been given him: to remain unconvinced, to perceive a contradiction, to require information, to emphasize different postulates, to point out faulty reasoning (FR, 381).

Elsewhere Foucault takes issue with Habermas's idealization of consensual communication, denying that "there could be a state of communication which would be such that the games of truth could circulate freely, without obstacles, without constraint and without coercive effects." Stated bluntly, Foucault thinks that Habermas's assessment of the prescriptive value to be accorded unconstrained consensus is too utopian.

It is being blind to the fact that relations of power are not something bad in themselves, from which one must free one's self. I don't believe there can be a society without relations of power, if you understand them as means by which individuals try to conduct, to determine the behavior of others. The problem is not of trying to dissolve them in the utopia of a perfectly transparent communication, but to give one's self the rules of law, the techniques of management, and also the ethics, the *ethos,* the practice of self, which would allow these games of power to be played with a minimum of domination.[42]

Several remarks in the above passage alert us to the possibility of a verbal disagreement between Foucault and Habermas. As noted above, both Foucault and Habermas distinguish power from domination, both affirm emancipation from domination as a goal of enlightenment, and both tacitly accept the strategic inducements necessary for initiating and sustaining dialogue. For Habermas, the unconstrained *force* of the better argument succeeds in persuading only to the extent that the arguer successfully anticipates the reactions of her interlocutor(s).[43] Thus it is not unreasonable to suppose that even an impoverished game theory might shed light on the Prisoners' Dilemmas and strategic bottlenecks that prevent agents from resolving conflicts consensually.

To be sure, consensual communication was not the only activity countenanced by Foucault in which validity claims are raised and justified. In his last course at the Collège de France in 1984 he talked about a different kind of self-justification modeled on the *parrhesia* practiced by ancient Greek and Roman ethicists. The emphasis here is on producing a "true life" through one's bearing and demeanor. Although some have seen in this bearing-witness-to-truth an esthetic alternative to what they regard as the overly rationalistic concept of justification implicit in consensual communication, it seems inconceivable that this rhetoric of exemplification could resolve moral disagreements arising from strategic conflicts.[44] In Habermas's scheme, such a notion of truth-telling bears a stronger resemblance to the raising of esthetic-expressive claims to truthfulness (*Wahrhaftigkeit*) and authenticity (*Eigentlichkeit*).

Foucault's interest in parrhesia as a nondiscursive form of justification might be construed as devaluing rational consensus-oriented communication in relation to expressive communication. It would be hard to square this assessment with his assertion that consensus remains "a critical idea to maintain at all times." Foucault seems to affirm a parity between communicative, strategic, and expressive action, adding that one must "ask oneself what proportion of nonconsensuality is implied in such a power relationship, and whether the degree of nonconsensuality is necessary or not" so that "one may question every power relationship to that extent" (*FR*, 379). But the affirmation of a parity between expressive and consensual communication still indicates a tension between esthetic self-realization and ethical self-determination whose resolution will require further examination of the rational subject's freedom to consent.

IV. CONCLUDING REMARKS: THE SUBJECT EMPOWERED

The mutual entwinement of consensus and power raises important questions about the extent to which the rational subject is empowered to choose its identity. For Foucault, the exercise of power is irreducible to "a consent which, implicitly, is renewable" in the form of a "renunciation of freedom, a transference of rights." Consisting of "obligatory tasks, of gestures, imposed by tradition or apprenticeship, [and] of subdivisions," it is the very inducement that structures free consent in the first place (*SP*, 218). Yet Foucault never doubts that some power relations are less obligatory than others. The power relations embedded in particular traditions can be criticized; their continuing efficacy for members of post-traditional society may well depend on voluntary consent. But what about the continuing efficacy of those obligations requisite for criticism as such?

Habermas, we know, denies that the inducements, constraints, and obligations regulative of the "unconstrained force of the better argument" are themselves a matter of consent; that is why he, like Kant, calls them a "fact of reason."[45] But is this not an oxymoron? How can reason remain bound by the very pragmatic assumptions it seeks to *critically* reconstruct and freely affirm?

Surely Habermas cannot have it both ways. He cannot appeal to an evolutionary logic to show that the moral facts of modern society are somehow superior to those of premodern society without begging important questions. Even if, for the sake of argument, we grant the validity of inferring obligations from facts, the question remains whether history reveals a progressive logic of moral problem-solving and, if so, whether it does so independently of the contingent and freely contested viewpoint of the present. Foucault put it eloquently in his late essay, "What Is Enlightenment?"

Criticism indeed consists of analyzing and reflecting upon limits. But if the Kantian question was that of knowing what limits knowledge has to renounce transgressing, it seems to me that the critical question today has to be turned back into a positive one: in what is given to us as universal, necessary, obligatory, what is occupied by whatever is singular, contingent, and the product of arbitrary constraints? The point, in brief, is to transform the critique conducted in the form of necessary limitation into a practical critique that takes the form of a possible trangression.... This entails the obvious consequence: that criticism is no longer going to be practiced in the search for formal structures with universal value, but rather as a historical investigation into the events that have led us to constitute ourselves and to recognize ourselves as subjects of what we are doing, thinking, saying. In that sense criticism is not transcendental, and its goal is not that of making a metaphysics possible.... it will not seek to identify the universal structures of all knowledge or of all possible moral action, but it will seek to treat the instances of discourse that articulate what we think, say, and do as so many historical events. And this critique will be genealogical in the sense that it will not deduce from the form of what we are to what it is impossible for us to do and to know; but it will separate out, from the contingency that has made us what we are, the possibility of no longer being, doing, or thinking what we are. . . . It is seeking to give new impetus, as far and wide as possible, to the undefined work of freedom (*FR*, 46).

Let us be very clear about what Foucault is saying here. He is not denying the existence of universal structures. The "universalizing tendencies" he discovers at the root of Western civilization – "the acquisition of capabilities and the struggle for freedom" – have constituted, in his opinion, "permanent elements" (*FR*, 48). That is why he characterizes "our" freedom as an "ascetic task" of self-production that is also a discipline *and* limit. As he puts it, "modernity does not 'liberate man in his own being'; it *compels* him to face the task of producing himself" (*FR*, 42 – my emphasis).

Yet it is precisely this compulsion that renders any justification of modernity itself problematic. Although one might provide formal interpretations of interactive competencies that suggest their functionality with respect to modern subjectivity, one could not claim any transcendental certainty for them.[46] Even less could one show in the manner of Habermas that modernity and its postconventional ethos culminate an irreversible logic. As Foucault never ceases to reiterate, since the Enlightenment is part of the "historical ontology of ourselves" that has determined who we are, it makes no sense to be for or against it (*FR*, 43).[47] At best we are compelled to reinterpret it, and, by implication, ourselves as well.[48]

The ontological inevitability of the hermeneutic circle returns us to the paradox of humanism. Hegel was right, after all: reason is inherently reflexive and self-transcending. Yet the circle in which it moves is neither as vicious nor as self-contained as the paradox of humanism would lead us to believe. For if the constraints of ethical substance and the powers of ethical subjectivity are lifeless and abstract apart from their mutual interpretation and affectation, the same is equally true of the abstract freedom of juridical self-determination and the concrete caring of esthetic sensibility.[49] To paraphrase Gadamer, the ontological relationship between interpreting subject and interpreted substance is as much a game of dialogue as it is a play of effects (or affectations).

Here we detect a final convergence between Foucault and Habermas. At first glance, it seems as though Foucault has no other recourse than to "bodies and pleasures" on which to base his Nietzschean critique of moral rationalism (*HS*, 157).[50] If this esthetic appeal is to avoid any question-begging reference to naturalism, it must rest on the "undefined work of freedom that is condemned to creating its self-awareness and its norms out of itself" (*TAHP*, 106). By the same token, it seems as though Habermas has no other recourse than to moral rationalism on which to base his critique of heteronomous estheticism. If this ethical appeal is to avoid any question-begging reference to transcendentalism, it must rest on the democratic freedom that collectively determines the legitimate needs of its own subjects.

Both of these conceptions of self-empowerment are abstract (*TCA*2, 96ff). The esthetic subject that creates its norms out of itself is impossible since, as Habermas reminds us, its own expressive creativity is partly conditioned by its objective, juridical identity.[51] Indeed, if it were not conditioned by moral reason, the esthetic subject could not possibly resist cooptation by the libidinal regime of disciplinary power (*PDM*, 285). Thus, as universal subject possessing abstract rights, it is essentially free, if not compelled, to reproduce the peculiar values constitutive of its unique personality.

The moral subject that determines itself democratically is equally abstract. Even if a general will could be rationally formed to ground our moral and legal obligations, the integrity of its content would depend on the extent to which citizens had freely cultivated their own esthetic sensibilities. Such cultivation could not be restricted to argumentation about needs. It would require a different – judgmental, intuitive, and affective – competency, one prescinding from the exercise of procedural rights regulating the democratic resolution of moral conflict. This means that no ethic of intimate caring is adequately compassed by the abstract social concern (or solidarity with others, as Habermas puts it) demanded of speakers who knowingly share a common fate.[52] For, in addition to this humanitarian concern, the social concern implicated in communication requires receptivity to our "bodies and pleasures" as well as intimate care for ourselves and others as unique persons.[53]

NOTES

1 Foucault, "The Discourse on Language," in *The Archaeology of Knowledge and The Discourse on Language*, trans. A.M. Sheridan Smith and Rupert Sawyer, 235. Hereafter *AK*.

2 Foucault, "What Is Enlightenment," in *The Foucault Reader*, ed. Paul Rabinow, hereafter *FR*. Other works of Foucault cited in this essay include *Discipline and Punish: The Birth of the Prison*, trans. Alan Sheridan, hereafter *DP*; *Language, Counter-Memory, Practice: Selected Essays and Interviews by Michel Foucault*, ed. D. Bouchard, hereafter *LCP*; *The Order of Things: An Archaeology of the Human Sciences*, hereafter *OT*; *Power/Knowledge: Selected Interviews and Other Writings 1972–1977*, ed. Colin Gordon, hereafter *PK*; *The History of Sexuality, Volume I: An Introduction*, trans. R. Hurley, hereafter *HS*; *The Use of Pleasure: The History of Sexuality, Volume II*, trans. R. Hurley, hereafter *UP*; *The Care of the Self: The History of Sexuality, Volume III*, trans. R. Hurley, hereafter *CS*; and "The Subject and Power," afterword to *Michel Foucault: Beyond Structuralism and Hermeneutics* by Hubert L. Dreyfus and Paul Rabinow, hereafter *SP*.

3 See J. Habermas, "Taking Aim at the Heart of the Present," in *Foucault: A Critical Reader*, ed. David Couzens Hoy, hereafter *TAHP*. Other works of Habermas cited in this essay include *The Philosophical Discourse of Modernity: Twelve Lectures*, trans. Frederick Lawrence, hereafter *PDM*; *Legitimation Crisis*, trans. T. McCarthy, (Boston: Beacon, 1975), hereafter *LC*); *The Theory of Communicative Action*, 2 vols., trans. T. McCarthy, (Boston: Beacon, 1984/87), hereafter *TCA1/2*; and "Modernity versus Postmodernity," *New German Critique* 22 (Winter 1981), hereafter *MP*.

4 The humanism Foucault criticizes is cognate with the romantic Image of Man that emerged late in the eighteenth century and must be distinguished from the civic humanism characteristic of the Renaissance.

5 For a concise summary of Marx's views on this score, see my "Rights and Privileges, Marx and the Jewish Question," *Studies in Soviet Thought* 35 (1988):125–45.

6 Compare Theodor W. Adorno, "Freudian Theory and the Pattern of Fascist Propaganda," in *Critical Theory: The Essential Readings*, ed. David Ingram and Julia Simon-Ingram (New York: Paragon House, 1992), 84–102; Erich Fromm, "The Method and Function of an Analytic Social Psychology," *The Essential Frankfurt School Reader*, ed. Andrew Arato and Eike Gebhardt (New York: Continuum, 1982), 477–97; T.W. Adorno and Max Horkheimer, *Dialectic of Enlightenment* (New York: Herder and Herder, 1947); and David Ingram, *Critical Theory and Philosophy* (New York: Paragon House, 1990), chs. 2 and 3.

7 In a 1978 interview with Duccio Trombadori, Foucault duly noted that first-generation critical theorists "had tried ahead of time to assert things" that he too had been working for years to sustain, among them "the effects of power that are connected to a rationality that has been historically and geographically defined in the West." In the interview Foucault also lamented his ignorance of the School's work during his formative years (he read with difficulty some of Horkheimer's texts) and added: "If I had encountered the Frankfurt School while young, I would have been seduced to the point of doing nothing else in life but the job of commenting on them." On the less complimentary side, Foucault revealed his unhappiness with their humanism and laxness with respect to historical sources. See M. Foucault, *Remarks on Marx: Conversations with Duccio Trombadori*, trans. R. James Goldstein and James Cascaito (New York: Semiotexte, 1991), 115–29. Hereafter *RM*.

8 Foucault rightly deplored first-generation critical theorists' neglect of archival research in their dependence on secondary historical sources. However, his belief that they were economic reductionists and idealists (who ostensibly insulated philosophy from the historical process) is clearly mistaken (*RM*, 125–26).

9 However, Foucault adds that Rusche and Kirchheimer "were right to see [public tortures and executions] as the effect of a system of production in which labour power, and therefore, the human body, has neither the utility nor the commercial value that are conferred upon them in an economy of an industrial type" (*DP*, 54). He also shares their view that formal notions of retributive justice foundational for criminal law during the liberal phase of capitalism have since been replaced by more substantive approaches aimed at evaluating, reforming, and preempting future behavior rather than at rectifying past acts. This restoration of judicial discretion on a large scale has been abetted by the introduction of psychology into the judicial process – an event that coincides with the decline of bourgeois notions of individual responsibility (*DP*, 17–19).

10 Among critical theorists, Adorno comes closest to Foucault in his analysis of the inherent dialectic underlying both subjective (instrumental) and objective (essentialist) forms of reason. For a discussion of the Nietzschean sympathies that unite Adorno's critique of reason to Foucault's critique of humanism, see T.W. Adorno, *Negative Dialectics* (New York: Continuum, 1973) and my "Foucault and the Frankfurt School: A Discourse on Nietzsche, Power and Knowledge," *Praxis International* 6/3 (Fall 1986):311–27.

11 I discuss this aspect of Hegel's logic in "Hegel and Leibniz on Individuation," *Kant-Studien* 4 (1985): 420–35.

12 For a sympathetic treatment of Foucault and first-generation critical

theory on this score, see Paul Bové, "The Rationality of Disciplines" in *After Foucault: Humanistic Knowledge, Postmodern Challenges*, ed. Jonathan Arac (Rutgers University Press, 1988), 42–70.

13 Sartre's notion of a non-positional (obliquely reflexive) consciousness was intended to address a similar problem in Husserl's account of transcendental reflection. But because Sartre operates within the framework of philosophy of consciousness, he cannot establish a deeper grounding for this oblique relationship of self to self.

14 First, Habermas notes that the welfare state has succeeded partially in uncoupling its own legitimacy from the Classical ideal of democratic self-determination in the manner suggested by Foucault. Voter apathy is partly symptomatic of a widespread belief that the proper business of government is to ensure long-term economic growth and prosperity for all. And who is better able to decide policy than those scientific and technological elites who have at their disposal the arcane wisdom of human science? Second, he shows how the spread of bureaucratic regulation in all its forms implies a more subtle detachment from legitimating ideals. In this case, the mere form of the law, that is, its enactment according to accepted procedure, is taken as self-justifying, apart from any belief about its having justly represented the interests of citizens. The spread of commercial law is one example of this. It facilitates the efficient pursuit of whatever strategic aims happen to predominate. But efficiency that affords entrepreneurs maximum predictability is no substitute for legitimacy. The colonization of health care by private insurance companies is mute testimony to this fact. For a more detailed account of Habermas's discussion of legitimation problems in the welfare state, see my "Dworkin, Habermas, and the CLS Movement on Moral Criticism in Law," *Philosophy and Social Criticism* 16:4 (1990):237–68.

15 Habermas here reiterates an objection developed by Axel Honneth in *Kritik der Macht* (Frankfurt: Suhrkamp, 1986), 182.

16 As I argue in Part III, Foucault does not deny the worthiness of inquiring into the issue of *domination* (or the question of *who* exercises power over *whom*). Rather, he chooses to address a different question: *How* do persons exercise power over other persons? Or better, *How* do the effects (intended and unintended) of a given action structure the field of possible responses? In contrast to the theory of power or, more specifically, the theory of domination developed by theorists in the Marxist tradition, such as Steven Lukes and Habermas, Foucault's "analytic of power" does not conceptualize power as something that certain subjects possess and consciously exercise in the repression of others. Although the *critical rhetoric* that accompanies Foucault's own analysis of power *does* presuppose a normative distinction between oppres-

254 THE CAMBRIDGE COMPANION TO FOUCAULT

sive and nonoppressive power relations, the *analysis* as such does not. Cf. Steven Lukes, "Power and Structure," in his *Essays in Social Theory* (Columbia University Press, 1977). For a defense of Foucault's structuralist account of power against the charge of fatalism leveled by Lukes, see David Hoy, "Power, Repression, Progress: Foucault, Lukes and the Frankfurt School" in *Foucault: A Critical Reader*, ed. Hoy, 123–47.

17 Habermas's critique of Foucault's cryptonormativism develops a theme first discussed by Nancy Fraser in "Foucault on Modern Power: Empirical Insights and Normative Confusions." Fredric Jameson observes a similar contradiction between the critical rhetoric of genealogical method, which encourages resistance, and the fatalistic rhetoric of a totalizing theory of power, which encourages resignation. See his "Postmodernism, or, the Cultural Logic of Late Capitalism," *New Left Review* 147 (September 1984):159.

18 "Whereas grammatical construction needs only elements and rules in order to operate . . . there is no statement in general, no free, neutral, independent statement; but a statement always belongs to a series or a whole" (*AK*, 99). This contextualist view of language is further reinforced by Foucault's assertion that "the regularity of statements is defined by the discursive formation itself" so that "the fact of its belonging to a discursive formation and the laws that govern it are one and the same thing" (ibid, 116).

19 Sometimes Foucault suggests that discursive relations between speech-acts possess an autonomous intelligibility. Elsewhere he implies that their meaning is mediated by *primary* relations involving *non-discursive* social practices (such as institutions, economic and social processes, behavioral patterns, techniques, and social norms) and *secondary* relations that articulate the way subjects reflectively define their behavior (*AK*, 45, 53, 68). This latter position already anticipates the turn to genealogy.

20 Charles Taylor ("Foucault on Freedom and Truth" in Hoy, 68–102) and Hilary Putnam (*Reason, Truth, and History*, 162–63) reiterate this objection.

21 These difficulties also vitiate Ernesto Laclau and Chantal Mouffe's attempt to define social hegemony on archaeological principles. See their *Hegemony and Socialist Strategy: Towards a Radical Democratic Politics* (London: Verso, 1985), 105–7; and Barry Smart, "The Politics of Truth and the Problem of Hegemony," in Hoy, 157–73.

22 For commentaries that stress the incompatibility of archaeology and genealogy, see Richard Rorty, "Foucault and Epistemology" in Hoy; and H. L. Dreyfus and P. Rabinow, *Michael Foucault: Beyond Structuralism and Hermeneutics*. For commentaries that stress their compatibility

and complementarity, see Arnold Davidson, "Archaeology, Genealogy, and Ethics," in Hoy (1986); and Ian Hacking, "The Archaeology of Foucault," in Hoy.

23 It is curious that Foucault's romantic side seems to mirror the antirealist, constructivist view of the history of science that he inherited from Georges Canguilhem and Gaston Bachelard. See Foucault, "Gaston Bachelard, le philosophe et son ombre: 'Piéger sa propre culture'," *Le Figaro* 1376 (Sept. 30, 1972 Litt. 16); and "Introduction" to Georges Canguilhem's *On the Normal and the Pathological*, trans. C. Fawcett (Boston: Reidel, 1978), ix–xx. For critical treatments of this influence, see Gary Gutting, *Michel Foucault's Archaeology of Scientific Reason* (Cambridge University Press, 1989); and Walter Privatera, *Stilprobleme. Zur Epistemologie Michel Foucaults* (Frankfurt am Main: Äthenaeum, 1990).

24 Nancy Fraser submits that "Habermas's charge misses the mark" inasmuch as "Foucault is not necessarily aspiring to a total break with modern values and forms of life just because he rejects a foundationalist metainterpretation of them." Yet she goes on to say that, whenever Foucault is read as a "strategic" or "normative" antihumanist who rejects modern values because they either produce counter-emancipatory effects or produce emancipatory effects that are cognate with disciplinary normalization, the charge sticks. In any case, cynicism might not be the only reaction provoked by Foucault's critique of modernity. Hoy, for one, argues that genealogy is best interpreted as a form of immanent social criticism: "Foucault paints the picture of a totally normalized society, not because he believes our present society to be one, but because he hopes we will find the picture threatening" (Hoy, 14). See also "Foucault: A 'Young Conservative'?" in Nancy Fraser, *Unruly Practices: Power, Discourse, and Gender in Contemporary Social Theory* (Minneapolis: University of Minnesota Press, 1989):52.

25 For similar criticisms of Foucault's functionalism, see Michael Walzer, "The Politics of Michel Foucault," in Hoy, 51–68; and Charles Taylor, ibid., 68–102. For a defense of Foucault (especially the later Foucault) against the charge of reductive functionalism, see H.L. Dreyfus and P. Rabinow (1982), and David Hoy (1986), 1–25.

26 *The Final Foucault*, ed. Bernauer and Rasmussen, 18.

27 Whether these theoretical and methodological shifts in Foucault's thought constitute radical changes or just refinements is a matter of some dispute. In one retrospective summation of his life's work, Foucault stressed his abiding interest in the relationship between the subject and truth but acknowledged that his analysis of this relationship over the years stressed different angles: the role of the theoretical human sciences in constituting the image of man, the role of coercive practices

256

THE CAMBRIDGE COMPANION TO FOUCAULT

and institutions (penology, medicine, and psychology) in normalizing behavior, and the role of ascetic practices in constituting the ethical subject (M. Foucault, "The Ethic of Care for the Self as a Practice of Freedom: An Interview with Michel Foucault on January 20, 1984," in *The Final Foucault*, 1–2). Elsewhere he said that his aim had been the creation of a history of the different modes of objectification by which human beings are made subjects: the scientific objectification of the subject in linguistics, economics, medicine, etc.; the coercive objectification of the self in exclusionary and disciplinary practices; and the self-objectification of the subject in the hermeneutics of desire (*SP*, 208). Again, in the introduction to *The Use of Pleasure*, Foucault describes these "theoretical shifts" as expanding the scope of genealogy, on the one hand, while specifying more precisely its method and goal, on the other (6, 9). For further discussion of the question of continuity in Foucault's thought, see Davidson (1986); Hoy (Introduction, 1986); Garth Gillian, "Foucault's Philosophy" in *The Final Foucault*, 34–44; and James Bernauer, "Foucault's Ecstatic Thinking" (ibid., 45–82).

28 More precisely, the ethos depends on the *mode of subjection* the way in which the individual recognizes his obligation), the *form of ethical work* (the way in which the individual transforms himself into an ethical subject), and the *telos* of the ethical conduct (*UP*, 27).

29 C. Gilligan, *In A Different Voice: Psychological Theory and Women's Development* (Cambridge: Harvard University Press, 1982), esp. chapters 1 and 2.

30 The passage cited seems incompatible with the strong, practical holism Dreyfus attributed to Foucault. Dreyfus argues that once we abandon the kind of theoretical holism that Quine, Davidson, Habermas, and Gadamer hold (or the view that the meaning of action can be captured in terms of non-context-specific true or false beliefs) and reduce the core meaning of actions to a prediscursive network of context-specific know-how (Heidegger's *Vorhabe*, Bourdieu's *habitus*, or Foucault's prediscursive practices), the debate between relativists and universalists becomes obsolete. Dreyfus may well be right about the precognitive aspects of some features of our practical lifeworld, but he underestimates the extent to which these competencies can be rationally reconstructed. Moreover, he appears to conflate praxical and linguistic competencies (as transcendental enabling conditions) with linguistic contents (as limiting conditions), thereby concluding that different language games (or forms of life) are somehow *radically* incommensurable. See H. Dreyfus, "Holism and Hermeneutics," *Review of Metaphysics* 34 (1980):3–23. For a detailed argument against strong holism, see J. Bohman, *New Philosophy of Social Science* (Cambridge: MIT Press, 1991), 115ff.

31 J. Habermas, "Knowledge and Human Interests: A General Perspective," in *Critical Theory: The Essential Readings*, 263.

32 Cf. J. Habermas, "Hannah Arendt's Communicative Concept of Power," *Social Research* 44 (1977), and *TCA*2, 153–97.

33 J. Habermas, "A Reply," in *Communicative Action*, ed. Axel Honneth and Hans Joas (Cambridge: MIT Press, 1991), 239.

34 According to Habermas, one must distinguish normative expectations accompanying the acceptance of *meaningful* utterances (illocutionary force in the narrow sense) from normative expectations accompanying the acceptance of *morally binding* obligations (illocutionary force in the broad sense). Even borderline cases involving *immoral* demands, such as a bankrobber's "Hands up!", accord with *norms* of correct speech *as a condition for their being successfully understood*. However, since the conditions of pragmatic (illocutionary) meaningfulness *ultimately* include the conditions for successful interaction as well (illocutionary meaning broadly construed), Habermas says that the bankrobber's demand remains *parasitic* on the structure of mutual moral obligation inherent in voluntary speech action. As we shall see, Habermas's characterization of the rules of discourse as a "fact of reason" perfectly illustrates the sense in which a generalized, *customary* practice of communicative action *within the historical context of Western rationalized culture and society* also assumes the status of a normatively binding authority (*ibid.*).

35 For a detailed discussion of Habermas's subtle analysis of the different kinds of strategic force (*Gewalt*) that accompany the use of systemic media of money and power, on the one hand, and influence and prestige, on the other, see J. Nicolas Kaufmann, "Formations discursives et dispositifs de pouvoir: Habermas critique Foucault," 41–57.

36 Cf. "Reply," 254–58.

37 Bernauer and Rasmussen, *The Final Foucault* 3, 18–19.

38 Gilligan, *In a Different Voice*, 168.

39 See Thomas McCarthy, "The Critique of Impure Reason: Foucault and the Frankfurt School," 455ff. Earlier in his career, Habermas himself appealed to the philosophical hermeneutics of H.-G. Gadamer, who argued that consensual dialogue can be understood as a strategic game in which the structure of play and reciprocity predominate over the subjective aim of winning. Not coincidentally, the concept of a language game was originally introduced by Wittgenstein to capture the rule-governed, consensual nature of speech. By contrast, J-F. Lyotard has recently emphasized the agonistic (or contestatory) nature of language games. Although Foucault often formulates his theory of strategic relations in confrontational terms, his remarks about preserving the freedom of the

other without dominating him (see below) suggest a more Gadamerian phrasing. See H.-G. Gadamer, *Truth and Method* (Continuum, 1986), 91–119; J.-F. Lyotard, *The Postmodern Condition: A Report On Knowledge* (University of Minnesota Press, 1984), sec.5; David Ingram, "The Possibility of a Communicative Ethic Reconsidered: Habermas, Gadamer, and Bourdieu On Discourse," *Man and World* 15 (1982):149–61; and "Legitimacy and the Postmodern Condition: The Political Thought of Jean-François Lyotard," *Praxis International* 7:3/4 (Winter 1987/ 88):284–303.

40 "Reply," 254–59. For Habermas, actors resort to communicative action *precisely in order to coordinate the pursuit of personal aims*. Here, however, the orientation toward personal success is subordinated to the orientation toward reaching mutual agreement. Stated differently, the ideal constraints of communicative reciprocity are superimposed over the real, empirical constraints that impinge at the level of mundane purposes. Only when strategic and communicative orientations are pursued on the same level, as it were, does contradiction occur. Still, Habermas also recognizes that there are borderline cases, such as the hortatory rhetoric of the politician, that mix orientations. Here the orientation toward reaching mutual understanding is pursued reservedly, at best (291, n. 63). In this regard it bears noting that Habermas by no means neglects the subordination of strategic speech acts to communicative aims that occurs whenever one "gives another to understand something" indirectly. The opening up and preservation of communicative interaction often depends on such non-verbalized *perlocutionary* effects. The unannounced power, or indirect influence, that stems from the (relatively independent) meaning of the speech act and/or its context of deployment cannot be conceived merely as a strategic accretion in the narrow sense, as Habermas once thought. Rather, it constitutes, as he himself now realizes, an indirect communication in its right, one that is perhaps best captured by the very different notion of strategic action alluded to by Foucault (239ff.).

41 Donald Davidson makes this point persuasively by arguing against the very idea of language, conceived as a system of conventional rules. As noted above, Habermas, too, plays on the irregularity of communicative competence in criticizing Foucault's "structuralist" account of language. However, neither Davidson's notion of a passing theory (that is, contextualized truth conditions) nor Habermas's notion of a communicative validity claim (that is, contextualized satisfaction conditions) captures the full range of pragmatic meaning implied in Foucault's notion of a practice (at most, they provide evidence for it). Compare n. 29 and D. Davidson, "A Nice Derangement of Epitaphs," *Truth and Interpreta-*

tion, ed. E. LePore (Oxford: Basil Blackwell, 1986), 433–46; T. Schatzki, "The Rationalization of Meaning and Understanding: Davidson and Habermas," *Synthese* 69 (1986):51–79.

42 "The Ethic of Care for the Self as a Practice of Freedom: An Interview with Michel Foucault on January 20, 1984," in *The Final Foucault*, 18.

43 Some of Foucault's defenders seem to have misunderstood the thrust of Habermas's discourse ethic and its appeal to unconstrained consensus. Dreyfus and Rabinow, for example, argue that Habermas's advocacy of enlightenment requires replacing *phronesis*, rhetoric, and art with rational communication. As they understand it, such communication would issue in a kind of transparent self-understanding in which all persons would necessarily agree on the criteria for evaluating their societies. Habermas, however, does not advocate replacing *phronesis*, rhetoric, and art with rational communication; indeed he says that the art of acting ethically, which embraces the former competencies, is a necessary component of moral life, the other being the capacity to justify one's conduct by appeal to general reasons. Nor does he think that (a) rational communication is always preferable to strategic action in dealing with conflict, (b) perlocutionary speech is merely incidental to the raising of illocutionary claims, (c) transparent understanding of one's lifeworld is possible, or (d) consensus in rational dialogue is inevitable. He *does* think that persons of average reason and intellect would agree on the most abstract assumptions underlying rational communication. Nevertheless, he concedes that these assumptions are still too abstract to provide concrete criteria of justice and happiness requisite for evaluating societies. See Dreyfus and Rabinow, "What Is Maturity? Habermas and Foucault on 'What Is Enlightenment?' " in Hoy, 110–11, 119–21; J. Habermas, *Moral Consciousness and Communicative Action*, trans. Christian Lenhardt and Shierry Weber Nicholsen (Cambridge: MIT Press, 1990 – hereafter *MC*), 98, 133, 175, 195ff; and Ingram, *Habermas and the Dialectic of Reason* (Yale University Press, 1987), 39, 101, 131, 172.

44 See T. Flynn, "Foucault as Parrhesiast: His Last Course at the College de France (1984)," in Bernauer and Rasmussen, *The Final Foucault*, 102–18.

45 Habermas, *Moral Consciousness*, 96–97.

46 The transcendental-empirical dialectic is especially evident in *Knowledge and Human Interests* (1968). The latter conceived nature both teleologically (as the natural history of the human species that transcends itself in the direction of a free, self-constitution of humanity), and objectively (as a system of causally determined events).

47 Hoy suggests that this feature of Foucault's post-modernism enables him to avoid the charge of pragmatic contradiction (or self-referential

paradox) leveled against him by Habermas. As a post-modernist Foucault can both accept the inescapability of rational notions of truth and legitimacy – something the anti-modernist can't do – and deny that they can (or need) be given any transcendental or teleological justification. Habermas seems to miss this aspect of Foucault's position, classifying him as an "anti-modernist" and "young conservative" (one who yearns for the "archaic, the spontaneous powers of imagination, of experience and emotionality") who nonetheless departs from a modern concept of emancipated subjectivity. See David Hoy, "Foucault: Modern or Postmodern?" in *After Foucault*, 12–41.

48 Since Habermas himself acknowledges that the task of rationally reconstructing formal rationality is a collective process of interpretation, he, too, must grant the inevitable circularity, historicity, and contextuality of reason (*MC*:97). See my "The Limits and Possibilities of Discourse Ethics for Democratic Reform," *Political Theory* (forthcoming).

49 For a Hegelian reading of the ontological significance of the hermeneutic circle, see Gadamer, *Truth and Method*, 310–25.

50 Habermas compares Foucault's appeal to a different economy of bodies and pleasures to Georges Bataille's appeal to the heterogeneous and Peter Sloterdijk's to the Cynics' bodily-expressive forms of protest. The fascination of such an idea also informs Foucault's late interest in *parrhesia* as a nondiscursive form of truth-telling. Foucault's criticism of the modern economy of sexuality-desire resonates with Marcuse's critique of repressive desublimation, in that both envisage an estheticization of the body and pleasure free of the constraints of genital sexuality (this despite the fact that Marcuse's critique operates within the conceptual parameters of Freud's theory of instincts). Elsewhere Habermas cites Foucault's own rejection of a "primordial vitality" (or "purity of desire") beneath sexual prohibitions. See B.-H. Levy, "Power and Sex: An Interview with Michel Foucault," *Telos* 32 (1977):158; Herbert Marcuse, *One Dimensional Man: Studies in the Ideology of Advanced Industrial Society* (Boston: Beacon, 1964), 56–83; and P. Sloterdijk, *Kritik der zynischen Vernunft*, 2 vols. (Frankfurt, 1982). For a critique of Foucault's appeal to "a posthumanist political rhetoric of body language" see Nancy Fraser, "Foucault's Body Language: A Posthumanist Political Rhetoric?" in *Unruly Practices*, 55–66.

51 Cf. *TCA*2, 40ff and 57ff., where Habermas appeals to Mead's account of the relationship between "me" and "I" to explain the complementarity of moral individuation and autonomy, on the one hand, and esthetic self-realization and creativity, on the other.

52 Cf. Habermas's response to Kohlberg and Gilligan in "Justice and Solidar-

ity: On the Discussion Concerning Stage," *The Philosophical Forum* 21, nos. 1–2 (Fall-Winter 1989–90): 47.

53 This statement must be qualified in light of certain ambiguities affecting Gilligan's account of an ethic of care. Do the ethics of care and of justice designate distinct moral theories of the caliber, say, of hedonistic and deontological theories? Or do they designate complementary – but abstract – aspects of a more inclusive and complete account of moral justification and deliberation? Inclining toward this latter alternative, Habermas proposes a two-step process of moral deliberation: the *justification* of just (universalizable) rules followed by their contextual application. Both steps involve real or simulated dialogue incorporating the perspectives of generalized and concrete other. This position seems to resonate with Gilligan's own views. For, although she distinguishes between social concern and intimate caring (p. 155), she shares Habermas's opinion that communicative openness is basic to both (pp. 29–30). In this context see Seyla Benhabib, "The Utopian Dimension in Communicative Ethics," in *Critical Theory: The Essential Readings;* Habermas's response to Gilligan in *MC,* 175–82; and my discussion of Gilligan, Benhabib, and Habermas in *Critical Theory and Philosophy,* 207–11. On a somewhat different point, it seems too facile to say, as Habermas and McCarthy do, that Foucault ended up embracing the esthetic side of the enlightenment in opposition to the cognitive and moral sides. Conversely, one must not overlook the role that esthetic experience plays in Habermas's account of moral discourse and critical enlightenment. See McCarthy (1990), 463; and my "Completing the Project of Enlightenment: Habermas on Aesthetic Rationality," *New German Critique* 53 (Spring/Summer 1991):67–103, and *Critical Theory and Philosophy,* 183ff.

10 "Between tradition and oblivion": Foucault, the complications of form, the literatures of reason, and the esthetics of existence

I

In a 1983 interview Michel Foucault characterized his work by connecting it with the complicated status of formalism in twentieth-century thought, claiming that the latter marked "one of the most powerful and complex forces in twentieth-century Europe" (*FL*, 234). Included under this rubric were a wide variety of expressions and esthetics, rational and political – all infinitely disrupting the continuities of tradition. The emergence of structuralism itself was equally aligned with this trend in an attempt to clarify its status (ibid., 235). The complicity between Michel Foucault's authorship and such formalism (like that with "structuralism," equally itself a complex force ceaselessly claiming a mathematical base) is long-standing,[1] and his major works attested to it from the outset (see *OT*, 384). It doubtless too figures Foucault's own complicity with modernism. Indeed, from the beginning to the end of his work Foucault was concerned with what he called in 1967 "the complex relations of forms" (*FL*, 27). Even his notorious denial of the subject for the sake of a certain authorial anonymity would not only be identified by him with the "revolutionaries" of esthetic modernism like Mallarmé or Roussel but also with the discoveries of Bourbaki.

What ultimately distinguishes Michel Foucault's own commitment to formalism was doubtless its complexity: one uniting the complexity in the play between syntax and semantics, figure and constraint, discourse and event. Unlike the structuralists, who had platonized structure – and yet unlike the positivists, with whom he was, initially in any case, too often aligned – Foucault realized that, were the analysis of language and language-like entities in terms of their formal properties to be carried out, the success of such projects depended upon realizing, as he had put it as early as 1967, that "discourses are unities of function" (*FL*, 26). Grasping such "functions" depended upon grasping the complexity of the dispersions in question. This complexity is far from being reducible from without (either to an authorial intention or a preexisting set of objects) or from within (to semiotic or logical relations). To account for this complexity it would be necessary to grasp a certain residuum or materiality that exceeds in the concrete practices from which such significative events emerge (*OT*, 16). The sayable relies not simply upon its syntactic or truth-functional possibilities; it remains bound equally to the specificity and the materiality of the said, to a certain residue that escapes such analyses, one that *inter alia* would form the object of an enquiry reducible or limited to the latter, the *analysandum* of an archaeology and genealogy "other" than representation. Equally, such an investigation would open the limits of language from within, and link it to the traditions of both formalist accounts of "rationality" and modernist forms of "esthetic" disencumberment, as much to Bataille or Roussel as to Husserl and Canguilhem, and perhaps to both at the same time.

To grasp this account it is necessary to map its emergence. Foucault's path was by no means a simple one and, as he attested on a number of occasions, was one that in many respects had been cleared before him. It originated in its own specific rupture with the internal formulations of French phenomenology. As late as 1969 Foucault declared that the "aim" of his project was "to free history from the grip of phenomenology" and its transcendentally reductive pretensions (*AK*, 203). In a number of contexts, in fact, Foucault identified his precursors not with the romantic lineage of the existential subject he encountered in the writings of Sartre or Merleau-Ponty, but with those who had been concerned less with the ambiguity of the "lived" than with the historicity of rationality, as had Bachelard, Canguilhem, and Cavaillès – less the content of a "living" intention than a matter of the dialectic of the concept, as Cavaillès put it. Throughout, the complex relations that had united this itinerary with the formalism of modernism never simply disappeared, but instead, it might be claimed, remained "constitutive," albeit it undercut the constitutive reductions of phenomenology.

From the beginning, the research program inaugurated by Edmund Husserl under the rubric of phenomenology contested such formalism, abandoning inference for intuition (*Schau*) in the name of strict science and (foundational) "radicality." Husserl's French critics, even those identified in the 1960s with post-structuralism, never simply denied those links. Nor had Foucault himself simply denied such claims, anymore than did others like Derrida, who contested the simplicity of such origins, whether they are understood in terms of the problem of absolute beginnings or the theme of philosophy of infinite task, both of which (as Foucault too put it) are "linked to the history of our rationality" (*AK*, 237).[2] The point as he had learned from his predecessors, and perhaps especially Cavaillès, is the discontinuity that belies their closure. Cavaillès' role in this regard, perhaps too often omitted from standard accounts, can in fact be seen as pivotal. Moreover, it can be witnessed most forcefully in the posthumous manuscript given (by Bachelard) the title "On Logic and the Theory of Science."

II

The manuscript Jean Cavaillès wrote while under arrest in 1942 for his resistance activity remains fragmentary and incomplete. Even so Bachelard, in agreement with Foucault, claimed in a 1960 Preface to this work that it inspired French Husserlian scholarship in the same moment that it "reveals the problems of Husserlian philosophy in an incomparable way" (*TS*, 354), one in which, to use Bachelard's own term, the "desubstantialization" of reason becomes most directly apparent.[3] Indeed, the remnants of Cavaillès work are to be found not only in the figures with whom Foucault aligned himself, but also in those authors of his youth with which he had broken. If, as Cavaillès related in a letter to Albert Lautmann, this treatise was written somewhat in opposition to Husserl, it too never simply broke with him.[4] Indeed its origins can be traced back at least a year, provoked by a *memoire* of Tran duc Thao's on Husserl that was "a little Hegelianized – or Finkized." Cavaillès now intended to adjudicate once more "an old quarrel against transcendental logic," now predicated on the basis of an "exhorbitant usage of the Cogito" which he found in Husserl's *Krisis*.[5] And yet, while this new treatise on the remnants of transcendental logic would remain phenomenological, directing its ultimate criticism at what he called "the old enemy," specifically citing the Carnap of the *Logical Syntax*, he realized too that the complicity between the reductions of logical empiricism, its naive logicist heritage, and phenomenology was likewise in the end equally insurmountable.[6] While it seemed clear too from this rupture that *l'expérience mathématique* required a certain interface with intuitionism, he likewise knew that the indeterminacy of his teacher Brunschwicg's creativist reaction against Frege and Russell's "Aristoteleanism" remained too subjectivist: "But is there still room for a philosophy which is not a simple explication of the scientist's intentions?" (*TS*, 369). The problem remains, as it would in the wake of all such "deconstructions," the status of the "indetermination" that results.

To such "formalist" intuitions Bolzano's project still furnished, if not the requisite counterexamples, at least the systematic antithesis (ibid., 368–70), radicalizing the issues at stake in transforming issues of "verification" into issues of demonstration. The antinomies that resulted between intuitionism and platonism, conventionalism and logicism, extensionalism and intensionalism, Cavaillès claims, rely upon a certain dogmatism: "either the absolute of intelligibility which legitimizes the Spinozist superimposition (*superposition*) of the idea of an idea, or the reference to a generative consciousness which has the property of grasping itself immediately in act" (ibid.). Moreover, Cavaillès' treatment immediately shows the effect not only of Husserl and Hegel, but equally of the dilemmas that had undercut Husserl and Heidegger, whose work had been a factor in Cavaillès' deliberations at least since 1929.[7] On either of these views, he claims, either on the appeal to the Idea of Science or its reduction or correlation to the generative grammer of consciousness, an ontology seems necessary. And yet such ontological appeals remain inevitably impoverished: "no answer is given to the questions of epistemology." Instead what results is a dialectic between demonstration and invention, interpretation and justification, experience and explication, Being and judgment.

Cavaillès also shows himself to be skeptical of the "abuse of dialectical conflict" as a resolution to such conflict, replacing deductive necessity.[8] Like many in Kojevean Paris, Cavaillès's account appealed to a "dialectic of the concept" that results from such antinomies. Unlike Classical accounts of dialectic, however, his account belies, without simply dissolving, the univocity or "profound homogeneity" between "the rational evidence of a mathematical demonstration and the sensory evidence of a historical perception" (ibid., 395), thus undercutting the exorbitant extensions of the *cogito*, articulating an in-principle inadequacy to all such demonstration.

Husserl himself in his last works had begun to realize both the problem of this inadequatability and the complicity between the historicity of reason and the impoverished judgments of perception, a matter developed not only by Cavaillès but more directly by Merleau-Ponty. Unlike in Cavaillès's work, in Merleau-Ponty's phenomenology of perception this "homology" became understood literally, an event regulated by what Foucault too would call the logic of superimposition or reduction. Hence Foucault claimed that what would be at stake in his own analysis of the archaeology of reason could not be contained within the transcendental status the meanings of the perceived world had held since Merleau-Ponty.[9] As Bachelard had seen as early as 1940, such a "dialectic" would involve a desubstantialization of the rational and the admission of a certain relative character to the category of unity.[10] The result would involve a disequilibrium in the relations between intension and extension, the opening of a certain indefinite plasticity in the extensions of reason (ibid., 409). While the problem of the articulation of form and hence the invocation of what Cavaillès called "syntactic imagination" would then become irreducible in the delineation of the rational, it would likewise take its revenge on the modernist project. The result is that the *ars analytica* became irreducibly linked to the indeterminacy of synthetics, resulting in a pluralization into "several transcendental logics" and hence "an irremediable relativity" (ibid., 399). As another posthumous document relates, unlike the foundational pretensions that had formed the protocols for modern (Cartesian) research programs, there would be no closed system, nor transcendental absolute, but at most the rational unity of a specific multiplicity where all "transcendentality" and "objectivity" would be schema-specific, all "solutions" as much as transformations (*PM*, 274–77). The practice that results, while never simply lacking legitimation, could never be predetermined, guaranteed, univocally bound in advance; its teleology, in short, lacks a *telos*. In effect, to speak Kantian but precisely against neo-kantianism, reason becomes purposiveness without a purpose.

As Foucault would later concur, no given form of reason exhausts the rational (*FL*, 250–51). Instead, reason remains "suspended" between origin and explication, intention and event, evidence and hypothesis, theory and observation, a complication precluding the return to origins. Cavaillès, in advance of Foucault, had likewise outlined the paradox of its inadequation:

no consciousness is a witness of the production of its content by an act, since the phenomenological analysis will always move only in the world of acts or, for corresponding noemas, be able to dissociate architectures of contents. But in both instances, it will stop before the simple elements, i.e. the realities of consciousness which refer to nothing which is other (*TS*, 407).

For reasons already evident, it must be emphasized that this cannot be confused with the return of the failures of historicism (*OT*, 372). If anything can be said, if the principle of expressibility invoked by Platonists remains transcendentally pure, it remains too formal, omitting "discursive practices in their complexity and their density" (*AK*, 209). Specifically, what is omitted are the determinate sequences and practices in accord with which statements emerge, not simply as limits or historical conditions but as constitutive features of utterances. If, consequently, all things are in principle both knowable and expressible, in fact "everything is never said" (ibid., 118). Between the sayable and the said, in other words, there remains the contingency of material practice. And phenomenologically there remains a fundamental "lived impossibility": to speak classically, an in-principle *Ich≠Ich* that haunts all analysis, forcing consciousness to be "exhorbitant" – beyond static analysis, beyond origins – and transforming its science of the experiential *arche* into archaeology (*TS*, 308).[11] The foundational (and tautological) *Ich kan nicht anders*, which Husserl articulated at the foundations of phenomenology, "however legitimate it may be is an abdication of thought" [*si legitime soit il est une abdication de la pensée*] (ibid., 408) before its own unthought, the articulation of "lived experience" irretrievably bound to its conditions, divided between the empirical and the transcendental. Moreover, if not contradictorily then ambiguously, Husserl's "system" remained divided between two archives. Although his transcendental articulemes for epistemic events remained "strictly" Cartesian – presentational, certain, univocal and foundational, those of his accounts of its conditions – of "nature," the "lifeworld," and "spirit" –

remained problematically (and indeterminately) Aristotelean. As a result, phenomenology as a science of infinite tasks remained interminably divided between the analytic requisites of presentation and the synthetic depth of *similitudo* and the figures of analogy, ones doubtless inherited from the figures of German Idealism.

Foucault's account of the positivity of the phenomenological remainder concluded exactly this. Contesting the categories of foundationalism in which it remained encased, "phenomenology is therefore much less the resumption of an old rational goal of the West than the sensitive and precisely formulated acknowledgment of the great hiatus that occurred in the modern *episteme* at the turn of the eighteen and the nineteenth centuries" (*OT*, 325). As Derrida similarly put it in the same year, phenomenology was from the beginning constituted on a warp and woof that is not its own.[12] Both openly traded upon the unstable "dialectic" that Cavaillès had seen in its equivocal origins, one lacking in ultimate articulemes, one in which

the term "consciousness" does not admit of univocity of application – no more than does the thing, as the unity which can be isolated. There is no consciousness which generates its products or is simply immanent to them. In each instance it dwells in the immediacy of the idea, lost in it, and losing itself with it, binding itself to other consciousness (which one would be tempted to call other moments of consciousness) only through the internal bonds of the ideas to which these belong. The progress is material or between singular essences, and its driving force is the need to surpass each of them. It is not a philosophy of consciousness but a philosophy of the concept which can provide a theory of science. The generating necessity is not the necessity of an activity, but the necessity of a dialectic (*TS*, 409).

The position would both prefigure and predetermine the dispersions awaiting the philosophy of consciousness.[13] Although, as Foucault clearly understood, the claim that "all theory is ideology" is ideological in the extreme (see *OT*, 328; *AK*, 184f), doubtless what remains central to its classical remainder is the hope to escape the historicity of reason itself. To speak to the point: what Bachelard aptly called phenomenology's "will to clarity" missed both the materiality and the underdeterminacy of rational practices.[14] And, as a result, reason would be divided by an event that the nascent logos all phenomenologies attempted to adequate and that would be available neither to formal tautology nor to narrative allegory. Although Cavaillès's treatise on the foundations of mathematics had made the former obvious, the source of the latter is an event of much more complicated formalism, one, it could be argued, that provides the order of reasons for *The Order of Things* and its recognition of the failure of Renaissance hermeneutics: implicit in its claim that neither tautology nor allegory could suffice for this "infinity." At stake would be less an infinity of Being than the irrecuperable excess of language. Consequently, the search for a "pure grammar" that would form the ground zero of the phenomenologist's semantic fields would now encounter an event that belongs as much to the figures of literature as to the implicatory sequences of science, as much to Mallarmé as to Bolzano. And yet this too cannot be seen as an exchange of phantasy for logic, *mythos* for *logos*, as a certain skepticism that always accompanied the inversions of philosophy had always hoped. Indeed, testimony both to the achievement and the effect of formalism, the point about the "being" of literature, becomes clear and demonstrable only on the basis of the latter, in the proof of its own indeterminacy – its own "desubstantialization." The "phantasm" cannot be bound (transcendentally or otherwise) to correspondence, the classical distinctions of the real and the fictional, fact and invention, the letter and the spirit. The event of the phantasm already involves the explication of a series whose ultimate resolution remains absent, an event then fully exorbitant before the demands of the "literal" (*L,C,P,* 178).

Instead, fully "desacrilized" (*FL,* 116), beyond all strict theory, the "literary" would now be grasped and historically denoted, Foucault claims, as a silence that eludes the representational requisites of strict science – as precisely "that which must be thought: but equally and for the same reason, as that, which can never in any circumstance, be thought in accordance with a theory of signification" (*OT,* 44). That is, the "excess" explicated by literature invokes a silence that both eludes and contests representation, demonstration, reduction, and proof – and doubtless consequently becomes no less experimental in this regard than the latter. Accordingly, if Foucault aligned himself with the tradition that runs from Comte to Cavaillès and Bachelard in its commitment to a rationality that had contested its substantialist past, it is precisely for these reasons that he aligned his work equally with an "experimental" tradition in literature that ran from Hölderlin to Mallarmé, Artaud and Roussel or Bataille, recognizing in the question of the literary not simply a "counter-discourse" before the classical but equally one whose excess involves a retrieval of "truths" that remain beyond or outside reason and "recalls the memory" of proto-modern accounts of language (ibid., 43–44).

Doubtless his complex account of the formalism and the complications in the relationships between syntax and semantics must then be sought by thinking both of these together. The event would need to be grasped less by antinomy, dialectic, and resolution, than the paradoxes that had run through its past – and not simply formal paradoxes but, more specifically, the paradoxes that await determinability in the transition to semantic actualization: *dedoubleture, coupure, and jeu*. These complications are precisely understood as those that delineate both the underdeterminacy and excess of the rational, an excess that opens in the rupture between form (*morphe*) and substance (*ousia*), complicated between the canons of proof and the codes that underlie its object language – a rupture that consequently circulates through the metamorphoses of modernism. If *The Order of Things* first assigns this rupture between the formal and the formless to surrealism, it likewise finds its development in Kafka, Bataille, and Blanchot (ibid., 383–84). It can be found early, in fact openly, in Bataille. In a 1930 article on "*L'Esprit moderne et le jeu des transpositions*," Bataille had complained of the facile understanding that had turned symbolic transposition into mere play, in effect the naiveté of a certain platonism whose remainder could only be nostalgic, without grasping the effect that had resulted – one not without its own abyssal and horrifying implications.[15] Only Foucault, it could be claimed, could grasp Bataille's insight without succumbing to its romanticism.

III

If Foucault's thought centered itself in the question of this *coupure*, it is not true that he did it without difficulty, nor even consistently. His work on Roussel, for example, in a posthumous interview, was in fact disconnected from his scientific work. We can nonetheless find Foucault's position at its heart. In referring to a certain deferral at the heart of classification and hearkening to the infinite impoverishment of Renaissance hermeneutics, Foucault notes a certain retrieval:

Eighteenth-century grammarians well understood this marvelous property of language [*cette merveilleuse propriété du langage*] to extract wealth from its own poverty. In their purely empirical concept of signs, they admired the way a word was capable of separating itself from the visible form to which it was tied by its "signification" in order to settle on another form, designating it with an ambiguity which is both its resource and limitation. At this point language indicates the source of an internal movement; its ties to its meaning can undergo a metamorphosis without its having to change its form, as if it had turned in on itself, tracing around a fixed point (the "meaning" of the word as they used to say) a circle of possibilities which allows for change, coincidence, effects, and all the rules of the game (*R,* 15).

Similarly *The Order of Things* had explicated this tropological "wealth" in its analysis of Renaissance hermeneutics (doubtless anticipating its account of the surrealist's *merveilleuse*). It involved an infinite circle of inter-signification articulated by analogy and simile, one (like the reductive phantasm of phenomenology, as has been seen) infinitely self-confirming and thereby "plethoric yet absolutely poverty stricken" (*OT,* 30). Yet confirmation itself remained regulated throughout by the infinite guarantee of the "primary, that absolutely initial, Word upon which the infinite movement of discourse was founded and by which it was limited" (ibid., 43). Moreover, the event that overcomes what the eighteenth-century grammarians "saw but did not see" is linked elsewhere more explicitly to the proper name of Hölderlin:

It seems to me that a change was produced in the relationship of language to its indefinite repetition at the end of the eighteenth century – nearly coinciding with the moment in which works of language became what they are now for us, that is, literature. This is the time (or very near so) when Hölderlin became aware, to the point of blindness, that he could only speak in the space marked by the disappearance of the gods and that language could only depend on its power to keep death at a distance. Thus an opening was traced on the horizon toward which our speech has ceaselessly advanced (*LCP,* 59).[16]

Here we should be precise. This disappearance of the gods belongs to no specific discipline. The birth of literature is by no means simply a theological event, if it may need to be inextricably linked with the sacred, as French thought beginning with Bataille's and Leiris's de-

bates in the *College de Sociologie* had suspected.[17] Still, Foucault's
position must be distinguished precisely in its emphasis upon its
complexity. While Bataille, for example, had been led in this regard to
mediate on a *Summa atheologique*, Foucault had been led to return to
the archive of Hölderlin, to a certain "a-logology."[18] And precisely
here occurs the event of "desacrilization" or desubstantiation of the
sacred that the axioms of the Roussel book invoke, the opening of an
economics without reserve: "Roussel's experiment is located in what
could be called the " 'tropological space' of vocabulary." He attempted not to "duplicate the reality of another world, but in the
spontaneous duality of language, he wanted to *discover* an unex-
pected space, and to *cover* it with things never said before" (*R*, 16).
Moreover it is not accidental that the description – or selection – of
objects distinguishes theories. The interpretations of artistic modernism were equally complicated in this regard, and none were more
complicated than Foucault's. While Bataille sought out primitive
"transgression" and "sacrifice" in the caves of Lescaux, and Merleau-
Ponty the painterly prose of the world in the visual *Gestalten* of
Cezanne, and Deleuze in the dispersed – and yet Rousseauian – logic
of sensation in Francis Bacon; while Lyotard sought a logic of "inconsistency" or "incommensurability" and "autochrony" in Duchamp's
transformations of Poincaré and Dedekind; Foucault sought the question of infinite transposition and complication of tropological (or het-
erotopical) space, as he called it, in Magritte and Roussel.[19] Here he
discovered a space delimitable neither by pure form, as for example in
Mondrian, nor its ruptures, neither in the rupture of resemblance (undermined, he claimed, by Klee) nor the tautological tropics of simili-
tude (undermined by Kandinsky). The hierarchical structure of these
canons instead became disrupted from within: neither the simple
separation of image or thing nor their identity, neither plasticity nor
signification, neither text nor image, neither commentary nor presentation; neither hermeneutics nor semiotic rules. And yet Magritte's
art is foreign to neither. Between *les mots et les choses*: "it constitutes, facing them and on the basis of a system common to them all, a
figure at once opposed and complementary" (*Pipe*, 35). Rather than
simple invention or simple reduction, it is the complication itself
that provokes thought, the event in which, rather than being simply
disgarded or denied, the hierarchy itself has turned paradoxical.

Beyond the homogeneous space of demonstrative representation (and again, to repeat Cavaillès's insight, without simply denying its legitimacy [*AK*,202]), the complication of language devoid of substance or guarantee – the infinite transposition or formal dispersion – is traced. Unlike the algebraic formalism of Russell or Hjelmslev, this inner form mutates – drifts – from function to metamorphosis. In fact, Foucault claims, unlike the latter – and disfigured before the master proportions (*analogiae*) of the ancients – the field of chance discovered by Roussel "is no longer proportionate to anything known": the preestablished harmonies of Leibniz's algebraic labyrinth have been transformed into Nietzsche's eternal return. In relation to the principles of nature and grace upon which it depended, "the eponymous sentence is irretrievably lost" (*R*,42). Hence the complex status of its desacrilization.

Before Foucault, Heidegger (led by Kant's critique of ontotheology and equally privileging Hölderlin and already conscious of the paradoxes that lurked for an account of representation) had similarly sought out the complex remainder of the theological within the rational. The domain that resulted remained similarly diremped: its multiplicity dispersed within a series of *Doppelgesichten* – between concealing and revealing, presence and withdrawal, errancy and truth – hence its failure before a "Tarskian" semantics of presentation. Granted the disjuncture between the metaphysics of analogy and transcendental representation, the result will be indefinitely complicated. As Heidegger realized in discussing the ontotheological overdeterminations of Nietzsche, "Nietzsche's 'God is dead' means anything but God is dead."[20] And yet despite the logical paradoxes that haunted metaphysics, Heidegger remained ever hopeful before its semantic, if not its literal, return: if not Being, then "Being" *sur rature*. But if in any case the literary "sacred" (like any predicate that concerns the sacred) is then always an institutional effect, it is never simply semantically reducible to those constraints. Literature (or esthetics) is precisely the experiment and the exploration of this labyrinth, one that both stands behind and reemerges in the paradoxical task of an "esthetics of existence."

IV

This "synthesis" in Foucault manifests itself again not only in his complex proximity to structuralism, but equally in the complicated status of its link with literary formalisms – both evident in the conjunct that is signaled by Foucault's reservation and his commitments before what he acknowledged to be the "legitimate limits" of structuralism (*AK*,200). Indeed, as this syntagm itself attests, it is a synthesis in which Foucault inextricably linked together the Kantian and the Enlightenment problem of the limits of the demonstrable, the extensions of the literary, and the ensuing complication of the phantasm. While in this regard, as he put it in a interview, his writing finds a certain *rapprochment* with that of the Frankfurt School, it nonetheless carries with it the itinerary he gleaned from that of French philosophy of science and the *Collège de Sociologie* and the latter's expression of the French *avant garde*.[21] This interface explains the argument by which Mallarmé provided Foucault's (critical) answer to Velazsquez in *The Order of Things*.

In fact Barthes had already similarly privileged Mallarmé in this regard for having tied critique and literature together.[22] Or, as Mallarmé himself had put it: "Science having found in language a confirmation of itself must now become a confirmation of language.[23] Still, the account is complex and indicative of the collision between formalism and classicism. And yet, despite its own complexity, *The Order of Things* is clear about formalism – perhaps even despite its Conclusion's ambiguities. As a result of the complications of formalism, the link between the multiplicity of language and the unicity of Being would be lost, thus dissolving the always depended-upon reserve of the transcendental tradition. The problem of the unicity of the phantasm, inherited from phenomenology, is one whose explication now betrays equally, to use Canguilhem's word, the latter's "exhaustion."[24] Moreover this event, as has been seen, links the articulation of language and the image not simply to Husserl but equally to Hölderlin and Novalis, and in turn to the phenomenologies (speculative or reductive) whose archive they share and contest, those of Kant, Fichte, Hegel, et al. As has become evident in retracing it here, it is the very idea of such a phenomenology that Foucault now contests: the attempt to make the phantasm a pure intentional act and this, in turn, the simple recuperation of Being. The visible, the unsaid, is never simply recuperable, never adequatable, never the simple result of an evidential seeing, never, that is, phenomenological. Nor again will it suffice to project its deferral upon the semantic abundance of a hermeneutic: "it is in vain that we attempt to

show, by the use of images, metaphors, or similes, what we are saying; the space where they achieve their splendor is not that deployed
by our eyes but that defined by the sequential elements of syntax"
(OT,9). Instead the fragmentation that results is a fragmentation between the sayable and the unsaid, where Foucault perhaps meets the
early Wittgenstein within the problem of fragmentation itself and its
concerns with the poetics (and the ethics) of silence. Michel Serres
was right in 1962 to claim of *Madness and Civilization* that, not
withstanding its own lingering romanticisms, "this is the book of
every solitude." The same of course can be said of the *oeuvre*.[25]

The question of the ineffable – logically, the issue of determinacy –
was a long-standing one that had haunted French thought, ciphered in
to the interface between the phenomenologies of Hegel and Husserl.
Doubtless it continually returned here, not only in Foucault's attempts to think outside the "subject" and the teleologies of reason
and the positivities of the unthought but equally in his hopes regarding "a leap towards a wholly new form of thought" (OT,307). Doubtless too it is not without its link with that other figure of French
Hegelianism to whose "influence" Foucault openly attested, Jean
Hyppolite. Hyppolite's 1952 *Logique et existence*, a book Foucault
regarded as "one of the great books of our time" was also a book on
Hegel, centered on the question of a logic of the concept.[26] It opened
by rewriting Hegel's *Phenomenology* as a logic of silence, a logic of
the ineffable. What Foucault adds to this silence is the complexity of
its eventhood, the interruption of its representation. This silence
would never be converted to a singular, nor would the disarticulation
of form be recuperable into an idea. The literary would remain strictly
taken "formless, mute, unsignifying" and epistemically "insufficient" and "inadequate" (ibid.,383). If there is a reading by which even
Mallarmé is a Hegelian, there is equally now the opening in which the
Idea is cast wholly adrift within the semantic field, the word culminating and dispersing Being, appearing "always in the objectivity that
manifests and conceals it, that denies it and yet forms its basis"
(BC,198). Hence the complexity of the question that now stares
Heidegger in the face: "What relation is there between being and
language and is it really to being that language is always addressed –
at least when we speak truly? [*Quel rapport y a-t-il entre le langage et
l'être, et est-ce bien a l'être que toujours s'adresse le langage, celui,
du moins, qui parle vraiment*]? (OT,306).

Between the ancients and the moderns, between analogy and representation, between the protentions of constitutive phenomenology and the *memoria* of hermeneutic retention – and between the dispersion of their antinomies – no simple choice can be made. What remains in one sense, as has been seen, is simply the question of the *transcendens* of the *word*. But it opens within a project that is as much a double as any representation.

There appear, like so many projects (or chimeras, who can tell as yet?), the themes of a universal formalization of all discourse, or the themes of an integral exegesis of the world which would at the same time be its total demystification, or those of a general theory of signs; or again, the theme (historically probably the first) of a transformation without residuum, of a total reabsorption of all forms of discourse into a single word, of all books into a single page, of the whole world into one book (*OT*,305).

V

The Order of Things doubtless attested most openly to this complexity. And yet it would be wrong, for reasons already evident, to think that Foucault's works ever simply abandoned it: the series they constitute is more its metamorphoses than its resolution. For reasons equally evident, it can be seen that the famous set of questions concerning transcendental and anthropological dispersion inaugurated in that book's conclusion, as romantic (and apocalyptic) as they were, in fact were never answered, let alone simply abandoned. But this was the case less because they were formulated within "an incomplete project" than because they were unanswerable, the function of a dispersion in which research projects, paradigms, and epistemes would in the end be without covering laws and bridging principles. Which answer would suffice to bridge the distance, the hiatus, the rupture, to use Foucault's articulemes for this event, to closure? Instead thought itself became recognized to be a perilous act, an event devoid not only of worldly foundation but of the codes of an *ethos*, the univocal consensus of a *polis*, or demonstrable laws (*OT*,328). In this respect the silence that ends this work prefigures the divided space of the ethical (see *AK*,193) as much as the affirmation of the literary anticipated the latter's potential. Still, Foucault had in fact delineated the formal conditions of the peril dangerous to both, an event that never escapes "syntactics" and yet never remains simply reducible to it.

In this sense, formal, intentional, empirical, or ideal attempts to reconstitute "the lost unity of language" will always fail, the effect of an illusion that was transcendental in the Kantian sense, losing sight of the belonging-together of discourse and figure. Hence Foucault's commitment, that Mallarmé's effaced answer in the anonymity of the word remains always a response to Nietzsche's question "Who speaks?", that archaeology, the archaeology of "truth" or "objectivity" remains always already inscribed within genealogical relations. For the same reason the human sciences become, to use Canguilhem's terms, parasitic, and their ideology, among other ideologies, a "scientific ideology."[27] It is equally for this reason that the theoretical polyvalence of Reason itself is neither simply vindicated nor simply dissolved, that literature no more reduces to the scientific than it can be opposed to it. Finally, it is precisely for this reason that the question of language in all its underdeterminacy "arises with such heavy overdetermination [*resurgit avec une si forte surdétermination*] (*OT*,382). The "literal" and the "literary" neither exclude one another nor reduce to one or the other, nor replace or supersede one another. The logic of such superimposition has been contested from the outset. "Literature" is not the event in which fictions become more true than facts, more legitimate than fact, more real than fact; neither is it a discipline whose veridical "subject matter" becomes, because of this, simply immune from scientific incursion; nor finally does literary criticism replace epistemology.

If nothing prevents us from articulating science as a narrative, nothing prevents us from converting fictions into experimental hypotheses, into science "fiction," if the hope for univocal reduction or intertranslatability has been dashed. Nor, however, does their testability or formalizability simply articulate their veracity – if it does articulate the shifting thresholds of epistemologization and formalization.[28] The relations between theory and evidence are multiple and complex. Moreover, this complexity marks, as Foucault had learned from Serres, the closure of Husserl's hopes for determinacy and the opening instead of a development in which "recurrent distributions reveal several pasts, several forms of connection, several hierarchies of importance, several networks of determination, several teleologies for one and the same science" (*AK*,5). And yet it remains to Foucault's credit to have realized, too, that knowing all this does not interfere with the validity of scientific achievement, if it does begin to articulate the complexity in which its truth claims emerge. The obverse likewise must be asserted: the tropological and heterological space of the literary escapes theory, the complexity of an event is not simply nor sufficiently grasped at the level of the proposition.

It is a mistake, consequently, simply to impose the thresholds of "scientificity" as the *telos* of reason. Nor can this demarcation denote the opposition of knowledge to ignorance, fantasy to demonstration (*AK*,192). The invention of the Classical, after all, was not simply concommitant with the invention of objective method (*OT*, 319), nor was the latter simply limited to the modern. Neither, of course, was the exclusion of the literary merely an expulsion of the rational from the tropic sphere – nor finally, would the critique of reason be reducible to the critique of literature. The logic is then complex indeed. Truth claims, that is, are both *de jure* and *de facto* a "complicated and costly gesture" (*AK*,209). If knowing that the ideological and power relations that underwrite scientific objectivity by no means dissolve its legitimacy, in the end perhaps the risk it entails likewise explains its danger. At the same time, this recognition forces the acknowledgment that the excess it also ventures (understood either as "literature" or more broadly construed in terms of what Foucault later called an "aesthetics of existence") is by no means, as apparently even Foucault himself occasionally believed, the inverted world of truth. The art of existence is not the contrary of the fictions of science. To use Bachelard's term, the "sanctioned" history of scientific accomplishment is complicated by the historical relations in which it is intertwined; reason and unreason, in short, are never simply opposable. The excess at stake does not simply lie beyond the pale of reason and critique, but involves the figural extension in which "truth" becomes invested, invented, and transformed. Hence it becomes clear: if the *Archaeology*, for example, concentrated in its descriptions of the statement upon the already said, upon the functional limits of linguistic form beyond all interpretation; indeed if its author admitted thereby to a certain dislike for interpretation (*AK*,202), he likewise acknowledged, distinguished, and delimited at the level of the sentence the realm of what again belies a theory of signification – but not *sensu stricto* legitimation.

Polysemia – which justified hermeneutics and the discovery of another meaning – concerns the sentence, and the semantic fields that it employs: the same group of words may give rise to several meanings, and to several possible constructions; there may be, therefore, interwoven or alternating, different meanings operating on the same enunciative bases (*AK*, 110).

Foucault had likewise demonstrated the failures of such appeals to polysemic excess. The account of such an event could not reinvoke – as *The Order of Things* had discovered in its analysis – the "superimposition" of either hermeneutics or semiology (see *OT*, 66). The failure of such superimposition had become manifest in Foucault's expositions of the significative practices in both the Renaissance (regulated either by analogy and resemblance) and the Classical Age (by representation), in both cases a logic in fact undermined, as has become evident, by a *complicatio* reducible by neither. The "hermeneutic" sentence never sufficiently dominates – nor adequates – the semantic field it transforms. Moreover, it is doubtless here that we can untangle this narrative's complex relation to Saussure, and this in turn to the complications of formalism. If, after all, Saussure's binary definition of the sign can rightly be understood as reconstituting by representation the classical paradigm (ibid., 67), then its *signe/signifié* opposition, understood diacritically and not just functionally – not simply synchronically but diachronically, and not consequently just mathematically – still reinvoked a premodern ancestry. At stake, to use Foucault's gloss, was an event in which "Words group syllables together, and syllables letters, because there are virtues placed in individual letters that draw them towards each other or keep them apart, exactly as the marks found in nature also repel or attract one another" (*OT*, 35).

This "virtue," both desacrilized and desubstantialized, becomes evident now as the virtue (or the experiment) of "literature," yet lacking the infinite, "literal" word that might ultimately reconcile its intrinsic differences, its "nature." Derrida too, it should be added, likewise in explicating Mallarmé, had similarly grappled with what he also called "the irreducible excess of the syntactic over the semantic," an event articulated equally by medieval accounts of the syncategorical which resulted in an "absolute extension of writing."

Equally desubstantialized, literature here too was said to be "without essence, no truth, no literary-being or being literature of literature."[29] It was the opening instead of "allegory" and "tautology" only in the sense of extrinsic difference, a dispersion whose "virtue" doubtless lies in both explicating and complicating reason – attesting again to the disequilibrium, the underdeterminacy of form, in which any attempt to return to origins would call forth the need for diagnosis (see *AK*,206). Precisely thereby, as has been seen, reason and interpretation – objectivity and ideology, legitimacy and exclusion, power and knowledge, the canons of proof and the dangers of theory – become intertwined. And yet as has also been seen, if "to interpret is a way of reacting to enunciative poverty," by appealing to inventions, that is, to "an inexhaustible treasure from which one can always draw new and unpredictable riches" (*AK*,120), Foucault himself, drawing upon the riches of both his pre-Classical and post-Classical analyses, complicates the infinite positivity upon which such investments could depend and disarticulates both a certain extension and a certain risk.

Beyond all dialectical resolution, the antinomies his analysis had grasped strike deep. Beyond neopositivism, it attests to the complication of facts by theories, beyond phenomenology to the complication of intentional description by "idea." Beyond hermeneutics it refuses the "grammatical" reduction of the present to the past or the future, attesting to the complication of explication itself (*LCP*,175). Neither syntax nor semantics, neither "hermeneutics" nor "seminology" can be reduced or superimposed. If *The Order of Things* had in this respect faced the recognition that interpretation and formalism were to be considered together under a sort of "double obligation" (*FL*,4–5), it is also true that its effect was overdetermined. Neither words nor things can be reduced to "order" *simpliciter*. The investments of form, inextricably necessary and unavoidable, are equally then as "legitimate" as the hermeneutic dependence upon polysemy. The point is, how could we do without either? Their coalescence, their "thought," always remains perilous, neither a reduction of the phantasm to the lived nor its infinite extension into an "imaginary density" to which hermeneutics classically sought to link itself (the flip side of Höderlin, after all, is Schleiermacher), nor finally, to speak Hegelian, their "reconciliation." Instead, as Foucault said of Deleuze's philosophy (and as he said of Magritte's painting), grasping the event at stake requires the complicated "belonging-together," that is, "the disjunctive affirmation, of both" (*LCP*,181). And to this extent, the extent that it contests the well-formed formulation or representation, this event marks the rupture of the political. Precisely, that is, to the extent to which discourse in all its disequilibrium involves "conditions of appropriation and operation; an asset that consequently from the moment of its existence (and not only in its 'practical application') poses the question of power; an asset that is, by nature, the object of a struggle, a political struggle" (*AK*,120). Reason is inextricably "literature" and "proof," truth and fiction, narrative and demonstration, figure and proof, knowledge and power – an event truly "understructured and ill-structured" (*BC*,195).

The result is paradoxical; its premises, as has been seen, the premises of a certain dispersion. If the antinomies of formalism were unanswerable, it is because both are equally affirmable without resolution. This impossibility, as Derrida would also say with respect to formalism, "is practiced."[30] The task, always local, always fragmentary, always discontinuous, remains always perilous, doubtless sublimely modern in this respect. But we should beware of false antinomies. Foucault's later project, researching not only our discontinuous modernity but that of the ancients, was after all an investigation of our past, even the remnants of tradition, precisely now as transposition and counter-memory, and found in the fragments of friendship, ascetics, and so on, a certain relevance – indeed as had Batallie before him.

In this respect, as Cavaillès put it in the midst of dismantling Husserl's Platonism, history reveals authentic meaning to the extent that it permits us to rediscover lost links [*TS*,408]. And yet such "rediscovery" or metamorphoses will surely lack, as Foucault knew, "the weight of tradition" (*AK*,130). Beyond all such impossible imaginary densities, however, it would be mistaken to think that it was simply its rupture. Neither coherence nor discontinuity claim the last word in the fragmentary logic of the event. Hence the complexity of a Foucaultian account of this sequence of transformation, the trans-mission or metamorphoses of tradition – despite all that he had imparted concerning the discontinuity of form. And nowhere did it become more evident than in the final works' investigations of the residuum of traditional forms. It can be witnessed, for example,

282 THE CAMBRIDGE COMPANION TO FOUCAULT

in his transposition of the ancient virtue of friendship, or the morality of *acesis* and its assertion that "there are different truths and different ways of saying it" (*FL*,314) – and, it should be added, new truths and old truths. And both of the latter become attested to, not only with respect to the Greeks but to the *avant garde* and the complicated effects of both in our's (and Foucault's) narratives. In all this, after all, both Aristotle and Bataille became connected, discontinuously and starkly, once more in disjunctive affirmation.[31]

ABBREVIATIONS

Works by Foucault. (For standard translations, see the bibliography.)

Books

AK   *The Archaeology of Knowledge*
BC   *The Birth of the Clinic*
OT   *The Order of Things*
MC   *Madness and Civilization*
R   *Death and the Labyrinth: The World of Raymond Roussel*
Pipe *This is not a Pipe*
CS   *The Care of the Self*

Interviews and Collected Essays
P/K   *Power/Knowledge*
LCP   *Language, Counter-Memory, Practice*
FL   *Foucault Live: Interviews, 1966–1984.* Ed. Sylvère Lotringer.

Works by Jean Cavaillès

TS   "On Logic and the Theory of Science," trans. Theodor J. Kisiel, *Phenomenology and the Natural Sciences*, ed. J. Kocklemans, T. Kisiel (Evanston: Northwestern University Press, 1970).
PM   "Transfini et Continu," *Philosphie mathématique* (Paris: Hermann, 1962)

NOTES

1 The mathematical models of structuralism are perhaps best explicated in Michel Serres' *Hermès ou la communication* (Paris: Minuit, 1968), a work Foucault cites (*AK*, 190). Moreover, the itinerary of Foucault's own work likewise bears witness to this complexity. The 1972 edition of *BC*, for example, eliminated all positive references to structural analysis.

2 Despite these ultimate theoretical differences, the identities between Derrida and Foucault's works are too often underestimated.

3 See Gaston Bachelard, "Preface" to Cavaillès "On logic and the Theory of Science" (*TS*, 354).

4 Cavaillès's correspondence can be found in the intellectual biography written by Cavaillès's sister, Gabrielle Ferrières, *Jean Cavaillès philosophe et combattant (1903–1944) avec une étude de son oeuvre par Gaston Bachelard* (Paris: Presses Universitaires de France, 1950). In general this book not only confirms Foucault's description of the interface of Cavaillès, Canguilhem, and Bachelard but provides further materials for the background of his theoretical divergence from existentialism and the complex relation to phenomenology that results.

5 Ibid., 169. Thao's important memoire doubtless finds expression in part one, "The Phenomenological Method and Its Actual Content," of his eventually published work, *Phenomenology and Dialectical Materialism*, trans. Daniel J. Hermann and Donald V. Morano (Dordrecht: D. Reidel, 1986).

6 Ibid., 15. Compare Martin Heidegger's similar descriptions of Husserl's shortcomings and his (similar) affirmation of the work of Weyl and Brouwer in *The History of the Concept of Time*, trans. Theodore Kisiel (Bloomington: Indiana University Press, 1985), 3.

7 Cavaillès had been present at Husserl's Paris lectures and the Davos exchange between Heidegger and Cassirer, had gone to Freiburg to study Heidegger, and had interviewed Husserl.

8 See Ferrières, *Jean Cavaillès philosophe*, 85.

9 See, for example, Maurice Merleau-Ponty, *Phenomenology of Perception*, trans. Colin Smith; rev. Forrest Williams and David Guerrière (New York: Humanities Press, 1981).

10 Gaston Bachelard, *La philosophie du non*, 90.

11 Cavaillès's manuscript explicitly refers the account of phenomenology as archeology to Fink (*TS*, 408), precisely in articulating the paradoxes, irresolvable by noematic analysis, that would render it "dialectical." Such concerns again date to as early as 1941. See Ferrières, *Jean Cavaillès*, 169.

12 See Jacques Derrida, *Of Grammatology*, trans. Gayatri Chakravorty Spivak (Baltimore: Johns Hopkins, 1976), 67.

13 Hence the "Spinozist" objections against representation raised by Althusser, Deleuze, et al.

14 Bachelard, *La philosphie du non*, 25.

15 Georges Bataille, "L'Esprit moderne et le jeu des transpositions," *Documents* (Paris: Gallimard, 1968), 198.

16 *The Birth of the Clinic* similarly invoked Hölderlin in delineating an event excessive before Reason, albeit one undermining the "old Aristotelian law which prohibited the application of science to the individual" (*BC*,111). "Hölderlin's Empedocles is the death of the last mediator between mortals and Olympus" (ibid.,198). Henceforth "the destiny of individuality will be to appear always in the objectivity that manifests and conceals it" (ibid). And henceforth literature becomes the explication of its "irreconcilable intermediate state."

17 See the documents of Bataille and Michel Leiris in *The College of Sociology 1937–1939*. ed. Denis Hollier, trans. Betsy Wang (Minneapolis: University of Minnesota Press, 1988).

18 *Summa athéologique* is Bataille's title for the three volumes: *L'Expérience intérieur* (Paris: Gallimard, 1942), *Le coupable* (Paris: Gallimard, 1944), and *Sur Nietzsche* (Paris: Gallimard, 1945).

19 See Georges Bataille, *Lascaux or the Birth of Art*, trans. Austryn Wainhouse (Lausanne: Skira, 1955; Maurice Merleau-Ponty "The Doubt of Cezanne" in *Sense and Non-Sense*, trans. H.L. Dreyfus, P.A. Dreyfus (Evanston: Northwestern University Press, 1964); Gilles Deleuze, *Francis Bacon: Logique de la sensation* (Paris: Editions de la difference, 1981); Jean-François Lyotard, *Duchamp's TRANS/formers* (Venice, CA: The Lapis Press, 1990).

20 See Martin Heidegger, "The Word of Nietzsche: 'God is Dead' " in *The Question Concerning Technology and Other Essays*, trans. William Louitt (New York: Harper & Row, 1972). Compare Foucault's claim that "Heidegger has always been the essential philosopher" and that if Nietzsche ultimately prevailed over him "I probably wouldn't have read Nietzsche if I hadn't read Heidegger" (*FL*,326). On the account of Being as *Doppel-gesicht*, see Heidegger's *Nietzsche*, Vol. 1: *The Will to Power as Art*, trans. David Farrell Krell (New York: Harper & Row, 1979), 74. Still, as has been seen, what "limits" finitude here, as has become evident, is not the tragedy of Being, but the limits of objectivity. In the latter perhaps the dialog with Michel Serres which took place in the writing of *OT* makes itself most forcefully apparent. Finally, compare Foucault's similar remarks on the complexity of Nietzsche's "word" in *OT*,385: "Rather than the death of God – or rather in the wake of that death and

in profound correlation with it – what Nietzsche's thought heralds is the death of his murderer."

21 All which makes Foucault's claim that if had he known the Frankfurt School he 'would have been spared a lot of work" surely ironic (FL,241). His interface between the problems of the *Collège de Socialogie* and French philosophy of science surely reiterates much of the Frankfurt School, if not, as has been seen, its anathemas to Benjamin (and ultimate fear of aesthetic formalism). Equally, however, French philosophy of science provided Foucault with a much more sophisticated account than would emerge before Habermas – while not succumbing to his neo-positivisms. Doubtless by relying upon all this, Foucault is able to say in the same interview that, while Kant and Weber cannot be laid aside – while the question of legitimacy, in short, cannot be circumvented – neither will it suffice for an adequate theory of the rational. The dangers of theory remain nonetheless nondefeasible, a point (Kantian enough it should be acknowledged) he had recognized, as he states, more from Nietzsche, Blanchot, Bataille, and Canguilhem (FL,238–39).

22 See Roland Barthes, *Critique et Vérité* (Paris: Editions du Seuil, 1966), 45.

23 Stéphane Mallarmé, *Oeuvres Complètes* (Paris: Gallimard, 1945), 852.

24 See Georges Canguilhem, "Death of Man or Exhaustion of the Cogito" (Review of the *Order of Things*) which likewise appears in this volume.

25 Serres, *Hermès ou la communication,* 176.

26 See Jean Hyppolite, *Logique et existence* (Paris: Presses Universitaires de France, 1952), and Michel Foucault, "Jean Hyppolite 1907–1968," *Revue de Mètaphysique et de Morale* (April-June 1969):136.

27 See Georges Canguilhem, *Idéologie et rationalité* (Paris: Vrin, 1977).

28 See the discussion of these issues in Gary Gutting, *Michel Foucault's Archaeology of Scientific Reason,* 252ff.

29 See Jacques Derrida, "The Double Session" [1970] in *Disseminations,* trans. Barbara Johnson (University of Chicago Press, 1981), 221–23.

30 Derrida, "The Double Session."

31 See Georges Bataille, *Inner Experience,* trans. Anne Boldt (Albany: SUNY Press, 1988), 218. Compare Foucault's "Friendship as a Way of Life" in *FL* and *CS*.

11 Foucault, feminism and questions of identity

Each of my works is part of my own biography.[1]

The main interest in life is to become someone else that you were not at the beginning. . . . The game is worthwhile insofar as we don't know what will be the end.[2]

— Michel Foucault

A movement for change lives in feelings, actions and words. Whatever circumscribes or mutilates our feelings makes it more difficult to act, keeps our actions reactive, repetitive: abstract thinking, narrow tribal loyalties, every kind of self-righteousness, the arrogance of believing ourselves at the center. It's hard to look back on the limits of my understanding a year, five years ago – how did I look without seeing, hear without listening? It can be difficult to be generous to earlier selves, and keeping in faith with the continuity of our journeys is especially hard in the United States, where identities and loyalties have been shed and replaced without a tremor, all in the name of becoming American. *Yet how, except through ourselves, do we discover what moves other people to change?* Our old fears and denials – what helps us let go of them? What makes us decide we have to reeducate ourselves, even those of us with "good" educations? A politicized life ought to sharpen both the senses and the memory.[3]

— Adrienne Rich

To many of his readers, Foucault's preoccupations with subjectivity and practices of the self in his later writings have been puzzling and disappointing – even embarrassing. His turn toward an esthetics of the self appeared on the surface to fly in the face of his earlier proclamation of the death of man and his anti-authoritarian predilections for anonymous authorship. Moreover, it seemed to mark a retreat into the self and away from the more politically engaged texts such as *Discipline and Punish* and *The History of Sexuality, Vol. I*. Had Foucault, the notorious "post-humanist" critic, recanted? This very question manifests a now outmoded concern for coherence and continuity – in short, for identity – in an author's work and life. Yet, if we are to take Foucault at his word, each of his works can be understood as "part of [his] own biography."

It requires no great stretch of the imagination to appreciate the truth of Foucault's remark. One has to think only of his preoccupations with the role of the intellectual, the function of theory, the historical production of homosexual identity in the context of the disciplinary apparatuses of modern sexuality, the status of sexual liberation struggles, and questions of literary, epistemic, and political authority. His effort to make the role of intellectuals, historians, social theorists, and activists the focus of a general historical and critical analysis reveals a remarkable degree of self-consciousness. These were all roles that he occupied with varying degrees of discomfort.

But Foucault's was no traditional heremeneutics of the self. He did not plumb the depths of self in order to discover inner truth – an authoritative, authentic experience. Nor did he write simply in order to express himself, as one of his most sensitive commentators, John Rajchman, has observed. Rajchman describes the shift of focus – the "crisis" – in Foucault's later period as a search for a new style, for "other rhetorical methods" that would include both his earlier questions about knowledge and power and "the question of the subject."[4] He links Foucault's critique of subjectivity (and his critical philosophy in general) to the Socratic injunction to know oneself.[5] He writes:

There arise moments when people cease to accept the practices that define them, moments of 'difficulty" in our historical constitution of ourselves. It was just in such moments that Foucault thought people had a particular kind of experience of critical thinking. For this reason, he presented his own difficulty with himself as intellectual and historian as part of a more general crisis or difficulty in the "function" of the intellectual and the historian, connected with the experience of a failure in progressive utopian ideals. His difficulty would then be part of *our* difficulty as critical thinkers or philosophers.[6]

The key is to know how to practice this critical concern for one-self. Foucault's self-knowing took the form of questioning dominant forms of self-understanding available in the modern West because he was skeptical about the efficacy of Enlightenment humanism as a philosophy of freedom. In his historical research he had identified forms of domination that operate through mechanisms of subjectification, objectification, and normalization. As a result, he preferred Nietzschean genealogy to Hegelian narratives of the progress of freedom – whether liberal or Marxist. Whereas his earlier genealogies focused on the anonymous processes through which individuals are constituted by each other, his genealogies of the self disclosed historical processes through which individuals establish particular relationships to themselves. This "subjectivity" is thoroughly historical and by no means monolithic or private; it is not a Cartesian but rather a Nietzschean or Heideggerian subjectivity. It is formed through multiple "practices of the self" – ways of knowing and governing ourselves that are inherited from historical traditions. Foucault remarks: "the subject is constituted through practices of subjection, or, . . . through practices of liberation, of freedom . . . starting of course from a certain number of rules, styles and conventions that are found in the culture."[7]

Foucault brings to our attention historical transformations in practices of self-formation in order to reveal their contingency and to free us for new possibilities of self-understanding, new modes of experience, new forms of subjectivity, authority, and political identity. Thus, the aim of Foucault's self-interrogations was not self-discovery, but rather self-refusal – "to become someone else you were not at the beginning." What he shares with the Enlightenment is the call to criticism that he finds in Kant's essay "What Is Enlightenment?" What he rejects is its appeals to universals and to grounding in a transcendental subject.

I have here highlighted the centrality of questions of identity in Foucault's life and work because they represent a particularly fruitful starting point for describing the reception of his work by feminist theorists. Questions of identity have become the focal point, a point of profound tension, within feminism for more than a decade. After all, feminism is a gender-based identity politics with an ambivalent relationship to the Enlightenment, humanism, traditional forms of authority, and even to femininity itself.[8] Feminists have learned about the dangers of essentialism and universalism in epistemology and politics in the context of their own political struggles. They have good reason to be suspicious of the universalist, absolutist, and foundationalist features of Enlightenment epistemologies and political theories. Nonetheless, they have also made use of them. White, middle-class feminists often unwittingly embraced universal categories and concepts of femininity that erase differences among women (differences of race, class, sexual orientation, ethnicity, religion, and so on) in ways that parallel their own erasure within androcentric humanisms.

Yet feminism is principally a modern Western movement with origins in the humanist philosophies of Classical liberalism and Marxism. Despite the fact that there are good reasons to believe that "femininity" itself is a masculinist construction, many feminists are reluctant to abandon appeals to absolute foundations – to some essential, liberatory subject rooted in "women's experience" (or nature) – as a starting point for an emancipatory theory. Thus, although questions of identity, and of the technologies of power/knowledge that produce them, prompted many of the feminist appropriations of Foucaultian analysis early in the 1980s, they also mark points of tension in the relationship between Foucault and feminism (and within feminism itself). As feminist theorist Linda Zirelli observes in another context: "Perhaps the radical politics of any feminist tale, so to speak, lies less in the text itself than in the debates it occasions, less in the movement of any specific narrative than in the contested interpretations generated by contentious feminist communities of readers."[9]

Debates among feminists about the implications of Foucault's theories and politics highlight tensions concerning questions of identity such as the following: In what sense, if any, are identity-based politics viable? Are any identities available as a basis for political organizing, for building a unified movement? Must we jettison appeals to the category of gender in order to avoid essentialism? What role do experiential narratives of oppressed groups play in a post-humanist politics? Do we need a transcendental or quasi-transcendental notion of subjectivity to "ground" political agency and critique? Can one define a workable politics without any form of foundational epistemology, feminist or otherwise? Without any grounding in theories of international or national so-

290 THE CAMBRIDGE COMPANION TO FOUCAULT

cial, economic, and political structures and their interrelation-
ships? Do we need a theory of resistance? What is the role of the
feminist theorist in women's struggles? In what follows I shall map
part of the terrain of Foucaultian feminisms in an effort to address
these questions.

FEMINISM AND FOUCAULT: CONVERGENCES
AND CRITICISMS

The work of Foucault has been of special interest to feminist social
and political theorists.[10] Among the many influential post-modern
discourses, Foucault's stand out insofar as they are self-consciously
presented as interventions in specific struggles of oppressed groups
such as homosexuals, prisoners, and mental patients. His analyses of
disciplinary forms of power exercised outside the confines of the
narrowly defined political realm of the modern liberal state overlap
with feminist insights about the politics of personal life. His emphasis on the sexual body as a target and vehicle of this new form of
power/knowledge is reproduced in feminist analyses of modern forms
of patriarchal control over women's minds and bodies in the context
of the emergence of the sciences of medicine, social work, and psychology. Further, as I have already indicated, his critique of Enlightenment humanism and its appeals to an autonomous subject of knowledge and history mirrors to some extent the radical challenges that
feminism has posed to the fundamental epistemological and political
assumptions in modern Western thought. Foucault's skepticism regarding universalism and essentialism in modern emancipatory theories coincides with feminist skepticism about the use of liberalism
and Marxism for feminist emancipatory politics.

Feminist appropriations of Foucault have relied principally on the
genealogies of power/knowledge found in his writings (books and
interviews) from the 1970s. They fall roughly into two camps: those
that use his analyses of disciplinary power to isolate disciplinary
technologies that subjugate women as both subjects and objects of
knowledge, and those that acknowledge domination but center on
cultures and strategies of resistance to hegemonic regimes of power/
knowledge.

The "subjection" of women

Examples of the former are Sandra Bartky's study of the "fashion/ beauty complex" in contemporary America and Susan Bordo's cultural analysis of anorexia nervosa.[11] Bartky gives compelling descriptions of disciplinary technologies that produce specifically feminine forms of embodiment, such as dietary and fitness regimens, expert discourse on how to walk, talk, style one's hair, care for one's skin, and wear one's makeup. These technologies subjugate women by developing norms and competencies, not simply by taking power away. Women become attached to them partly because they involve the acquisition of skills. More important, they are tied to a central component of normative feminine identity, namely, sexual attractiveness. Bartky suggests that many women have resisted or ignored feminist critiques of prevailing standards of fashion and beauty because abandoning them challenges their very sense of identity. Thus, patriarchal power operates by attaching women to certain paradigms of feminine identity.

Susan Bordo uses Foucaultian insights to show how the "fashion/ beauty complex" with its "tyranny of slenderness" produces pathological forms of subjectivity that might also be understood as a crystallization of the cultural production of "normal" femininity. Bordo has written a gripping analysis of the current epidemic of eating disorders as disciplinary technologies of the body. Following Foucault, she treats the body as a product of cultural practices that shape and manipulate not only the physical body but also women's lived experiences of their bodies. She argues that social manipulation of female bodies has been a key strategy for maintaining power relations between the sexes for more than a century. Anorexia nervosa represents the pathological, and thus extreme, imposition of widely encouraged dietary and fitness regimes that have come to be associated with new norms of the healthy, attractive, and disciplined individual in contemporary America. The dietary and fitness regimes of the anorexic enhance her sense of willpower and self-mastery as they destroy her physical body. Her soul literally becomes the prison and torturer of her body.

Many anorexics represent this "torturer" as male. Bordo cites Hilde Bruch, who reports that:

many anorexics talk of having a "ghost" inside them or surrounding them, a "dictator who dominates me," as one woman describes it; "a little man who objects when I eat" is the description given by another. . . . The little ghost, the dictator, (the "other self" as he is often described) is always male. . . . The anorexic's *other* self – the self of the uncontrollable appetites, the impurities and taints, the flabby will and tendency to mental torpor – is the body. . . . But it is also (and here the anorexic's associations are surely in the mainstream of Western culture) the *female* self. These two selves are perceived as at constant war. But it is clear that it is the male side – with its associated values of greater spirituality, higher intellectuality, strength of will – that is being expressed and developed in the anorexic syndrome.[12]

Bordo analyzes the meaning of these gender associations on two levels – the anorexic's disdain for tradional female roles and the social constraints associated with them, and her fear of "the Female" insofar as it conjures images of "voracious hungers and sexual insatiability," that is, images of women (and feminism?) as "too much."[13] To be sure, in the anorexic's symptoms there is a degree of feminine protest against social constraints placed upon women. Yet this is not a self-conscious political protest, as Bordo reminds us, but rather one "written on the bodies of anorexic women."[14] It reflects no political or social understanding. In fact, anorexia is so overwhelming that it precludes the possibility of gaining such understanding and participating in political protest. Thus, both the anorexic's pathological protest and even more moderate examples of the pursuit of slenderness are counterproductive because they take time and energy away from personal growth and social and political achievement. The impulse to resistance is rechanneled and thereby neutralized.

Finally, Bordo does not claim that these cultural practices have been imposed in any conscious way by men. They do not represent the machinations of a male conspiracy. Again, following Foucault, she describes them as intentional but non-subjective. There is a patriarchal logic to the historical power relations exhibited in them, but this logic is not the invention of any individual or group.

Bartky's and Bordo's uses of Foucault correct a deficiency that all feminists find in his writings. They note the gender-specific character of some of the disciplinary technologies developed at the micropolitical level in the modern period. Yet they also reproduce a dimension of the Foucaultian account of modern disciplinary practices that many have found to be problematic. Despite his rejection of totalizing theory and teleological narratives of closure, Foucault's holistic rhetoric and sometimes shrill condemnations of the carceral society in *Discipline and Punish* lend support to those who claim that in this book Foucault describes a wholly disciplined society. He does at times seem to evoke a disciplinary power infinitely capable of enlisting forces of resistance in the service of domination. In short, he provides no convincing account of how effective resistance to power is possible. Similarly, one could argue, Bartky and Bordo have portrayed forms of patriarchal power that insinuate themselves within subjects so profoundly that it is difficult to imagine how they (we) might escape. They describe our complicity in patriarchal practices of victimization without providing suggestions about how we might resist it. Nor is there a sustained account of resistance in their stories.

Elsewhere I have argued that despite the holistic rhetoric in *Discipline and Punish*, Foucault's comments about this book indicate that it was not intended as a portrait of the whole of society, but rather as a genealogy of the emergence of the ideal of a perfectly administered society. Bentham's Panopticon functions not as a metaphor for modern society, but as a theoretical model that should be analyzed in terms of its impact.[15] Moreover, the dystopian narrative of decline might be understood as a rhetorical counter to Whiggish histories of progress. Power, in Foucault's analysis, is neither deterministic nor systemic in a closed sense.

Bartky's response to the charge of "pessimism" in her own work might also be enlisted to support Foucault, who, after all, referred to himself as a "hyperactive pessimist." She writes:

Most of my papers . . . focus not on what is positive in women's experience, but on what is not, on characteristically feminine anxieties, fears, and obsessions: in a word, on the internalization of pervasive intimations of inferiority. Women's joys and triumphs are not my theme. I realize that this may give the collection as a whole a rather pessimistic cast. But this is not the whole story. Theoretical work done in the service of political ends may exhibit a "pessimism of the intellect," but the point of doing such work at all is that "optimism of the will" without which any serious political work is impossible.[16]

Both Bartky and Foucault want to maintain that there is a value in negative criticism, criticism that does not provide a policy or strategy for resolving the difficulties in a situation. John Rajchman's fitting description of the task of Foucault's critical thought provides another defense for this view:

One task for "critical thought" is thus to expose [the costs of our self-constitution], to analyze what we did not realize we had to say and do to ourselves in order to be who we are. . . . The experience of critical thought would start in the experience of such costs. Thus, before asking, or at least when asking, what we must do to behave rationally, this kind of thinking would ask: What are "the forms of rationality" that secure our identity and delimit our possibilities? It would ask what is "intolerable" about such forms of reason?[17]

The point here is the very simple one that oppression must be experienced before it can be effectively resisted. Thus, one necessary role for the intellectual is to exercise critical thought in specific areas of modern experience in order to create an experience of their intolerability. Through the analysis, description, and criticism of existing power/knowledge relations Foucault hoped to create the space necessary for resistance, for taking advantage of what he referred to as the "tactical polyvalence" of discourses and practices, and for developing oppositional strategies and new forms of experience.

Bartky hints at the possibility that even the disciplinary technologies of the "fashion/beauty complex" may produce possibilities of resistance. Images of women as strong and muscular may destabilize feminine bodily identities and confuse gender in ways that open up the space for alternative gender arrangements. The bodily experience of fitness can lead to enhanced self-esteem and individual empowerment in ways that contribute to feminist goals.

Foucault also claims that power is never won once and for all; there are always possibilities of resistance.[18] Nonetheless, the themes of resistance and political agency remain undeveloped and rather vague in Foucault's writings. He waffles between descriptions of power (domination?) that seem to emphasize its capacity to coopt all forms of resistance and reproduce hegemonic discourses and those that emphasize micropolitical forces of resistance. There is also the famous and confusing invocation of "bodies and pleasures" at the end of *The History of Sexuality, Vol. I*, which many commentators have understood as an unwitting appeal to a pre-discursive body.[19] Finally, there are comments that imply that identity politics involve participation in dominating practices of "subjection." Of course, negative criticism already presupposes some notion of critical agency and critical self-reflection.[20] Although Foucault refused any legislative or prophetic roles for himself, the aim of his writings was to offer interpretations of specific practices and ideas that could be used politically, to offer descriptions that suggested "possible paths of attack." He described his aim thus: "I would like to produce some effects of truth which might be used for a possible battle, to be waged by those who wish to wage it, in forms yet to be found and in organizations yet to be defined."[21] Foucault appears to be challenging those committed to emancipatory movements to develop alternative forms and understandings of political struggle.

In order to see the themes of identity, subjectivity, resistance, and agency developed in ways that build upon and develop Foucault's position, we must turn to another set of feminist texts. In contrast to Bartky's and Bordo's uses of Foucault to describe particular forms of male domination and feminine "subjection" are those that attempt to develop the outlines of a post-humanist politics implicit in his writings.

Post-humanism and politics: The subject of feminism

One of the key debates within feminism being played out in the encounter with Foucault is the debate about the desirability of developing feminist epistemologies, in particular, standpoint epistemologies grounded in the historically constituted labor and practices of women in the context of a gendered division of labor. A brief rehearsal of the key points in this debate will serve not only to clarify the basis of the feminist critiques of Foucault but also to highlight those feminist discourses that, Foucaultian in spirit, respond to his challenge to think beyond existing emancipatory traditions and categories. Judith Butler, Wendy Brown, and Donna Haraway have each developed the outlines of a post-humanist feminism based on criticisms of modern emancipatory theories. What is remarkable about their efforts is their willingness to respond to the challenge to begin to think beyond the categories and practices of modernist social and political theory. Each of their positions can be read in part as a response – whether indirect or direct – to feminists' reluctance to give up their claims to innocent origins and a unified identity as a basis for epistemological, moral, and political struggles. Much of what they object to in contemporary feminism is found in the theoretical efforts of feminist standpoint theorists such as Nancy Hartsock. In the following section I shall lay out Hartsock's critique of Foucault and then use these post-humanist feminists to develop a response. Here I shall be less concerned with developing my own critical response to post-humanist feminism than with presenting it as a viable, if problematic, direction for future feminist practice. In the final section I offer my own critical assessment of the debates concerning the future of identity politics occasioned by the feminist encounter with Foucault.

My aim is less to defend Foucault, for much remains implicit and vague in his own remarks about identity and politics, than to defend the importance of taking seriously the questions that he raises. Many feminist responses to Foucault have begged the radical questions that he introduces, preferring to dismiss much of what he said because he does not provide a systematic alternative to traditional liberal or Marxist emancipatory theories. Others have seriously engaged the questions he is raising by imagining the outlines of a politics that could flow from his writings. Whether such a politics is workable or necessary remains an open question. Nonetheless, responses to Foucault that keep open the questions that he raises are certainly more useful than those that merely beg them.

Nancy Hartsock, a leading feminist standpoint theorist and prominent critic of post-structuralism, argues that Foucault's alleged "wholesale" rejection of modernity and its emancipatory theories, his refusal to envision alternative orders, and his emphasis on resistance and destabilization over transformation rob feminism of elements that are indispensable to its emancipatory goals. Hartsock observes: "systematically unequal power relations ultimately vanish from [Foucault's] work."[22] She also alleges that his ascending analysis of power leads to victim-blaming insofar as it highlights agents' participation in their own oppression. Like feminist literary critic Barbara Christian, Hartsock is suspicious of Foucault's moves to reject the subject and universal theories of history at a time when many marginal groups are finally breaking silence, rejecting their object status within dominant discourses, and constructing oppositional political subjectivities, theories, and progressive visions of their own.[23] Ultimately, she claims that Foucault's analytic of power fails feminism because it is not a theory developed *for* women. It is the theory of a colonizer who rejects and resists the colonizers, but who, because he does not think from the perspective of the colonized, "fails to provide an epistemology which is usable for the task of revolutionizing, creating and constructing."[24] She regards his Hobbesian vision of struggle as a "war of all against all" as dystopian and unacceptable. In a more sympathetic reading of Foucault's contributions to critical theory, Joan Cocks echoes Hartsock when she comments upon the limitations of Foucault's anarchistic tendencies:

> We must be clear on his two great weaknesses, both constitutional weaknesses of anarchism. These are the inability to support any movement that through its massiveness and disciplined unity would be popular and yet powerful enough to undermine an entrenched legal-political regime; and the inability to stand on the side of any positive new cultural-political order at all, such an order's always being at once a new system of imposed prohibitions and permissions, with respect to which opposition properly can respond only negatively. Both inabilities are symptoms of a basic failure of nerve before the whole question of order – which, after all, every tolerable as well as intolerable mode of social life must and will have, and which any serious countermovement at some juncture will have to develop as well.[25]

Thus, the most trenchant criticisms of Foucault by feminists identify two major defects in his work: his rejection of modern foundationalist epistemologies (and their philosophies of the subject) and the related question of the adequacy of his politics of resistance. (Who resists power? What is its source? Toward what ends should resistance aim?) These feminist critiques of Foucault overlap significantly with critiques from non-feminist social and political theorists.[26] Thus, they point to the dangers of relativism, pessimism, and nihilism often associated with his work.

What does Hartsock propose instead? It is noteworthy that Hartsock links the inadequacy of Foucault's account of power and knowledge to his social location as a privileged white male, for the logic of her standpoint epistemology commits her to the view that certain situations are more likely to produce distortions and partial visions than others. Employing a feminist revision of Marxian standpoint epistemology, she argues for the epistemic privilege of the feminist standpoint. Among the features that she identifies as essential to this revised theory are the following:

First, rather than getting rid of subjectivity or notions of the subject, as Foucault does, and substituting his notion of the individual as an effect of power relations, we need to engage in the historical, political, and theoretical process of constituting ourselves as subjects as well as objects of history. . . . Second . . . if we are to construct a new society, we need to be assured that some systematic knowledge about our world and ourselves is possible. . . . Third . . . we need a theory of power that recognizes that our practical daily activity contains an understanding of the world . . . a "standpoint" epistemology [based upon] the claim that material life . . . not only structures but sets limits on the understanding of social relations, and that, in systems of domination, the vision available to the rulers will be both partial *and will reverse the real order of things* [emphasis mine].[27]

According to Hartsock, Foucault's theory of power is deficient insofar as he allegedly rejects subjectivity (and the possibility of transformative agency), systematic knowledge, and epistemological foundationalism.

What responses to Hartsock's critique are available to a Foucaultian feminist? Does Foucault's emphasis on the productive processes through which individuals and subjectivities are produced indeed entail a wholesale rejection of subjectivity?

In a brilliant and imaginative, if problematic, effort to think beyond modernist conceptions of politics and identity, Judith Butler provides a compelling response to this question. Butler argues that feminist politics without a feminist subject is possible and desirable. In Butler's framework, the notion of a "feminist subject" refers to a fixed and stable identity (whether natural or social) that serves as the ground and reference point of feminist theories and politics. What she objects to about identity-based politics is their tendency to appeal to a pre-discursive "I" as their ground and support, that is, their tendency "to assume that an identity must first be in place in order for political interests to be elaborated and, subsequently, political action to be taken."[28] In Nietzschean fashion, she argues that feminism need not assume that there is a "doer behind the deed," but rather that "the 'doer' is variably constructed in and through the deed."[29]

Feminist and other critics of post-structuralist critiques of the subject are wrong to conclude that the view that the subject is discursively constituted precludes the possibility of agency. Socio-linguistic constructionism does not entail historical determinism. To the contrary, Butler states: "Construction is not opposed to agency; it is the necessary scene of agency."[30] Feminists have mistaken social constructionism for determinism because they have been caught in the binary logic of Western thought in which the idea of free will presupposes a form of agency that escapes the world in which it must negotiate its identity – an I that is at most "embedded" and "mired" within discourse, as in Sartre's existentialism, but never wholly constituted by it.[31] (Again, "constitution" is not a deterministic notion.) Elaborating upon this Foucaultian view of the self, Butler describes identities as self-representations, "fictions" that are neither fixed nor stable. The subject is not a thing, a substantive entity, but rather a process of signification within an open system of discursive possibilities. The self is a regulated, but not determined, set of practices. One such practice involves the reification of the subject itself. We have mistaken the self for a thing because of our participation in Cartesian and ultimately Hegelian discursive traditions, which postulate a subject/object dichotomy and identify liberation with the epistemological project of the subject's discovery of itself in the objective world.

Although Hartsock is neither Cartesian nor ahistorical, her view of the subject of feminism draws upon the Hegelian and Marxist tradition in appealing to an essential ground of critique, namely, the standpoint of the oppressed. The essentializing moment in her standpoint epistemology is her effort to ground critique in "women's labor" – a realm of practices that, she claims, contains the basis for a transformative and emancipatory knowledge of society.

Why should we challenge this tradition? Following Heidegger, Butler links this subject/object thinking with an instrumental rationality that leads to domination of the Other. She states: "The language of appropriation, instrumentality, and distanciation germane to the epistemological mode also belongs to a strategy of domination that pits the 'I' against and 'Other' and, once that separation is effected, creates an artificial set of questions about the knowability and recoverability of that Other."[32] The binary logic of subject/object is itself an historically contingent logic embedded within a discursive tradition that conceals its productive function by reifying and naturalizing its effects. This discursive tradition is so much a part of us that we find it difficult to think in any other terms, or to recognize it when someone else does so.

Butler appears to be recommending that feminists regard the epistemological account of identity as merely one possible discursive practice, and that it not serve as the adjudicator of all other possibilities. Moreover, Butler's central argument is that any feminist politics that operates by installing alternative gender identities as a basis for identity politics is likely to reproduce the normative, hence, exclusionary practices associated with the masculinist gender configurations that it seeks to overcome.

There is no ontology of gender on which we might construct a politics, for gender ontologies always operate within established political contexts as normative injunctions, determining what qualifies as intelligible sex, invoking and consolidating the reproductive constraints on sexuality, setting the prescriptive requirements whereby sexed or gendered bodies come into cultural intelligibility. Ontology is, thus, not a foundation, but a normative injunction that operates insidiously by installing itself into political discourse as its necessary ground.[33]

Much of Butler's book consists of critical analyses of influential accounts of gender production, which, despite their radical intentions, continue to reproduce unexamined heterosexist and normative ontologies of gender.

Of course, to claim that the subject and its identifications are mere effects of practices of signification is not to claim that these effects are not real or that identity is artificial and arbitrary. Discursive practices that construct gender are rule-governed structures of intelligibility that both constrain and enable identity formation. Seeing identity as neither wholly determined nor wholly arbitrary, the view promulgated here attempts to move beyond the dichotomy of free will versus determinism and to recognize the possibilities for critical and transformative agency that do not require us to establish an absolute and incontestable ground of knowledge and experience beyond relations of power.

What postmodern conception of agency does Butler find within this view of the subject as a regulated practice of signification? That of parodic repetition or repetition with a difference. She remarks:

If the rules governing signification not only restrict, but enable the assertion of alternative domains of cultural intelligibility, i.e., [in the case of gender] new possibilities for gender that contest the rigid codes of hierarchical binarisms, then it is only within the practices of repetitive signifying that a subversion of identity becomes possible. The injunction to be a given gender produces necessary failures, a variety of incoherent configurations that in their multiplicity exceed and defy the injunction by which they are generated.[34]

Examples of repetitive signification that defy and exceed dominant cultural injunctions might include the practices associated with such liminal types as the "assertive female," the "effeminate man," the "lipstick lesbian," and the "macho gay." These are all figures – lived realities, "subjugated experiences" – that lie outside the hegemonic gender norms, challenge its coherence and stability, and prefigure other identities – perhaps, other genders.

In effect, Butler recommends Foucaultian-style critical genealogies of the domination relations involved in the mechanisms of identity production as a way of bringing such liminal identities into play. She is attempting to politicize the processes and categories through which identity is formed. A feminist identity politics that appeals to a founding subject "presumes, fixes and constrains the very 'subjects' that it hopes to represent and liberate."[35] Thus, essentialist versions of identity politics constrain the possibilities for alternative political configurations. "If identities were no longer fixed as the premises of a political syllogism, and politics no longer understood as a set of practices derived from the alleged interests that belong to a set of ready-made subjects, a new configuration of politics would surely emerge from the ruins of the old."[36]

What I find particularly illuminating in Butler's position is its articulation of the post-structuralist argument against the humanist subject. It is the foundationalist subject that is challenged, not the practices of assuming subject positions and representing oneself. Indeed, the latter are inevitable. Nor is agency denied; it is simply reformulated as enactments of variation within regulated, normative, and habitual processes of signification. Post-structuralists like Foucault do not deny that we can or should "constitute ourselves as subjects" as Hartsock alleges, for this is unavoidable. It is the epistemological move to ground our politics in a foundational subject that is challenged. Foucault and Butler want to shift the focus of political analysis from the epistemological project of grounding political and social theories to analyzing the production of certain forms of subjectivity in terms of their costs. Both conclude that the costs associated with modernist practices of identity formation are too high. Finally, both seem to be suggesting that we develop an understanding of politics that is not grounded in modernist foundational epistemological projects.

Wendy Brown, another feminist theorist who accepts Foucault's challenge to think beyond modernist emancipatory projects, is also very attentive to feminist assessments of the cost of abandoning such grounding projects. In a provocative analysis of the motivations behind feminist rejections of post-structuralism, she suggests that feminist anti-post-modernism betrays a modernist attachment to a very anti-political vision:

> it betrays a preference for extrapolitical terms and practices: for truth . . . over politics . . . ; for certainty and security . . . over freedom . . . ; for discoveries (science) over decisions (judgments); for separable subjects armed with established rights and identities over unwieldy and shifting pluralities adjudicating for themselves and their future on the basis of nothing more than their own habits and argument.[37]

Brown challenges feminists to develop a politics without foundational appeals to truth and authenticity. Her diagnosis of the feminist anti-post-modern condition is noteworthy for two reasons. On the one hand, unlike Foucault or Butler, she calls for a more robust and collective vision of political struggle – one that moves beyond the merely reactive strategies of resistance and subversion. On the other, she highlights the inconsistency in feminists' reluctance to overthrow the very self-determining, rational, willing, autonomous agent of modernity, which they have continually challenged for its masculinist tendencies.

What is her diagnosis? Brown argues that the feminist attachment to the subject is rooted in a reluctance to give up the project of grounding the moral and epistemological authority of "women's experiences, feelings and voices as sources and certifications of postfoundational political truth."[38] While most feminist theorists embrace some version of the social construction of gender, many have been unwilling to relinquish their understanding of feminist consciousness-raising as revealing the hidden truths of women's experiences. Thus, they participate in what Foucault described as "the ruse of confession," namely, the idea that "[c]onfession frees, but power reduces to silence."[39] In attempting to secure a ground of truth that is beyond the realm of social construction, and thus is incontestable, feminist theories are involved in a paradoxical inconsistency. On the one hand, they acknowledge that feminine identities are constructed under patriarchal conditions, and on the other hand, they attempt to secure a ground of truth that is beyond this scene of construction. Again Brown comments: "Within the confessional frame, even when social construction is adopted as a method for explaining the making of gender, 'feelings' and 'experiences' acquire a status that is politically if not ontologically essentialist – beyond hermeneutics."[40] Further, she asks: "What is it about feminism that fears the replacement of truth with politics, philosophy with struggle, privileged knowledge with a cacophony of unequal voices clamoring for position?"[41]

Brown turns to Nietzsche to develop her diagnosis. Borrowing his analysis of morality as an invention of the powerless designed to avenge their lot in life, she concludes that "much North Atlantic feminism partakes deeply of both the epistemological spirit and political structure of *ressentiment.*"[42] Simply put, Brown claims that feminists do not want to give up the epistemic privilege of their moral claims against domination. Lacking confidence in their ability to succeed without the force of such absolutist claims, they continue to seek "knowledge accounts that are innocent of power, that position us outside power, [that] make power *answer* to reason/ morality and prohibit demands for accountability in the other direction."[43] In response to feminist efforts to preserve the modern myth of a truth free of power, Brown asks: "What would be required for us to live and work politically without such myths, without claiming that our knowledge is uncorrupted by a will-to-power, without insisting that our truths are less partial and more moral than 'theirs'? Could we learn to contest domination with strength and an alternative vision of collective life, rather than through moral reproach?"[44]

Thus, Brown embraces Foucault's Nietzschean vision of the boundless contest of interpretations concerning identity and how to live. Nonetheless, she finds the Nietzschean position excessively individualistic. In contrast, she calls for the development of "postmoral and antirelativist political spaces, practices of deliberation, and modes of adjudication."[45] Foucault's politics of resistance is insufficient as well. Like Joan Cocks, Brown regards Foucault's failure of nerve before the question of order and authority as an effort to eschew demands for accountability and justification. The politics of resistance is more a reaction to power than an effort to wield it. Post-modernist feminists must supplement the politics of resistance with deliberate efforts to create democratic spaces for inventing and contesting political visions and norms. Moreover, they must replace the politics of identity, and its postulation of an uncontestable private experience and interest, with a politics of diversity that begins from a vision of the common good. Brown concludes: "I am suggesting that only political conversation oriented toward diversity and the common, toward world rather than self, and involving conversion of one's knowledge of the world from a situated (subject) position into a public idiom, offers us the possibility for countering postmodern social fragmentations and political disintegrations."[46] Feminist identity politics with its emphasis on an emancipatory subject and its "private" interests has overshadowed other crucial feminist projects, namely, developing practices of public argument and creating public spaces for conversations among diverse and complex constituencies.

Both Butler's and Brown's post-structuralist critiques of the subject of feminism shift our focus toward the dominating features (the "costs") of modern feminist epistemological projects such as Hartsock's. Butler decries feminist participation in the exclusionary and normative practices of gender identification and attempts to salvage feminist politics by appealing to strategies for subverting identities. She questions whether the political costs associated with retaining gender-based identity politics might outweigh its benefits. Brown goes beyond Butler and Foucault in explicitly articulating the demand for the creation of new public spaces for a collectivist and democratic feminist political practice.

What distinguishes these post-humanist feminist projects is their imaginative and bullet-biting effort to meet Foucault's critique of modern humanism head on. Both make convincing arguments that feminism is caught in the paradoxical position of using the master's tools to dismantle his house. Both conclude that one of these tools, the project of developing foundationalist epistemologies grounded in an essentialist feminist subject, is hopelessly counterproductive. What remains unclear is the status of identity-based politics, and the practices associated with them, in the aftermath of these critiques.

Do these efforts to develop a post-humanist politics require that we jettison appeals to gender as a basis for struggling against oppression? Are any identities available as a basis of political organizing, for building unified political movements? What, if any, unities are desirable? Butler and Brown have both challenged feminist efforts to build a total emancipatory theory on the foundations of women's experiences and interests, but neither has argued that gender is not a category of oppression, nor that feminist politics is impossible without a unified and grounding subject. To the contrary, Butler simply warns against the oppressive features of current gender norms defined as they have been under conditions of oppression. She rejects appeals to a reified or naturalized gender. She also challenges the idea that "unity" is a prerequisite for political action. She asks: "What sort of politics demands that kind of advance purchase on unity? Perhaps a coalition needs to acknowledge its contradictions and take action with these contradictions intact?"[47] Butler is clearly sensitive to the tendencies toward exclusivity, narrowness, closure, self-preoccupation, and self-righteousness often found in identity-based political groups. She argues for an anti-foundationalist approach to coalition politics.

As we have seen, Brown too challenges appeals to fixed notions of identity, or to an authentic and incontestable and innocent ground of feminism. Presumably, she too admits the value of self-consciously political bases of identification, including our identifications with other women, insofar as they attempt to avoid the destructive sense of community extant in contemporary feminist political cultures.

In the place of identity politics based on some naturalized or essentialized identification, Donna Haraway, another feminist influenced by post-structuralism, has introduced the notion of a politics based on "affinities" or political kinship.[48] She recommends that we draw upon the writings of women of color, women who have been denied unproblematic access to the identities such as "African-American," "Asian," and "woman" because of their sexist or racist connotations, to learn how to construct political unities "without relying on a logic of appropriation, incorporation, and taxonomic classification."[49] What distinguishes these modes of identity formation is their self-consciously political character. What they attempt to avoid is the reduction of politics to projects of self-discovery and personal transformation, or to the formation of narrowly defined counter-cultural communities.[50]

This new political identity offered by Haraway is crystallized in the image of the "cyborg." The cyborg is a political identity created by the very forces that we oppose in post-industrial capitalist patriarchal societies. Neither wholly human, machine, or animal, it defies categorization and takes pleasure in the fusion of boundaries (human-animal, human-machine, nature-culture), but also takes responsibility for their construction. It is an identity stripped of innocent origins and yet opposed to domination. Haraway describes its perspective as one of hopeful possibility:

From the perspective of cyborgs, freed of the need to ground politics in "our" privileged position of the oppression that incorporates all other dominations, the innocence of the merely violated, the ground of those closer to nature, we can see powerful possibilities. Feminisms and Marxisms have run aground on Western epistemological imperatives to construct a revolutionary subject from the perspective of a hierarchy of oppressions and/or a latent position of moral superiority, innocence, and greater closeness to nature. With no available original dream of a common language or original symbiosis promising protection . . . to recognize "oneself" as fully implicated in the world, frees us of the need to root politics in identification, vanguard parties, purity, and mothering.[51]

Haraway's cyborg politics is especially interesting because it retrieves and subversively repeats elements of humanistic identity politics. It is an identity politics with a difference. For example, cyborg politics involves a continuation of the practice of advocating the writing of narratives of members of oppressed groups. Partially rooted as it is in the experiences of women of color, Haraway's vision emphasizes the significance of story-telling for liberatory politics, indeed, for the very survival of oppressed groups. The power to signify, to enter into the struggle over meanings is crucial to any feminist politics. Yet, these stories do not participate in the origin myths of essentialist feminisms and humanisms; instead, they explore the theme of identity on the margins of hegemonic groups and thereby deconstruct the authority and legitimacy of dominant humanist narratives by exposing their partiality. Thus, narratives of oppressed groups are important insofar as they empower these groups by giving them a voice in the struggle over interpretations without claiming to be epistemically privileged or incontestable. They are not denied the "authority" of experience if, by "authority," one means the power to introduce that experience as a basis for analysis, and thereby to create new self-understandings. What is denied is the unquestioned authority of unanalyzed experience. Rather than "construct defenses of . . . experience," to use Edward Said's phrase, they promote knowledge of it.[52] Here "knowledge" is understood as fully implicated in relations of power and not as an autonomous, power-neutral, domain of inquiry.

As for consciousness-raising, I believe that it too can be salvaged from the remnants of humanist emancipatory politics. As I have argued elsewhere, a post-structuralist account of subjectivity is compatible with the insights underpinning the feminist practice of consciousness-raising. In some models the aim of consciousness-raising is simply to develop critical consciousness and a recognition of oppression, not to uncover an authentic and shared experience. More often, consciousness-raising leads to the destabilization of one's sense of identity, not to a unified sense of self. Indeed, this notion of consciousness-raising is not unlike Foucault's genealogy. Both are designed to challenge current self-understandings and to create the space for new forms of subjectivity.

Telling our stories to one another has been a crucial instrument for healing and for building grassroots feminist movements. Too narrow a focus on the Nietzschean embrace of flux and chaos within the subject overlooks even Nietzsche's sensitivity to the need for an illusion or "fiction" of unity to stave off complete loss of identity. Although we are denied metaphysical comfort in Foucault's pessimistic politics of finitude and uncertainty, there is no reason why we must be denied the sense of stability and provisional integrity that comes from ordering the chaos. From a feminist perspective, the notable absence of attention to the logics of desire and feeling in Foucault's texts represents a significant gap. He dismissed preoccupations with the psyche and a "core self" as hopelessly disciplinary. Indeed, this absence contributes to the detached and ascetic tone in his early desire for anonymity and self-erasure. In later texts on the subject, his focus shifts from self-erasure to self-overcoming. Still, he lacks Nietzsche's pathos and sensitivity to the role of pain and anger in projects of identity formation. Moreover, one could interpret his inattention to the stability and continuity of the self as an expression of an implicit *ressentiment* against the past. Regardless of its etiology, Foucault's emphasis on self-detachment must be coupled with such sensitivity in order to be useful to feminism. Foucault ignores the importance of maintaining the generosity "to earlier selves" that, according to Adrienne Rich, is necessary for "healthy" projects of personal transformation. Recalling the quotations with which this essay began, one might say that Foucault has "sharpened" the memory necessary to a politicized life, but he fails to sharpen the senses.

Feminists must continue to address the personal costs of patriarchal domination, through attention to developing empowering practices of self-creation, while at the same time avoiding the tendency to reduce politics to personal transformation. In their efforts to challenge the disabling features of identity politics, post-humanist critics have overlooked this crucial function, which counter-cultural communities serve. Of course, simply using our voices and asserting ourselves in the face of the violence and trauma associated with oppression sometimes seems radical enough when compared to our silences and submissions. But although self-assertion and the self-esteem that it entails are crucial to the constitution of subjects able to enter the political arena, they are not the same thing. As Adrienne Rich points out: "Breaking the silences, telling our tales, is not enough. We can value the process – and the courage it may require – without believing that it is an end in itself."[53] The political implications of these individual narratives will be a function of their being collectively analyzed and strategically deployed in feminist political struggles. The value for feminism of building identities will depend upon how it is done.

The post-humanist challenge to modernist feminisms that I have associated with the influence of Foucault begins from our experiences of the limits of identification and with political movements based on such identifications. Efforts to envision alternative political strategies prompted by these experiences are still in their early stages, but many of the problems are clear. At this point, I have shown that feminists who have developed some of the radical insights of Foucault's post-structuralism are not obviously left without useful tools for furthering feminist projects of social transformation. The major weaknesses in his analyses revealed by those feminists who are most sympathetic to his project include (a) his failure to address the gender specificity of many of the political technologies of the body that he described, and (b) his emphasis on the reactive strategy of resistance over the more constructive project of envisioning alternative orders. A charitable interpretation of these failures would link them to Foucault's self-conscious preoccupations with the identity and role of the intellectual.

As we have seen, Foucault envisioned his task as one of providing tools for others to use in the contexts and struggles in which they find themselves. Does his critique of the totalizing features of emancipatory social theories and his emphasis on a local micropolitics of resistance leave us without the resources to identify any global structures of domination? Do we need a theory of resistance in order to know which coalitions are likely to produce desired political results? I shall conclude by responding to these remaining questions concerning identity.

Foucault's answers to such questions consistently refer us to the historical and practical contexts out of which any theorizing and political judgments emerge. He does not reject the need for justifications and norms in political theory and struggle. He simply stresses that the justifications and norms that we appeal to will always be internal to the practices that we are criticizing. Our judgments will inevitably involve comparative historical and social analysis. Thus, there will be no transhistorical universals to ground our critiques, no incontestable theory of global domination to guide a unified revolutionary praxis, to bring history within our control. Moreover, he stresses the dangerous features of efforts to provide such theories. In our political struggles against injustice and oppression, feminists may continue to appeal to the standards of rationality and justice that are available in the contexts in which we find ourselves. These standards do not univocally determine one decision rather than another – how they are interpreted is a matter of political struggle – but they do constitute grounds for critique.

Attentive as he was to the tendency of dominant theoretical approaches to overlook certain domains of experience and practice – subjugated knowledges – Foucault preferred to write cautionary tales rather than to endorse particular "isms." As feminists, we too have good reason to be wary of the dangers of theoretical imperialism. Women engaged in struggles in the Third World constantly remind Western feminists of the limits of our particular understandings of justice, rights, and liberation for their own movements. Foucault's reluctance to proffer global diagnoses, to attempt to represent universal interests, is less an injunction to avoid thinking about global structures of domination than it is an effort to cultivate sensitivity to the need to allow local constituencies the freedom to develop their own strategies, priorities, visions, and understandings of oppression. Rather than begin with global pronouncements and presumptions of universality, he recommends that intellectuals attempt to provide tools for local critique within the specific sectors in which their life and work situates them. This is how he describes the aims of his own historical projects. Michael Kelly aptly characterizes Foucault's position when he remarks:

As for the more specific norms governing resistance – who should resist what, when, and how, and whether some forms of resistance are more desirable then others – Foucault argues that critique "should be an instrument for those who fight." That is, he addresses these normative questions about resistance as practical not theoretical issues . . . [as] justified in the context of a practice.[54]

Indeed, Foucault's rhetoric is often masculine, his perspective androcentric, his vision pessimistic. Nonetheless, what I claim to have shown is that his methods and cautionary tales have been useful and productive for feminist intellectuals struggling to combat dangerous and de-politicizing trends within feminist theory and practice – feminist intellectuals who share neither his androcentrism nor his reluctance to offer guiding visions. Nonetheless, he raises the question whether there are not alternative ways of understanding the identity of the intellectual and the functions of theory. Moreover, he compels us to reconsider the value of the emancipatory practices and theories that have been handed down to us within Western capitalist patriarchal traditions. In this regard, his work has fueled self-critical impulses within feminism that are indispensable.

NOTES

1 Michel Foucault, "Truth, Power, Self: An Interview with Michel Foucault," in *Technologies of the Self*, eds. Luther Martin, Huck Gutman, and Patrick Hutton (Amherst: The University of Massachusetts Press, 1988), 11.
2 Ibid., 9.
3 Adrienne Rich, "The Politics of Location," in *Blood, Bread, and Poetry* (New York: Norton, 1986), 223–24.

4 John Rajchman, *Truth and Eros: Foucault, Lacan, and the Question of Ethics*, 4.

5 Ibid., 7.

6 Ibid., 9.

7 Michel Foucault, *Foucault Live*, ed. Sylvère Lotringer, 313.

8 See Susan Hekman, *Gender and Knowledge: Elements of a Postmodern Feminism* (Boston: Northeastern University Press, 1990), 186 ff..

9 Linda Zirelli, "Rememoration or War? French Feminist Narrative and the Politics of Self-Representation," in *Differences: A Journal of Feminist Cultural Studies* (Spring 1991): 17.

10 Foucault's critical philosophy has been alluring, but also troubling, to feminists. In one of the most balanced assessments of the implications of his middle writings (*Discipline and Punish* and *The History of Sexuality*) for emancipatory political theory found in the critical literature, Nancy Fraser provocatively asserts that while she would not recommend marrying him, Foucault "makes a very interesting lover indeed" (*Unruly Practices: Power, Discourse and Gender in Contemporary Social Theory*, 65.) Why "lover" rather than "husband"? We can tolerate qualities in a lover that are unacceptable in a husband. As a lover, Foucault's "very outrageousness in refusing standard humanist virtues, narrative conventions, and political categories provides just the jolt we occasionally need to dereify our usual patterns of self-interpretation and renew our sense that, just possibly, they may not tell the whole story" (65). Fraser's point is that although the feminist encounter with Foucault provides excitement and occasions self-reflection on the part of feminist theorists, he is ultimately too selfish, inconsistent, and unreliable to make commitment advisable. We should love him, learn what we can, and leave him.

The metaphors of marriage or love affair strike me as inappropriate characterizations of the relationship between feminism and Foucault, principally because they obscure his homosexuality. Many feminists found Foucault's work intriguing precisely because, like them, he too challenged compulsory heterosexuality and dominant paradigms of masculinity. Neither lover, husband, nor father figure, Foucault seems more like an older brother or friend with whom we have common struggles. Yet, like many gay men, he is predominantly male-identified. As we shall see, this androcentrism limits the possiblities for successful collaboration. It creates tensions in the relationship.

Of course, the central relationships at stake in the feminist appropriations of Foucault are those that develop among feminists as a result of this encounter.

11 Sandra Lee Bartky, "Foucault, Femininity and the Modernization of Pa-

triarchal Power," in *Femininity and Domination: Studies in the Phenomenology of Oppression* (New York: Routledge Press, 1990), 63–82; and Susan Bordo, "Anorexia Nervosa: Psychopathology as the Crystallization of Culture," in Diamond and Quinby (eds.), *Feminism and Foucault: Reflections on Resistance,* 87–117.

12 Bordo, "Anorexia Nervosa," 101.

13 Ibid., 102.

14 Ibid., 105.

15 Jana Sawicki, "Feminism and the Power of Foucauldian Discourse: Foucault and Mothering Theory," in *Disciplining Foucault: Feminism, Power and the Body* (New York: Routledge Press, 1991), 58.

16 Bartky, "Introduction" in *Femininity and Domination,* 7.

17 Rajchman, *Truth and Eros,* 11.

18 As I argue in my book, in response to criticisms of *Discipline and Punish* Foucault ultimately made a distinction between relations of domination and relations of power. The former allow no room for effective struggle, whereas the latter are contestable and alterable.

19 See Judith Butler, "Foucault and the Paradox of Bodily Inscriptions," *Journal of Philosophy* 86, no. 11, 601–7.

20 Whether Foucault's notion of resistance is incoherent because it presupposes an account of subjectivity that he has already rejected is a question that will be addressed below.

21 *Foucault Live,* ed. Sylvère Lotringer, 191.

22 Nancy Hartsock, "Foucault on Power: A Theory for Women?" in *Feminism/Postmodernism,* ed. Linda Nicholson, 168.

23 Hartsock asks: "Why is it that just at the moment when so many of us who have been silenced begin to demand the right to name ourselves, to act as subjects rather than objects of history, that just then the concept of subjecthood becomes problematic? Just when we are forming our own theories about the world, uncertainty emerges about whether the world can be theorized. Just when we are talking about the changes we want, ideas of progress and the possibility of systematically and rationally organizing human society become dubious and suspect. Why is it only now that critiques are made of the will to power inherent in the effort to create theory?" See "Foucault on Power," 163–64. See also Barbara Christian, "The Race for Theory," *Cultural Critique* 6 (Spring 1987): 51–63.

24 Hartsock, "Foucault on Power," 164.

25 Joan Cocks, *The Oppositional Imagination: Feminism, Critique and Political Theory* (New York: Routledge, 1989), 74. See also Ann Ferguson, *Blood at the Root: Motherhood, Sexuality, and Male Domination* (London: Pandora Press, 1989), for a similar criticism.

26 For examples of this non-feminist criticism, see the articles by Taylor, Walzer, and Habermas in *Foucault: A Critical Reader*, ed. Hoy.

27 Hartsock, "Foucault on Power," 171–72.

28 Judith Butler, *Gender Trouble: Feminism and the Subversion of Identity* (New York: Routledge Press, 1990), 142.

29 Ibid.

30 Ibid., 147.

31 This account of a non-Cartesian subjectivity that is always in a world and to which the distinctions of inner/outer, and active/passive do not apply in any familiar sense is also found in Heidegger. In the last chapter of *Disciplining Foucault*, I suggested that the subject to which Foucault appeals is a critical, creative, nihilating subject similar to the Sartrian decentered subject. I now think that Foucault's subject is more Nietzschean than Sartrian.

32 Butler, *Gender Trouble*, 147.

33 Ibid., 148.

34 Ibid., 145.

35 Ibid., 148.

36 Ibid., 149.

37 Brown, "Feminist Hesitations," 69.

38 Ibid., 71.

39 Michel Foucault, quoted in Brown, "Feminist Hesitations," 73.

40 Brown, 'Feminist Hesitations," 73.

41 Ibid.

42 Ibid., 75.

43 Ibid., 76.

44 Ibid., 77.

45 Ibid.

46 Ibid., 81.

47 Butler, *Gender Trouble*, 14.

48 Donna Haraway, "A Cyborg Manifesto: Science, Technology, and Socialist Feminism in the Late Twentieth Century," in *Simians, Cyborgs, and Women: The Reinvention of Nature* (New York: Routledge Press, 1991), 156.

49 Ibid., 157.

50 See Diana Fuss, *Essentially Speaking: Feminism, Nature, and Difference* (New York: Routledge Press, 1989), 101.

51 Haraway, "A Cyborg Manifesto," 176.

52 See Diana Fuss, p. 115, for Said quote.

53 Rich, "Resisting Amnesia," in *Blood, Bread, and Poetry*, 144.

54 Michael Kelley, "A Critique of Habermas' Interpretation of Foucault," unpublished manuscript.

12   Foucault, Michel, 1926–

It is doubtless too early to assess the break introduced by Michel Foucault, who has been Professor at the Collège de France (he holds the Chair of the History of Systems of Thought) since 1970, in a philosophic landscape previously dominated by Sartre and by what Sartre called the unsurpassable philosophy of our time, Marxism. From the outset, starting with *The History of Madness* (1961), Michel Foucault situates himself elsewhere. It is no longer a question of basing philosophy on a new cogito, or of developing a system of things previously hidden from the eyes of the world, but rather of interrogating the enigmatic gesture – a gesture that may be characteristic of Western society – through which true discourses (thus also those of philosophy) are constituted, with their familiar power.

If Foucault is indeed perfectly at home in the philosophical tradition, it is within the *critical* tradition of Kant, and his undertaking could be called *A Critical History of Thought*. This is not meant to imply a history of ideas that would be at the same time an analysis of errors that could be measured after the fact, or a deciphering of the misunderstandings to which they are related and on which what we think today might depend. If by thought is meant the act that posits a subject and an object in their various possible relations, a critical history of thought would be an analysis of the conditions under which certain relations between subject and object are formed or modified, to the extent that these relations are constitutive of a possible knowledge. It is not a matter of defining the formal conditions of a relation to objects; it is not a matter, either, of determining the empirical conditions that at a given moment might have permitted the subject in general to become conscious of an object already given in reality. The question is one of determining what the subject must be, what condition is imposed on it, what status it is to have, and what position it is to occupy in reality or in the imaginary, in order to become the legitimate subject of one type of knowledge or another. In short, it is a matter of determining its mode of "subjectivization"; for the latter will obviously vary according to whether the knowledge in question takes the form of exegesis of a sacred text, observations in natural history, or analysis of a mental patient's behavior. But the question is also and at the same time one of determining under what conditions something can become an object of a possible knowledge, how it could be problematized as an object to be known, to what procedure of division it could be subjected, and what part of it is considered pertinent. It is thus a matter of determining its mode of objectivization, which varies, too, according to the type of knowledge involved.

This objectivization and this subjectivization are not independent of one another; it is from their mutual development and their reciprocal bond that what we might call "truth games" arise: not the discovery of true things, but the rules according to which, with respect to certain things, what a subject may say stems from the question of truth and falsehood. In short, the critical history of thought is neither a history of the acquisitions of truth nor a history of its occultations; it is the history of the emergence of truth games. It is the history of "veridictions," understood as the forms according to which discourses capable of being deemed true or false are articulated with a domain of things: what the conditions of that emergence have been; what price has been paid for it, as it were; what effects it has had on the real; and the way in which, linking a certain type of object with certain modalities of the subject, it has constituted for a time, a space, and particular individuals, the historical a priori of a possible experience.

Now that question – or that series of questions – which is that of an "archaeology of knowledge" has never been posed by Michel Foucault with regard to just any truth game, nor would he pose it except with regard to those truth games in which the subject itself is posited as an object of possible knowledge: what are the processes of subjectivization and objectivization that allow the subject to become, as subject, an object of knowledge? Of course it is not a matter of knowing how "psychological knowledge" is constituted in the course of history, but of knowing how various truth games have taken shape, truth games in the course of which the subject has become an object of knowledge. Michel Foucault began by attempting to carry out this analysis in two ways. With regard to the appearance and the insertion – within the realms of knowledge having a scientific status and according to the forms of such knowledge – of the question of the speaking, working, living subject: it was then a matter of the formation of certain of the "human sciences," examined with reference to the practice of the empirical sciences and their particular discourse in the seventeenth and eighteenth centuries (*The Order of Things*). Michel Foucault also tried to analyze the constitution of the subject as it might appear on the other side of a normative distribution and become an object of knowledge – as an insane, ill, or delinquent individual: here his approach involved practices such as psychiatry, clinical medicine, and the penal system (*The History of Madness, The Birth of the Clinic, Discipline and Punish*).

Still pursuing the same overall project, Michel Foucault has now undertaken to study the constitution of the subject as its own object: the formation of the procedures by which the subject is led to observe itself, to analyze itself, to decipher itself, to recognize itself as a domain of possible knowledge. At issue, in short, is the history of "subjectivity," if by that word is meant the way in which the subject experiences itself in a truth game in which it has a relation to itself. The issue of sex and sexuality doubtless seemed to Michel Foucault to constitute not the only possible example, but at least a fairly privileged case: in fact it is in relation to sexuality that, throughout the Christian era and perhaps even earlier, all individuals have been called upon to recognize themselves as subjects of pleasure, desire, lust, temptation. And it is in relation to sexuality that they have been summoned by various practices (self-examination, spiritual exercises, avowal, confession) to apply the game of truth and falsehood to themselves, to the most private and personal elements of their subjectivity.

In brief, Foucault's history of sexuality undertakes to constitute the third panel of a triptych, joining his other analyses of the relations between subject and truth, or, more precisely, the study of the modes according to which the subject could be inserted as an object in truth games.

Taking the question of the relations between the subject and truth as the guiding thread of all these analyses implies certain methodological choices. First is a systematic skepticism with respect to all anthropological universals – which does not mean that they are all rejected at the outset, only that nothing along those lines must be allowed if it is not rigorously indispensable. In the realm of our knowledge, everything presented to us as having universal validity, insofar as human nature or the categories that can be applied to the subject are concerned, has to be tested and analyzed: to refuse the universals of "madness," "delinquency," or "sexuality" does not mean that these notions refer to nothing at all, nor that they are only chimeras invented in the interest of a dubious cause. Yet the refusal entails more than the simple observation that their content varies with time and circumstances; it entails wondering about the conditions that make it possible, according to the rules of truth-telling, to recognize a subject as mentally ill or to cause subjects to recognize the most essential part of themselves in the modality of their sexual desire. The first methodological rule for this sort of work is thus the following: to circumvent anthropological universals to the greatest extent possible, so as to interrogate them in their historical constitution (and of course also the universals of a humanism that would put forward the rights, privileges, and nature of a human being as an immediate and nontemporal truth of the subject). It is also necessary to overturn the philosophic procedure of moving back toward the constitutive subject in which one is seeking an account of what any object of knowledge in general may be; what is required, on the contrary, is to return toward the study of the concrete practices by which the subject is constituted in the immanence of a domain of knowledge. Here again one has to be careful: to deny the philosophic recourse to a constitutive subject does not amount to behaving as if the subject did not exist nor to setting it aside in favor of a pure objectivity. The aim of this refusal is to bring to light the processes proper to an experience in which subject and object "form and transform themselves" in relation to and as functions of one another. The discourses of mental illness, delinquency, or sexuality say what the subject is only within a very particular truth game; but these games do not impose themselves on the subject from the outside in accord with necessary causal or structural determinations. Instead they open up a field of experience in which subject and object alike are constituted only under certain simultaneous conditions, but in which they go on changing in relation to one another, and thus go on modifying this field of experience itself.

From this a third methodological principle follows: that of appealing to "practices" as a domain of analysis, of approaching one's study from the angle of what "was done." Thus, what was done with mental patients, criminals, or sick people? Of course we can use the representation of them that is available to us, or knowledge we thought we had about them, to try to reconstruct the institutions in which they were placed and the treatments to which they were subjected; we can also try to find out what form "real" mental illnesses took, or to discover the modalities of actual criminality in a given period in order to explain what people thought about it then. Michel Foucault's approach is quite different. He first studies the practices – ways of doing things – that are more or less regulated, more or less conscious, more or less goal-oriented, through which one can grasp the lineaments both of what was constituted as real for those who were attempting to conceptualize and govern it, and of the way in which those same people constituted themselves as subjects capable of knowing, analyzing, and ultimately modifying the real. These "practices," understood simultaneously as modes of acting and of thinking, are what provide the key to understanding a correlative constitution of the subject and the object.

Now as soon as it is a matter of studying, through these practices, the various modes of objectivization of the subject, the important role that the analysis of power relations has to play becomes clear. It is obviously not a matter of interrogating "power" as to its origin, its principles, or its legitimate limits, but of studying the devices and techniques that are used in different institutional contexts to act on the behavior of individuals taken separately or in groups; to shape, direct, and modify their behavior, to impose limits on their inaction, or to inscribe it within overall strategies that are thus multiple in their forms and zones of enactment. Such strategies are diverse as well in the procedures and techniques they deploy: these power relations characterize the way human beings "govern" one another, and their analysis shows how, through the use of certain patterns of "governance" with madmen, sick people, criminals, and so on, the mad, ill, or delinquent subject is objectivized. Such an analysis does not mean, therefore, that the abuse of one sort of power or another created madmen, sick people, or criminals where there were none before, but that the various and particular forms of "governing" individuals were determining factors in the various modes of the subject's objectivization.

It is clear how the theme of a "history of sexuality" can be inscribed within Michel Foucault's overall project: he analyzes "sexuality" as a historically singular mode of experience in which the subject is objectivized for itself and for other subjects, through certain precise procedures of "governance."

BIBLIOGRAPHY

The following bibliography is extensive but by no means complete. I have tried to include all of Foucault's books and his most important articles and interviews. The list of secondary writings is much more selective, although I trust the most important pieces in English are included. For the most complete bibliography of Foucault's writing currently available, see James Bernauer and Thomas Keenan, "The Works of Michel Foucault, 1954–1984" in James Bernauer and David Rasmussen, eds., *The Final Foucault*. Another very extensive list is given by J. Lagrange, "Les oeuvres de Michel Foucault," *Critique* 42 (1986): 942–69. Michael Clark's *Michel Foucault: An Annotated Bibliography* provides an essentially complete listing of and very helpful annotations on primary and secondary sources through 1981. A more recent but much more limited list is found in J. Nordquist, *Michel Foucault: A Bibliography.*

BOOKS BY FOUCAULT

Maladie mentale et personnalité. Paris: PUF, 1954. Revised as *Maladie mentale et psychologie*. Paris: PUF, 1962. (*Mental Illness and Psychology*, trans. Alan Sheridan, foreword by H. Dreyfus. Berkeley: University of California Press, 1987.)

MC   *Folie et déraison: Histoire de la folie à l'âge classique*. Paris: Plon, 1961. Second edition with new preface and appendices: *Histoire de la folie à l'âge classique*. Paris: Gallimard, 1972; without appendices, 1976. (*Madness and Civilization*, trans. by R. Howard. New York: Pantheon, 1965. A greatly abridged edition.)

BC   *Naissance de la clinique: une archéologie du régard médical*. Paris: PUF, 1963. (*The Birth of the Clinic*, trans. A. Sheridan. New York: Vintage, 1973.)

R   *Raymond Roussel*. Paris: Gallimard, 1963. (*Death and the Labyrinth: The World of Raymond Roussel*, trans. C. Ruas. Garden City,

321

N.Y.: Doubleday & Co., 1986. Also includes an interview with Foucault.)

OT   *Les mots et les choses: une archéologie des sciences humaines.* Paris: Gallimard, 1966. (*The Order of Things,* trans. A. Sheridan. New York: Random House, 1970.)

AK   *L'archéologie du savoir.* Paris: Gallimard, 1969. (*The Archaeology o; Knowledge,* trans. A. Sheridan. New York: Pantheon, 1972. Also in cludes "The Discourse on Language," a translation of *L'ordre du discours,* Foucault's inaugural address at the Collège de France, Paris: Gallimard, 1971.)

Pipe   *Ceci n'est pas une pipe: deux lettres et quatre desseins de René Magritte.* Montpellier: Fata Morgana, 1973. (*This Is Not a Pipe,* trans. and ed. J. Harkness. Berkeley: University of California Press, 1981.)

DP   *Surveiller et punir: naissance de la prison.* Paris: Gallimard, 1975. (*Discipline and Punish,* trans. A. Sheridan. New York: Pantheon, 1977.)

HS   *Histoire de la sexualité. I: la Volonté de savoir.* Paris: Gallimard, 1976. (*The History of Sexuality, Vol. I: An Introduction,* trans. R. Hurley. New York: Pantheon, 1978.)

UP   *L'usage des plaisirs: histoire de la sexualité, II.* Paris: Gallimard, 1984. (*The Use of Pleasure. History of Sexuality, Vol. 2.* Trans. Robert Hurley. New York: Pantheon, 1985.)

CS   *Le souci de soi: histoire de la sexualité, III.* Paris: Gallimard, 1984. (*The Care of the Self: History of Sexuality, Vol. 3.* Trans. R. Hurley. New York: Pantheon, 1986.)

BOOKS EDITED BY FOUCAULT

Moi, Pierre Rivière, ayant égorgé ma mère, ma soeur et mon frère: une cas de parricide au XIXe siècle. Paris: Gallimard-Julliard, 1975. Includes a Foreword and an essay by Foucault. (*I, Pierre Rivière, Having Slaughtered My Mother, My Sister and My Brother: A Case of Parricide in the 19th Century.* Trans. F. Jellinik. New York: Pantheon, 1975.)

Herculine Barbin, dite Alexina B. Paris: Gallimard, 1978. (*Herculine Barbin: Being the Recently Discovered Memoirs of a Nineteenth-Century French Hermaphrodite,* trans. R. McDougall. New York: Pantheon, 1980. Includes an Introduction to the English edition and a note by Foucault.)

(With A. Farge) *Le désordre des familles: lettres de cachet des Archives de la Bastille.* Paris: Gallimard-Julliard, 1982.

COLLECTIONS OF FOUCAULT'S ARTICLES,
LECTURES, AND INTERVIEWS

LCP   Bouchard, Donald, ed., and Sherry Simon. *Language, Counter-Memory, and Practice: Selected Essays and Interviews*. Ithaca, N.Y.: Cornell University Press, 1977.
       Résumé des cours 1970–1982. Paris: Julliard, 1989. Foucault's summaries of the courses he offered at the Collège de France.
P/K   Gordon, Colin, ed. *Power/Knowledge: Selected Interviews and Other Writings, 1972–1977*. New York: Pantheon, 1980.
PPC   Kritzman, Lawrence, ed. *Politics, Philosophy, and Culture: Interviews and Other Writings, 1977–1984*. New York: Routledge, 1988.
FL   Lotringer, Sylvère, ed. *Foucault Live: Interviews, 1966–1984*. New York: Semiotext(e), 1989.
PTS   Morris, M., and Patton, P. *Michel Foucault: Power, Truth, and Strategy*. Sydney, Australia: Feral Publications, 1979.
FR   Rabinow, Paul, ed. *The Foucault Reader*. New York: Pantheon, 1985.

SELECTED ARTICLES AND ESSAYS BY FOUCAULT, BY
YEAR OF PUBLICATION

"Introduction" to Ludwig Binswanger, *Traum und Existenz* (*Le rêve et l'existence*), trans. J. Verdeaux. Bruges: Desclée de Brouwer, 1954, 9–128. ("Dream, Imagination and Existence," trans. F. Williams, *Review of Existential Psychology and Psychiatry* 19 [1984–85]: 29–78.)

"La recherche scientifique et la psychologie," in *Des chercheurs français s'interrogent*, ed. J.-E. Morère. Paris: PUF, 1957, 171–201.

"Le 'non' du père," *Critique* 178 (1962): 195–209. ("The Father's 'No'," in *LCP*, 68–86.)

"Préface à transgression," *Critique* 195 (1963): 751–69. ("A Preface to Transgression," in *LCP*, 29–52.)

"Un 'Fantastique de bibliothèque'," *Cahiers Renaud-Barrault* 59 (1967): 7–30. ("Fantasia of the Library," in *LCP*, 87–109.)

"Le langage à l'infini," *Tel quel* 15 (1963): 44–53. ("Language to Infinity," in *LCP*, 53–67.)

"Distance, aspect, origine," *Critique* 198 (1963): 931–45.

"La prose d'Actéon," *La Nouvelle revue française* 130 (1964): 444–59.

"Le langage de l'espace," *Critique* 203 (1964): 378–82.

"La folie, l'absence d'oeuvre," *La Table ronde* 196 (1964): 11–21. (Reprinted as an appendix to the 1972 edition of *Histoire de la folie*, 575–82.)

"Nietzsche, Freud, Marx," *Cahier de Royaumont 6: Nietzsche*. Paris: Éditions de Minuit, 1967, 183–200. ("Nietzsche, Freud, Marx" trans. Jon Anderson and Gary Hentzi, *Critical Texts* 3 [1986]: 1–5.)

"La pensée du dehors," *Critique* 229 (1966): 523–46. ("Maurice Blanchot, the Thought from Outside," trans. Brian Massumi, in *Foucault/Blanchot* [New York: Zone Books, 1987], 7–60.)

"Réponse à une question," *Esprit* 371 (1986): 850–74. ("Politics and the Study of Discourse," trans. Colin Gordon, *Ideology and Consciousness* 3 [1978]: 7–26. A revised version of this translation appears in Graham Burchell, Colin Gordon, and Peter Miller, eds., *The Foucault Effect* [Chicago: University of Chicago Press, 1991], 53–72.)

"Réponse à Cercle d'épistémologie," *Cahiers pour l'analyse* 9 (1968): 9–40. ("On the Archaeology of the Sciences," *Theoretical Practice* 3–4 [1971]: 108–27, abridged translation.)

"Qu'est-ce qu' un auteur?" *Bulletin de la Société française de Philosophie* 63 (1969): 73–104. ("What Is an Author?" in *LCP*, 113–38, translation abridged and following discussion omitted.)

"Theatrum philosophicum," *Critique* 282 (170): 885–908. ("Theatrum Philosophicum," in *LCP*, 165–96.)

"Nietzsche, la généalogie, l'histoire," in *Hommage à Jean Hyppolite*. Paris: PUF, 1971, 145–72. ("Nietzsche, Genealogy, History," in *LCP*, 149–64.)

"Mon corps, ce papier, ce feu," *Paideia* (September 1971). Reprinted as an appendix to the 1972 edition of *Histoire de la folie*, 583–603. ("My Body, This Paper, This Fire," trans. Geoff Bennington, *Oxford Literary Review* 4 [1979]: 5–28.)

"Monstrosities in Criticism," reply to George Steiner's review of *The Order of Things*. Trans. Robert J. Mathews, *Diacritics* 1 (1971): 57–60.

"Foucault Responds 2," *Diacritics* 1 (1971): 59. Reply to a response by Steiner.

"La maison de la folie," in Basaglia and Basaglia-Ongaro, eds., *Les Criminels de paix: Recherches sur les intellectuels et leurs techniques comme préposés à l'oppression*. Paris: PUF, 1980, 145–60. (Full original French version of a text published in Italian in 1975 as "La casa della follia.")

"Two Lectures," trans. Kate Soper, in *P/K*, 78–108. (First published in 1977 in an Italian translation from the unpublished French original.)

"La vie des hommes infâmes," *Les cahiers du chemin* 29(1977): 12–29. ("The Life of Infamous Men," trans. Paul Foss and Meaghan Morris, in *PTS*.)

"Pouvoirs et stratégies,' *Les révoltes logiques* 4 (1977): 89–97. ("Powers and Strategies," trans. Colin Gordon, in *P/K*.)

"Introduction" to George Canguilhem, *On the Normal and the Pathological* (an English translation by Carolyn Fawcett of *Le normal et la pathologique* [Paris: PUF, 1966].) Dordrect: D. Reidel, 1978, ix–xx. A somewhat different French version later appeared as "La vie: l'expérience et la science," *Revue de métaphysique et de morale* 90 (1985): 3–14.

"Governmentality," trans. Rosi Braidotti, in *Ideology and Consciousness* 6 (1979): 5–12. Reprinted in Graham Burchell, Colin Gordon, and Peter Miller, eds., *The Foucault Effect.* (Chicago: University of Chicago Press, 1991), 87–104.

"Le poussière et le nuage," in Michelle Perot, ed., *L'impossible prison: recherches sur le système pénitentiaire au XIXe siècle.* Paris: Seuil, 1980. Followed by a discussion entitled "Table ronde du 20 mai 1978," 40–56. (Trans. by Colin Gordon as "Questions of Method," *Ideology and Consciousness* 8 [1981]: 3–12. Reprinted with slight revisions in Graham Burchell, Colin Gordon, and Peter Miller, eds. *The Foucault Effect* [Chicago: University of Chicago Press, 1991], 73–86.)

"Omnes et singulatim: Towards a Criticism of 'Political Reason.' " In Sterling McMurrin, ed., *The Tanner Lectures on Human Values II* (Salt Lake City: University of Utah Press, 1981), 225–54. Reprinted as "Politics and Reason" in *PPC.*

"Sexuality and Solitude," *London Review of Books* 3 (1981): 3, 5–6. Reprinted in David Rieff, ed., *Humanities in Review* 1. (New York: Cambridge University Press, 1982), 3–21.

"The Subject and Power," afterword to H. Dreyfus and P. Rabinow, *Michel Foucault: Beyond Structuralism and Hermeneutics* (Chicago: University of Chicago Press, rev. ed., 1983), 214–32.

"La combat de la chasteté," *Communications* 35 (1982): 15–25. ("The Battle for Chastity" in P. Ariès and André Béjin, *Western Sexuality: Practice and Precept in Past and Present Times,* trans. Anthony Foster [Oxford: Basil Blackwell, 1985], 14–25. Reprinted in *PPC.*)

"Technologies of the Self," in L. H. Martin, H. Gutman, and P. H. Hutton, eds., *Technologies of the Self: A Seminar with Michel Foucault* (Amherst: University of Massachusetts Press, 1988), 9–15.

"L'écriture de soi," *Corps écrit* 5 (1983): 3–23.

"Un cours inédit," *Magazin littéraire* 207 (1984): 35–39. ("Kant on Enlightenment and Revolution," trans. Colin Gordon, *Economy and Society* 15 [1986]: 88–96. Also translated by Alan Sheridan as "The Art of Telling the Truth" in *PPC.*)

"What is Enlightenment?," trans. Catherine Porter from an unpublished French original, in *FR,* 31–50.

SELECTED INTERVIEWS AND DISCUSSIONS

These are listed according to the year (as best I can determine it) in which the interview was conducted, even if publication occurred later.

1965

"Philosophie et vérité," *Dossiers pédagogiques de la radio-télévision scolaire* (March 27, 1965): 1–11. Discussion among Foucault, J. Hyppolite, G. Canguilhem, P. Ricouer, et al.

1966

"Entretien: Michel Foucault, 'les mots et les choses'," *Les lettres françaises* 1125 (March 31, 1966): 3–4. An interview with Raymond Bellour. Reprinted in Raymond Bellour, *Le livre des autres* (Paris: Éditions de l'Herne, 1971), 135–44. ("The order of things," translated by John Johnston, in *FL*.)

"Entretien," with Madeleine Chapsal, *Le quinzaine littéraire* 5 (May 16, 1966): 14–15.

"Michel Foucault et Gilles Deleuze veulent rendre à Nietzsche son vrai visage." Interview with C. Jannoud. *Le Figaro littéraire* 1065 (1966): 7.

1967

"Deuxième entretien: Sur les façons d'écrire l'histoire." With Raymond Bellour, *Les lettres françaises* 1187 (1967): 6–9. Reprinted in Raymond Bellour, *Le livre des autres* (Paris: Éditions de l'Herne, 1971), 189–207. ("The Discourse on History," trans. John Johnston, in *FL*.)

"Conversazione con Michel Foucault." With P. Caruso, *La fiera letteraria* 39 (1967). Reprinted in P. Caruso, *Conversatione con Lévi-Strauss, Foucault, Lacan* (Milan: U. Mursia and Co., 1969), 91–131.

1968

"Foucault répond à Sartre." Interview with Jean-Pierre El Kabbach. *La quinzaine littéraire* 46 (March 1–15, 1968): 20–22. ("Foucault Responds to Sartre," trans. John Johnston, in *FL*.) See Foucault's objection to the publication of this interview, "Une mise au point de Michel Foucault," *La quinzaine littéraire* 46 (March 15–31, 1968): 21.

1971

"A Conversation with Michel Foucault." Interview with John Simon. *Partisan Review* 38 (1971): 192–201.

"Human Nature: Justice versus Power." Televised discussion with Noam Chomsky, moderated by Fons Elders. In Fons Elders, ed., *Reflexive Water: The Basic Concerns of Mankind* (London: Souvenir Press, 1974), 139–97.

"Par delà le bien et le mal." Interview with M. A. Burnier and P. Graine. *Actuel* 14 (1971): 42–47. ("Revolutionary Action: 'Until Now'," in *LCP*, 218–33.)

1972

"Les intellectuels et le pouvoir." Conversation with Gilles Deleuze. *L'Arc* 49 (1972). ("Intellectuals and Power," in *LCP*, 205–17.)

"Sur la justice populaire," *Les temps modernes* 310 (1972): 335–60. (On Popular Justice: A Discussion with Maoists," in *P/K*, 1–36.)

1975
"Entretien sur la prison." With J.J. Brochier. *Magazine littéraire* 101 (1975): 10–15. ("Prison Talk," in *P/K*, 37–54.)
"Pouvoir et corps." Interview in *Quel corps?* 2 (1975). ("Body/power," in *P/K*, 55–62.)

1976
"Questions à Michel Foucault sur la géographie," *Hérodote* 1 (1976): 71–85. ("Questions on Geography," *P/K*, 63–77.)
"Vérité et pouvoir." Interview with A. Fontana and P. Pasquino. *L'Arc* 70 (1977): 16–26. ("Truth and power," in *P/K*, 109–133.)

1977
"L'oeil du pouvoir." Conversation with J.-P. Barou and M. Perrot. Introduction to French translation of Jeremy Bentham, *Le panoptique* (Paris: Pierre Belfond, 1977), 7–31. ("The Eye of Power," *P/K*, 146–65.)
"Le jeu de Michel Foucault." Discussion with Alain Grosrichard et al. *Ornicar?* 10 (1977): 62–93. ("The Confession of the Flesh," in *P/K*, 194–228.)
"Foucault: Non au sexe roi." An interview with B.-H. Lévy. *Le nouvel observateur*, March 12, 1977. ("Power and Sex," trans. David J. Parent, *Telos* 32 (1977): 152–61. Reprinted in *PPC*.)

1978
Colloqui con Foucault. Interviews with Duccio Trombadori, Salerno, 10/17. Cooperative editrice, 1981. (*Remarks on Marx: conversations with Duccio Tombadori*, trans. R. James Goldstein and James Cascaito [New York: Semiotext(e), 1991].)
"L'esprit d'un monde sans esprit." Discussion with Claire Brière and Pierre Blanchet. Published as an appendix to their *Iran: la révolution au nom de Dieu* (Paris: Seuil, 1979), 225–41. ("Iran: the Spirit of a World without Spirit," trans. Alan Sheridan in *PPC*.)

1980
"Le philosophe masqué." Anonymous interview with Christian Delacampagne. *Le monde dimanche* (April 6, 1980), 945. ("The Masked Philosopher," in *PPC*.)

1981
"L'Intellectuel et les pouvoirs." Interview with Christian Panier and Pierre Watté. *La revue nouvelle* 80 (1984): 338–45.
"Est-il donc important de penser?" Interview with Didier Eribon, *Libération*

(May 30–31, 1981), 21. ("Is It Really Important to Think?," trans. Thomas Keenan, *Philosophy and Social Criticism* 9 (1982): 29–40. Trans. Alan Sheridan as "Practicing Criticism" in *PPC*.)

"An inteview," with Stephen Riggins. *Ethos* 1 (1983): 4–9. (Reprinted as "The Minimalist Self" in *PPC*.)

1983

"Structuralism and Post-structuralism: An Interview with Michel Foucault." With Gérard Raulet, trans. Jeremy Harding, *Telos* 55 (1983): 195–211. (Reprinted as "Critical Theory/Intellectual History" in *PPC*.)

"Politics and Ethics: An Interview." Trans. Catherine Porter, in Paul Rabinow, ed., *The Foucault Reader* (New York: Pantheon, 1984), 373–80.

"On the Genealogy of Ethics: An Overview of Work in Progress." An interview with H. Dreyfus and P. Rabinow in their *Michel Foucault: Beyond Structuralism and Hermeneutics* (Chicago: University of Chicago Press, rev. ed., 1983), 229–52.

"An Interview with Michel Foucault." With Charles Ruas. Printed as a postscript to his English translation of Foucault's *Raymond Roussel.*

"How Much Does It Cost for Reason to Tell the Truth." With Gerard Raulet. First published in a German translation in *Spuren* (May, June, 1983). (In *FL*.)

1984

"L'éthique du souci de soi comme practique de liberté." Interview with R. Fornet-Betancourt, H. Becker, and A. Gomez-Müller. *Concordia* 6 (1984): 99–116. ("The Ethics of Care of the Self as a Practice of Freedom," trans. J. Gauthier, *Philosophy and Social Criticism* 12 (1984): 2–3, 112–31.)

"Le souci de la vérité." Interview with François Ewald. *Magazine littéraire* 207 (May 1984): 18–24. ("The Concern for Truth," in *PPC*.)

"Le retour de la morale." Interview with Gilles Barbedette and André Scala. *Les nouvelles* 2937 (1984): 36–41. ("The Return of Morality," in *PPC*.)

BOOKS ABOUT FOUCAULT

Auzias, Jean-Marie. *Michel Foucault: qui suis-je?* Lyon: La Manufacture, 1986.

Baudrillard, Jean. *Oublier Foucault.* Paris: Edition Galilée, 1977. ("Forgetting Foucault," trans. N. Dufresne. *Humanities in Society* 3 [1980]: 87–111.)

Bernauer, James W. *Michel Foucault's Force of Flight: Towards an Ethics for Thought.* Atlantic Highlands, N.J.: Humanities Press, 1990.

Blanchot, Michel. *Michel Foucault tel que je l'imagine.* Paris: Fata Morgana,

1986. (In *Foucault/Blanchot*, trans. Jeffrey Mehlman and Brian Massumi [New York: Zone Books, 1987].)

Boyne, Roy. *Foucault and Derrida: The Other Side of Reason.* London: Unwin Hyman, 1990.

Brede, Rüdinger. *Aussage und Discours: Untersuchungen zu Discours – Theorie bei Michel Foucault.* Frankfurt am Main: Peter Lang, 1985.

Carroll, David. *Paraesthetics: Foucault, Lyotard, Derrida.* New York: Methuen, 1988.

Clark, Michael. *Michel Foucault, An Annotated Bibliography.* New York: Garland, 1983.

Cook, Deborah. *The Subject Finds a Voice: Foucault's Turn Toward Subjectivity.* New York: P. Lang, 1992.

Cooper, Barry. *Michel Foucault: An Introduction to the Study of His Thought.* New York: Edwin Mellen Press, 1981.

Cousins, Mark, and Athar Hussain. *Michel Foucault.* London: Macmillan, 1984.

Dauk, Elke. *Denken als Ethos und Methode: Foucault lesen.* Berlin: D. Reimer, 1989.

Deleuze, Gilles. *Foucault,* trans. Sean Hand. Minneapolis: University of Minnesota Press, 1988.

Dreyfus, Hubert L., and Paul Rabinow. *Michel Foucault: Beyond Structuralism and Hermeneutics,* 2nd ed. Chicago: University of Chicago Press, 1983.

During, Simon. *Foucault and Literature: Towards a Genealogy of Writing.* London, New York: Routledge, 1992.

Eribon, Didier. *Michel Foucault,* trans. Betsy Wing. Cambridge: Harvard University Press, 1991.

Fink-Eitel, Hinrich. *Foucault zur Einführung.* Hamburg: Junius Verlag, 1989.

Gillan, Garth, and Charles Lemert. *Michel Foucault: Social Theory as Transgression.* New York: Columbia University Press, 1982.

Guédez, Annie. *Foucault.* Paris: Editions Universitaires, 1972.

Gutting, Gary. *Michel Foucault's Archaeology of Scientific Reason.* Cambridge: Cambridge University Press, 1989.

Honneth, Axel. *The Critique of Power: Reflective Stages in a Critical Social Theory.* Cambridge: MIT Press, 1991.

Kammler, Clemens. *Michel Foucault: eine kritische Analyse seines Werke.* Bonn: Bouvier, 1986.

Kremer-Marietti, Angèle. *Foucault et l'archéologie et genéologie.* Paris: Livre de Poche, 1985.

Künzel, Werner. *Foucault liest Hegel: Versuch einer polemischen Dekonstruktion dialektischen Denkens.* Frankfurt am Main: Haag and Herchen, 1985.

Kusch, Martin. *Foucault's Strata and Fields: An Investigation into Archaeo-logical and Genealogical Science Studies.* Dordrecht: Kluwer, 1991.

Lanigan, Richard L. *The Human Science of Communicology: A Phenome-nology of Discourse in Foucault and Merleau-Ponty.* Pittsburgh: Du-quesne University Press, 1992.

Lemert, Charles C., and Garth Gillan. *Michel Foucault: Social Theory and Transgression.* New York: Columbia University Press, 1982.

Lentricchia, Frank. *Ariel and the Police: Michel Foucault, William James, Wallace Stevens.* Madison: University of Wisconsin Press, 1988.

Lyantey, P. *Foucault.* Paris: Editions Universitaires, 1973.

Mahon, Michael. *Foucault's Nietzschean Genealogy: Truth, Power, and the Subject.* Albany: SUNY Press, 1992.

Major-Poetzl, Pamela. *Michel Foucault's Archaeology of Western Culture: Toward a New Science of History.* Chapel Hill: University of North Carolina Press, 1983.

Marti, Urs. *Michel Foucault.* Munich: Beck, 1988.

Martin, Luther H., Huck Gutman, and Patrick Hutton. *Technologies of the Self: A Seminar with Michel Foucault.* Amherst: University of Massa-chusetts Press, 1988.

McNay, Lois. *Foucault and Feminism.* Boston: Northeastern University Press, 1993.

Megill, Allan. *Prophets of Extremity: Nietzsche, Heidegger, Foucault, Der-rida.* Berkeley: University of California Press, 1985.

Merquior, J. G. *Foucault.* London: Fontana, 1985.

Miller, James. *The Passion of Michel Foucault.* New York: Simon & Schuster, 1993.

Minson, Jeffrey. *Genealogies of Morals: Nietzsche, Foucault, Donzelot and the Eccentricity of Ethics.* New York: St Martin's Press, 1985.

Nordquist, Joan. *Michel Foucault: A Bibliography.* Santa Cruz, Calif.: Refer-ence and Research Services, 1986.

O'Farrell, Clare. *Foucault: Historian or Philosopher?* London: Macmillan, 1990.

O'Hara, Daniel T. *Radical Parody: American Culture and Critical Agency after Foucault.* New York: Columbia University Press, 1992.

Otto, Stephan. *Das Wissen des Ähnlichen: Michel Foucault und die Renais-sance.* Frankfurt am Main, New York: P. Lang, 1992.

Perrot, Michel, ed. *L'impossible prison: recherches sur le système péni-tentiaire au XIXe siècle. Débat avec Michel Foucault.* Paris: Seuil, 1980.

Poster, Mark. *Foucault, Marxism, and History.* Cambridge: Polity Press, 1984.

    Critical Theory and Poststructuralism: In Search of a Context. Ithaca, N.Y.: Cornell University Press, 1989.

Privitera, Walter. *Stilprobleme zur Epistemologie Michel Foucaults*. Frankfurt am Main: Anton Hain, 1990.

Quinby, Lee. *Freedom, Foucault, and the Subject of America*. Boston: Northeastern University Press, 1991.

Racevskis, Karlis. *Michel Foucault and the Subversion of Intellect*. Ithaca, N.Y.: Cornell University Press, 1983.

Rajchman, John. *Michel Foucault: The Freedom of Philosophy*. New York: Columbia University Press, 1985.

Truth and Eros: Foucault, Lacan, and the Question of Ethics. New York: Routledge, 1991.

Russ, Jacqueline. *Histoire de la folie: Michel Foucault*. Paris: Hatier, 1979.

Sawicki, Jana. *Disciplining Foucault: Feminism, Power, and the Body*. New York: Routledge, 1991.

Schmid, Wilhelm. *Die Geburt Der Philosophie im Garten der Lüste: Michel Foucault's Archäologie des platonischen Eros*. Frankfurt am Main: Athenäum, 1987.

Auf der Suche nach einer neuen Lebenskunst: die Frage nach dem Grund und die Neubegründung der Ethik bei Foucault. Frankfurt: Suhrkamp, 1991.

Scott, Charles E. *The Question of Ethics: Nietzsche, Foucault, Heidegger*. Bloomington: Indiana University Press, 1990.

Sheridan, Alan. *Michel Foucault: The Will to Truth*. London: Tavistock, 1980.

Shumway, David R. *Michel Foucault*. Boston: Twayne Publishers, 1989.

Smart, Barry. *Foucault, Marxism, and Critique*. London: Routledge and Kegan Paul, 1983.

Michel Foucault. London: Tavistock, 1985.

COLLECTIONS OF ESSAYS AND ISSUES OF JOURNALS

Arac, Jonathan, ed. *After Foucault: Humanistic Knowledge, Postmodern Challenges*. New Brunswick, N.J.: Rutgers University Press, 1988. (Essays by E. Said, D. Hoy, P. Bové, D. O'Hara, M.-R. Logan, H. Harootunian, I. Balbus, J. Sawicki, and S. Wolin.)

Bernauer, James, and David M. Rasmussen, eds. *The Final Foucault*. Cambridge: MIT Press, 1988. Originally published as *Philosophy and Social Criticism* 12 (1987), nos. 2 and 3. (Essays by K. Racevskis, G. Gillan, J. Bernauer, D. Rubenstein, and T. Flynn.)

Burchell, Graham, Colin Gordon, and Peter Miller, eds. *The Foucault Effect: Studies in Governmentality*. Chicago: University of Chicago Press, 1991. (Essays by C. Gordon, M. Foucault, P. Pasquino, G. Burchell, G. Procacci, J. Donzelot, I. Hacking, F. Ewald, D. Defert, and R. Castel.)

Critique 31 (1975): 343: *A propos d'un livre de Michel Foucault [Surveiller et punir]*. (Essays by G. Deleuze, F. Ewald, and P. Meyer.)

Critique 42 (1986): 471–72: *Michel Foucault du monde entier*. (Essays by A. Jaubert, J. Piel, P. Machery, J. Colombel, F. Ewald, J. Habermas, A. Honneth, W. Miklenitsch, C. Gordon, H. Sluga, H. Dreyfus and P. Rabinow, R. Rorty, R. Bodei, A. Rovatti, M. Vegetti, and P. Veyne.)

Le débat 41 (Sept.–Nov. 1986). ("Etudes" by G. Canguilhem, R. Castel, J. Donzelot, F. Ewald, J. Habermas, P. Pasquino, H. Joly; "Témoinages" by M. Pinguet, E. Burin des Roziers, M. Fano, M. de Certeau, H. Cixous, J. Almira, A. Farge, K. von Bülow, and P. Boulez.)

Deutsche Zeitschrift für Philosophie 38 (1990).

Diamond, I., and L. Quinby, eds. *Feminism and Foucault: Reflections on Resistance*. Boston: Northeastern University Press, 1988. (Essays by B. Martin, M. Morris, F. Barkowski, S. Bartky, S. Bordo, K. Jones, M. Lydon, P. Kamuf, W. Woodhull, J. Sawicki, L. Quinby, and S. Welch.)

Erdmann, Eva, Rainer Forst, and Axel Honneth, eds. *Ethos der Moderne: Foucault's Kritik der Aufklärung*. Frankfurt, New York: Campus, 1990.

Evolution psychiatrique 36 (1971): 2: *La conception idéologique de "l'Histoire de la folie" de Michel Foucault*. (Essays by J. Laboucarie, H. Ey, G. Daumézon, and H. Sztulman.)

Gane, Mike, ed. *Towards a Critique of Foucault*. London: Routledge and Kegan Paul, 1986. (Essays by M. Gane, M. Donnelly, B. Brown and M. Cousins, P. Dews, J. Minson, and G. Wickham.)

Giard, Luce, ed. *Michel Foucault: lire l'oeuvre*. Grenoble: Jérôme Millon, 1992. (Essays on *Histoire de la folie, Naissance de la clinique, Les mots et les choses*, and *Surveiller et punir* by L. Giard, J. Le Brun, M. David-Ménard, A. Tardits, P. Lardet, Judith Revel, C. Sinding, Jacques Revel, Y. Roussel, J.-J. Courtine, R. Reid, C. Ménard, C. Chevalley, J.-G. Petit, A. Farge, T. Conley, G. Vigarello, and F. Ewald.)

Hoy, David C., ed. *Foucault: A Critical Reader*. Oxford: Basil Blackwell, 1986. (Essays by D. Hoy, R. Rorty, C. Taylor, I. Hacking, M. Waltzer, A. Davidson, M. Jay, E. Said, M. Poster, J. Habermas, B. Smart, H. Dreyfus and P. Rabinow.)

Humanities in Society 3 (Winter 1980). *On Foucault*. (Essays by M. Sprinker, P. Bové, K. Racevskis, M. Cavallari, J. Arac, and J. Baudrillard.)

Journal of Medicine and Philosophy 12 (Nov. 1987): *Michel Foucault and the Philosophy of Medicine*. (Articles by H. Dreyfus, C. Scott, E. Casey, C. Spitzack, M. Rawlinson, and S. Spicker.)

Magazine littéraire 101 (1975). (Essays by B.-H. Lévy, J. Revel, M. Kravetz, P. Venault, and R. Bellour.)

Michel Foucault, Philosopher, trans. Timothy J. Armstrong. New York: Routledge, 1992. (Papers from an international conference on Foucault held in Paris, January 8–10, 1988, sponsored by the Centre Michel Foucault.) *Michel Foucault: une histoire de la vérité/conception graphique.* Paris: Syros, 1985. (Contributions by R. Badinter, P. Bourdieu, J. Daniel, F. Ewald, A. Farge, B. Kouchner, E. Maire, C. Mauriac, and M. Perrot; also contains photos and other illustrations.)

Revue Internationale de Philosophie 44 (1991). (Essays by J.-M. Auzias, S. Delivoyatsis, H. Dreyfus, A. Kremer-Marietti, P. Major-Poetzel, and K. Racevskis.)

SCE Reports, Spring/Summer 1982. (Essays by R. Knapp, C. Chase, et al.)

Schmid, Wilhelm, ed. *Denken und Existenz bei Michel Foucault.* Frankfurt: Suhrkamp, 1991.

Still, Arthur, and Irving Velody, eds. *Rewriting the History of Madness: Studies in Foucault's "Histoire de la folie."* London: Routledge, 1992. (Replies to Colin Gordon, *"Histoire de la folie:* An Unknown Book by Michel Foucault.")

ARTICLES AND CHAPTERS IN BOOKS

Aladjem, Terry K. "The Philosopher's Prism: Foucault, Feminism, and Critique." *Political Theory* 19 (1991): 277–291.

Albury, W.R. and D.R. Oldroyd. "From Renaissance Mineral Studies to Historical Geology, in the Light of Michel Foucault's *The Order of Things.*" British Journal of Historical Science 10 (1977): 187–215.

Allen, Barry. "Government in Foucault." *Canadian Journal of Philosophy* 21 (1991): 421–440.

Almansi, G. "Foucault and Magritte." *History of European Ideas* 3 (1982): 303–310.

Amariglio, Jack L. "The Body, Economic Discourse, and Power: An Economist's Introduction to Foucault." *History of Political Economy* 20 (1989): 583–613.

Amiot, M. "Le relativisme culturaliste de Michel Foucault." *Temps modernes* 22 (1967): 1271–1298.

Arac, Jonathan. "The Function of Foucault at the Present Time." *Humanities in Society* 3 (1980): 73–86.

Archambault, Paul J. "Michel Foucault's Last Discourse on Language." *Papers on Language & Literature* 21 (1985): 433–42.

Ariès, Phillipe. "A propos de *La volonté de savoir.*" *Arc* 70 (1977): 27–32.

Armstrong, D. "The Subject and the Social in Medicine: An Appreciation of Michel Foucault." *Sociology and Health and Illness* 7 (1) (1985): 108–117.

Auzias, Jean-Marie. "Le non-structuralisme de Michel Foucault." Pages 128–46 in *Clefs pour le structuralisme*, 3rd ed. Paris: Seghers, 1975.
  "Les gisants et les pleureuses: pour un tombeau de Michel Foucault." *Revue Internationale de Philosophie* 44 (1990): 262–276.
Babin, Daniel. "Au-delà des Lumières." *De Philosophia* 7 (1987–88): 1–30.
Balbus, Isaac D. "Disciplining Women: Michel Foucault and the Power of Feminist Discourse." *Praxis International* 5 (1986): 466–483.
Barthes, Roland. "Savoir et folie." *Critique* 17 (1961): 915–922. ("Taking Sides," pp. 163–70 in Roland Barthes, *Critical Essays*, trans. R. Howard. Evanston, Ill.: Northwestern University Press, 1972.)
Bellour, Raymond. "L'homme, les mots." *Magazine littéraire* 101 (1975): 20–23.
Bernauer, James, W. "Foucault's Political Analysis." *International Philosophical Quarterly* 22 (1982): 87–96.
  "Michel Foucault's Ecstatic Thinking." *Philosophy and Social Criticism* 12 (1987): 156–193.
  "The Prisons of Man: An Introduction to Foucault's Negative Theology." *International Philosophical Quarterly* 27 (1987): 365–380.
  "Beyond Life and Death: On Foucault's Post-Auschwitz Ethic." *Philosophy Today* 32 (1988): 128–142.
Bernstein, Richard. *The New Constellation: The Ethical-Political Horizons of Modernity/Postmodernity*. Cambridge: MIT Press, 1992, chapter 5.
Bersani, Leo. "The Subject of Power." *Diacritics* 7 (1977): 2–21.
  "Pedagogy and Pederasty." *Raritan* 5 (1985): 14–21.
Bertherat, Yves. "La pensée folle." *Esprit* 36 (1967): 862–881.
Beyssade, J. M. "Mais quoi ce sont des fous." *Revue de métaphysique et de morale* 78 (1973): 273–294.
Birken, Lawrence. "Foucault, Marginalism, and the History of Economic Thought: A Rejoinder to Amariglio." *History of Political Economy* 22 (1990): 557–569.
Blair, Carole, and Martha Cooper. "The Humanist Turn in Foucault's Rhetoric of Inquiry." *Quarterly Journal of Speech* 73 (1987): 151–171.
Bogard, William. "Discipline and Deterrence: Rethinking Foucault on the Question of Power in Contemporary Society." *Social Science Journal* 28 (1991): 325–346.
Bordo, Susan. "Docile Bodies, Rebellious Bodies." In Hugh J. Silverman, ed., *Writing the Politics of Difference*. Albany: SUNY Press.
Botwinick, Aryeh. "Nietzsche, Foucault and the Prospects of Postmodern Political Philosophy." *Manuscrito* 12(1989): 117–154.
Bouchard, Donald. "For Life and Action: Foucault, Spectacle, Document." *Oxford Literary Review* 4 (1980): 20–28.

Bové, Paul. "The End of Humanism: Michel Foucault and the Power of Disciplines." *Humanities in Society* 3 (1980): 23–40.

"Intellectuals at War: Michel Foucault and the Power of Disciplines," *Sub-stance* 11–12 (1980): 23–40.

"Mendacious Innocents: Or, the Modern Genealogist as Conscientious Intellectual: Nietzsche, Foucault, Said." Pages 359–388 in Daniel O'Hara, ed., *Why Nietzsche Now?* Bloomington: Indiana University Press, 1985.

Brague, Remi. "Le fou stoicien." *Revue Philosphique de la France et de l'étranger* 180 (1990): 175–184.

Breuer, Stefan. "Foucault and Beyond: Towards a Theory of the Disciplinary Society." *International Social Science Journal* 41 (1989): 235–247.

Brodeur, Jean-Paul. "McDonnell on Foucault's Philosophical Method: Supplementary Remarks." *Canadian Journal of Philosophy* 7(1977): 555–568.

Bruzina, Ron. "Comments on 'On the Ordering of Things: Being and Power In Heidegger and Foucault' by Hubert Dreyfus." *Southern Journal of Philosophy, Supplement* 28 (1989): 97–104.

Buker, Eloise A. "Hidden Desires and Missing Persons: A Feminist Deconstruction of Foucault." *Western Political Quarterly* 43 (1990): 811–832.

Burgelin, Pierre. "L'archéologie du savoir." *Esprit* 35 (1967): 843–861.

Butler, Judith. "Foucault and the Paradox of Bodily Inscriptions." *Journal of Philosophy* 86, (1989): 601–607.

Carroll, David. "The Subject of Archaeology or the Sovereignty of the Episteme." *MLN* 93 (1978): 695–722.

Casey, E.S. "The Place of Space in the *Birth of the Clinic.*" *The Journal of Medicine and Philosophy* 12 (1987): 351–356.

Cavallari, Hector Mario. "Savoir' and 'pouvoir': Michel Foucault's Theory of Discursive Practice." *Humanities in Society* 3 (1980): 55–72.

"Understanding Foucault: Same Sanity, Other Madness." *Semiotica* 56 (1985): 315–346.

Certeau, Michel de. "Les sciences humaines et la mort de l'homme," *Études* 326 (1967): 344–360.

Chidester, David. "Michel Foucault and the Study of Religion." *Religious Study Review* 12 (1986).

Clark, Elizabeth A. "Foucault, the Fathers, and Sex." *Journal of the American Academy of Religion* 56 (1988): 619–641.

Clifford, Michael. "Crossing (out) the Boundary: Foucault and Derrida on Transgressing." *Philosophy Today* 31 (1987): 223–233.

Close, Anthony. "Centering the De-centerers: Foucault and 'Las meninas'." *Philosophy and Literature* 11 (1987): 21–36.

Cohen, Richard. "Merleau-Ponty, the Flesh and Foucault." *Philosophy Today* 28 (1984): 329–338.

Colburn, Kenneth. "Desire and Discourse in Foucault: The Sign of the Fig Leaf in Michelangelo's 'David'." *Human Studies* 10 (1987): 61–79.

Coles, Romand. "Shapiro, Genealogy, and Ethics." *Political Theory* 17 (1989): 575–579.

Comay, Rebecca. "Excavating the Repressive Hypothesis: Aporias of Liberation in Foucault." *Telos* 67 (1986): 111–119.

Connolly, William E. "Discipline, Politics, and Ambiguity." *Political Theory* 11 (1983): 325–342.

"Michel Foucault: An Exchange: Taylor, Foucault, and Otherness." *Political Theory* 13 (1985): 365–376.

Cook, Deborah. "The Turn Towards Subjectivity: Michel Foucault's Legacy." *Journal of the British Society for Phenomenology* 18 (1987): 215–225.

"Nietzsche, Foucault, Tragedy." *Philosophy and Literature* 13 (1989): 140–150.

"Madness and the Cogito: Derrida's Critique of *Folie et deraison*." *Journal of the British Society for Phenomenology* 21 (1990): 164–174.

"Nietzsche and Foucault on *Ursprung* and Genealogy." *Clio* 19 (1990): 299–309.

"History as Fiction: Foucault's Politics of Truth." *Journal of the British Society for Phenomenology* 22 (1991): 139–147.

"Umbrellas, Laundry Bills, and Resistance: The Place of Foucault's Interviews in His Corpus." *Clio* 21 (1992): 145–155.

Corlett, William S. "Pocock, Foucault, Forces of Reassurance." *Political Theory* 17 (1989): 77–100.

Corvez, M. "Le structuralisme de M. Foucault." *Revue Thomiste* 66 (1968): 101–124.

Cottier, Georges. "La mort de l'homme: une lecture de Michel Foucault." *Revue Thomiste* 86 (1986): 269–282.

Cranston, Maurice. "Michel Foucault: A Structuralist View of Reason and Madness." Pages 137–155 in *The Mask of Politics and Other Essays.* New York: Liberty Press, 1973.

D'Amico, Robert. "Desire and the Commodity Form." *Telos* 35 (1978): 88–122.

[Survey review of Foucault's writings]. *Telos* 36 (1978): 169–183.

"Text and Context: Derrida and Foucault on Descartes." In John Fekete, ed., *The Structural Allegory.* Manchester: Manchester University Press, 1984.

Dagognet, François. "Archéologie ou histoire de la medicine." *Critique* 21 (1965): 436–447.

Dallmayr, Fred R. *Polis and Praxis.* Cambridge: MIT Press, 1984, Chapter 3.

"Democracy and Post-Modernism." *Human Studies* 10 (1987): 143–170.

Daraki, M. "Foucault's Journey to Greece." *Telos* 67 (1986): 87–110.

Daumézon, G. "Lecture historique de *L'histoire de la folie* de Michel Foucault." *Evolution psychiatrique* 36 (1971): 227–242.

Davidson, Arnold. "Conceptual Analysis and Conceptual History: Foucault and Philosophy." *Stanford French Review* 8 (1984): 105–122.

Delivoyatsis, Socratis. "Le pouvoir de la difference." *Revue Internationale de Philosophie* 44 (1990): 179–197.

Derrida, Jacques. "Cogito et l'histoire de la folie." *Revue de métaphysique et de morale* 3–4 (1964): 460–494. Reprinted in Jacques Derrida, *Ecriture et la différence* (Paris: Seuil, 1967). (*Writing and Difference* [Chicago: University of Chicago Press, 1978].)

Descombes, Vincent. *Modern French Philosophy*, trans. L. Scott-Fox and J.M. Harding. Cambridge: Cambridge University Press, 1980, Chapter 4.

"Je m'en Foucault." *London Review of Books*, March 5, 1987.

Dews, Peter. *Logics of Disintegration*. London: Verso, 1987, Chapters 5–7.

"The Return of the Subject in Late Foucault." *Radical Philosophy* 51 (1989): 37–41.

Digeser, Peter. "The Fourth Face of Power." *Journal of Politics* 54 (1992): 977–1007.

Dreyfus, Hubert L. "Foucault's Critique of Psychiatric Medicine." *Journal of Medicine and Philosophy* 12 (1987): 311–333.

"On the Ordering of Things: Being and Power in Heidegger and Foucault." *Southern Journal of Philosophy, Supplement* 28 (1989): 83–96.

"Foucault et la psychotherapie." *Revue Internationale de Philosophie* 44 (1990): 209–230.

"Beyond Hermeneutics." Pages 66–83 in Gary Shapiro, ed. *Hermeneutics* (Amherst, Mass.: University of Massachusetts Press, 1984).

Dumm, Thomas L. "The Politics of Post-modern Aesthetics: Habermas contra Foucault." *Political Theory* 16 (1988): 209–228.

Duvivier, Roger. "La mort de Don Quichotte et *l'Histoire de la folie*." *Marche romane* 20 (1970): 69–83.

El Kordi, M. "L'archéologie de la pensée classique selon Michel Foucault." *Revue d'histoire économique et sociale* 51 (1973): 309–335.

Ewald, François. "Anatomie et corps politiques." *Critique* 343 (1975): 1228–1265.

Ey, H. "Commentaires critiques sur *L'histoire de la folie* de Michel Foucault." *Evolution psychiatrique* 36 (1971): 243–258.

Felman, Shoshana. "Madness and Philosophy or Literature's Reason." *Yale French Review* 52 (1975): 206–228.

"Foucault/Derrida: The Madness of the Thinking/Speaking Subject." Pages 35–55 in *Writing and Madness: Literature/Philosophy/Psychoanalysis*. Ithaca, N.Y.: Cornell University Press, 1985.

Fine, Bob. "Struggles Against Discipline: The Theory and Politics of Michel Foucault." *Capital and Class* 9 (1979): 75–96.

Finkelstein, Joanne L. "Biomedicine and Technocratic Power (Views of Michel Foucault)." *The Hastings Center Report* 20 (1990): 13–16.

Flaherty, Peter. "(Con)textual Contest: Derrida and Foucault on Madness and the Cartesian Subject." *Philosophy and Social Science* 16 (1986): 157–175.

Flynn, Bernard. "Michel Foucault and the Husserlian Problematic of a Transcendental Philosophy of History." *Philosophy Today* 22 (1978): 224–238.

"Sexuality, Knowledge and Power in the Thought of Michel Foucault." *Philosophy and Social Criticism* 8 (1981): 329–348.

"Foucault and the Body Politic." *Man and World* 20 (1987): 65–84.

"Derrida and Foucault: Madness and Writing." Pages 201–218 in Hugh J. Silverman, ed., *Derrida and Deconstruction*. New York: Routledge, 1989.

Flynn, Thomas. "Truth and Subjectivation in the Later Foucault." *Journal of Philosophy* 82 (1985): 531–540.

"Michel Foucault and the Career of the Historical Event." Pages 178–200 in Bernard P. Dauenhauer, ed., *At the Nexus of Philosophy and History*. Athens: University of Georgia Press, 1987.

"Foucault as Parrhesiast: His Last Course at the Collège de France (1984)." *Philosophy and Social Criticism* 12 (1987): 213–276. Reprinted in Bernauer and Rasmussen, eds., *The Final Foucault*.

"Foucault and the Politics of Postmodernity." *Nous* 23 (1989): 187–189.

"Foucault and Historical Nominalism." In H.A. Durfee and D.F.T. Rodier, eds., *Phenomenology and Beyond: The Self and Its Language*. Dordrecht: Kluwer, 1989.

"Foucault and the Spaces of History." *Monist* 45 (1991): 165–186.

Forrester, J. "Michel Foucault and Psychoanalysis." *History of Science* 18 (1980): 286–303.

"Foucaultian Politics (symposium)." *Political Theory* 15 (1987): 5–80.

Frank, Arthur. "The Politics of the New Positivity: A Review Essay of Michel Foucault's *Discipline and Punish*." *Human Studies* 5 (1982): 61–68.

Frank, Manfred. *What Is Neostructuralism?*, trans. Sabine Wilke and Richard Gray. Minneapolis: University of Minnesota Press, 1989, Chapters 7–12.

Fraser, Nancy. "Foucault on Modern Power: Empirical Insights and Normative Confusions." *Praxis International* 1 (1981): 272–287.

"Foucault's Body Language: A Posthumanist Political Rhetoric?" *Salmagundi* 61 (1983): 55–70. Reprinted in Fraser, *Unruly Practices: Power,*

Discourse, and Gender in Contemporary Social Theory. Minneapolis: University of Minnesota Press, 1989.

"Michel Foucault: A 'Young Conservative'?" *Ethics* 96 (1985): 165–184. Also in Fraser, *Unruly Practices.*

Freundlieb, Dieter. "Rationalism versus Irrationalism: Habermas's Response to Foucault." *Inquiry* 31 (1988): 171–192.

Frow, John. "Foucault and Derrida." *Raritan* 5 (1985): 31–42.

Gandal, Keith. "Michel Foucault: Intellectual Work and Politics." *Telos* 67 (1986).

Garland, David. "Criminological Knowledge and Its Relation to Power: Foucault's Genealogy and Criminology Today." *British Journal of Criminology* 32 (1992): 403–422.

Gearhart, Susan. "Establishing Rationality in the Historical Text: Foucault and the Problem of Unreason." Pages 29–56 in Gearhart, *The Open Boundary of History and Fiction: A Critical Approach to the French Enlightenment.* Princeton: Princeton University Press, 1984.

Gillan, Garth. "Foucault's Philosophy." *Philosophy and Social Criticism* 12 (1987): 145–155.

Girardin, Benoit. "*Les Mots et les choses,* à propos du livre de Michel Foucault." *Freiburger Zeitschrift für Philosophie und theologie* 16 (1969): 92–99.

Goldstein, Jan. "Foucault among the Sociologists: The 'Disciplines' and the History of the Professions." *History and Theory* 23 (1984): 170–192.

" 'The Lively Sensibility of the Frenchman': Some Reflections on the Place of France in Foucault's *Histoire de la folie.*" *History of the Human Sciences* 3 (1990): 333–341.

Gordon, Colin. "Birth of the Subject." *Radical Philosophy* 17 (1977): 15–25.

"Question, Ethos, Event: Foucault on Kant and Enlightenment." *Economy and Society* 15 (1986): 71–87.

"*Histoire de la folie:* An Unknown Book by Michel Foucault." *History of the Human Sciences* 3 (1990): 3–26. (See also the series of responses by various writers in *History of the Human Sciences* 3, no.1 and no. 3.)

Gould, James A. "Explanatory Grounds: Marx versus Foucault." *Dialogos* 25 (1990): 133–138.

Greene, John. "Les mots et les choses." *Social Science Information* 6 (1967): 131–138.

Gruber, David F. "Foucault and Theory: Genealogical Critiques of the Subject." Pages 189–196 in Arleen B. Dallery, ed., *The Question of the Other.* Albany: SUNY Press, 1989.

"Foucault's Critique of the Liberal Individual." *Journal of Philosophy* 86 (1989): 615–621.

Guédon, Jean-Claude. "Michel Foucault: The Knowledge of Power and the Power of Knowledge." *Bulletin of the History of Medicine* 51 (1977): 245–277.

Gutting, Gary. "Michel Foucault and the History of Reason." In Ernan McMullin, ed., *Construction and Constraint*. Notre Dame, Ind.: University of Notre Dame Press, 1988.

"Continental Approaches to the History and Philosophy of Science." Pages 127–147 in G. H. Cantor et al., eds., *Companion to the History of Modern Science*. London: Routledge, 1989.

"Continental Philosophy of Science." Pages 94–117 in Peter Asquith and Henry Kyburg, eds., *Current Research in Philosophy of Science*. East Lansing, Mich.: Philosophy of Science Association, 1979.

"Foucault's Genealogical Method." Pages 327–344 in P. French, T. Uehling, and H. Wettstein, eds., *Midwest Studies in Philosophy* 15 (1990).

Habermas, Jürgen. "Taking Aim at the Heart of the Present." *University Publishing* 13 (1984): 5–6. Reprinted in David Hoy, ed., *Foucault: A Critical Reader*. Oxford: Basil Blackwell, 1986.

"Genealogical Writing of History: On Some Aporias in Foucault's Theory of Power." *Canadian Journal of Political and Social Theory* 10 (1986): 1–9.

The Philosophical Discourse of Modernity: Twelve Lectures, trans. Frederick Lawrence. Cambridge: MIT Press, 1987, Chapters 9 and 10.

Hacking, Ian. "Michel Foucault's Immature Science." *Nous* 13 (1979): 39–51.

"Biopower and the Avalanche of Printed Numbers." *Humanities in Society* 5 (1982): 279–295.

"Five Parables." Pages 103–124 in Richard Rorty et al., eds., *Philosophy in History*. New York: Cambridge University Press, 1984.

"The Archaeology of Foucault." In David Hoy, ed., *Foucault: A Critical Reader*. Oxford: Basil Blackwell, 1986.

Halperin, David M. "Sexual Ethics and Technologies of the Self in Classical Greece." *American Journal of Philology* 107 (1986): 274–286.

"Is There a History of Sexuality?" *History and Theory* 28 (1989): 257–274.

Harpham, Geoffrey Galt. "Foucault and the 'Ethics' of Power." Pages 71–81 in Robert Merrill, ed., *Ethics/Aesthetics*. Washington: Maisonneuve Press, 1988.

Hartsock, Nancy. "Foucault on Power: A Theory for Women?" In L. Nicholson, ed., *Feminism/Postmodernism*. London: Routledge, 1990.

Hattiangadi, J.H. "Language Philosophy: Hacking and Foucault." *Dialogue* 17 (1978): 513–528.

Hekman, Susan. "Foucault: Moral Nihilism." Pages 171–186 in *Hermeneutics and the Sociology of Knowledge*. Cambridge: Polity Press, 1986.

Hiley, David R. "Foucault and the Analysis of Power: Political Engagement Without Liberal Hope or Comfort." *Praxis International* 4 (1984): 192–207.
"Foucault and the Question of Enlightenment." *Philosophy and Social Criticism* 11 (1985): 63–83.
Hill, R. Kevin. "Foucault's Critique of Heidegger." *Philosophy Today* (1990): 334–341.
Hinkle, Gisela J. "Foucault's Power/Knowledge and American Sociological Theorizing." *Human Studies* 10 (1987): 35–59.
Hirsch, Eli. "Knowledge, Power, Ethics." *Manuscrito* 12 (1989): 49–63.
Hirst, P., and P. Wooley. *Social Relations and Human Activities*. London: Tavistock, 1982, Chapter 9.
Hodge, Joanna. "Habermas and Foucault: Contesting Rationality." *Irish Philosophical Journal* (1990): 60–78.
Hollier, Denis. "Foucault: The Death of the Author." *Raritan* 5 (1985): 22–30.
Holub, R.C. "Remembering Foucault." *German Quarterly* 58 (1985): 238–56.
Honneth, Axel. *Kritik der Macht*. Frankfurt am Main: Suhrkamp, 1985, Chapters 4–6.
Hooke, Alexander E. "The Order of Others: Is Foucault's Antihumanism Against Human Action?" *Political Theory* 15 (1987): 38–60.
Horowitz, Gad. "The Foucaultian Impasse: No Sex, No Self, No Revolution." *Political Theory* 15 (1987): 61–80.
Hoy, David. "Power, Repression, Progress: Foucault, Lukes, and the Frankfurt School." *Triquarterly* 52 (1981): 43–63.
Huppert, George. " 'Divinatio et eruditio': Thoughts on Foucault." *History and Theory* 13 (1974): 191–207.
Ignatieff, Michael. "State, Civil Society, and Total Institutions: A Critique of Recent Social Histories of Punishment." Pages 75–105 in Stanley Cohen and Andrew Scull, eds., *Social Control and the State*. New York: St. Martin's Press, 1983.
Ijsseling, S. "Foucault with Heidegger." *Man and World* 19 (1986): 413–424.
Ingram, David. "Foucault and the Frankfurt School: A Discourse on Nietzsche, Power and Knowledge." *Praxis International* 6 (1986): 311–327.
Isenberg, Bo. "Habermas on Foucault: Critical Remarks." *Acta Sociologica* 34 (1991): 299–308.
Johnson, J. Scott. "Reading Nietzsche and Foucault: A Hermeneutics of Suspicion? (Comment on L. P. Thiele)." *American Political Science Review* 85 (1991): 581–584.
Johnston, Craig. "Foucault and Gay Liberation." *Arena* 61 (1982): 54–70.
Johnston, John. "Discourse as Event: Foucault, Writing, and Literature." *MLN* 105 (1990): 800–818.

Kaufmann, J. N. "Foucault historien et 'historien' du present." *Dialogue* 25 (1986): 223–237.

"Formations discursives et dispositifs de pouvoir: Habermas critique Foucault." *Dialogue* 27 (1988): 41–57.

Kearney, Richard. "Michel Foucault." Pages 283–298 in *Modern Movements in European Philosophy.* Manchester: Manchester University Press, 1986.

Keat, Russell. "The Human Body in Social Theory: Reich, Foucault, and the Repressive Hypothesis." *Radical Philosophy* 42 (1986): 24–32.

Keeley, James F. "Toward a Foucauldian Analysis of International Regimes." *International Organization* 44 (1990): 83–105.

Keenan, Tom. "The 'Paradox' of Knowledge and Power: Reading Foucault on a Bias." *Political Theory* 15 (1987): 5–37.

Kelkel, Arion L. "La fin de l'homme et le destin le la pensée: la mutation anthropologique de la philosophie de M Heidegger et M Foucault." *Man and World* 18 (1985): 3–38.

Kemp, Peter. "Michel Foucault." *History and Theory* 23 (1984): 84–105.

Kennedy, Deveraux. "Michel Foucault." *Theory and Society* 8 (1979): 269–290.

Kent, Christopher A. "Michel Foucault: Doing History, or Undoing It?" *Canadian Journal of History* 21 (1986): 371–395.

Knee, Philip. "Le cercle et le doublet: note sur Sartre et Foucault." *Philosophiques* 17 (1990): 113–126.

"Le Probleme politique chez Sartre et Foucault." *Laval Théologique et Philosophique* 47 (1991): 83–93.

Kremer-Marietti, Angèle. "De la matérialité du discours saisi dans l'institution." *Revue Internationale de Philosophie* 44 (1990): 241–261.

Krips, Henry. "Power and resistance." *Philosophy and Social Science* 20 (1990): 170–182.

Kurzweil, Edith. "Michel Foucault: Ending the Era of Man." *Theory and Society* 4 (1977): 395–420.

"Michel Foucault: Structuralism and Structures of Knowledge." Pages 193–226 in *The Age of Structuralism: Lévi-Strauss to Foucault.* New York: Columbia University Press, 1980.

"Michel Foucault and Culture." *Current Perspectives in Social Theory* 4 (1983): 143–179.

"Michel Foucault's History of Sexuality as Interpreted by Feminists and Marxists." *Social Research* 53 (1986).

LaCapra, Dominick. "Foucault, History, and Madness." *History of the Human Sciences* 3 (1989): 32–34.

La Chance, Michael. "Deploiement et resistances chez Foucault." *Philosophiques* 14 (1987): 33–56.

Lacharité, Normand. "Les conditions de possibilité du savoir: deux versions structuralistes de ce problème." *Dialogue* 7 (1968): 359–373.

Laforest, Guy. "Regards généalogiques sur la modernité: Michel Foucault et la philosophie politique." *Canadian Journal of Political Science* 18 (1985): 77–97.

"Gouverne et liberté: Foucault et la question du pouvoir." *Canadian Journal of Political Science* 22 (September 1989): 547–562.

Lash, Scott. "Genealogy and the Body: Foucault/Deleuze/Nietzsche." *Theory, Culture, and Society* 2 (1984): 1–17.

Leary, D.E. "Michel Foucault: An Historian of the Science Humaines." *Journal of the History of Behavioral Sciences* 12 (1976): 286–293.

Le Bon, Sylvie. "Un positiviste désespéré: Michel Foucault." *Les Temps modernes* 22 (1967): 1299–1319.

Lecourt, Dominique. "Sur l'archéologie et la savoir (à propos de Michel Foucault)." *Pensée* 152 (1970): 69–87. (Translated by Ben Brewster in D. Lecourt, *Marxism and Epistemology: Bachelard, Canguilhem, Foucault* [London: NLB, 1975].)

Leigh, David. "Michel Foucault and the Study of Literature and Theology." *Christianity and Literature* 33 (1983): 75–85.

Leland, Dorothy. "On Reading and Writing the World: Foucault's History of Thought." *Clio* 4 (1975): 225–243.

Lemaigre, B. "Michel Foucault, ou les malheurs de la raison et les prospérités du langage." *Revue des Sciences Philosophique et Théologique* 51 (1967): 440–460.

Lemert, Charles, and Garth Gillan. "The New Alternative in Critical Sociology: Foucault's Discursive Analysis." *Cultural Hermeneutics* 4 (1977): 309–320.

Lentricchia, Frank. "Reading Foucault (Punishment, Labor, Resistance)." *Raritan* 1 (1982): 5–32.

Leonard, Jacques. "L'historien et le philosophe: à propos de *Surveiller et punir.*" *Annales historiques de la révolution française* 288 (1977): 163–181.

Leroux, Georges. "Le sujet du souci: à propos de L'historie de la sexualité de Michel Foucault." *Philosophiques* 14 (1987): 5–32.

Levin, David. "The Body Politic: The Embodiment of Praxis in Foucault and Habermas." *Praxis International* 9 (1989): 112–132.

Levy, Silvano. "Foucault on Magritte on Resemblance." *Modern Language Review* 85 (1990): 50–56.

Lévy, B.-H. "Le système Foucault." *Magazine littéraire* 101 (1975): 7–9.

Lilly, Reginald. "Foucault: Making a Difference." *Man and World* 24 (1991): 267–284.

Lunn, Forrest. "Foucault and the Referent." *Gnosis* (1990): 73–88.

Lydon, M. "Foucault and Feminism: A Romance of Many Dimensions." *Humanities in Society* 5 (1982): 245–256.

Macherey, Pierre. "Aux sources de 'L'histoire de la folie': une rectification et ses limites." *Critique* 43 (1986): 752–774.

Maher, Winifred, and Brendan Maher. "The Ship of Fools: 'stultifera navis' or ignis fatuus?" *American Psychologist* 37 (1982): 756–761.

Maidan, Michael. "Michel Foucault on Bentham and Beccaria." *Rivista Internazionale di Filosofia del Diritto* 65 (1988): 329–331.

Major-Poetzl, Pamela. "The Disorder of Things." *Revue Internationale de Philosophie* 44 (1990): 198–208.

Mall, James. "Foucault as Literary Critic." Pages 197–204 in Philip Crant, ed., *French Literary Criticism*. Columbia: University of South Carolina Press, 1977.

Mandrou, Robert. "Trois clefs pour comprendre la folie à l'époque classique." *Annales* 4 (1962): 761, 771–772.

Margolin, J.-C. "L'homme de Michel Foucault." *Revue des sciences humaines* 128 (1967): 497–522.

Margot, Jean Paul. "Hermeneutique et fiction chez M. Foucault." *Dialogue* 23 (1984): 635–648.

"La lecture foucaldienne de Descartes: ses présupposés et ses implications." *Philosophiques* 11 (1984): 3–40.

Martin, B. "Feminism, critique, and Foucault." *New German Critique* 26 (1982): 3–12.

Martin, Bill. "Foucault: Power/Counterpower." *Arena* 73 (1985): 138–153.

Maslin, M. "Foucault and Pragmatism." *Raritan* 7 (1988): 94–114.

Massé Alain. "La representation chez Foucault." *De Philosophia* 6 (1985–86): 85–91.

McCarthy, Thomas. "The Critique of Impure Reason: Foucault and the Frankfurt School." *Political Theory* 18 (1990): 437–469.

McDonell, Donald J. "On Foucault's Philosophical Method." *Canadian Journal of Philosophy* 7 (1977): 537–553.

McHugh, Patrick. "Dialectics, Subjectivity and Foucault's Ethos of Modernity." *Boundary* 2, 16 (1989): 91–108.

McNay, Lois. "The Foucauldian Body and the Exclusion of Experience." *Hypatia* 6 (1991): 125–139.

McWhorter, Ladelle. "Culture or Nature: The Function of the Term 'Body' in the Work of Michel Foucault." *Journal of Philosophy* 86 (1989): 608–614.

"Foucault's Move Beyond the Theoretical." Pages 197–203 in Arleen B. Dallery, ed., *The Question of the Other*. Albany: SUNY Press, 1989.

Megill, Allan. "Foucault, Structuralism, and the Ends of History." *Journal of Modern History* 51 (1979): 451–503.

"Recent Writing on Michel Foucault." *Journal of Modern History* 56 (1984): 499–511.

"The Reception of Foucault by Historians." *Journal of the History of Ideas* 48 (1987): 117–141.

"Foucault, Ambiguity, and the Rhetoric of Historiography." *History of the Human Sciences* 3 (1990): 343–361.

Meisel, Perry. "What Foucault Knows." *Salmagundi* 44–45 (1979): 235–241.

Meynell, Hugo. "On Knowledge, Power and Michel Foucault." *Heythrop Journal* 30 (1989): 419–432.

Midelfort, H.C. Eric. "Madness and Civilization in Early Modern Europe: A Reappraisal of Michel Foucault." Pages 247–265 in Barbara Malament, ed., *After the Reformation: Essays in Honor of J.H. Hexter.* Philadelphia: University of Pennsylvania Press, 1980.

Miel, J. "Ideas or Epistemes: Hazard versus Foucault." *Yale French Studies* 49 (1973): 231–245.

Miller, James. "Carnivals of Atrocity: Foucault, Nietzsche, Cruelty." *Political Theory* 18 (1990): 470–491.

"Michel Foucault: The Heart Laid Bare." *Grand Street* 10 (1991): 53–64.

"Foucault: The Secrets of a Man." *Salmagundi* 88/89 (1991): 311–332.

Miller, James, et al. "A Symposium on James Miller's *The Passion of Michel Foucault*" (J. Miller, L. Hunt, A. MacIntyre, R. Rorty, D. Halperin). *Salmagundi* 97 (Winter 1993): 30–99.

Moore, Mary Candace. "Ethical Discourse and Foucault's Conception of Ethics." *Human Studies* 10 (1987): 81–95.

Murphy, John W. "Foucault's Ground of History." *International Philosophical Quarterly* 24 (1984): 189–196.

Nehamas, Alexander. "What an Author Is." *Journal of Philosophy* 83 (1986): 685–692.

Noujain, Elie Georges. "History as Genealogy: An Exploration of Foucault's Approach to History." *Philosophy* 21 (1987): 157–174.

O'Brien, Patricia. "Foucault's History of Culture." Pages 25–46 in Lynn Hunt, ed., *The New Cultural History.* Berkeley: University of California Press, 1989.

O'Hara, Daniel T. "Michel Foucault and the Fate of Friendship." *Boundary* 2, 18 (1991): 83–103.

Olivier, Lawrence. "La question du pouvoir chez Foucault: espace, stratégie et dispositif." *Canadian Journal of Political Science* 21 (1988): 83–98.

Olivier, Lawrence, and Sylvain Labb. "Foucault et l'Iran: à propos du désir de révolution." *Canadian Journal of Political Science* 24 (1991): 219–236.

Ophir, Adi. "The Semiotics of Power: Reading Michel Foucault's *Discipline and Punish.*" *Manuscrito* 12 (1980): 9–34.

"Michel Foucault and the Semiotics of the Phenomenal." *Dialogue* 27 (1988): 387–415.

Paden, Roger. "Surveillance and Torture: Foucault and Orwell on the Methods of Discipline." *Social Theory and Practice* 10 (1984): 261–271.

"Locating Foucault – Archeology vs. Structuralism." *Philosophy and Social Criticism* 11 (1986): 19–37.

"Foucault's Anti-humanism." *Human Studies* 10 (1987): 123–141.

Palmer, Jerry, and Frank Pearce. "Legal Discourse and State Power: Foucault and the Juridical Relation." *International Journal of the Sociology of Law* 11 (1983): 361–383.

Parsons, S. "Foucault and the Problem of Kant." *Praxis International* 8 (1988): 317–328.

Pasquino, Pascale. "Michel Foucault [1926–84]: The Will to Knowledge." *Economy and Society* 15 (1986).

Paternek, Margaret A. "Norms and Normalization: Michel Foucault's Overextended Panoptic Machine." *Human Studies* 10 (1987): 97–121.

Patton, Paul. "Taylor and Foucault on Power and Freedom." *Political Studies* 37 (1989): 260–276.

Pelorson, Jean-Marc. "Michel Foucault et l'espagne." *Pensée* 152 (1970): 88–99.

Peterson, R.T. "Foucault and the Politics of Social Reproduction." *Humanities in Society* 5 (1982): 231–243.

Phelan, Shane. "Foucault and Feminism." *American Journal of Political Science* 34 (1990): 421–440.

Philp, Mark. "Foucault on Power: A Problem in Radical Translation?" *Political Theory* 11 (1983): 29–51.

"Michel Foucault." Pages 65–81 in Quentin Skinner, ed., *The Return of Grand Theory in the Human Sciences.* Cambridge: Cambridge University Press, 1985.

Piaget, Jean. *Le structuralisme.* Paris: PUF, 1968, pp. 108–115. (*Structuralism*, trans. C. Maschler [New York: Basic Books, 1970], pp. 128–135.)

Pierart, Marcel. "Michel Foucault et le morale sexuelle des anciens." *Freiburger Zeitschrift für Philosophie und Theologie* 33 (1986): 23–43.

Plumpe, Gerhard. "Wissen ist Macht." *Philosophische Rundschau* 27 (1980): 185–218.

Polan, Dana. "Fables of Transgression: The Reading of Politics and the Politics of Reading in Foucauldian Discourse." *Boundary* 2, 10 (1982): 361–382.

Pollis, Carol A. "The Aparatus of Sexuality: Reflections on Foucault's Contributions to the Study of Sex in History." *The Journal of Sex Research* 23 (1987): 401–408.

Porter, Roy. "Foucault's Great Confinement." *History of the Human Sciences* 3 (1990): 47–54.

Poster, Mark. "Foucault's Science Without Scientists." Pages 334–340 in *Existential Marxism in Postwar France: From Sartre to Althusser*. Princeton: Princeton University Press, 1975.

"Foucault's True Discourses." *Humanities in Society* 2 (1980): 153–166.

"Foucault and History." *Sociological Research* 49 (1982): 116–142.

"The Future According to Foucault: The Archaeology of Knowledge and Intellectual History." Pages 137–152 in Dominick LaCapra and Steven Kaplan, eds., *Modern European Intellectual History: Reappraisals and New Perspectives*. Ithaca, N.Y.: Cornell University Press, 1982.

Pratt, John. "The Legacy of Foucault." *International Journal of the Sociology of Law* 13 (1985): 289–293.

Pratt, Vernon. "Foucault and the History of Classification Theory." *Studies in the History and Philosophy of Science* 8 (1976): 163–171.

Putnam, Hilary. *Reason, Truth, and History*. Cambridge: Cambridge University Press, 1981, Chapter 7.

Racevskis, Karlis. "The Discourse of Michel Foucault: A Case of an Absent and Forgettable Subject." *Humanities in Society* 3 (1980): 44–54.

"Michel Foucault, Rameau's Nephew, and the Question of Identity." *Philosophy and Social Criticism* 12 (1987): 132–144.

"The Conative Function of the Other in *Les mots et les choses*." *Revue Internationale de Philosophie* 44 (1990): 231–240.

Rajchman, John. "The Story of Foucault's History." *Social Text* 8 (1983–84): 3–24.

"Nietzsche, Foucault, and the Anarchism of Power." *Semiotext(e)* 3 (1978): 96–107.

"Approaching Michel Foucault." *Queen's Quarterly* 91 (1984): 623–634.

"Ethics after Foucault." *Social Text* 13 (1985): 165–183.

Philosophical Events: Essays of the '80s. New York: Columbia University Press, 1991.

Rawlinson, Mary C. "Foucault's Strategy: Knowledge, Power, and the Specificity of Truth." *Journal of Medicine and Philosophy* 12 (1987): 371–395.

Ray, Larry. "Foucault, Critical Theory and the Decomposition of the Historical Subject." *Philosophy and Social Criticism* 14 (1988): 69–110.

Redner, Harry. "Infernal Recurrence of the Same: Nietzsche and Foucault on Knowledge and Power." Pages 291–315 in Marcelo Dascal, ed., *Knowledge and Politics*. Boulder, Colo.: Westview Press.

Revel, Jacques, and Raymond Bellour. "Foucault et les historiens." *Magazine littéraire* 101 (1975): 10–13.

Richters, A. "Modernity-Postmodernity Controversies: Habermas and Foucault." *Theory, Culture, and Society* 5 (1988): 611–643.

Riley, Philip F. "Michel Foucault, Lust, Women, and Sin in Louis XIV's Paris." *Church History* 59 (1990): 35–50.

Rollet, Jacques. "Michel Foucault et la question du pouvoir." *Archives de Philosophie* 51 (1988): 647–663.

Rorty, Richard. "Beyond Nietzsche and Marx." *London Review of Books* 3 (1981): 5–6.

"Method, Science and Social Hope." *Canadian Journal of Philosophy* 16 (1981): 569–588. Reprinted in *Consequences of Pragmatism*. Minneapolis: University of Minnesota Press, 1982, pp. 191–210.

"Foucault and Epistemology." Pages 41–49 in David Hoy, ed., *Foucault: A Critical Reader.* Oxford: Basil Blackwell, 1986.

"Foucault/Dewey/Nietzsche." *Raritan* 9 (1990): 1–8.

"Moral Identity and Private Autonomy: The Case of Foucault." Pages 93–98 in Richard Rorty, *Essays on Heidegger and Others: Philosophical Papers*, vol. 2. New York: Cambridge University Press, 1991.

Ross, Stephen. "Foucault's Radical Politics." *Praxis International* 5 (1985): 131–144.

Roth, Michael S. "Foucault's 'History of the Present'." *History and Theory* 20 (1981): 32–46.

Review article on Michel Foucault. *History and Theory* 27 (1988): 70–80.

Rouse, Joseph. *Knowledge and Power: Toward a Political Philosophy of Science.* Ithaca, N.Y.: Cornell University Press, 1987, Chapter 7.

Rousseau, G.S. "Whose Enlightenment? Not Man's: The Case of Michel Foucault." *Eighteenth-Century Studies* 6 (1972–73): 238–256.

Rubenstein, Diane. "Food for Thought: Metonymy in the Late Foucault." *Philosophy and Social Criticism* 12 (1987): 194–212.

Russo, François. "L'archéologie du savoir de Michel Foucault." *Archives de Philosophie* 36 (1973): 69–105.

Rybalka, M. "Michel Foucault: Philosopher of Exclusion." *Contemporary French Civilization* 9 (1985): 192–198.

Said, Edward. "*Abecedarium Culturae:* Structuralism, Absence, Writing." *Triquarterly* 20 (1971): 33–71.

"Michel Foucault as an Intellectual Imagination." *Boundary* 2 (1972): 1–36. Reprinted in Edward Said, *Beginnings: Intention and Method.* New York: Basic Books, 1975.

"An Ethics of Language." *Diacritics* 4 (1974): 28–37.

"The Problem of Textuality: Two Exemplary Solutions." *Critical Inquiry* 4 (1978): 673–714.

"Travelling Theory." *Raritan* 1 (1982): 41–67.

"Michel Foucault, 1926–1984: In Memoriam." *Raritan* 4 (1984): 1–11.

Sartre, Jean-Paul. "Jean-Paul Sartre répond." *Arc* 30 (1966): 87–96.
Sawicki, Jana. "Foucault and Feminism: Towards a Politics of Difference." *Hypatia* 1 (1986): 23–36.
"Heidegger and Foucault: Escaping Technological Nihilism." *Philosophy and Social Criticism* 13 (1987): 155–173.
Sax, Benjamin C. "Foucault, Nietzsche, History: Two Modes of the Genealogical Method." *History of European Ideas* (1989): 769–781.
"On the Genealogical Method: Nietzsche and Foucault." *International Studies in Philosophy* (1990): 129–141.
Schaub, Uta Liebmann. "Foucault's Oriental Subtext." *PMLA* 104 (1989): 306–316.
Schneck, Stephen F. "Michael Foucault on Power/Discourse, Theory and Practice." *Human Studies* 10 (1987): 15–33.
Schneider, Ulrich Johannes. "Eine Philosophie der Kritik: Zur Amerikanischen und Franzosischen Rezeption Michel Foucaults." *Zeitschrift für Philosophische Forschung* 42 (1988): 311–317.
Schurmann, Reiner. " 'What Can I Do?' in an Archaeological-Genealogical History." *Journal of Philosophy* 82. (1985): 540–547.
"On Constituting Oneself an Anarchistic Subject." *Praxis International* 6 (1986): 294–310.
Scott, Charles E. "Structure and Order." Pages 16–27 in Hugh J. Silverman, ed., *Piaget, Philosophy and the Human Sciences.* Atlantic Highlands, N.J.: Humanities Press, 1980.
"Foucault's Practice of Thinking." *Research in Phenomenology* 14 (1984): 75–85.
"The Power of Medicine, the Power of Ethics." *Journal of Medicine and Philosophy* 12 (1987): 335–356.
"Foucault and the Question of Humanism." In David Goicoechea, John Luik, and Tim Madigan, eds., *The Question of Humanism: Challenges and Possibilities.* Buffalo, N.Y.: Prometheus, 1991.
"The Question of Ethics in Foucault's Thought." *The Journal of the British Society for Phenomenology* 22 (1991): 33–43.
Sedgwick, Peter. "Michel Foucault: The Anti-History of Psychiatry." Pages 125–148 in Sedgwick, *Psycho Politics.* New York: Harper & Row 1982.
Seigel, Jerrold. "Avoiding the Subject: A Foucaultian Itinerary." *Journal of the History of Ideas* 51 (1990): 273–299.
Seltzer, Mark. "Reading Foucault: Cells, Corridors, Novels." *Diacritics* 14 (1984): 78–89.
Serres, Michel. "Géometrie de l'incommunicable: La folie" and "Le retour de la nef." Pages 167–190, 191–275 in Serres, *Hermes I: La communication.* Paris: Editions de Minuit, 1968.

Shaffer, Elinor S. "The Archaeology of Michel Foucault." *Studies in History and Philosophy of Science* 7 (1976): 269–275.

Shapiro, Michael J. "Michel Foucault and the Analysis of Discursive Practice." Pages 127–164 in Shapiro, *Language and Political Understanding*. New Haven: Yale University Press, 1981.

Shiner, Larry. "Foucault and the Unconscious of History." *Psychohistory Review* 10 (1981): 3–17.

"Foucault, Phenomenology and the Question of Origins." *Philosophy Today* 26 (1982): 312–321.

"Reading Foucault: Anti-Method and the Genealogy of Power-Knowledge." *History and Theory* 21 (1982): 382–398.

Silverman, Hugh. "Jean-Paul Sartre versus Michel Foucault on Civilizational Study." *Philosophy and Social Criticism* 5 (1978): 161–171.

"Michel Foucault's Nineteenth Century System of Thought and the Anthropological Sleep." *Seminar III*, 1979: 1–8.

Simons, Jon. "From Resistance to Polaesthetics: Politics after Foucault." *Philosophy and Social Criticism* 18 (1991): 41–55.

Sluga, Hans. "Foucault, the Author, and the Discourse." *Inquiry* 28 (1985): 403–415.

Smart, Barry. "Foucault, Sociology, and the Problem of Human Agency." *Theory and Society* 11 (1982): 121–141.

"On the Subjects of Sexuality, Ethics, and Politics in the Work of Foucault." *Boundary* 2, 18 (Spring 1991): 201–225.

Sprinker, Michael. "The Use and Abuse of Foucault." *Humanities in Society* 3 (1980): 1–22.

Steiner, George. "Power Play." *New Yorker*, March 17, 1986, pp. 105–109.

Steinert, H. "Development of Discipline According to Michel Foucault: Discourse Analysis vs. Social History." *Crime and Social Justice* 20 (1983): 83–98.

Stempel, Daniel. "Blake, Foucault, and the Classical Episteme." *PMLA* 96 (1981): 388–407.

Stone, Laurence. "Madness." *New York Review of Books*, December 16, 1982, 36ff. See also the subsequent "Exchange" between Foucault and Stone, *New York Review of Books*, March 31, 1983, pp. 42–44.

Strong, Beret E. "Foucault, Freud, and French Feminism: Theorizing Hysteria as Theorizing the Feminine." *Literature and Psychology* 35 (1989): 10–26.

Struever, Nancy S. "Vico, Foucault, and the Strategy of Intimate Investigation." *New Vico Studies* 2 (1984): 41–57.

Sztulman, H. "Folie ou maladie mentale? Etude critique, psychopathologique et épistémologique des conceptions Michel Foucault." *Evolution psychiatrique* 36 (1971): 259–277.

Tambling, Jeremy. "Prison-Bound: Dickens and Foucault." *Essays in Criticism* 36 (1986): 11–31.

Taylor, Charles. "Foucault on Freedom and Truth." *Political Theory* 12 (1984): 152–183. Reprinted in David Hoy, ed., *Foucault: A Critical Reader.* Oxford: Basil Blackwell, 1986.

"Connolly, Foucault, and Truth." *Political Theory* 13 (1985): 377–386.

"Taylor and Foucault on Power and Freedom: A Reply." *Political Studies* 37 (1989): 277–281.

Thiele, Leslie Paul. "Foucault's Triple Murder and the Modern Development of Power." *Canadian Journal of Political Science* 19 (1986): 243–260.

"The Agony of Politics: The Nietzschean Roots of Foucault's Thought." *American Political Science Review* 84 (1991): 907–925.

Tjiattas, Mary, and Jean-Pierre Delaporte. "Foucault's Nominalism of the Sexual." *Philosophy Today* 32 (1988): 118–127.

Valdinoci, S. "Étude critique: les incertitudes de l'archéologie: arché et archive." *Revue de métaphysique et de morale* 83 (1978): 73–101.

Van De Wiele, Jozef. "L'histoire chez Michel Foucault: le sens de l'archéologie." *Revue Philosphique de Louvain* 81 (1983): 601–633.

Veyne, Paul. "Foucault revolutionne l'histoire." Appendix to *Comment on écrit l'histoire*, 2d ed. Paris: Seuil, 1978.

Visker, Rudi. "Can Genealogy Be Critical? A Somewhat Unromantic Look at Nietzsche and Foucault." *Man and World* 23 (1990): 441–452.

"From Foucault to Heidegger: A One-Way Ticket?" *Research in Phenomenology* 21 (1991): 116–140.

Wahl, François. "Y a-t-il une épistèmé structuraliste? ou d'une philosophie en déçà du structuralisme: Michel Foucault." In Oswald Ducrot et al., eds., *Qu'est-ce que le structuralisme?* Paris: Seuil, 1978.

Walzer, Michael. "The Politics of Michel Foucault." *Dissent* 30 (1983): 481–490.

Wapner, Paul. "What's Left: Marx, Foucault and Contemporary Problems of Social Change." *Praxis International* 9 (1989): 88–111.

Wartenberg, Thomas E. "Foucault's Archaeological Method: A Response to Hacking and Rorty." *Philosophical Forum* 15 (1984): 345–364.

Watson, Stephen. "Kant and Foucault: On the Ends of Man." *Tijdschrift voor Filosofie* 47 (1985): 71–102.

"Merleau-Ponty and Foucault: De-aestheticization of the Work of Art." *Philosophy Today* 28 (1984): 148–166.

Weightman, John. "On Not Understanding Michel Foucault." *The American Scholar* 58 (1989): 383–406.

Wellbery, David E. "Theory of Events: Foucault and Literary Criticism." *Revue Internationale de Philosophie* 41 (1987): 420–432.

White, Hayden V. "Foucault Decoded: Notes from Underground." *History and Theory* 12 (1973): 23–54. Reprinted in White, *Tropics of Discourse.* Baltimore: Johns Hopkins University Press, 1978, pp. 230–260.
"Power and the Word." *Canto* 2 (1978): 164–172.
"Foucault's Discourse: The Historiography of Anti-humanism." In White, *The Content of Form.* Baltimore: Johns Hopkins University Press, 1987.
"Michel Foucault." Pages 81–115 in John Sturrock, ed., *Structuralism and Since: from Lévi-Strauss to Derrida.* Oxford: Oxford University Press, 1980.
White, Stephen K. "Foucault's Challenge to Critical Theory." *American Political Science Review* 80 (1986): 419–432.
Willers, Jack Conrad. "The Constitution of Knowledge and Knower: Michel Foucault on Power and Discipline." *Philosophical Studies in Education* (1985): 199–210.
Wolin, S. "Foucault's Aesthetic Decisionism." *Telos* 67 (1986): 71–86.
Wolton, Dominique. "Qui veut savoir?" *Esprit* 7–8 (1977): 36–47.
Wright, Gordon. "Foucault in Prison." *Stanford French Review* 1 (1977): 71–78.
Yoon, Pyung-Joong. "Habermas and Foucault: On Ideology-Critique and Power/Knowledge Nexus." *Kinesis* (1987): 17, 87–103.
Ysmal, Colette. "Histoire et archéologie: note sur la recherche de Michel Foucault." *Revue française de science politique* 22 (1972): 775–804.
Zoila, A. F. "Michel Foucault, anti-psychiatre?" *Revue Internationale de Philosophie* 32 (1978): 59–74.

INDEX

abominations, 116
achievement, 200, 202
action, communicative, 216, 225–8;
  Foucault and Habermas on, 243–7;
  strategic, 242–6
activity, self-forming, 118, 122–3,
  124–5
Acton, Lord, 35
Adorno, T., 218, 252
aesthetics, *see* esthetics
age, 200, 202
agents, 106
agonism, 154
Aldrovandi, U., 36
alignment, 106–12; *see also*
  dispositive
Althusser, L., 36, 167
analytic of finitude, 12, 221
analytics, interpretative, 2–3
anatomy, 32, 79, 81
animality, 53–4, 58–9
Annales school, 6, 54
anorexia, 291–2
anthropological sleep, 90
anthropology, 90; philosophical, 44
anti-realism, 18–9
Apel, K.-O., 226
a priori, historical, 29, 30
Archaeology of Knowledge, 5, 17–18,
  29–31, 224, 230–32, 278–9
archaeology of knowledge, 2, 4, 6–7,
  9–10, 14, 29–33, 44, 73–5, 79, 81–
  2, 85, 160, 170, 231–4, 315; and
  practices, 30; as verdicative, 37; of
  psychoanalysis, 149
Archilochus, 24

archipelago, carceral, 151
architecture, 36, 41
archive, 29, 30
Ariosto, L., 72
Aristotle, 43, 141, 162, 282
art, 21–22, 153, 175, 180
ascetics, 122–3, 125–6, 129, 144, 175;
  homosexual, 125–6, 131
askésis, see ascetics
asylum, 10–11
authenticity, 153
author, 1, 4, 39
autonomy, 120, 154, 160, 169, 171, 185

Bachelard, G., 32, 89, 255, 263, 266,
  269
Barbin, H., 24, 146, 155
Bardo, S., 291–2, 295
Bartky, S., 291, 293–4, 295
Bataille, G., 22, 152, 270, 271–2, 282
Baudelaire, C., 173–6
Being, 199, 201, 202, 204
Bentham, J., 37, 41–2, 293
Berlin, I., 2
Bernauer, J., 256
Bethlem, 53, 57, 58, 63
Bicêtre, 58
Bichat, F., 75
Binswanger, L., 29, 142
biology, 9, 33, 73, 80, 155, 232; Comte
  and, 87; *see also* natural history
biopolitics, 117, 146
biopower, 203
Birth of the Clinic, 2, 9, 32, 41, 284
Blanchot, M., 22, 152
Blumenburg, H., 200–201, 207–209